enVisionmath 2.0

SCOTT FORESMAN · ADDISON WESLEY

Volume 1 Topics 1-8

Authors

Randall I. Charles
Professor Emeritus
Department of Mathematics
San Jose State University
San Jose, California

Jennifer Bay-Williams
Professor of Mathematics Education
College of Education and Human
Development
University of Louisville
Louisville, Kentucky

Robert Q. Berry, III
Associate Professor of
Mathematics Education
Department of Curriculum,
Instruction and Special Education
University of Virginia
Charlottesville, Virginia

Janet H. Caldwell
Professor of Mathematics
Rowan University
Glassboro, New Jersey

Zachary Champagne
Assistant in Research
Florida Center for Research in Science,
Technology, Engineering, and
Mathematics (FCR-STEM)
Jacksonville, Florida

Juanita Copley
Professor Emerita, College of Education
University of Houston
Houston, Texas

Warren Crown
Professor Emeritus of Mathematics
Education
Graduate School of Education
Rutgers University
New Brunswick, New Jersey

Francis (Skip) Fennell
L. Stanley Bowlsbey Professor
of Education and Graduate and
Professional Studies
McDaniel College
Westminster, Maryland

Karen Karp
Professor of Mathematics Education
Department of Early Childhood and
Elementary Education
University of Louisville
Louisville, Kentucky

Stuart J. Murphy
Visual Learning Specialist
Boston, Massachusetts

Jane F. Schielack
Professor of Mathematics
Associate Dean for Assessment and
Pre K-12 Education, College of Science
Texas A&M University
College Station, Texas

Jennifer M. Suh
Associate Professor for
Mathematics Education
George Mason University
Fairfax, Virginia

Jonathan A. Wray
Mathematics Instructional Facilitator
Howard County Public Schools
Ellicott City, Maryland

PEARSON

Glenview, Illinois   Boston, Massachusetts   Chandler, Arizona   Hoboken, New Jersey

Mathematicians

Roger Howe
Professor of Mathematics
Yale University
New Haven, Connecticut

Gary Lippman
Professor of Mathematics and
Computer Science
California State University, East Bay
Hayward, California

ELL Consultants

Janice R. Corona
Independent Education Consultant
Dallas, Texas

Jim Cummins
Professor
The University of Toronto
Toronto, Canada

Debbie Crisco
Math Coach
Beebe Public Schools
Beebe, Arkansas

Kathleen A. Cuff
Teacher
Kings Park Central School District
Kings Park, New York

Erika Doyle
Math and Science Coordinator
Richland School District
Richland, Washington

Reviewers

Susan Jarvis
Math and Science Curriculum Coordinator
Ocean Springs Schools
Ocean Springs, Mississippi

PEARSON

ISBN-13: 978-0-328-88709-5
ISBN-10: 0-328-88709-9

6 18

You'll be using these digital resources throughout the year!

Digital Resources

Go to PearsonRealize.com

 MP
Math Practices **Animations** to play anytime

Glossary
Animated Glossary in English and Spanish

 Help
Another Look **Homework Video** for extra help

ACTIVe-book
Student Edition online for showing your work

Solve
Solve & Share problems plus math tools

Tools
Math Tools to help you understand

Games
Math Games to help you learn

 Learn
Visual Learning Animation Plus with animation, interaction, and math tools

Assessment
Quick Check for each lesson

eText
Student Edition online

PEARSON
realize™ Everything you need for math anytime, anywhere

Contents

KEY

- Operations and Algebra
- Numbers and Computation
- Measurement and Data
- Geometry

Digital Resources at PearsonRealize.com

And remember your eText is available at PearsonRealize.com!

TOPICS

TOPIC 1
Fluently Add and Subtract Within 20

This shows how you can use ten-frames to make a 10.

TOPIC 2
Work with Equal Groups

This shows how you can use connecting cubes to show that a number is even or odd.

8 is even.

$4 + 4 = 8$

9 is odd.

$5 + 4 = 9$

TOPIC 3
Add Within 100 Using Strategies

This shows how you can add two-digit numbers using a hundred chart.

$54 + 18 = 72$

51	52	53	54	55	56	57	58	59	60
61	62	63	64	65	66	67	68	69	70
71	72	73	74	75	76	77	78	79	80

TOPIC 4
Fluently Add Within 100

This shows one way to model a 2-digit addition problem.

Tens	Ones		Tens	Ones
		+	3	7
			1	9
			5	6

PearsonRealize.com

TOPIC 5
Subtract Within 100 Using Strategies

This shows how you can add up to subtract on an open number line to find 57 − 28.

+2   +10   +10   +7

28 30   40   50   57

© Pearson Education, Inc. 2

Contents

TOPIC 6
Fluently Subtract Within 100

> This shows how addition and subtraction are related. You can use addition to check subtraction.

TOPIC 7
More Solving Problems Involving Addition and Subtraction

This shows how bar diagrams can be used to model and solve a two-step problem.

Mia sees 15 yellow birds and 16 red birds. Some birds fly away and now Mia sees 14 birds. How many birds flew away?

© Pearson Education, Inc. 2

Contents

TOPIC 8
Work with Time and Money

This shows how to count on to find the total value.

Micah has the coins shown below. How many cents does Micah have?

50¢ 75¢ 85¢ 90¢ 91¢

TOPIC 9 in Volume 2
Numbers to 1,000

TOPIC 10 in Volume 2
Add Within 1,000 Using Models and Strategies

Contents

TOPIC 13 in Volume 2
More Addition, Subtraction, and Length

TOPIC 14 in Volume 2
Graphs and Data

Contents

TOPIC 15 in Volume 2
Shapes and Their Attributes

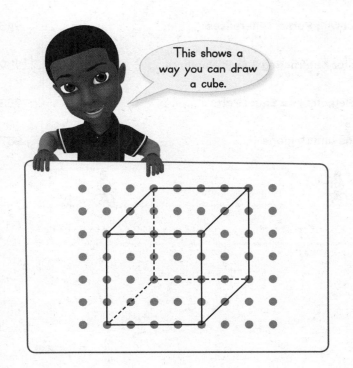

This shows a way you can draw a cube.

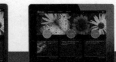

STEP UP to Grade 3 in Volume 2

These lessons help prepare you for Grade 3.

Problem Solving Handbook

Math Practices

1 Make sense of problems and persevere in solving them.

2 Reason abstractly and quantitatively.

3 Construct viable arguments and critique the reasoning of others.

4 Model with mathematics.

5 Use appropriate tools strategically.

6 Attend to precision.

7 Look for and make use of structure.

8 Look for and express regularity in repeated reasoning.

There are good Thinking Habits for each of these math practices.

▶ 1 Make sense of problems and persevere in solving them.

MP

Good math thinkers know what the problem is about. They have a plan to solve it. They keep trying if they get stuck.

My plan is to use counters as trucks. I can act out the problem.

A store has some toy trucks.
Mike buys 2 of the trucks.
Now the store has 3 trucks.
How many trucks did the store have at the start?

5 – 2 = 3
5 trucks

Thinking Habits

What do I need to find?

What do I know?

What's my plan for solving the problem?

What else can I try if I get stuck?

How can I check that my solution makes sense?

2 Reason abstractly and quantitatively.

I completed a part-part-whole model. It shows how things in the problem are related.

Good math thinkers know how to think about words and numbers to solve problems.

Tony has 10 apples. 6 are red. The rest are green. How many apples are green?

10 – 6 = 4

4 apples are green.

Thinking Habits

What do the numbers stand for?

How are the numbers in the problem related?

How can I show a word problem using pictures or numbers?

How can I use a word problem to show what an equation means?

3 Construct viable arguments and critique the reasoning of others.

I can use place-value blocks to check Paula's thinking. My explanation is clear and complete.

Good math thinkers use math to explain why they are right. They talk about math that others do, too.

Paula added $34 + 5$.
She says she had to regroup the ones.
Is she correct? Show how you know.

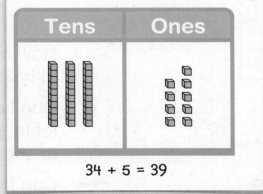

34 has 4 ones.
4 ones and 5 ones are 9 ones.
Paula is incorrect.
You do not need to regroup ones.

Tens	Ones

$34 + 5 = 39$

Thinking Habits

How can I use math to explain my work?

Am I using numbers and symbols correctly?

Is my explanation clear?

What questions can I ask to understand other people's thinking?

Are there mistakes in other people's thinking?

Can I improve other people's thinking?

4 Model with mathematics.

MP

I can use ten-frames and counters to show the problem.

Good math thinkers use math they know to show and solve problems.

14 dogs are playing at a park.
9 dogs go home.
How many dogs are still at the park?

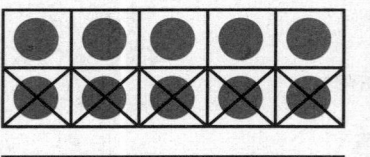
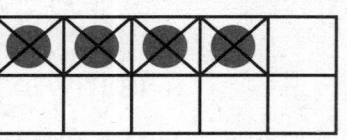

$14 - 9 = 5$

5 dogs

Thinking Habits

How can I use the math I know to help solve this problem?

Can I use a drawing, diagram, table, graph, or objects to show the problem?

Can I write an equation to show the problem?

5 Use appropriate tools strategically.

Good math thinkers know how to pick the right tools to solve math problems.

I chose connecting cubes to solve the problem.

Kai and Maddie each pick 6 apples.
Then Maddie picks 1 more apple.
How many apples do they pick in all?

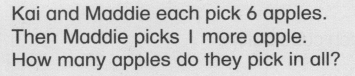

6 + 7 = 13

13 apples

Thinking Habits

Which tools can I use?

Is there a different tool I could use?

Am I using the tool correctly?

6 Attend to precision.

Good math thinkers are careful about what they write and say, so their ideas about math are clear.

I can use the definition of a cube to help me describe what it looks like.

Circle each cube below.

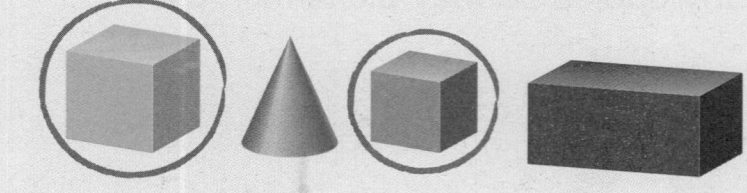

Describe what a cube looks like.

A cube has 6 flat surfaces.

Each flat surface is the same size.

A cube has 12 edges.

Thinking Habits

Am I using numbers, units, and symbols correctly?

Am I using the correct definitions?

Is my answer clear?

7 Look for and make use of structure.

MP

It is hard to add three numbers at once. I can add any two numbers first. I added 6 + 4 first to make the problem easier.

Good math thinkers look for patterns in math to help solve problems.

Jeff saw 6 brown frogs, 3 green frogs, and 4 spotted frogs.
How many frogs did Jeff see in all?

Show your work and explain your answer.

6 + 3 + 4 = 13
   10

I made 10 then added 3 to make the problem easier.

Thinking Habits

Is there a pattern?

How can I describe the pattern?

Can I break the problem into simpler parts?

8 Look for and express regularity in repeated reasoning.

MP

I can compare the tens first. If the tens are the same, I can compare the ones.

Good math thinkers look for things that repeat in a problem. They use what they learn from one problem to help them solve other problems.

Compare each pair of numbers.
Write <, >, or =. Tell how you will compare each pair of numbers.

57 $<$ 75   49 $<$ 52

36 $>$ 34   61 $=$ 61

Thinking Habits

Does something repeat in the problem?

How can the solution help me solve another problem?

Problem Solving Handbook

Problem Solving Guide

These questions can help you solve problems.

Make Sense of the Problem

Reason
- What do I need to find?
- What given information can I use?
- How are the quantities related?

Think About Similar Problems
- Have I solved problems like this before?

Persevere in Solving the Problem

Model with Math
- How can I use the math I know?
- How can I show the problem?
- Is there a pattern I can use?

Use Appropriate Tools
- What math tools could I use?
- How can I use those tools?

Check the Answer

Make Sense of the Answer
- Is my answer reasonable?

Check for Precision
- Did I check my work?
- Is my answer clear?
- Is my explanation clear?

Some Ways to Show Problems
- Draw a Picture
- Draw a Number Line
- Write an Equation

Some Math Tools
- Objects
- Rulers
- Technology
- Paper and Pencil

Problem Solving Recording Sheet

This sheet helps you organize your work.

Name __Mary__

Teaching Tool 1

Problem Solving Recording Sheet

Problem:
John bikes for 17 miles on Monday.
He bikes for 15 miles on Tuesday.
How many miles does John bike in all?

MAKE SENSE OF THE PROBLEM

Need to Find	Given
I need to find how many miles John bikes in all.	John bikes 17 miles on Monday and 15 miles on Tuesday.

PERSEVERE IN SOLVING THE PROBLEM

Some Ways to Represent Problems
☑ Draw a Picture
☐ Draw a Number Line
☑ Write an Equation

Some Math Tools
☐ Objects
☐ Rulers
☐ Technology
☑ Paper and Pencil

Solution and Answer

$17 + 15 = 32$

I made a 10.
John bikes 32 miles in all.

CHECK THE ANSWER

I checked my drawing of blocks.
They matched the problem and show 32 in all.

TT1

Fluently Add and Subtract Within 20

Essential Question: What are strategies for finding addition and subtraction facts?

Digital Resources

Solve · Learn · Glossary

Tools · Assessment · Help · Games

Look at the different types of paper!

Different papers have different properties.

Wow! Let's do this project and learn more.

Math and Science Project: Material Math

Find Out Collect different types of paper. Talk about the uses of paper. Tell how strong each type of paper is. Tell how the paper feels. Tell if the paper can soak up water.

Journal: Make a Book Show what you find out in a book. In your book, also:

• Glue samples of paper and tell what you found.

• Choose a type of paper to make flash cards of addition and subtraction facts.

Name _____

Review What You Know

Vocabulary

1. Circle the symbol for **equals**.

   −

   +

   =

2. Circle the symbol for **minus**.

   −

   +

   =

3. Circle the number that is the **whole**.

   $4 + 2 = 6$

Subtraction Stories

4. There are 7 birds on a fence. 2 fly away. How many birds are left?

   _____ birds

Addition Stories

5. Write an equation to solve the problem.

   Kate draws 4 big stars. Then she draws 2 small stars. How many stars does Kate draw in all?

   _____ + _____ = _____

Making 10

6. Write the numbers that show a way to make 10.

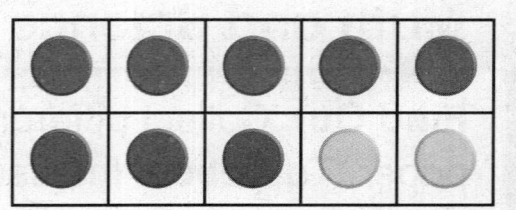

   _____ + _____ = _____

© Pearson Education, Inc. 2

My Word Cards Study the words on the front of the card. Complete the activity on the back.

A-Z Glossary

addend

$2 + 5 = 7$

addends

sum

$3 + 4 = 7$

$$\begin{array}{r} 4 \\ +\ 3 \\ \hline 7 \end{array}$$

sum ⟶ 7

equation

$3 + 4 = 7$

$14 - 6 = 8$

doubles

$4 + 4 = 8$

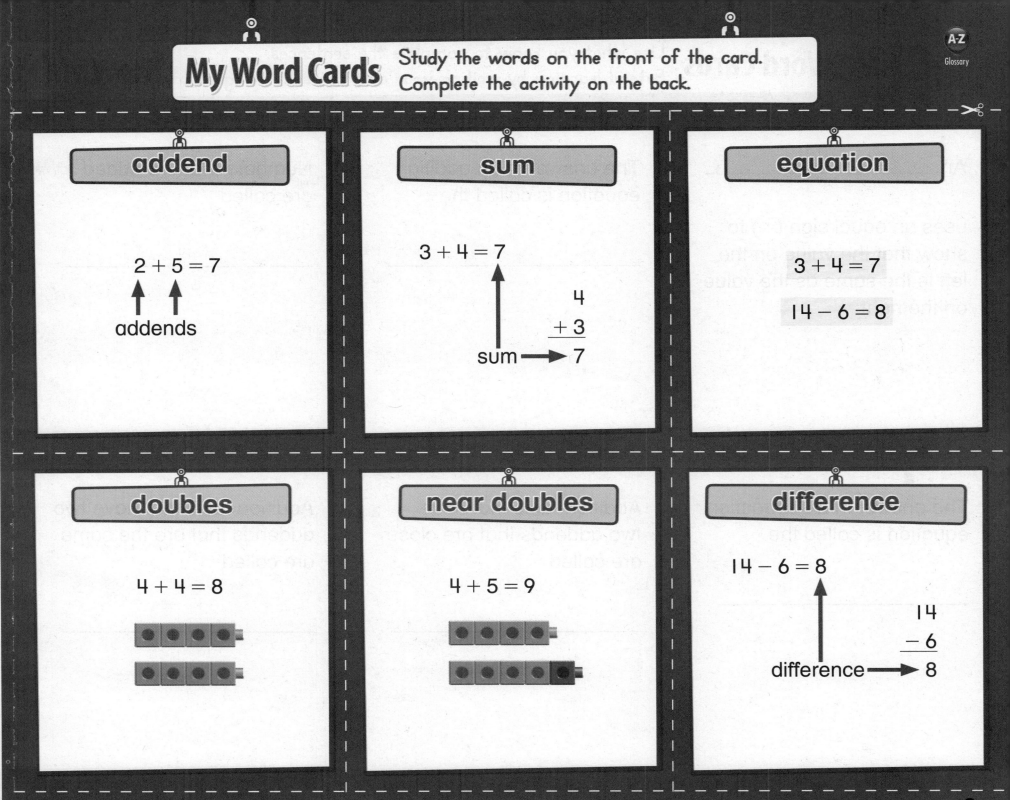

near doubles

$4 + 5 = 9$

difference

$14 - 6 = 8$

$$\begin{array}{r} 14 \\ -\ 6 \\ \hline 8 \end{array}$$

difference ⟶ 8

My Word Cards

Use what you know to complete the sentences.
Extend learning by writing your own sentence using each word.

An _____

uses an equal sign (=) to show that the value on the left is the same as the value on the right.

The answer in an addition equation is called the

_____.

Numbers that are added are called

_____.

The answer in a subtraction equation is called the

_____.

Addition facts that have two addends that are close are called

_____.

Addition facts that have two addends that are the same are called

_____.

Name _____

Solve & Share

Use cubes to show 4 + 5.

What will happen to the total number of cubes if you change the order of the numbers being added? Explain.

I can ...
count on to add and add in any order.

I can also reason about math.

4 + 5 = _____   _____ + _____ = _____

You can count on to find 6 + 3.

6 7 8 9

Or count on to find 3 + 6.

3 4 5 6 7 8 9

Counting on from the greater number is easier!

An **equation** uses an equal sign (=) to show that the value on the left is the same as the value on the right.

6 + 3 = 9

3 + 6 = 9

You can change the order of the **addends**.

6 + 3 = 9

3 + 6 = 9

addend addend **sum**

The sum is the same.

You can add numbers in any order, and the sum is the same.

So, 6 + 3 = 3 + 6.

You can write the facts this way, too.

6   3
+ 3   + 6
9   9

Do You Understand?

Show Me! Does 5 + 2 = 2 + 5? How do you know?

☆ **Guided Practice** ☆ Count on to find the sum. Then change the order of the addends.

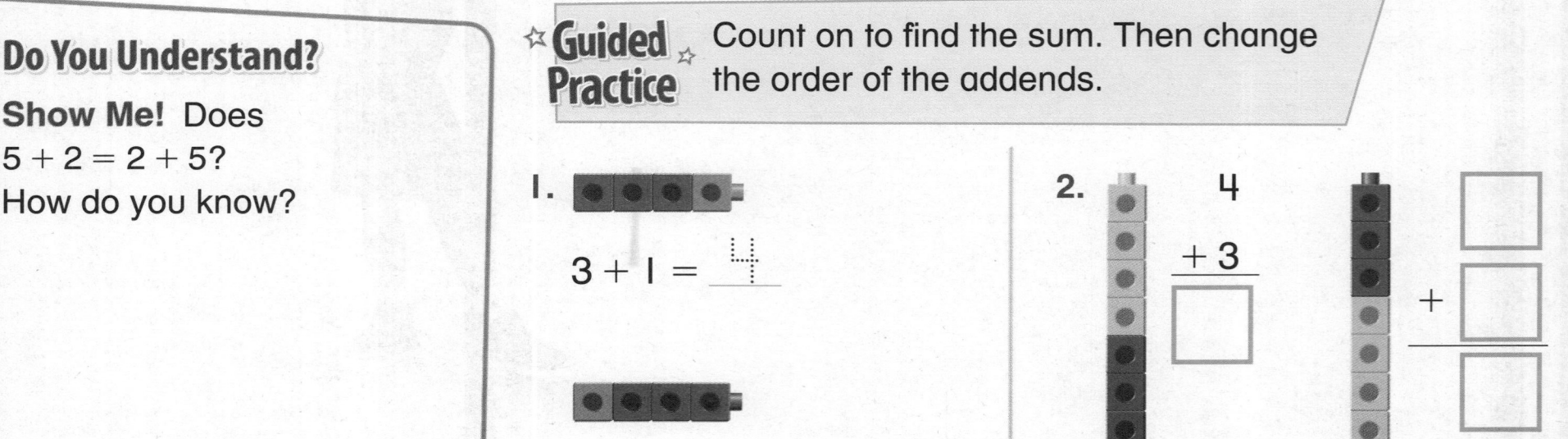

1. 3 + 1 = 4

1 + 3 = 4

2.   4
       + 3
       ___

       +
       ___

© Pearson Education, Inc. 2

Tools   Assessment

Independent Practice   Count on to find the sum. Then change the order of the addends. Use cubes if needed.

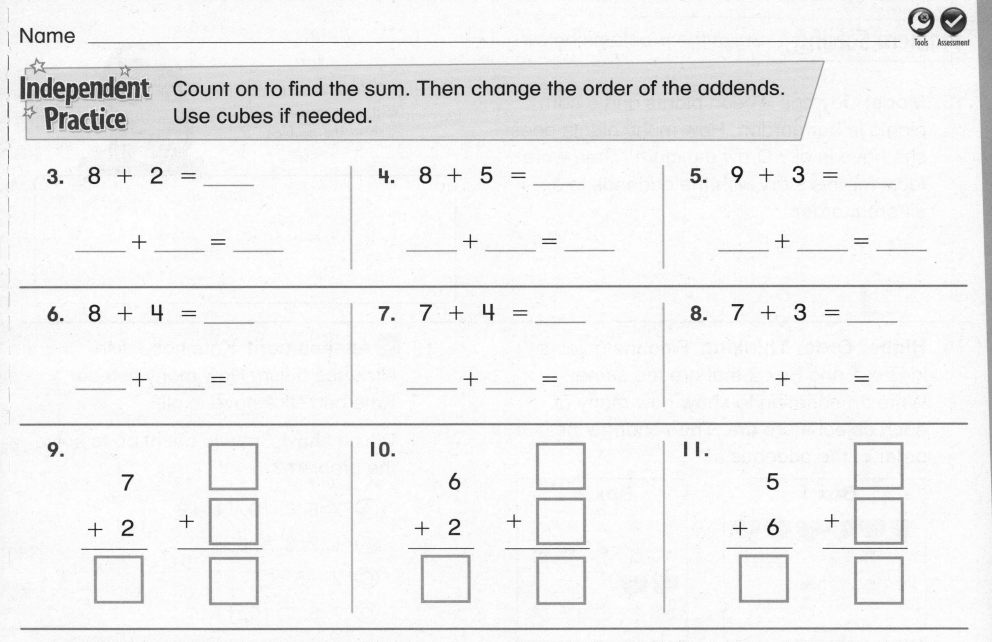

3. 8 + 2 = ____

___ + ___ = ___

4. 8 + 5 = ____

___ + ___ = ___

5. 9 + 3 = ____

___ + ___ = ___

6. 8 + 4 = ____

___ + ___ = ___

7. 7 + 4 = ____

___ + ___ = ___

8. 7 + 3 = ____

___ + ___ = ___

9.
```
   7            ☐
 + 2       +  ☐
 ───       ───
  ☐           ☐
```

10.
```
   6            ☐
 + 2       +  ☐
 ───       ───
  ☐           ☐
```

11.
```
   5            ☐
 + 6       +  ☐
 ───       ───
  ☐           ☐
```

12. **Algebra** Write the missing numbers.

6 + ____ = 4 + 6

8 + 2 = ____ + 8

6 + ____ = 5 + 6

____ + 7 = 7 + 4

9 + 3 = 3 + ____

____ + 8 = 8 + 4

13. **Model** Joy has 8 bean plants and 6 corn plants in her garden. How many plants does she have in all? Draw a picture. Then write facts for this story with the addends in a different order.

Your picture and your equation will show the problem.

_____ + _____ = _____

_____ + _____ = _____

14. **Higher Order Thinking** Find the objects in Box 1 and Box 2 that are the same. Write an equation to show how many of each object there are. Then change the order of the addends.

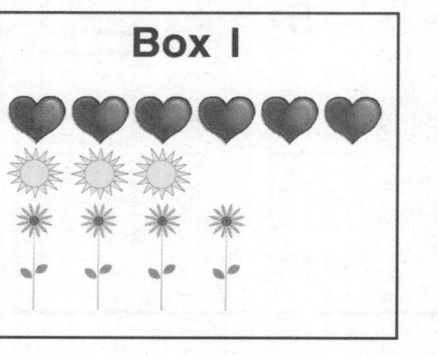

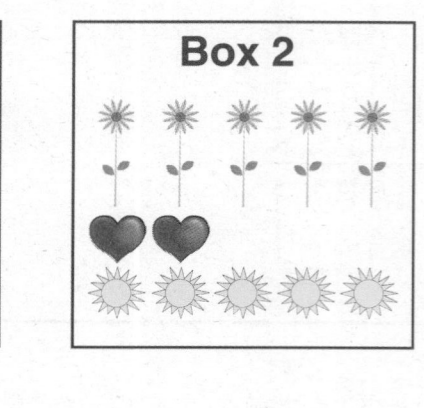

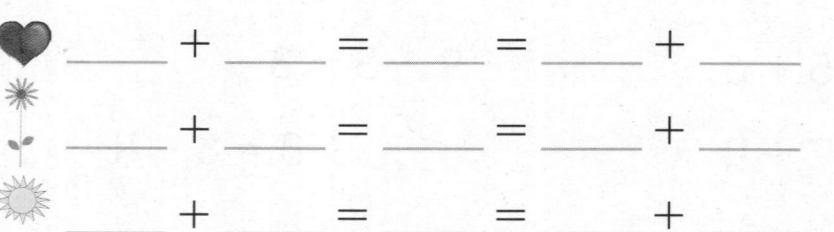

15. ✓**Assessment** Kate has 7 fish. Nick has 5 fish. How many fish do Kate and Nick have in all?

Which shows how to count on to solve the problem?

Ⓐ 7, 8, 9, 10, 11, 12

Ⓑ 1, 2, 3, 4, 5

Ⓒ 7 − 5

Ⓓ 7, 8, 9, 10, 11

Name _____

Another Look! You can count on to find a sum. Counting on from a greater number is easier.

I can add numbers in any order and get the same sum.

HOME ACTIVITY Have your child use small clothing items, such as socks or mittens, to model counting on to find $5 + 4$. Then ask your child to explain why $5 + 4$ and $4 + 5$ have the same sum.

5   6 7

2   3 4 5 6 7

$5 + 2 = \underline{7}$

$\underline{2} + \underline{5} = \underline{7}$

Count on to find the sum. Then change the order of the addends.

1.

$3 + 4 = \underline{}$

$\underline{} + \underline{} = \underline{}$

2.

$\begin{array}{r} 5 \\ + 4 \\ \hline \square \end{array}$

$\begin{array}{r} \square \\ + \square \\ \hline \square \end{array}$

3.

$7 + 6 = \underline{}$

$\underline{} + \underline{} = \underline{}$

Write two addition facts for each story. Then solve.

4. **Reasoning** Danny collects toy train cars. He has 9 red train cars and 5 black train cars. How many train cars does he have in all?

____ + ____ = ____

____ + ____ = ____

_____ train cars

5. **Reasoning** Ana draws 3 red circles and 8 blue circles. How many circles does Ana draw?

____ + ____ = ____

____ + ____ = ____

_____ circles

6. **Higher Order Thinking** Draw a picture to solve. Then write two addition facts for the story.

15 cows live at a farm. Some of the cows are brown and some are white. How many of each color could be at the farm?

____ + ____ = 15

____ + ____ = 15

_____ brown cows

_____ white cows

7. ✓**Assessment** Which shape belongs in the second equation?

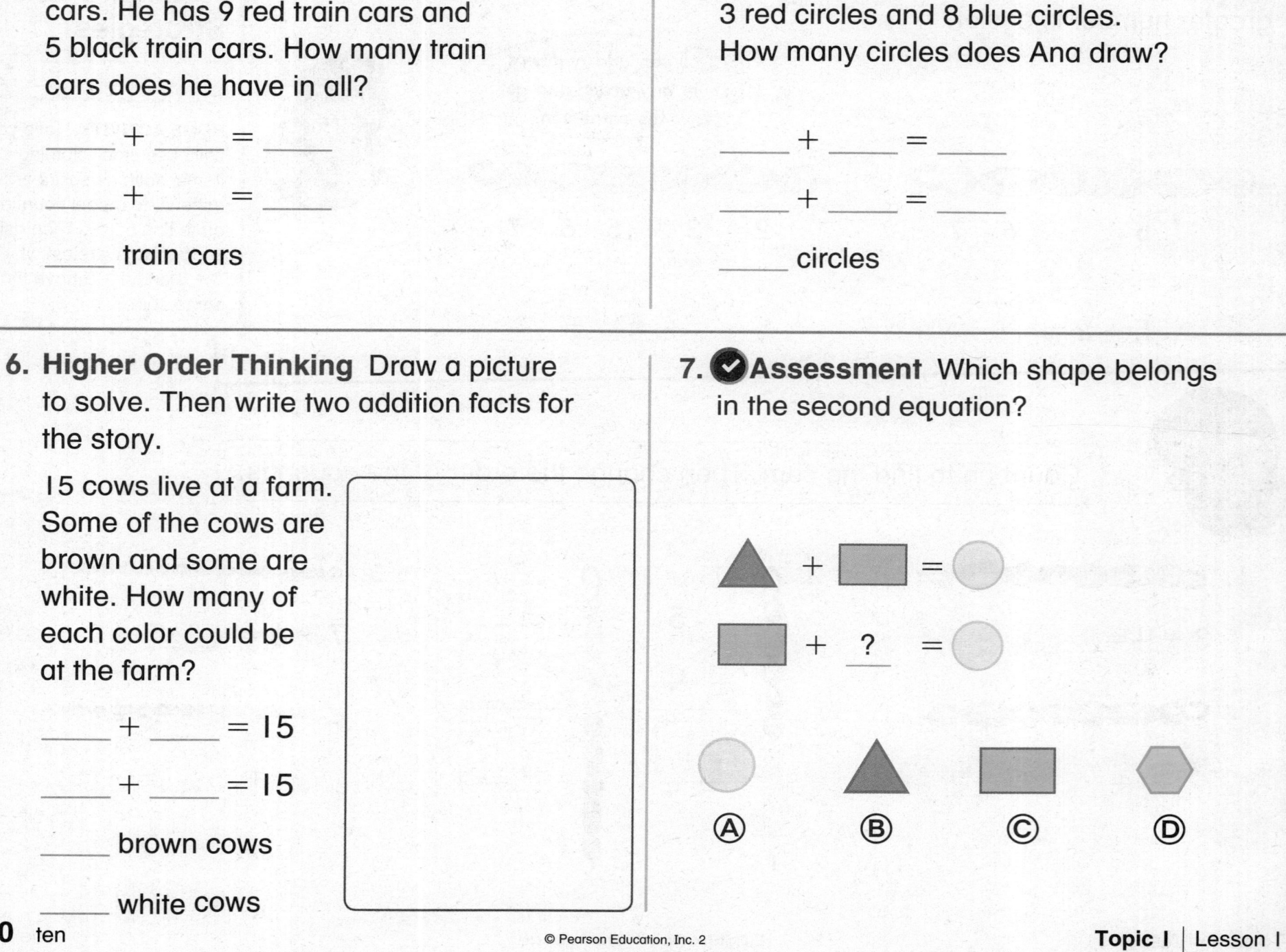

Ⓐ   Ⓑ   Ⓒ   Ⓓ

I can ...
use doubles and near doubles to add quickly and accurately.

I can also model with math.

Solve & Share

You know that $2 + 2 = 4$.
Tell how knowing that fact can help you find $2 + 3$.

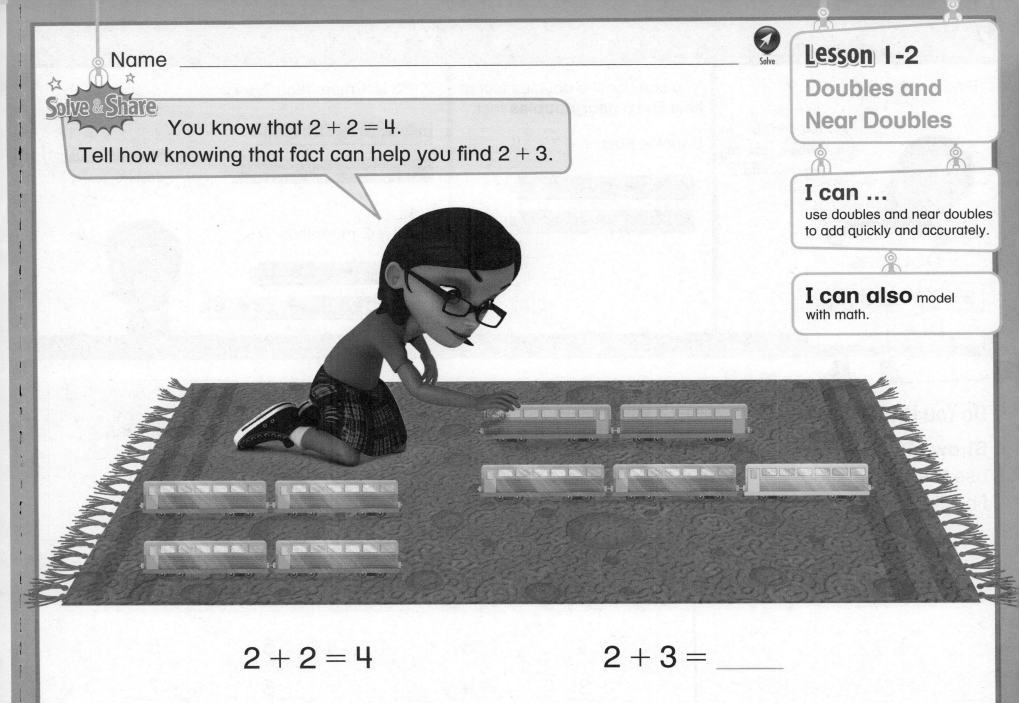

$2 + 2 = 4$

$2 + 3 = $ _____

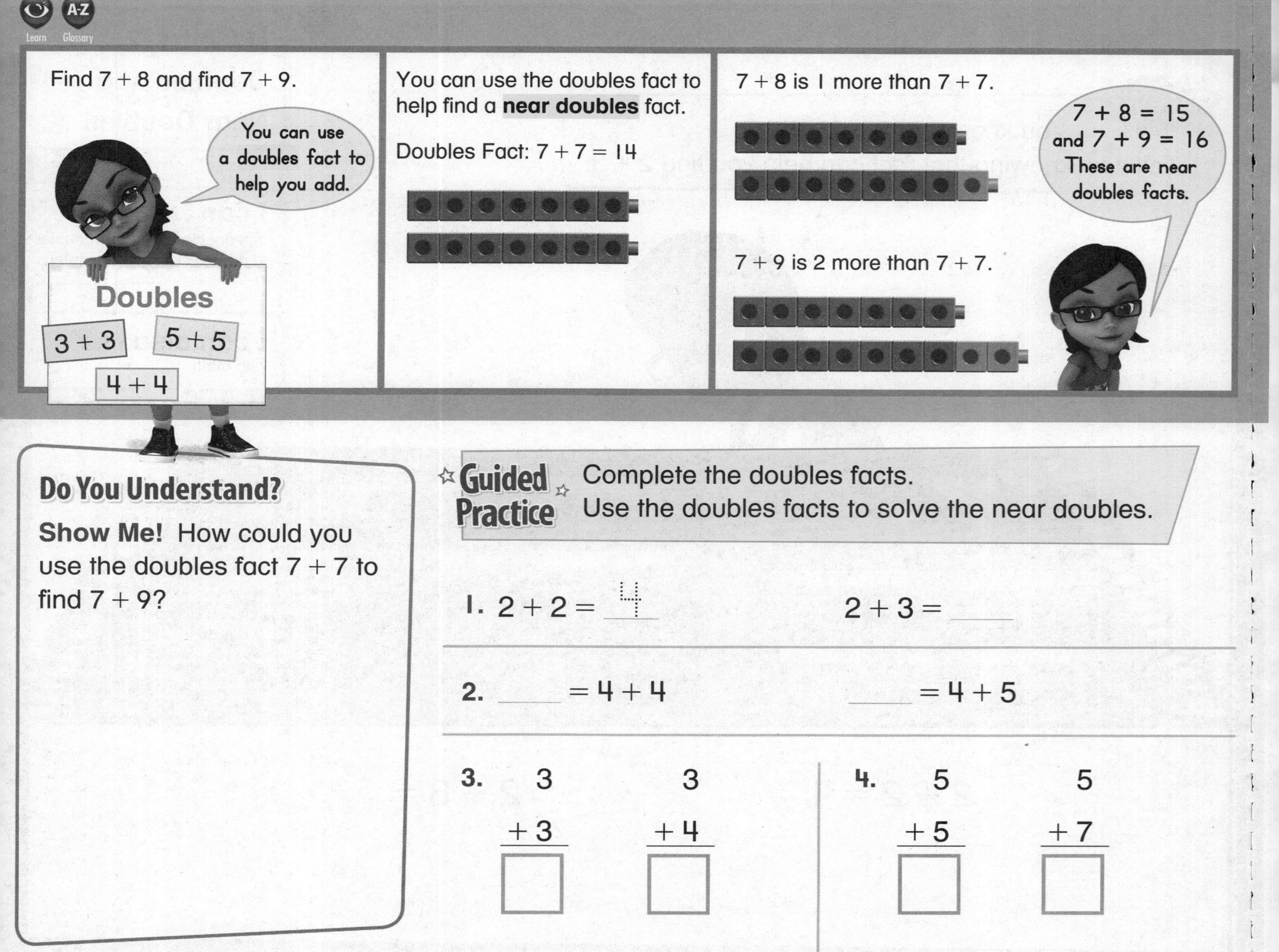

Find 7 + 8 and find 7 + 9.

You can use a doubles fact to help you add.

Doubles

3 + 3   5 + 5

4 + 4

You can use the doubles fact to help find a **near doubles** fact.

Doubles Fact: 7 + 7 = 14

7 + 8 is 1 more than 7 + 7.

7 + 9 is 2 more than 7 + 7.

7 + 8 = 15 and 7 + 9 = 16 These are near doubles facts.

Do You Understand?

Show Me! How could you use the doubles fact 7 + 7 to find 7 + 9?

☆ Guided Practice ☆

Complete the doubles facts.
Use the doubles facts to solve the near doubles.

1. 2 + 2 = __4__   2 + 3 = _____

2. _____ = 4 + 4   _____ = 4 + 5

3.   3   3
   + 3   + 4
   □   □

4.   5   5
   + 5   + 7
   □   □

12 twelve

© Pearson Education, Inc. 2

Topic 1 | Lesson 2

Name _____

Independent Practice

Complete the doubles facts. Use the doubles facts to solve the near doubles.

5. $6 + 6 =$ _____ $6 + 7 =$ _____ | **6.** $5 + 5 =$ _____ $5 + 6 =$ _____

7. $8 + 8 =$ _____ $8 + 10 =$ _____ | **8.** _____ $= 1 + 1$ _____ $= 1 + 3$

9.
$$
\begin{array}{r} 2 \\ +2 \\ \hline \end{array}
$$
$$
\begin{array}{r} 2 \\ +3 \\ \hline \end{array}
$$
10.
$$
\begin{array}{r} 4 \\ +4 \\ \hline \end{array}
$$
$$
\begin{array}{r} 4 \\ +5 \\ \hline \end{array}
$$
11.
$$
\begin{array}{r} 8 \\ +8 \\ \hline \end{array}
$$
$$
\begin{array}{r} 8 \\ +9 \\ \hline \end{array}
$$

12.
$$
\begin{array}{r} 3 \\ +3 \\ \hline \end{array}
$$
$$
\begin{array}{r} 3 \\ +5 \\ \hline \end{array}
$$
13.
$$
\begin{array}{r} 5 \\ +5 \\ \hline \end{array}
$$
$$
\begin{array}{r} 5 \\ +7 \\ \hline \end{array}
$$
14.
$$
\begin{array}{r} 7 \\ +7 \\ \hline \end{array}
$$
$$
\begin{array}{r} 7 \\ +9 \\ \hline \end{array}
$$

15. Algebra Complete the doubles and near doubles facts.

$9 + \boxed{} = 18$ $\boxed{} + \boxed{} = 19$

16. **Model** John drew 4 houses. Then he drew 5 more houses. How many houses did John draw in all?

Draw a picture and write an equation.

_____ + ____ = ____ houses

17. **Higher Order Thinking** Choose a doubles fact. Use that doubles fact to draw a picture that shows a near doubles story.

18. ✓ **Assessment** Kate's dog had 6 puppies. Jim's dog had 1 more puppy than Kate's dog.

Which equation shows how many puppies in all?

Ⓐ $6 + 1 = 7$

Ⓑ $6 + 6 = 12$

Ⓒ $6 + 7 = 13$

Ⓓ $7 + 7 = 14$

Name _____

Help Tools Games

Homework & Practice 1-2

Doubles and Near Doubles

Another Look! You can use a doubles fact to solve a near doubles fact.

To solve a near doubles fact, you can add 1 or 2 more to the doubles fact.

HOME ACTIVITY Have your child use common objects, such as pennies or buttons, to show doubles and near doubles. Then ask your child to write equations to show the facts.

$6 + 6 = \underline{12}$

Doubles Fact

$6 + 7 = \underline{13}$

Near Doubles Fact

Write and solve the doubles facts and the near doubles facts.

1. ____ + ____ = ____   ____ + ____ = ____

2. ____ + ____ = ____   ____ + ____ = ____

3. $7 + 7 = \underline{\hspace{1cm}}$

   $7 + 9 = \underline{\hspace{1cm}}$

4. $8 + 8 = \underline{\hspace{1cm}}$

   $8 + 10 = \underline{\hspace{1cm}}$

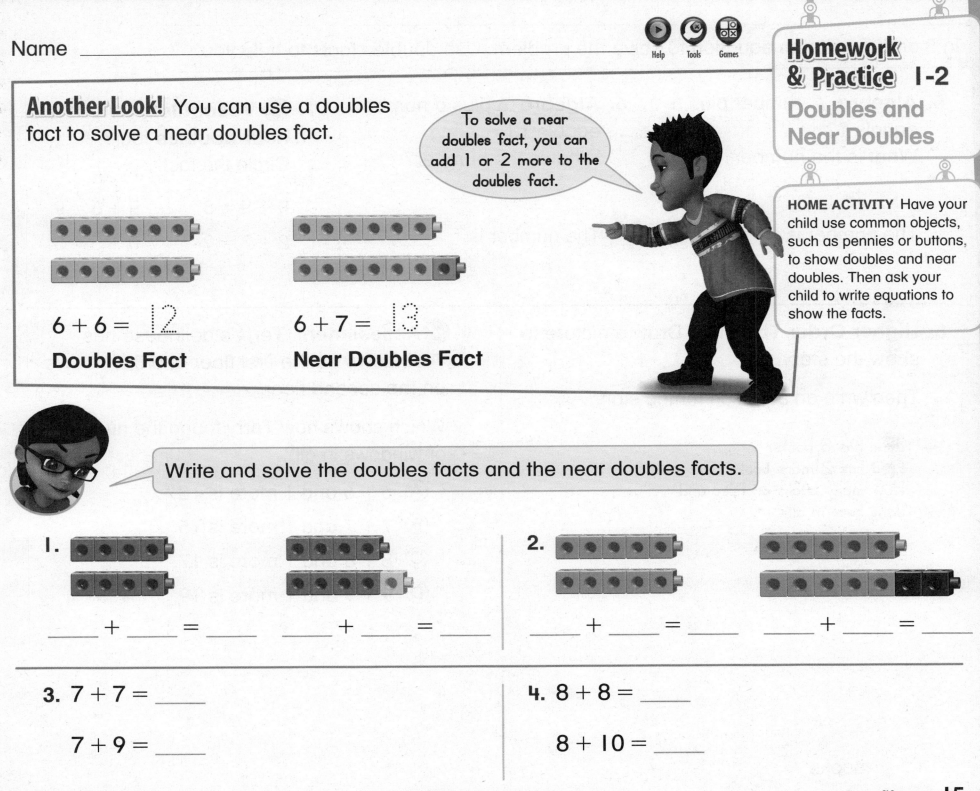

In 5 and 6, write an equation to solve the problem. Use doubles facts to help you.

5. **Algebra** A number plus 6 equals 12.
What is the number?

_____ + _____ = _____

The number is _____.

6. **Algebra** 6 plus a number equals 13.
What is the number?

_____ + _____ = _____

The number is _____.

7. **A-Z** **Vocabulary** Which is a **near doubles** fact?
Circle the fact.

$4 + 4 = 8$ $4 + 5 = 9$

$2 + 7 = 9$ $0 + 5 = 5$

8. **Higher Order Thinking** Draw a picture to show the story.

Then write an equation for the story.

Jane has 5 books.
Fred has 2 more books than Jane.
How many books do Fred and Jane have in all?

_____ + _____ = _____

_____ books

9. ✓**Assessment** Terry's dollhouse has 7 windows on the first floor and 8 windows on the second floor.

Which shows how Terry found the number of windows in all?

Ⓐ $6 + 6$ and 1 more is 13.

Ⓑ $7 + 7$ and 1 more is 15.

Ⓒ $8 + 8$ and 1 more is 17.

Ⓓ $9 + 9$ and 1 more is 19.

Name _____

Solve & Share

How can thinking about 10 help you find 9 + 3? Use the ten-frames and counters to show how.

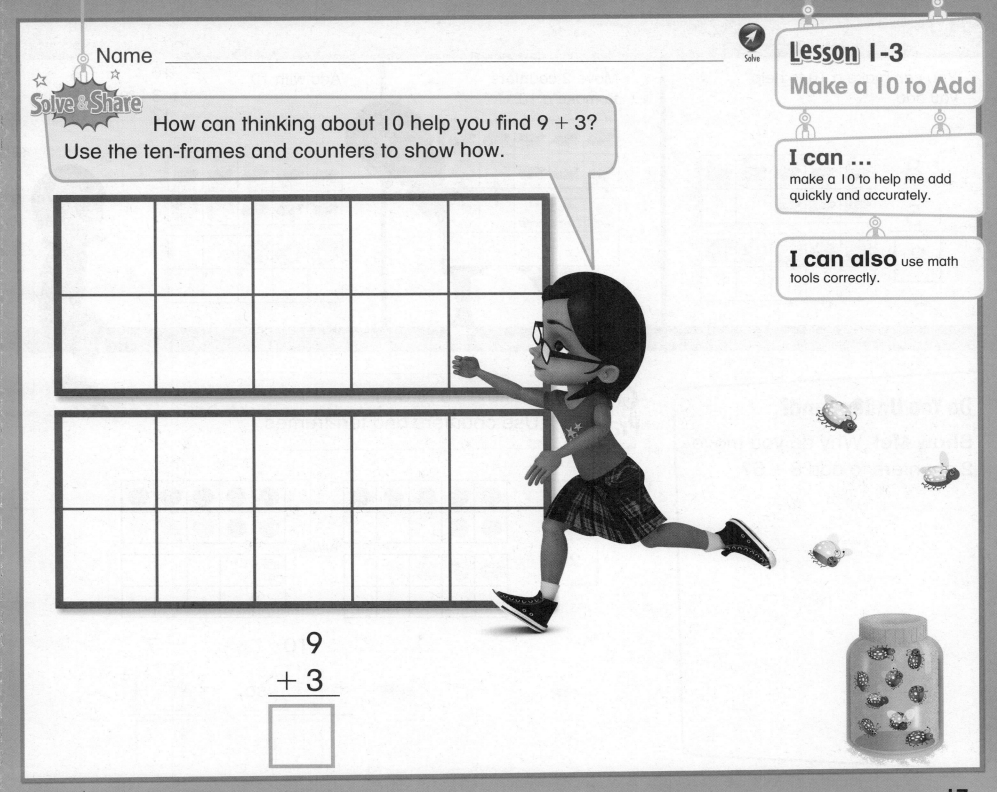

I can ...
make a 10 to help me add quickly and accurately.

I can also use math tools correctly.

$$\begin{array}{r} 9 \\ + 3 \\ \hline \end{array}$$

Learn Glossary

You can make a 10 to help you add.

8
+ 5

?

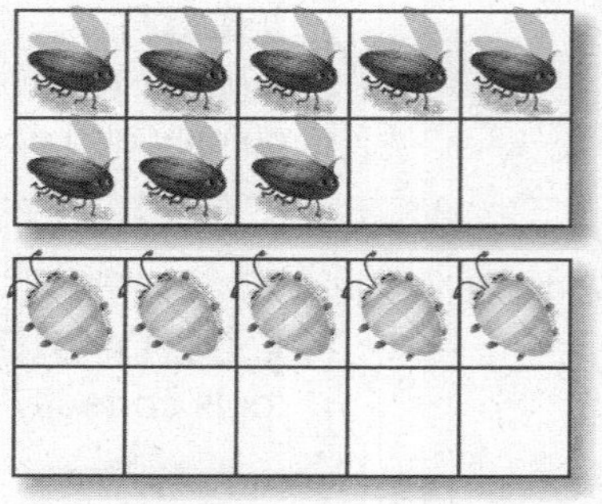

Move 2 counters to make a 10.

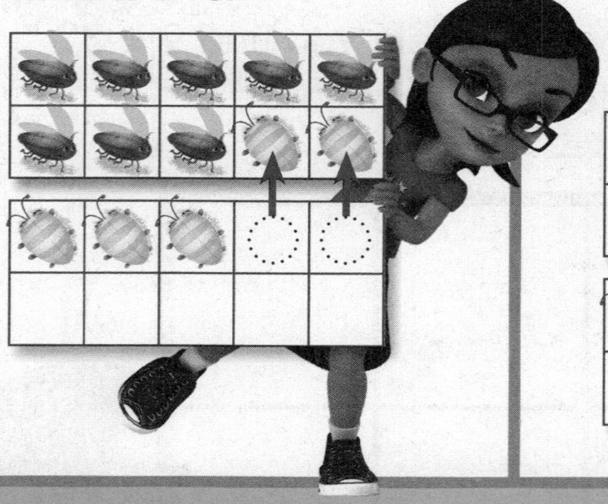

Add with 10.

$$\begin{array}{r} 10 \\ +3 \\ \hline 13 \end{array}$$ so, $$\begin{array}{r} 8 \\ +5 \\ \hline 13 \end{array}$$

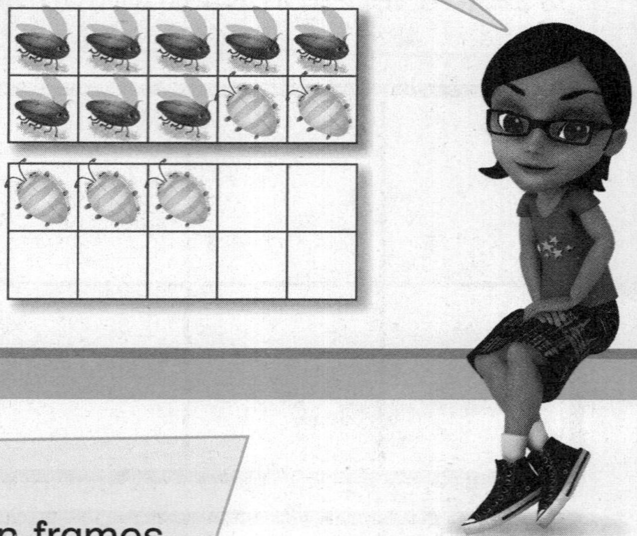

Do You Understand?

Show Me! Why do you move 2 counters to add 8 + 5?

☆ **Guided Practice** ☆ Make a 10 to add. Use counters and ten-frames.

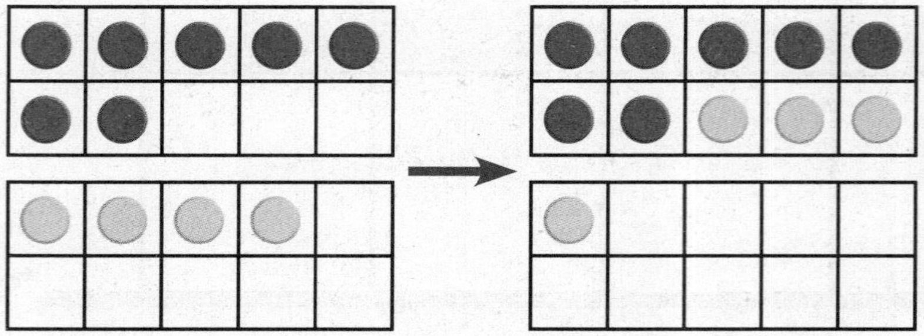

1.   7
     + 4

      ?

10   7

+ �... so,   +

☆ Independent Practice ☆ Make a 10 to add. Use counters and ten-frames.

2.   8
   + 4
□

3.   3
   + 9
□

4.   6
   + 7
□

5.   5
   + 8
□

6.   7
   + 5
□

7. 5 + 9 = ____

8. 3 + 8 = ____

9. 4 + 9 = ____

10. 7 + 9 = ____

Algebra Which number is missing?

11. 8 + 5 = □ + 3

12. 6 + 9 = 10 + □

13. 8 + 9 = 10 + □

14. **Higher Order Thinking** Can you make a 10 to help you add 7 + 4 + 5? Explain.

_____

_____

15. Tan's team scored 16 points in a game. During the first half, they scored 9 points. How many points did the team score in the second half of the game?

_____ points

16. Make Sense The school has a clothing drive for charity. Ana's class donates 8 coats. Nico's class donates 5 hats. Adam's class donates 8 coats. How many coats were donated in all?

_____ coats

17. Higher Order Thinking Draw a picture to show how you can make a 10 to help you add $3 + 5 + 9$.

18. ✅ **Assessment** Mary wrote an equation. Which number makes her equation true?

$$8 + 9 = 10 + \underline{\quad}$$

Ⓐ 5

Ⓑ 6

Ⓒ 7

Ⓓ 8

Think about making a 10. Find the missing addend!

Name _____

Another Look! You can make a 10 to help you add.

This shows $8 + 4$.

Show $10 + 2$.
Move 2 counters to make a 10.

The sums are the same!

$8 + 4$ is the same as $10 + 2$.

$8 + 4 = 12$ $10 + 2 = 12$

HOME ACTIVITY Have your child use buttons to make a group of 9 and a group of 5. Ask your child to show you how to make a group of 10 buttons to help find the sum.

Make a 10 to help you add.

1. Find $9 + 7$.   Move 1 counter to make a 10.

$9 + 7$ is the same as $10 +$ ____.

$9 + 7 =$ ____   ____ $+$ ____ $=$ ____

2. Find $7 + 5$.

Move ____ counters to make a 10.

$7 + 5$ is the same as $10 +$ ____.

$7 + 5 =$ ____   ____ $+$ ____ $=$ ____

Add. Then draw lines to match addition problems with the same sum.

3. $9 + 6 =$ _____ $10 + 2 =$ _____

4. $7 + 5 =$ _____ $10 + 3 =$ _____

5. $9 + 5 =$ _____ $10 + 4 =$ _____

6. $5 + 8 =$ _____ $10 + 5 =$ _____

7. **Explain** Blanca wants to add $5 + 8$. Describe how she can make a 10 to solve.

$5 + 8 =$ _____

_____

_____

_____

8. **Higher Order Thinking** Jay has 14 blocks in all. He has 6 yellow blocks. The rest of the blocks are green. How many green blocks does Jay have? Make a 10 to solve.

Jay has _____ green blocks.

Explain how you solved the problem!

_____

_____

_____

9. ✓**Assessment** Beth has 8 fish and 7 snails. How can Beth make a 10 to find how many fish and snails she has in all?

$10 + 9$ $10 + 8$ $10 + 7$ $10 + 5$

ⓐ   Ⓑ   Ⓒ   Ⓓ

10. ✓**Assessment** Use the ten-frames. Show how to find $7 + 6$ by making a 10.

Name _____

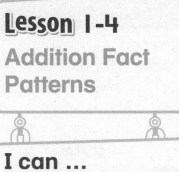

Lesson 1-4

Addition Fact Patterns

I can ...
use the patterns on an addition facts table to help me remember the addition facts.

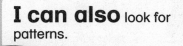

I can also look for patterns.

Solve & Share

Look at the sums on an addition facts table for addends 0 to 5. Describe one of the patterns that you see.

Use words, colors, or addition facts to describe the patterns.

+	0	1	2	3	4	5
0	0	1	2	3	4	5
1	1	2	3	4	5	6
2	2	3	4	5	6	7
3	3	4	5	6	7	8
4	4	5	6	7	8	9
5	5	6	7	8	9	10

_____

_____

_____

How can you describe a pattern for all the sums of six?

+	0	1	2	3	4	5	6	7	8	9	10
0	0	1	2	3	4	5	6	7	8	9	10
1	1	2	3	4	5	6	7	8	9	10	11
2	2	3	4	5	6	7	8	9	10	11	12
3	3	4	5	6	7	8	9	10	11	12	13
4	4	5	6	7	8	9	10	11	12	13	14
5	5	6	7	8	9	10	11	12	13	14	15
6	6	7	8	9	10	11	12	13	14	15	16
7	7	8	9	10	11	12	13	14	15	16	17
8	8	9	10	11	12	13	14	15	16	17	18
9	9	10	11	12	13	14	15	16	17	18	19
10	10	11	12	13	14	15	16	17	18	19	20

It makes a diagonal pattern.

You can write an addition equation.

$4 + 2 = 6$

4 and 2 are addends for the sum of 6.

+	0	1	2	3	4
0	0	1	2	3	4
1	1	2	3	4	5
2	2	3	4	5	6

Here are all the ways to make a sum of 6.

$6 + 0 = 6$
$5 + 1 = 6$
$4 + 2 = 6$
$3 + 3 = 6$
$2 + 4 = 6$
$1 + 5 = 6$
$0 + 6 = 6$

What pattern do you see?

Do You Understand?

Show Me! How can patterns on an addition facts table help you remember the addition facts?

☆ Guided Practice   Use fact patterns to complete each equation.

1. $10 + \underline{6} = 16$
   $9 + 7 = \underline{16}$
   $\underline{8} + 8 = 16$
   $7 + \underline{9} = 16$
   $6 + \underline{10} = 16$

2. $10 + \underline{} = 14$
   $\underline{} + 5 = 14$
   $8 + 6 = \underline{}$
   $7 + \underline{} = 14$
   $\underline{} + 6 = 14$
   $9 + \underline{} = 14$
   $\underline{} + 4 = 14$

3. $9 + \underline{} = 9$
   $\underline{} + 1 = 9$
   $7 + 2 = \underline{}$
   $6 + \underline{} = 9$
   $\underline{} + 4 = 9$
   $5 + \underline{} = 9$
   $3 + \underline{} = 9$
   $\underline{} + 2 = 9$
   $8 + 1 = \underline{}$
   $\underline{} + 0 = 9$

Tools Assessment

Independent Practice ☆ Use fact patterns to complete each equation.

4. $10 + \underline{\hphantom{00}} = 12$

$\underline{\hphantom{00}} + 3 = 12$

$8 + 4 = \underline{\hphantom{00}}$

$\underline{\hphantom{00}} + 7 = 12$

$6 + 6 = \underline{\hphantom{00}}$

$7 + \underline{\hphantom{00}} = 12$

$\underline{\hphantom{00}} + 4 = 12$

$9 + \underline{\hphantom{00}} = 12$

5. $7 + \underline{\hphantom{00}} = 7$

$\underline{\hphantom{00}} + 1 = 7$

$5 + 2 = \underline{\hphantom{00}}$

$\underline{\hphantom{00}} + 3 = 7$

$\underline{\hphantom{00}} + 4 = 7$

$\underline{\hphantom{00}} + 5 = 7$

$\underline{\hphantom{00}} + 6 = 7$

$0 + \underline{\hphantom{00}} = 7$

6. $10 + \underline{\hphantom{00}} = 15$

$\underline{\hphantom{00}} + 5 = 15$

$9 + 6 = \underline{\hphantom{00}}$

$9 + \underline{\hphantom{00}} = 15$

$7 + \underline{\hphantom{00}} = 15$

$\underline{\hphantom{00}} + 7 = 15$

7. Number Sense Find the 8 in the top row of the addition facts table. Complete all of the equations using the 8-column on the table. What pattern do you see?

$8 + \underline{\hphantom{00}} = 8$

$8 + \underline{\hphantom{00}} = 9$

$8 + \underline{\hphantom{00}} = 10$

$8 + 3 = \underline{\hphantom{00}}$

$8 + \underline{\hphantom{00}} = 12$

$8 + \underline{\hphantom{00}} = \underline{\hphantom{00}}$

$8 + 6 = \underline{\hphantom{00}}$

$8 + \underline{\hphantom{00}} = 15$

$8 + 8 = \underline{\hphantom{00}}$

$8 + \underline{\hphantom{00}} = \underline{\hphantom{00}}$

$8 + 10 = \underline{\hphantom{00}}$

_____

_____

_____

_____

8. **Reasoning** Lucy is sorting items by their texture. She finds 6 items that are bumpy. Lucy finds 5 items that are smooth. How many items does Lucy find in all?

_____ items

9. (A-Z) **Vocabulary** Look at the **equation** below. Circle the **addends**. Draw a square around the **sum**.

$$9 + 5 = 14$$

10. **Higher Order Thinking** Write 8 addition facts that have a sum of 12. How can patterns help you?

_____

_____

_____

_____

11. ✓**Assessment** Which have a sum of 17? Choose all that apply.

☐ $10 + 7 = ?$

☐ $7 + 6 = ?$

☐ $9 + 8 = ?$

☐ $8 + 8 = ?$

Think about fact patterns.

Name _____

Another Look! You can use your addition table to find the addition facts that have 7 as an addend.

Find the 7 in the top row of the table.
Write an equation for each sum in that column.

+	0	1	2	3	4	5	6	7	8	9	10
0	0	1	2	3	4	5	6	7	8	9	10
1	1	2	3	4	5	6	7	8	9	10	11
2	2	3	4	5	6	7	8	9	10	11	12
3	3	4	5	6	7	8	9	10	11	12	13
4	4	5	6	7	8	9	10	11	12	13	14
5	5	6	7	8	9	10	11	12	13	14	15
6	6	7	8	9	10	11	12	13	14	15	16
7	7	8	9	10	11	12	13	14	15	16	17
8	8	9	10	11	12	13	14	15	16	17	18
9	9	10	11	12	13	14	15	16	17	18	19
10	10	11	12	13	14	15	16	17	18	19	20

$0 + 7 = 7$ $5 + 7 = 12$
$1 + 7 = 8$ $6 + 7 = 13$
$2 + 7 = 9$ $7 + 7 = 14$
$3 + 7 = 10$ $8 + 7 = 15$
$4 + 7 = 11$ $9 + 7 = 16$
                       $10 + 7 = 17$

HOME ACTIVITY Have your child practice using an addition facts table by asking your child to write an equation for each sum that is 16.

You can add in any order. So, complete the list by switching the order of the addends.

Use fact patterns to complete each equation.

1. $9 + 6 =$ _____

   _____ $+ 7 = 15$

   $7 +$ _____ $= 15$

   $6 +$ _____ $= 15$

2. $0 +$ _____ $= 4$

   $1 + 3 =$ _____

   _____ $+ 2 = 4$

   $3 +$ _____ $= 4$

   _____ $+ 4 = 4$

3. $5 +$ _____ $= 6$

   $4 +$ _____ $= 6$

   $3 + 3 =$ _____

   _____ $+ 4 = 6$

   _____ $+ 5 = 6$

Look for Patterns Use fact patterns to complete each equation.

4. $10 + \underline{\quad} = 11$ $\quad$ $5 + \underline{\quad} = 11$

$\underline{\quad} + 2 = 11$ $\quad$ $4 + \underline{\quad} = 11$

$8 + 3 = \underline{\quad}$ $\quad$ $3 + \underline{\quad} = 11$

$7 + \underline{\quad} = 11$ $\quad$ $\underline{\quad} + 2 = 11$

$\underline{\quad} + 5 = 11$ $\quad$ $1 + 10 = \underline{\quad}$

$\quad\quad\quad\quad\quad\quad\quad$ $0 + \underline{\quad} = 11$

5. $9 + 9 = \underline{\quad}$ $\quad$ $\underline{\quad} + 4 = 13$

$9 + \underline{\quad} = 17$ $\quad$ $9 + 3 = \underline{\quad}$

$\underline{\quad} + 7 = 16$ $\quad$ $9 + \underline{\quad} = 11$

$9 + 6 = \underline{\quad}$ $\quad$ $\underline{\quad} + 1 = 10$

$9 + \underline{\quad} = 14$ $\quad$ $9 + 0 = \underline{\quad}$

6. **Higher Order Thinking** Write 8 equations with 2 addends that have a sum of 13. Use patterns to help you.

_____

_____

_____

7. ✓**Assessment** Which have a sum of 19? Choose all that apply.

☐ $10 + 9 = ?$

☐ $8 + 8 = ?$

☐ $9 + 9 = ?$

☐ $9 + 10 = ?$

8. ✓**Assessment** Which have a sum of 15? Choose all that apply.

☐ $7 + 8 = ?$

☐ $8 + 7 = ?$

☐ $9 + 6 = ?$

☐ $5 + 10 = ?$

Name _____

How can counting help you find 12 − 4?
Use the number line to show your work.

I can ...
count on and count back on a
number line to subtract.

I can also use
math tools.

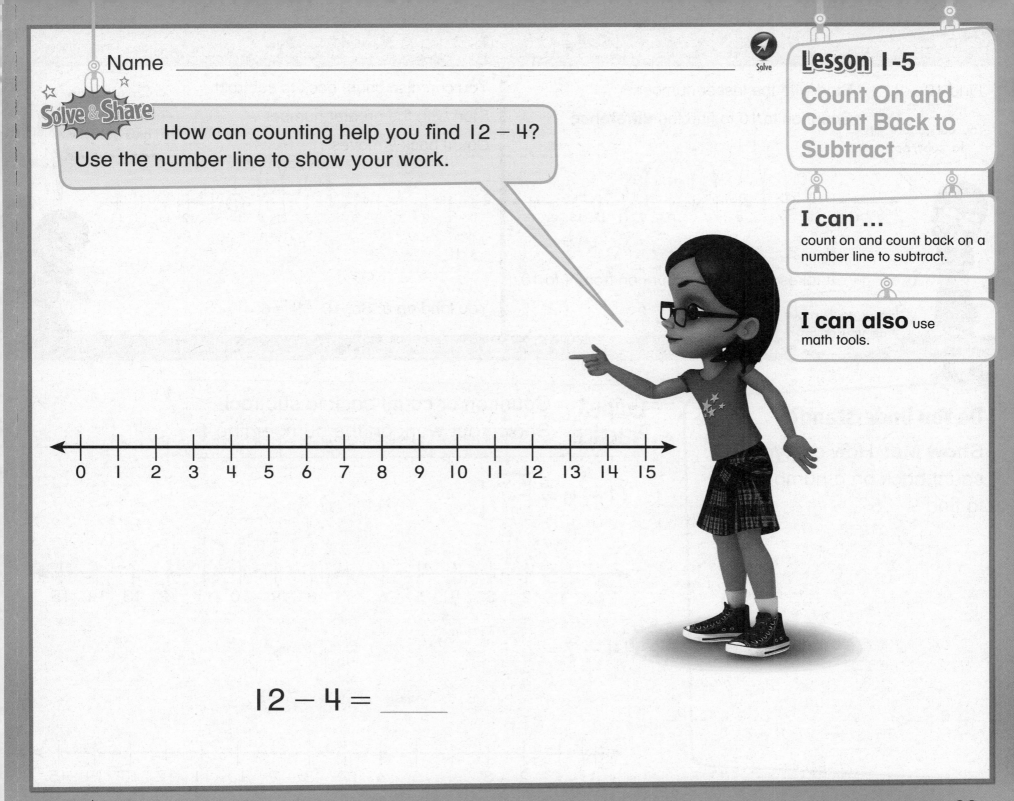

$$12 - 4 = \underline{}$$

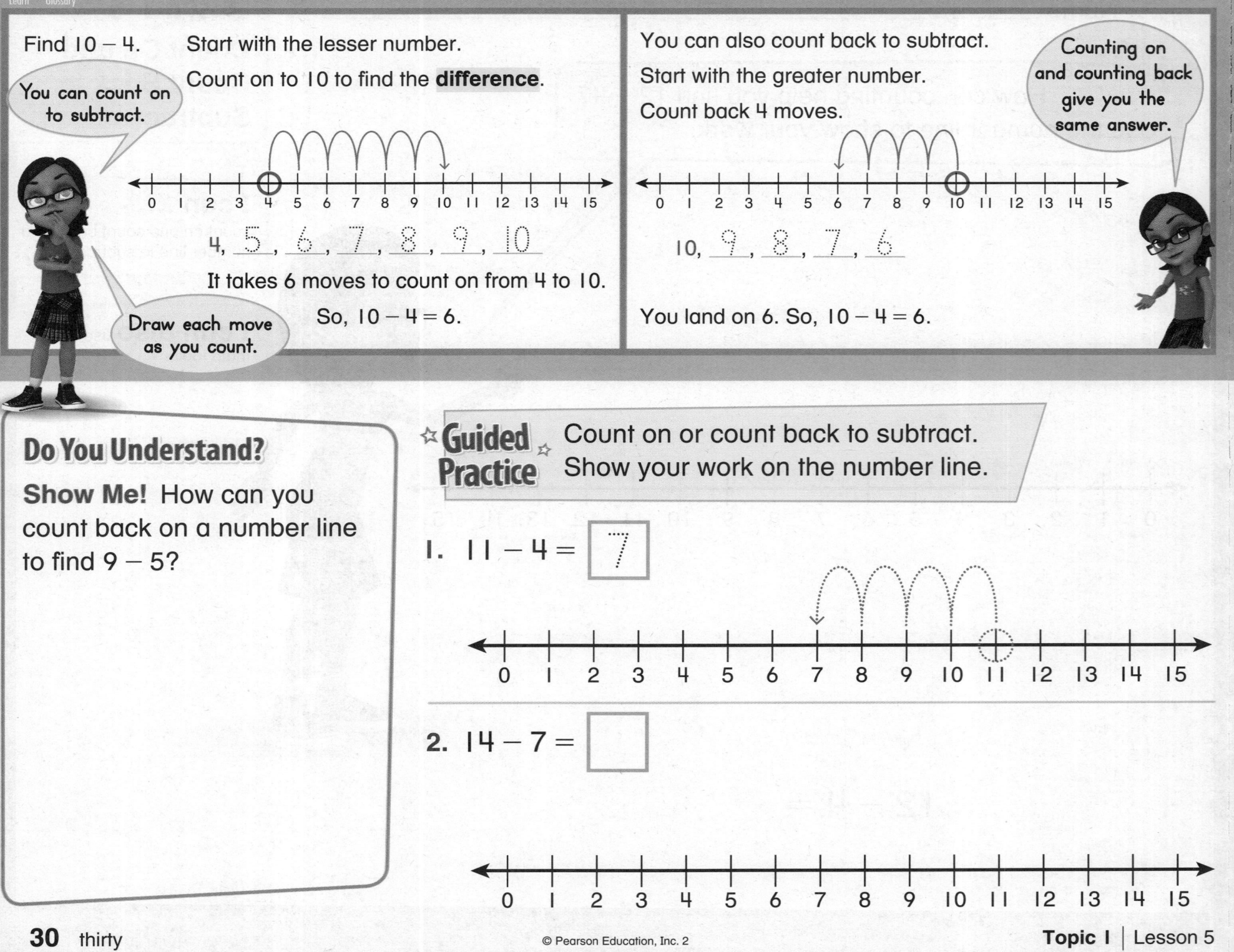

Find 10 − 4.   Start with the lesser number.

Count on to 10 to find the **difference**.

You can count on to subtract.

Draw each move as you count.

4, _5_, _6_, _7_, _8_, _9_, _10_

It takes 6 moves to count on from 4 to 10.

So, 10 − 4 = 6.

You can also count back to subtract.

Start with the greater number.

Count back 4 moves.

Counting on and counting back give you the same answer.

10, _9_, _8_, _7_, _6_

You land on 6. So, 10 − 4 = 6.

Do You Understand?

Show Me! How can you count back on a number line to find 9 − 5?

☆ Guided Practice ☆   Count on or count back to subtract. Show your work on the number line.

1. 11 − 4 = [7]

2. 14 − 7 = [ ]

© Pearson Education, Inc. 2

Tools Assessment

Independent Practice ☆ Count on or count back to subtract. Show your work on the number line.

3. $14 - 8 = \boxed{}$

0 1 2 3 4 5 6 7 8 9 10 11 12 13 14 15

4. $12 - 7 = \boxed{}$

0 1 2 3 4 5 6 7 8 9 10 11 12 13 14 15

5. $9 - 7 = \boxed{}$

0 1 2 3 4 5 6 7 8 9 10 11 12 13 14 15

6. $15 - 6 = \boxed{}$

0 1 2 3 4 5 6 7 8 9 10 11 12 13 14 15

7. **Higher Order Thinking** How can you count on to find $13 - 4$? Explain.

_____

_____

_____

8. Callie had 8 seeds.
She planted 2 of the seeds.
How many seeds does
Callie have now?

_____ seeds

9. **Make Sense** Peter has 16 grapes.
He eats some of the grapes. Peter has
10 grapes left. How many grapes did
Peter eat?

$16 - \underline{\quad} = 10$

_____ grapes

10. **Higher Order Thinking** Choose
2 numbers. Use the numbers to write
or draw a subtraction story. Write the
equation you used to solve your story.

_____ − _____ = _____

11. ✅**Assessment** Jake is playing with
6 marbles. He gives 3 marbles to Sam.
How many marbles does Jake have now?

Use the numbers on the cards to show
how to count on to solve the problem.

| 6 | 3 | 5 | 4 |

Begin with ⬜ . Then count on ⬜ ,

⬜ , ⬜ .

Jake has _____ marbles now.

© Pearson Education, Inc. 2

Name _____

Another Look! You can use a number line to count back to subtract.

Find 12 − 5.

Draw jumps on the number line as you count back!

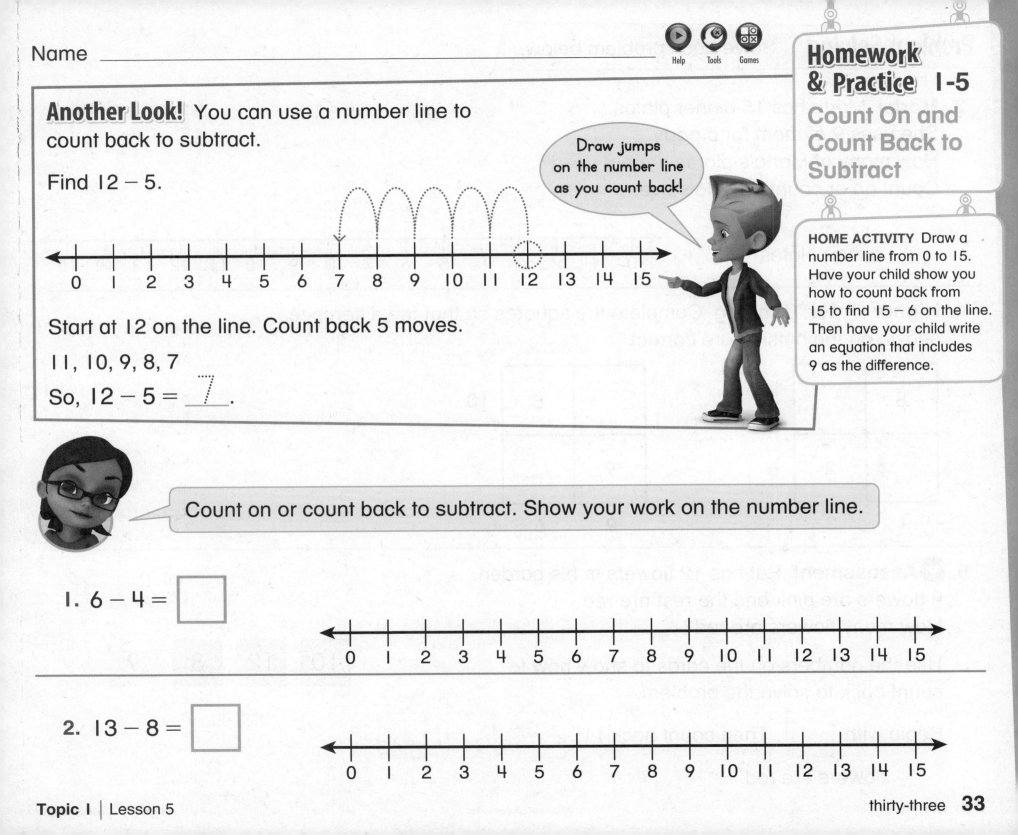

0 1 2 3 4 5 6 7 8 9 10 11 12 13 14 15

Start at 12 on the line. Count back 5 moves.

11, 10, 9, 8, 7

So, 12 − 5 = 7 .

HOME ACTIVITY Draw a number line from 0 to 15. Have your child show you how to count back from 15 to find 15 − 6 on the line. Then have your child write an equation that includes 9 as the difference.

Count on or count back to subtract. Show your work on the number line.

1. 6 − 4 = ☐

0 1 2 3 4 5 6 7 8 9 10 11 12 13 14 15

2. 13 − 8 = ☐

0 1 2 3 4 5 6 7 8 9 10 11 12 13 14 15

3. **Model** Marta has 15 dinner plates.
   She uses 9 of them for a party.
   How many of Marta's plates are not used?
   Count on or count back to solve.

_____ dinner plates

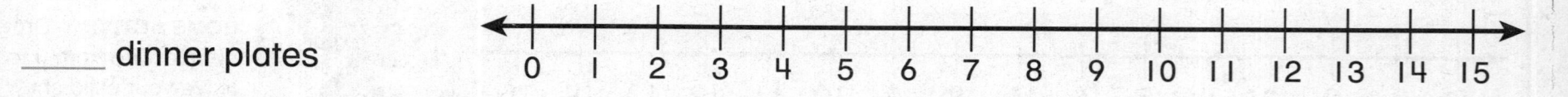

4. **Higher Order Thinking** Complete the squares so that the differences
   shown on the outside are correct.

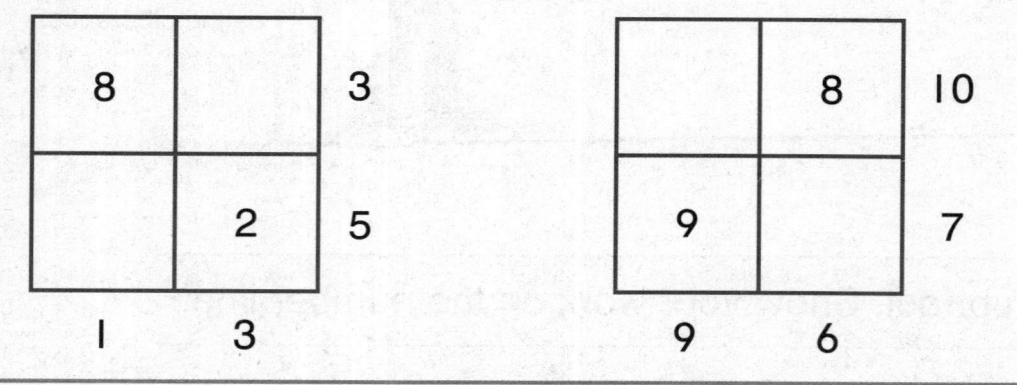

5. ✅**Assessment** Pat has 12 flowers in his garden.
   4 flowers are pink and the rest are red.
   How many flowers are red?

   Use the numbers on the cards to show how to
   count back to solve the problem.

   | 10 | 12 | 8 | 9 |

   Begin with ☐ . Then count back 11, ☐ , ☐ , ☐ .

   _____ flowers are red.

Name _____

Solve & Share

How can you use an addition fact to find 14 − 6? Use counters to help show how.

I can ...
use addition to help me subtract quickly and accurately.

I can also reason about math.

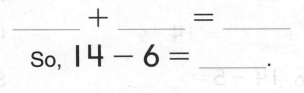

_____ + _____ = _____

So, 14 − 6 = _____.

Find $15 - 7$.

One way to subtract is to think about addition.

To find $15 - 7$, you can think:

7 plus how many more is 15?
or
$7 + \underline{} = 15$

The missing number is the same in both equations.

$7 + \underline{} = 15$

$15 - 7 = \underline{}$

You know the addition fact.

$7 + \underline{8} = 15$

You also know the subtraction fact.

$15 - 7 = \underline{8}$

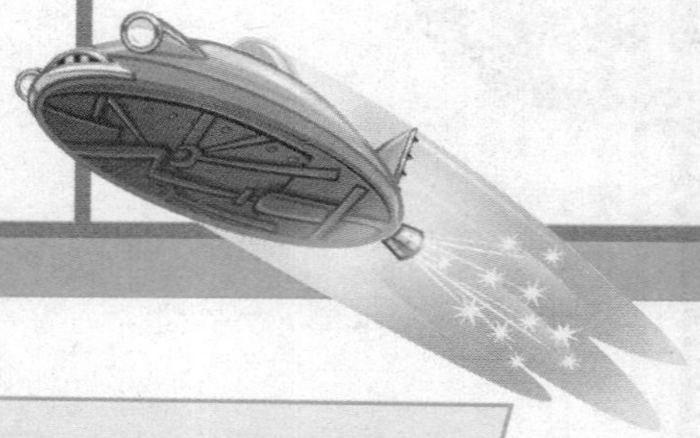

Do You Understand?

Show Me! How do you know which addition fact to use to complete the subtraction fact?

☆ Guided Practice   Think addition to help you subtract.

1. $6 - 4 = ?$

   $4 + \underline{2} = 6$

   So, $6 - 4 = \underline{2}$.

2. $9 - 3 = ?$

   $3 + \underline{} = 9$

   So, $9 - 3 = \underline{}$.

3. $14 - 5 = ?$

   $5 + \underline{} = 14$

   So, $14 - 5 = \underline{}$.

4. $12 - 4 = ?$

   $4 + \underline{} = 12$

   So, $12 - 4 = \underline{}$.

Independent Practice ☆ Subtract. Write the addition fact that can help you.

5. $8 - 1 =$ _____

$1 +$ _____ $= 8$

6. $10 - 2 =$ _____

$2 +$ _____ $= 10$

7. $15 - 6 =$ _____

$6 +$ _____ $= 15$

8. $17 - 7 =$ _____

$7 +$ _____ $= 17$

9. $14 - 8 =$ _____

$8 +$ _____ $= 14$

10. $9 - 5 =$ _____

$5 +$ _____ $= 9$

11.
$$\begin{array}{r} 18 \\ -\ 8 \\ \hline \square \end{array} \qquad \begin{array}{r} 8 \\ +\ \square \\ \hline 18 \end{array}$$

12.
$$\begin{array}{r} 16 \\ -\ 9 \\ \hline \square \end{array} \qquad \begin{array}{r} 9 \\ +\ \square \\ \hline 16 \end{array}$$

13.
$$\begin{array}{r} 19 \\ -\ 9 \\ \hline \square \end{array} \qquad \begin{array}{r} 9 \\ +\ \square \\ \hline 19 \end{array}$$

Higher Order Thinking Write a related addition fact to complete the subtraction fact.

14. $11 -$ _____ $= 5$

_____ $+$ _____ $=$ _____

15. $7 -$ _____ $= 2$

_____ $+$ _____ $=$ _____

16. $12 -$ _____ $= 8$

_____ $+$ _____ $=$ _____

17. Reasoning Kate had 6 pens.
She got 5 more pens from John.
How many pens does
Kate have in all?

_____ + _____ = _____

_____ pens

18. Reasoning John had 11 pens.
He gave 5 pens to Kate.
How many pens does
John have now?

_____ − _____ = _____

_____ pens

19. Higher Order Thinking Write a
subtraction story using the numbers
18 and 10. Then write an addition fact
that can help you solve the problem in
your story.

_____ + _____ = _____

20. ✅**Assessment** Pam has 16 cherries.
She eats 7 cherries.
Which addition fact can help you
find how many cherries Pam has left?

$7 + 4 = 11$
Ⓐ

$7 + 9 = 16$
Ⓒ

$7 + 6 = 13$
Ⓑ

$9 + 9 = 18$
Ⓓ

Name _____

Help Tools Games

Another Look! Addition facts can help you subtract.
Use the pictures to find the missing numbers.

HOME ACTIVITY Make up problems during daily activities such as, "If I have 12 eggs and I use 3 of them, how many eggs do I have left?" Have your child write and solve the subtraction sentence using addition facts.

Addition Fact

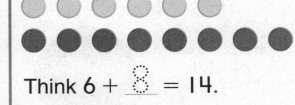

Think $6 + \underline{8} = 14$.

Subtraction Fact

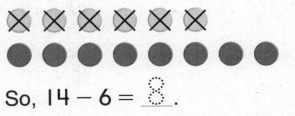

So, $14 - 6 = \underline{8}$.

Addition facts can help you subtract.
Use the pictures to find the missing numbers.

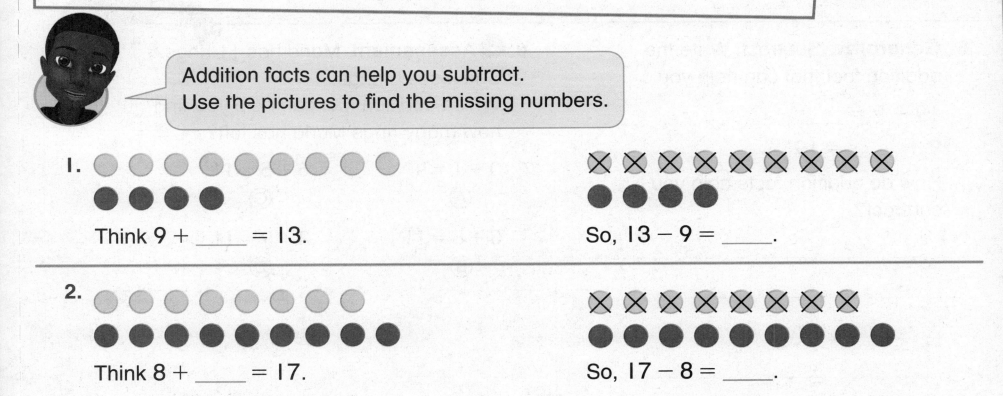

1. Think $9 + \underline{\hspace{1cm}} = 13$.

So, $13 - 9 = \underline{\hspace{1cm}}$.

2. Think $8 + \underline{\hspace{1cm}} = 17$.

So, $17 - 8 = \underline{\hspace{1cm}}$.

3. Lucy had 12 books. She gave 3 books to Michael. How many books does Lucy have now?

   3 + 12

   3 + 9

   6 + 6

   _____ − _____ = _____

   _____ books

4. Pam has 20 marbles. She puts 10 marbles in a jar. How many marbles are **NOT** in the jar?

   20 + 10

   9 + 9

   10 + 10

   _____ − _____ = _____

   _____ marbles

   > Think about the parts and the whole.

5. **Generalize** Subtract. Write the addition fact that can help you.

   $19 - 9 =$ _____

   $9 +$ _____ $= 19$

   How do addition facts help you subtract?

   _____

   _____

   _____

   _____

6. ✅**Assessment** Maria has 11 rings. She loses 3 rings. Which addition fact can help you find how many rings Maria has left?

   $3 + 1 = 4$ $6 + 5 = 11$

   Ⓐ   Ⓒ

   $3 + 8 = 11$ $2 + 9 = 11$

   Ⓑ   Ⓓ

Name _____

Solve & Share

14 ladybugs are on a leaf. 6 ladybugs fly away. How can thinking about 10 help you find how many ladybugs are left? Explain.

I can ...
make a 10 to help me subtract quickly and accurately.

I can also use math tools correctly.

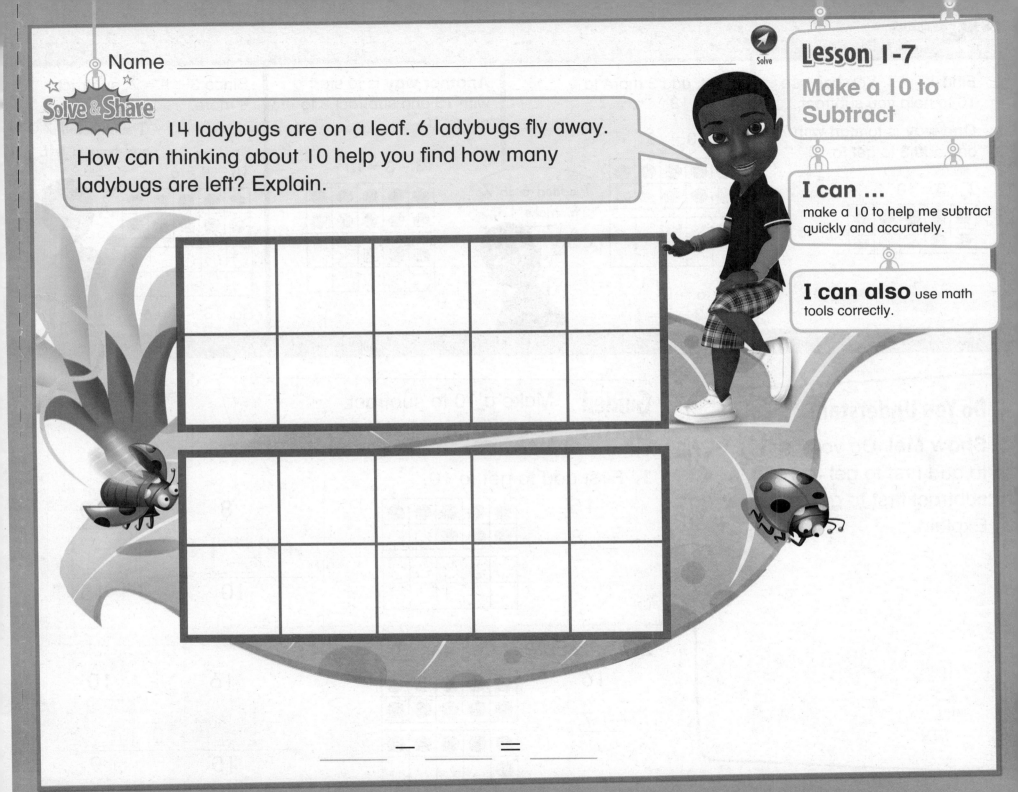

_____ − _____ = _____

Find 13 − 7. You can use 10 to help you subtract.

One way is to start with 7 and add 3 to get to 10.

7 + 3 = 10

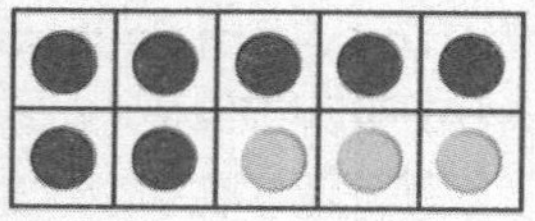

Next, add 3 more to make 13.

10 + 3 = 13

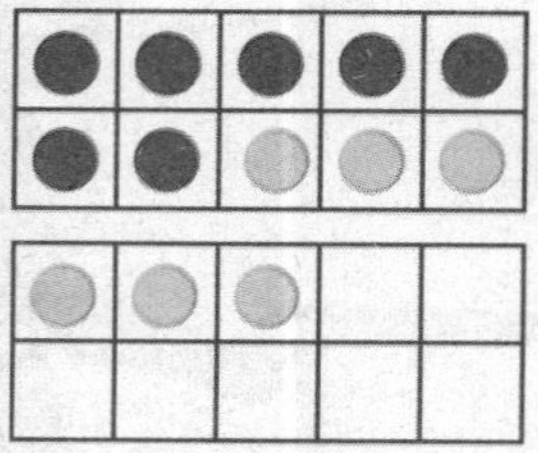

I added 6 to 7 to make 13.

7 + 6 = 13,
so 13 − 7 = 6.

Another way is to start with 13 and subtract 3 to get to 10.

13 − 3 = 10

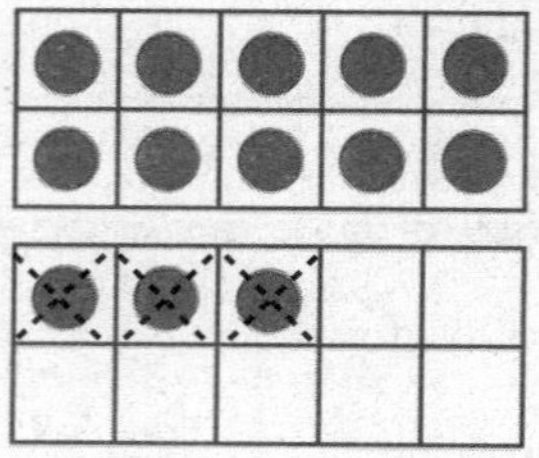

Since 3 + 4 = 7, subtract 4 more.

10 − 4 = 6

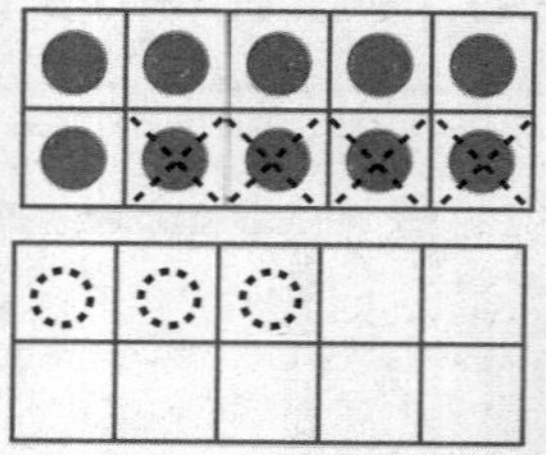

I subtracted 7 and have 6 left.

So, 13 − 7 = 6.

Do You Understand?

Show Me! Do you prefer to add first to get to 10 or subtract first to get to 10? Explain.

☆ Guided Practice ☆

Make a 10 to subtract.
Use counters and your workmat.

1. First add to get to 10.

$$\begin{array}{r} 15 \\ -\ \ 8 \\ \hline 7 \end{array}$$

$$\begin{array}{r} 8 \\ +\ \boxed{2} \\ \hline 10 \end{array} \quad \begin{array}{r} 10 \\ +\ \boxed{5} \\ \hline 15 \end{array}$$

2. First subtract to get to 10.

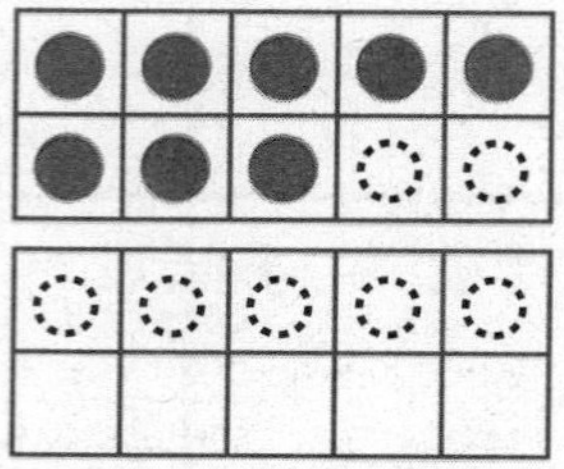

$$\begin{array}{r} 16 \\ -\ \ 7 \\ \hline \end{array}$$

$$\begin{array}{r} 16 \\ -\ \boxed{} \\ \hline 10 \end{array} \quad \begin{array}{r} 10 \\ -\ \boxed{} \\ \hline 9 \end{array}$$

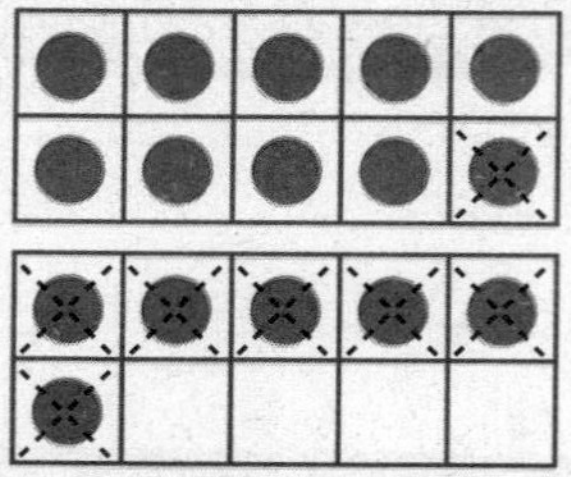

Topic 1 | Lesson 7

Independent Practice ☆ Make a 10 to subtract. Use counters and your workmat.

3. 11
   − 4
   ─────

4. 14
   − 8
   ─────

5. 12
   − 7
   ─────

6. 12
   − 4
   ─────

> Think of the ways you know to make 10.

7. 18
   − 9
   ─────

8. 17
   − 8
   ─────

9. 16
   − 8
   ─────

10. 13
    − 4
    ─────

11. 15
    − 9
    ─────

12. 14
    − 7
    ─────

13. 12
    − 8
    ─────

14. 16
    − 9
    ─────

15. **Higher Order Thinking** Carol subtracts
    6 from 15. First, she adds to get to 10.
    Then she adds again to find her answer.
    Her answer is 10. Is Carol correct?
    Explain.

_____

_____

_____

_____

16. Use Tools Chen had 12 animal stickers. He gave 5 of the stickers away. How many animal stickers does Chen have now?

_____ animal stickers

17. Use Tools Angie bought 13 strawberries. She ate 8 of the strawberries. How many strawberries does Angie have now?

_____ strawberries

18. Higher Order Thinking Show how you can make a 10 to find 17 − 9.

19. 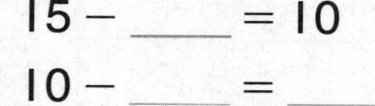**Assessment** Use the ten-frames. Show how to make a 10 to find 15 − 9. Start by subtracting to get to 10. Then complete the equations.

15 − _____ = 10

10 − _____ = _____

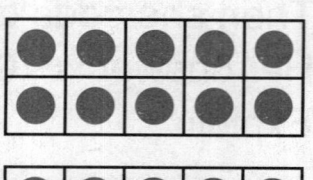
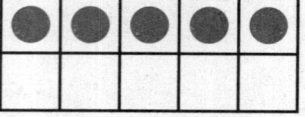

Name _____

Another Look! You can make a 10 to help you subtract. Find $13 - 5$.

One way

Subtract $13 - 3$ to make a 10.
Subtract 2 more to subtract 5 in all.
$10 - 2 = 8$

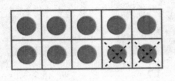
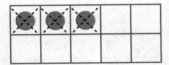

You have 8 left. So, $13 - 5 = 8$.

Another way

Add $5 + 5$ to make a 10.
Add 3 more to make 13.
$10 + 3 = 13$

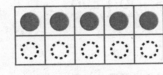
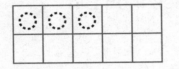

You added $5 + 8 = 13$. So, $13 - 5 = 8$.

HOME ACTIVITY Have your child use 12 small objects to explain how to find $12 - 8$ by first subtracting to get 10.

Use the ten-frames to subtract. Think about the parts and the whole.

1. $11 - 7 =$ _____

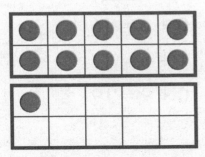

2. $14 - 6 =$ _____

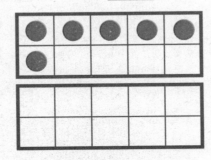

3. $12 - 5 =$ _____

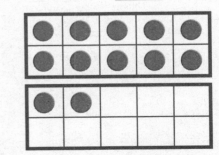

Higher Order Thinking For each problem, pick a bin from each row. Subtract to find how many more bottles are in the bin from the top row than the bin from the bottom row.

4. Bin _____ has _____ more bottles than Bin _____.

5. Bin _____ has _____ more bottles than Bin _____.

6. Bin _____ has _____ more bottles than Bin _____.

7. Bin _____ has _____ more bottles than Bin _____.

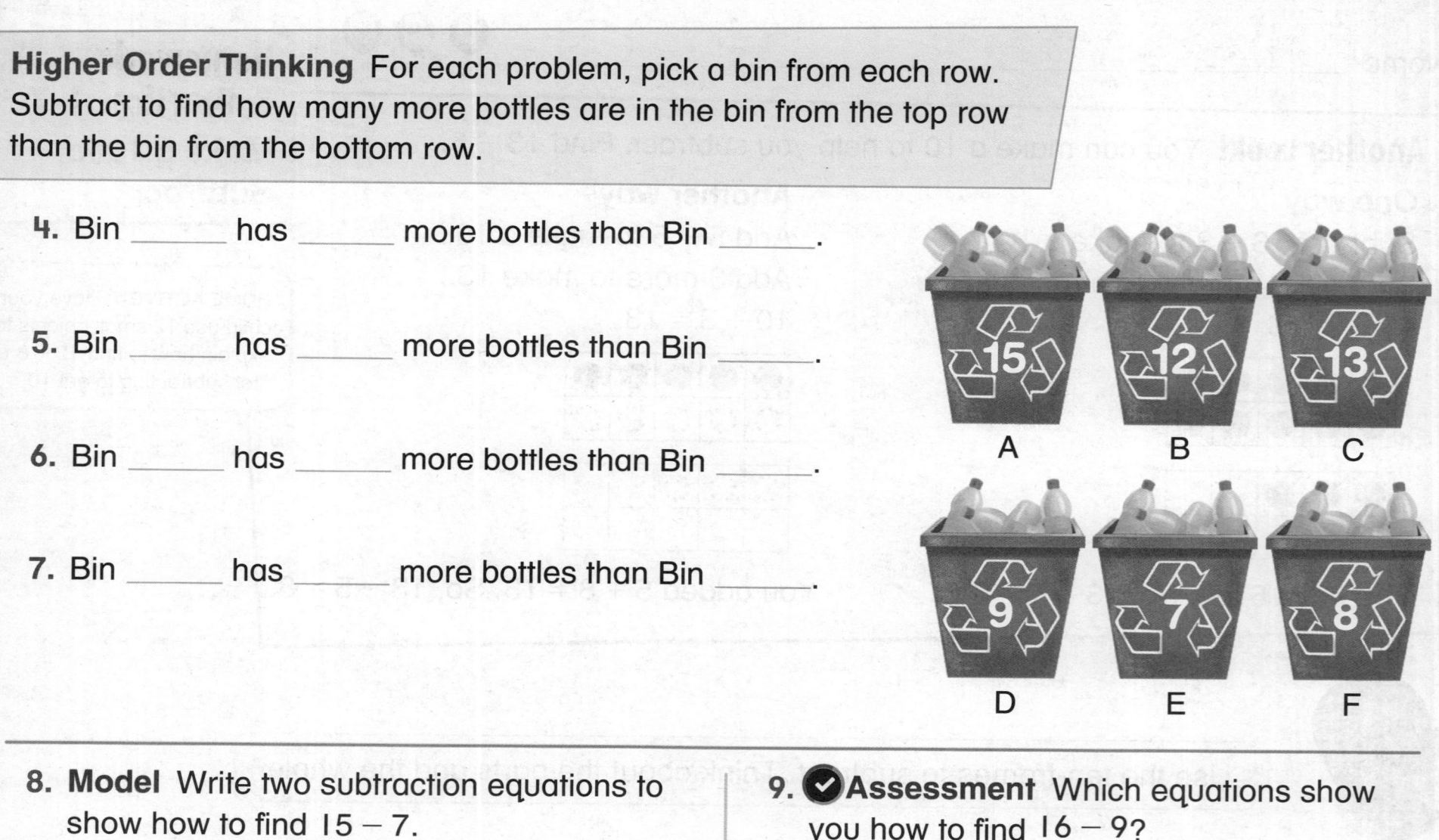

A   B   C

15   12   13

D   E   F

9   7   8

8. **Model** Write two subtraction equations to show how to find $15 - 7$.

_____ − _____ = _____

_____ − _____ = _____

9. ✅**Assessment** Which equations show you how to find $16 - 9$?

Ⓐ $9 + 1 = 10, 10 + 5 = 15$

Ⓑ $9 + 1 = 10, 10 + 6 = 16$

Ⓒ $9 + 2 = 11, 11 + 6 = 17$

Ⓓ $9 + 1 = 10, 10 + 9 = 19$

Name _____

Solve & Share

Write four related facts that use both the numbers 7 and 9 as quickly as you can. Hold up your hand when you are done. Then, tell how you found each fact.

I can ...
add and subtract quickly and accurately using mental math strategies.

I can also reason about math.

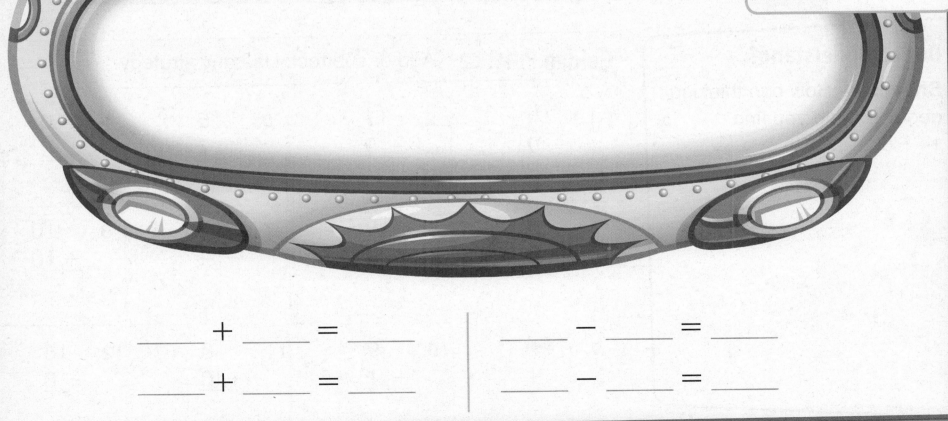

___ + ___ = ___   ___ − ___ = ___

___ + ___ = ___   ___ − ___ = ___

Digital Resources at PearsonRealize.com

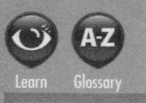
Practice your basic facts to recall them quickly.

Find 7 − 4.

Think of strategies to help you practice the facts.

One way to subtract is to think about addition.

| 7 |

$4 + \boxed{3} = 7$

So, $7 - 4 = \boxed{3}$.

Knowing doubles facts can help, too! Find 4 + 5.

4 + 4 and 1.

$4 + 5 = \boxed{9}$.

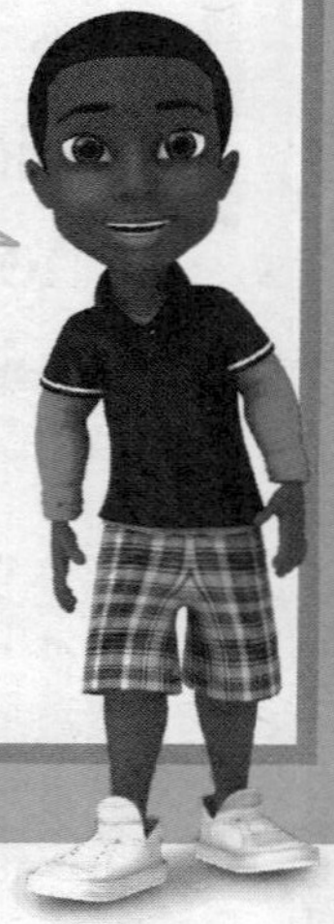

Practicing my basic facts will help me remember the facts quickly. Then my math problems will be easier.

Do You Understand?

Show Me! How can thinking about 10 help you find 14 − 8?

☆ Guided Practice   Add or subtract. Use any strategy.

1.
$$\begin{array}{r} 14 \\ -\ 9 \\ \hline 5 \end{array}$$

2.
$$\begin{array}{r} 17 \\ -\ 9 \\ \hline \end{array}$$

3.
$$\begin{array}{r} 5 \\ +\ 7 \\ \hline \end{array}$$

4.
$$\begin{array}{r} 10 \\ -\ 5 \\ \hline \end{array}$$

5.
$$\begin{array}{r} 6 \\ -\ 0 \\ \hline \end{array}$$

6.
$$\begin{array}{r} 9 \\ +\ 9 \\ \hline \end{array}$$

7.
$$\begin{array}{r} 12 \\ -\ 4 \\ \hline \end{array}$$

8.
$$\begin{array}{r} 10 \\ +10 \\ \hline \end{array}$$

9.
$$\begin{array}{r} 11 \\ -\ 4 \\ \hline \end{array}$$

10.
$$\begin{array}{r} 9 \\ +\ 1 \\ \hline \end{array}$$

11.
$$\begin{array}{r} 8 \\ +\ 0 \\ \hline \end{array}$$

12.
$$\begin{array}{r} 16 \\ -\ 8 \\ \hline \end{array}$$

Tools Assessment

Independent Practice ☆ Add or subtract. Use any strategy.

13. $14 - 7 =$ ____

14. $3 + 0 =$ ____

15. $8 + 7 =$ ____

16. $13 - 6 =$ ____

17. $10 + 9 =$ ____

18. $17 - 8 =$ ____

19. $18 - 9 =$ ____

20. $9 - 1 =$ ____

21. $7 + 4 =$ ____

22. $6 + 6 =$ ____

23. $16 - 9 =$ ____

24. $20 - 10 =$ ____

25. $16 - 7 =$ ____

26. $15 - 8 =$ ____

27. $7 + 3 =$ ____

28. $2 + 7 =$ ____

29. $9 + 6 =$ ____

30. $10 - 2 =$ ____

Higher Order Thinking Write the missing number.

31. $6 + \boxed{} = 14 - 5$

32. $12 - 4 = \boxed{} + 2$

33. $14 - \boxed{} = 5 + 4$

34. **Math and Science** Danielle had 17 pieces of paper. She changed 8 of the pieces by cutting them. How many pieces were not changed? Write an equation to solve.

_____ ◯ _____ = _____

_____ pieces of paper

35. **Model** Diego saw 5 frogs on a rock. He also saw 7 frogs in the grass. How many frogs did Diego see in all? Write an equation to solve.

_____ ◯ _____ = _____

_____ frogs

36. **Higher Order Thinking** Glen counts on to solve $9 + \boxed{} = 14$. Explain how he can do this. What is the missing addend?

_____

_____

_____

_____

_____

37. ✓**Assessment** Deshawn had some shells. He gave 3 shells to his brother. Now Deshawn has 8 shells.
How many shells did Deshawn have to begin with? Solve. Explain your solution.

Which operation will you use to solve this problem?

_____

_____

_____

Name _____

Help   Tools   Games

Homework
& Practice 1-8

Practice Addition
and Subtraction
Facts

Another Look! You can use strategies to help you practice addition and subtraction facts.

Find 12 − 7.

You can think about the relationship between addition and subtraction and use related facts.

HOME ACTIVITY Give your child the following numbers: 5, 6, and 11. Tell your child to write the fact family for these numbers as quickly as he or she can.

7 plus how many more is 12?

or

$7 + \underline{5} = 12$

So, 12 − 7 = 5.

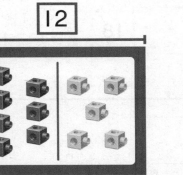

12

Add or subtract. Use any strategy.

1.	11	2.	12	3.	7	4.	2	5.	12	6.	8
	− 5		− 6		+ 6		+ 1		− 3		+ 8
	6										

7. $9 - 3 =$ ____

8. $10 + 9 =$ ____

9. $10 - 1 =$ ____

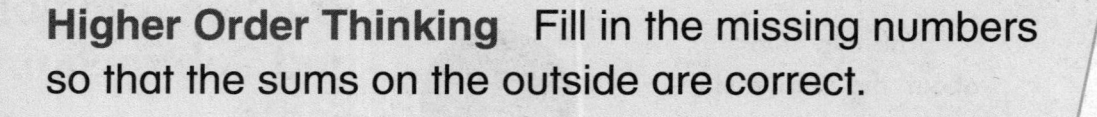

Higher Order Thinking Fill in the missing numbers so that the sums on the outside are correct.

10.

	3	11
0		3
8	6	

11.

6		10
	9	18
15		

12.

	7	12
8		17
13	16	

13.

6		14
	10	18
	18	

14. Explain What addition doubles fact can help you find $4 + 3$? Explain how you know.

_____

_____

_____

15. ✓**Assessment** Write an addition equation that can help you find $9 - 6$. Explain your answer.

_____

_____

_____

© Pearson Education, Inc. 2

Name _____

Solve & Share

Diego has 6 apples. Leslie has 9 apples.
How many more apples does Leslie have than Diego?

Will you add or subtract to solve this problem? Explain.

I can ...
use addition and subtraction to solve word problems.

I can also make sense of problems.

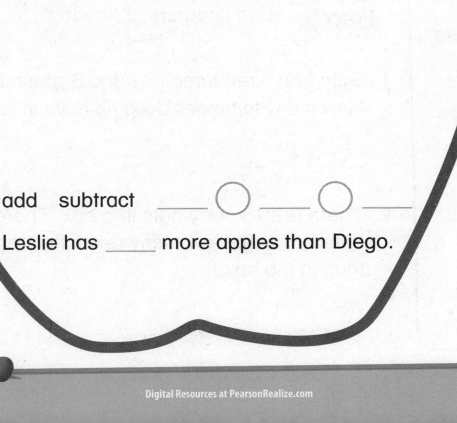

add   subtract   _____ ◯ _____ ◯ _____

Leslie has _____ more apples than Diego.

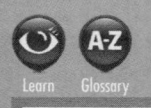

17 books are on a table. 8 books are on a shelf. How many fewer books are on the shelf than on the table?

You can use a bar diagram and an equation to model the problem.

The shelf has fewer books.

books on table

17

8	?

books on shelf   fewer books on shelf

You can write an addition or subtraction equation for the problem.

$17 - 8 = \underline{9}$

$8 + \underline{9} = 17$

17

8	9

So, there are 9 fewer books on the shelf.

Do You Understand?

Show Me! Why can you use addition OR subtraction to solve the problem above?

☆ Guided Practice ☆

Write an equation to solve each problem. Use counters, if needed.

1. Sam has 5 red tomatoes and 3 green tomatoes. How many tomatoes does he have in all?

$\underline{5} \ (+) \ \underline{3} \ (=) \ \underline{8}$ $\underline{8}$ tomatoes

2. There are 16 party hats in a box. There are 10 party hats in a bag. How many fewer hats are in the bag than in the box?

____ ◯ ____ ◯ ____   _____ fewer hats

Independent Practice Write an equation to solve each problem.
Use counters, if needed.

3. Cho has 3 more toy horses than Hakeem.
Cho has 9 toy horses.
How many toy horses does Hakeem have?

___ ◯ ___ ◯ ___

_____ toy horses

4. There are 12 peaches in a bowl.
The children eat some of them.
Now there are 8 peaches.
How many peaches did the children eat?

___ ◯ ___ ◯ ___

_____ peaches were eaten.

5. Juan reads 5 books.
Susan reads some books.
They read 11 books in all.
How many books did Susan read?

___ ◯ ___ ◯ ___

_____ books

6. Jack has 13 brushes.
Igor has 6 brushes.
How many fewer brushes
does Igor have than Jack?

___ ◯ ___ ◯ ___

_____ fewer brushes

7. **Number Sense** Jen had 3 animal
stickers in her collection. Her friend gave her
5 more stickers. Jen bought 7 more stickers.
How many stickers does Jen have now?
Show your work.

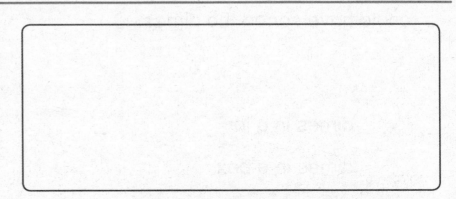

Problem Solving

8. **Higher Order Thinking** Sandy has 8 markers.
   Alex has 6 fewer markers than Sandy.
   Jill has 2 markers.
   How many markers do they have in all?

   Show your work. Then explain how you found the answer.

   _____

   _____

   _____

Use counters to solve.

9. **Make Sense** Annika saves 13 dimes.
   She put some of the dimes in a box and the rest in a jar.

   Write an equation to show one way she could have sorted the dimes.

   ____ ◯ ____ ◯ ____

   _____ dimes in a jar

   _____ dimes in a box

10. ✅**Assessment** Maria had 5 rings.
    She bought some more rings. Now she has 12 rings.

    Choose Yes or No to show if the equation can be used to find how many more rings Maria bought.

    $12 - 5 = 7$ ◯ Yes ◯ No

    $10 + 2 = 12$ ◯ Yes ◯ No

    $5 + 7 = 12$ ◯ Yes ◯ No

    $12 - 8 = 4$ ◯ Yes ◯ No

© Pearson Education, Inc. 2

Name _____

Another Look! You can use counters to solve this problem.

Francine has made 9 wristbands. Jon has made 5 wristbands. How many more wristbands has Francine made than Jon?

⬯ ⬯ ⬯ ⬯ ⬯ ⬯ ⬯ ⬯ ⬯
⬯ ⬯ ⬯ ⬯ ⬯

You can use an addition or subtraction strategy to help solve the problem.

Compare blue and red wristbands. Count on from 5 and add to find how many more wristbands Francine made.

5 ⊕ 4 ⊜ 9

You can also subtract. $9 - 5 = 4$

HOME ACTIVITY Make up addition and subtraction word problems. Ask your child to use small objects such as paper clips or pennies to add or subtract to solve the problems. For each problem, have your child write an equation to show how to solve it.

Write an equation to solve each problem. Use counters, if needed.

1. 6 bugs are on a leaf.
   2 bugs join them.
   How many bugs are there in all?

   ___ ◯ ___ ◯ ___

   ___ bugs

2. There are 13 baseballs in a box.
   There are 8 baseballs in a bag.
   How many more baseballs are in a box?

   ___ ◯ ___ ◯ ___

   ___ more baseballs

3. Be Precise Devin brought his snail collection to school. He has 10 snails.
How could he put them into 2 tanks so two classes could see them?

Write equations for all the possible ways.
One of the ways is given.

Explain how you know you have found all the ways.

_____

_____

_____

$$10 = 9 + 1$$

Write equations to solve the problem. Use counters, if needed.

4. Higher Order Thinking Pat has 9 cards.
Frank has 2 more cards than Steve.
Steve has 3 cards.
How many more cards does Pat have than Frank?

Cards Frank has: ____ ◯ ____ ◯ ____

More cards Pat has than Frank:

____ ◯ ____ ◯ ____

Pat has ____ more cards than Frank.

5. ✓Assessment Jan has 10 dolls.
Kat has 7 dolls. Choose Yes or No to show if the equation can be used to find how many fewer dolls Kat has than Jan.

$10 - 7 = 3$	◯ Yes	◯ No
$3 + 7 = 10$	◯ Yes	◯ No
$10 + 7 = 17$	◯ Yes	◯ No
$7 + 3 = 10$	◯ Yes	◯ No

© Pearson Education, Inc. 2

Name _____

Solve & Share

How can you use the **make a 10** strategy to find 7 + 9?

Explain your thinking and work.
Use pictures, numbers, or words.

I can ...
use pictures, numbers, and words to explain why my thinking and work are correct.

I can also add or subtract within 20.

Thinking Habits

How can I use math to explain why my work is correct?

Is my explanation clear?

_____

_____

_____

_____

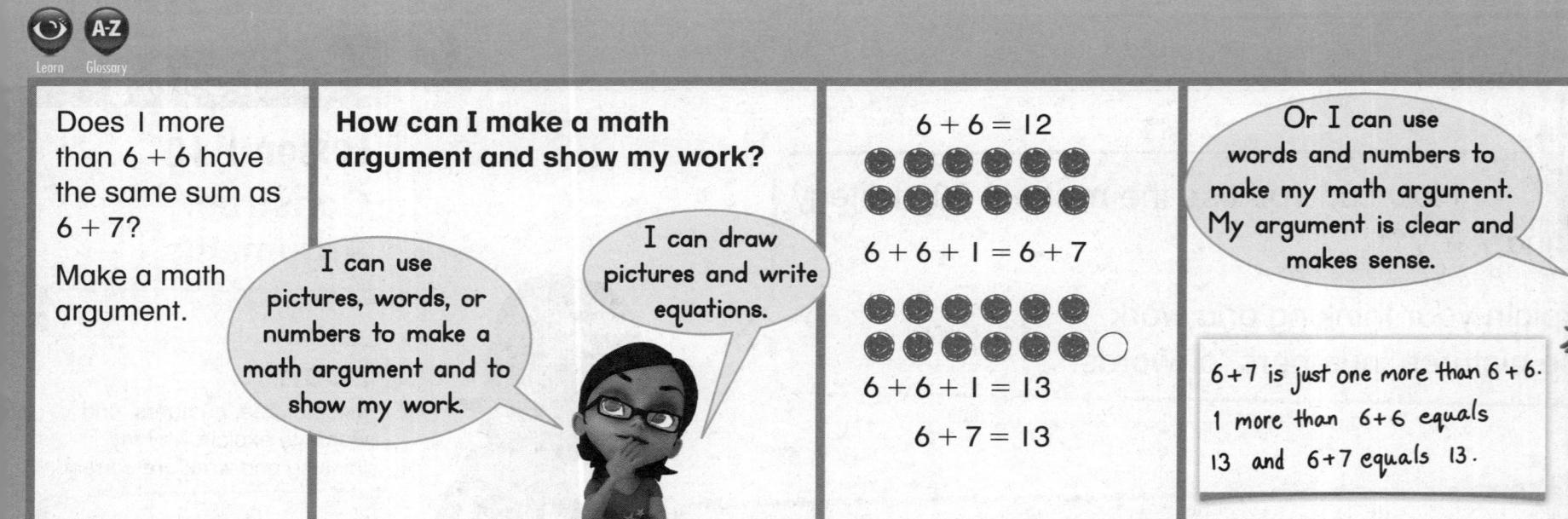

Does 1 more than 6 + 6 have the same sum as 6 + 7?

Make a math argument.

How can I make a math argument and show my work?

I can use pictures, words, or numbers to make a math argument and to show my work.

I can draw pictures and write equations.

6 + 6 = 12

6 + 6 + 1 = 6 + 7

6 + 6 + 1 = 13

6 + 7 = 13

Or I can use words and numbers to make my math argument. My argument is clear and makes sense.

6 + 7 is just one more than 6 + 6.
1 more than 6 + 6 equals 13 and 6 + 7 equals 13.

Do You Understand?

Show Me! Are both math arguments above clear and complete? Explain.

☆ **Guided Practice** ☆ Use the picture to help you solve the problem. Then use words and numbers to make a math argument.

1. Is the sum of 9 + 5 the same as the sum of 10 + 4?

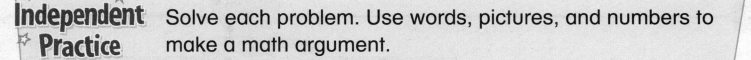

Independent Practice   Solve each problem. Use words, pictures, and numbers to make a math argument.

2. Lynn had 14 grapes. She ate 8 of them. She wants to eat 6 more grapes. Will Lynn have enough grapes? Explain.

3. The Lions scored 11 runs in a baseball game. The Tigers scored 7 runs. Did the Tigers score 3 fewer runs than the Lions? Explain.

4. Complete the explanation below for how to find 8 + 9. Use pictures, words, or numbers to complete the explanation.

I know that 8 + 8 = 16

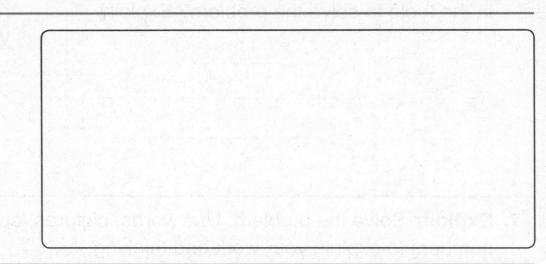

Problem Solving

Puppies Sold

The Sunset Pet Store sells puppies. The table shows how many puppies were sold Monday through Thursday.

Is the total number of puppies sold on Tuesday and Wednesday less than the number of puppies sold on Monday?

Number of Puppies Sold			
Monday	Tuesday	Wednesday	Thursday
16	10	7	15

5. **Make Sense** Will you use all the numbers in the table to solve the problem? Explain.

6. **Model** Write an equation to find the total number of puppies sold on Tuesday and Wednesday. Solve.

7. **Explain** Solve the problem. Use words, pictures, and numbers to explain your work and thinking.

Help Tools Games

Another Look! Tamra has 8 animal books and 4 sports books. Will she be able to give away 9 of her books?

Solve and explain your work and thinking.

> You can use words, pictures, and numbers when you explain.

> You can also write 8 + 4 = 12 and 12 − 9 = 3. These equations show that Tamara can give away 9 books.

8 animal books   4 sports books

Yes, Tamara can give away 9 of her books.

HOME ACTIVITY Tell your child this story: "Omar has 3 green stickers and 8 blue stickers. If he gives away 5 of these stickers, will Omar have 6 stickers left?" Have your child solve the problem and explain his or her thinking using words, pictures, and numbers.

Solve each problem. Use words, pictures, or numbers to make a math argument.

1. Alan has 17 stickers. He wants to give 6 stickers to Jean and 7 stickers to Matt. How many stickers will Alan give away? Explain.

2. Tasha has 12 minutes. She wants to jump rope for 8 minutes and play tag for 5 minutes. Will Tasha have enough time? Explain.

T-shirts

The number of T-shirts that four students own is given in the table.

Are there three students who have a total of 20 T-shirts? If so, which students are they?

Number of T-Shirts			
Will	Mandy	Greg	Cindy
4	7	12	9

3. **Make Sense** What operation will you use to solve the problem? Explain.

_____

_____

_____

4. **Reasoning** How will you go about solving the problem? Explain.

_____

_____

_____

5. **Explain** Solve the problem. Use words, pictures, and numbers to explain your work and thinking.

Name _____

Find a Match

Find a partner. Point to a clue. Read the clue.

Look below the clues to find a match. Write the clue letter in the box next to the match.

Find a match for every clue.

I can ...
add and subtract within 20.

Clues

A Near doubles with sums near 8

B Every difference is 6.

C Ways to make 12

D Exactly two differences equal 9.

E Every sum is greater than 14.

F Exactly three differences are equal.

G Near doubles with sums near 6

H Every difference equals $14-7$.

☐	5 + 7 6 + 6 8 + 4 9 + 3	☐	10 − 5 11 − 7 12 − 7 13 − 8	☐	11 − 5 10 − 4 12 − 6 9 − 3	☐	4 + 3 3 + 2 2 + 3 3 + 4
☐	13 − 3 9 − 0 14 − 6 16 − 7	☐	3 + 4 5 + 4 4 + 3 4 + 5	☐	8 + 9 7 + 8 8 + 7 6 + 9	☐	9 − 2 13 − 6 8 − 1 15 − 8

A-Z Glossary

Word List
- addend
- difference
- doubles
- equation
- near doubles
- sum

Understand Vocabulary

1. Circle a doubles fact.

$$7 + 7 = 14$$

$$6 + 7 = 13$$

$$7 + 0 = 7$$

2. Circle a near doubles fact.

$$4 + 4 = 8$$

$$4 + 1 = 5$$

$$4 + 5 = 9$$

3. Write a subtraction equation using numbers and symbols.

_____

4. Find the sum of $8 + 6$.

_____

5. Find the difference of $12 - 5$.

_____

Use Vocabulary in Writing

6. Describe how you can make a 10 to add $7 + 4$. Use a term from the Word List.

_____
_____
_____
_____

Set A

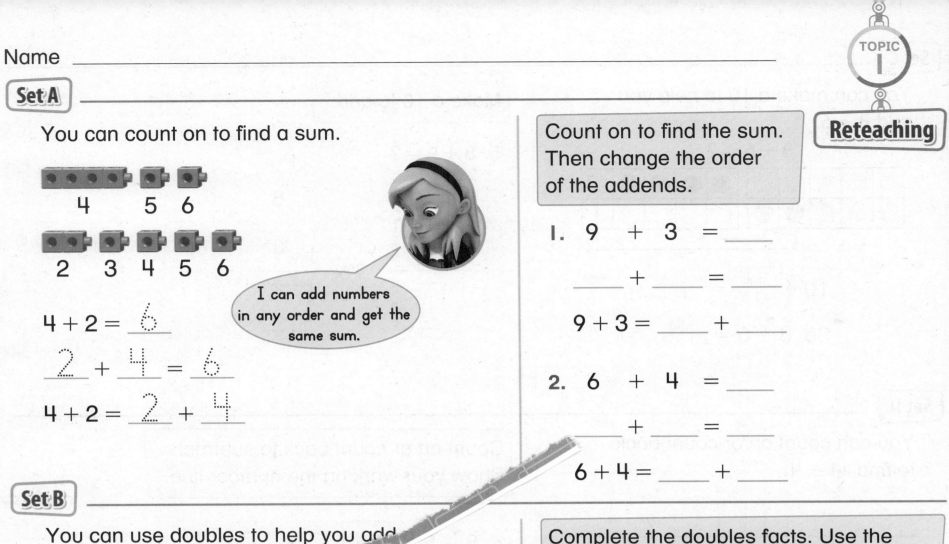

You can count on to find a sum.

4   5   6

2   3   4   5   6

I can add numbers in any order and get the same sum.

$4 + 2 = \underline{6}$

$\underline{2} + \underline{4} = 6$

$4 + 2 = \underline{2} + \underline{4}$

Reteaching

Count on to find the sum. Then change the order of the addends.

1. $9 + 3 = \underline{\hspace{1cm}}$

$\underline{\hspace{1cm}} + \underline{\hspace{1cm}} = \underline{\hspace{1cm}}$

$9 + 3 = \underline{\hspace{1cm}} + \underline{\hspace{1cm}}$

2. $6 + 4 = \underline{\hspace{1cm}}$

$\underline{\hspace{1cm}} + \underline{\hspace{1cm}} = \underline{\hspace{1cm}}$

$6 + 4 = \underline{\hspace{1cm}} + \underline{\hspace{1cm}}$

Set B

You can use doubles to help you add a near double.

$4 + 4 = \underline{8}$

So, $3 + 4 = \underline{7}$.

$3 + 4$ is one less than $4 + 4$.

So, $3 + 4 = 7$.

Complete the doubles facts. Use the doubles facts to solve the near doubles.

3. $8 + 8 = \underline{\hspace{1cm}}$

So, $7 + 8 = \underline{\hspace{1cm}}$.

4. $5 + 5 = \underline{\hspace{1cm}}$

So, $6 + 5 = \underline{\hspace{1cm}}$.

You can make a 10 to help you add $8 + 6$.

$$8 + 6 = ?$$

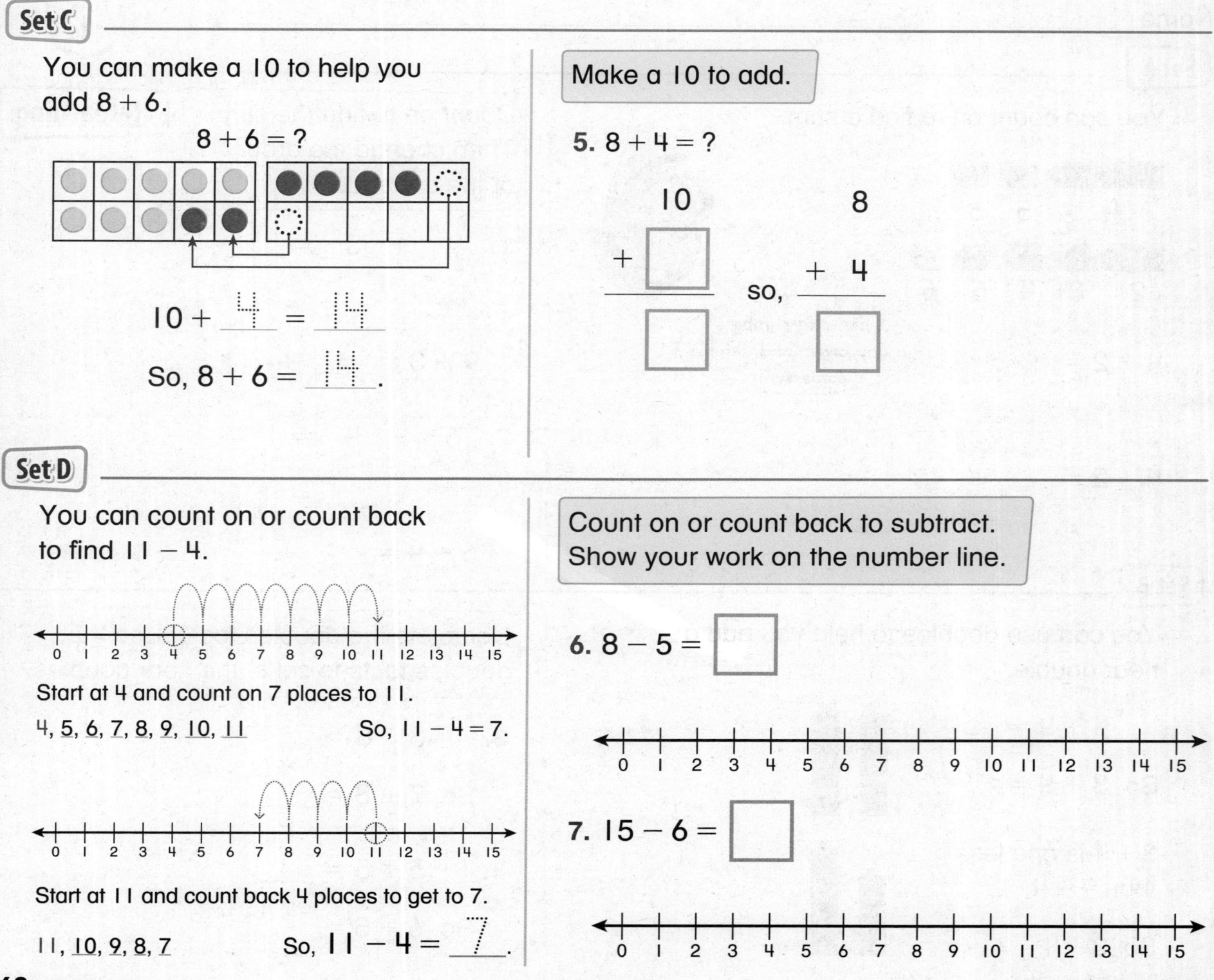

$$10 + \underline{4} = \underline{14}$$

So, $8 + 6 = \underline{14}$.

Make a 10 to add.

5. $8 + 4 = ?$

$$
\begin{array}{c}
10 \\
+ \ \square \\
\hline
\square
\end{array}
\qquad \text{so,} \qquad
\begin{array}{c}
8 \\
+ \ 4 \\
\hline
\square
\end{array}
$$

You can count on or count back to find $11 - 4$.

Start at 4 and count on 7 places to 11.

4, 5, 6, 7, 8, 9, 10, 11   So, $11 - 4 = 7$.

Start at 11 and count back 4 places to get to 7.

11, 10, 9, 8, 7   So, $11 - 4 = \underline{7}$.

Count on or count back to subtract. Show your work on the number line.

6. $8 - 5 = \square$

7. $15 - 6 = \square$

Set E

You can think addition to help you subtract.

Find: $16 - 9 = ?$

Think: $9 + \underline{7} = 16$

So, $16 - 9 = \underline{7}$

Subtract. Write the addition fact that helped you.

Reteaching
Continued

8. $13 - 7 = \underline{\quad}$

   $7 + \underline{\quad} = 13$

9. $17 - 9 = \underline{\quad}$

   $9 + \underline{\quad} = 17$

Set F

You can make a 10 to subtract.
Find $17 - 8$.

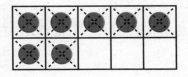

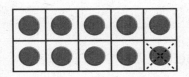

$17 - 7 = 10$

$10 - 1 = 9$

$17 - 8 = \boxed{9}$

Make a 10 to find $13 - 8$.
Draw counters to show your work.

10.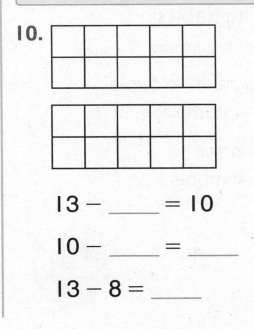

$13 - \underline{\quad} = 10$

$10 - \underline{\quad} = \underline{\quad}$

$13 - 8 = \underline{\quad}$

You can use addition or subtraction to solve word problems.

11 grapes are in a bowl.
9 grapes are in a cup.
How many fewer grapes are in the cup?

$$11 - 9 = 2 \qquad 9 + 2 = 11$$

So, 2 fewer grapes are in the cup.

Write an equation to solve each problem.

11. 13 shirts are in a closet.
8 shirts are in a box.
How many more shirts are in the closet?

_____ ◯ _____ ◯ _____ more shirts

12. Drake has 10 more books than Yuri.
Yuri has 10 books.
How many books does Drake have?

_____ ◯ _____ ◯ _____ books

Thinking Habits

Construct Arguments

How can I use math to explain why my work is correct?

Did I use the correct numbers and symbols?

Solve. Use words, pictures, or numbers to construct arguments.

13. Tyler read 15 pages of a book.
Ann read 9 pages of the same book.
Did Tyler read 4 more pages than Ann? Explain.

1. Tom draws 7 bugs. Gina draws 4 bugs. How many bugs did they draw in all?

Which shows how to *count on* to solve the problem?

Ⓐ 7, <u>8</u>, <u>9</u>, <u>10</u>, <u>11</u>

Ⓑ 4, <u>5</u>, <u>6</u>, <u>7</u>

Ⓒ 7 + 4

Ⓓ 4 + 7

2. Lilly has 7 fish. Jack has 1 more fish than Lilly.

Which equations show how many fish in all? Choose all that apply.

☐ 7 + 1 = 8

☐ 7 + 7 + 1 = 15

☐ 7 + 7 = 14

☐ 7 + 8 = 15

3. Use the ten-frames. Show how to find the sum of 8 + 7 by making a 10. Then fill in the gray boxes.

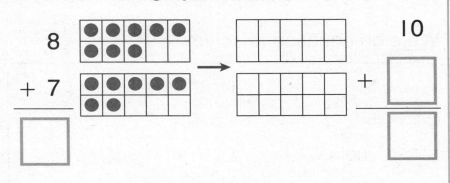

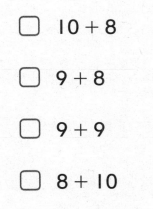

4. Which have a sum of 18? Choose all that apply.

☐ 10 + 8

☐ 9 + 8

☐ 9 + 9

☐ 8 + 10

5. 7 friends go to the movies. They have 4 tickets. How many more tickets do they need?

Draw lines to match each solution to how it was solved.

A. 7, 6, 5, 4   Use an addition fact.

B. 7 − 4 = 3

      Count back.

C. 4, 5, 6, 7

      Count on.

D. 4 + 3 = 7

      Use a subtraction fact.

6. Nita has 14 grapes. She eats 6 grapes.

Which addition fact can help you find how many grapes Nita has left?

Ⓐ   6 + 6 = 12

Ⓑ   6 + 7 = 13

Ⓒ   6 + 8 = 14

Ⓓ   8 + 8 = 16

7. Show how to make a 10 to find 13 − 7. Then complete the equation.

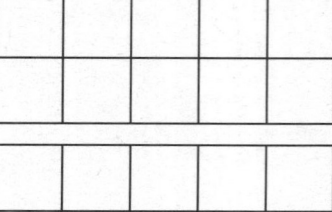

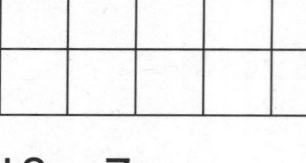

13 − 7 = _____

8. Bruce has some coins.
He gives 4 coins to his brother.
Now Bruce has 9 coins.
How many coins did Bruce have at first?

Write an equation to solve.

_____ ◯ _____ = _____

_____ coins

9. Maria has 4 pears.
She buys some more pears.
Now she has 12 pears.

How many pears does
Maria buy?

Part A
Draw a picture to model
the problem.

Part B
Write an equation to
solve the problem.

_____ ◯ _____ = _____

_____ pears

---

10. The team has 9 players.
Then 2 players quit.
After that, 5 players join the team.

How many players does the team
have now?

Use the numbers on the cards.
Complete both equations to solve the problem.

2	5
7	12

$9 - \boxed{} = \boxed{}$

$7 + \boxed{} = \boxed{}$ $\boxed{}$ players

---

11. Choose Yes or No to show if 7 will make
each equation true.

$8 + \boxed{} = 16$ ◯ Yes ◯ No

$7 + \boxed{} = 14$ ◯ Yes ◯ No

$14 - \boxed{} = 7$ ◯ Yes ◯ No

$15 - 8 = \boxed{}$ ◯ Yes ◯ No

12. Matt finds 9 sticks at the park.
Mabel finds 7 sticks.
How many sticks do they find in all?

_____ sticks in all

13. Choose Yes or No to show if 8 will make each equation true.

$6 + \boxed{} = 14$ $8 + 8 = \boxed{}$ $14 - \boxed{} = 6$ $16 - \boxed{} = 8$

○ Yes   ○ No   ○ Yes   ○ No   ○ Yes   ○ No   ○ Yes   ○ No

---

14. Josh ate 6 fewer cherries than Gail. Gail ate 15 cherries.

How many cherries did Josh eat?

Part A
Draw a picture to model the problem.

Part B
Write an equation to solve the problem.

_____ ◯ _____ = _____

_____ cherries

---

15. The table shows how many pictures 3 friends made.

Pictures Made			
	Horses	Cats	Dogs
Brian	9	1	3
Fernando	7	6	2
Laurel	4	0	8

Write an equation to solve the problem.

_____ ◯ _____ ◯ _____ = _____

_____ pictures

Choose one of the friends.
Write the name of the friend you choose.

_____

How many pictures did that friend make?

© Pearson Education, Inc. 2

Name _____

Farm Kittens

Many kittens are born each summer at the Sunshine Farm. The table shows the number of kittens born at the farm from June to August.

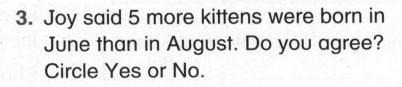

Number of Kittens Born		
June	July	August
13	8	7

1. During which two months were a total of 20 kittens born?

2. Write an equation to find the total number of kittens born in July and August. Solve.

_____

_____

_____

_____

3. Joy said 5 more kittens were born in June than in August. Do you agree? Circle Yes or No.

Show your work to explain.

Yes   No

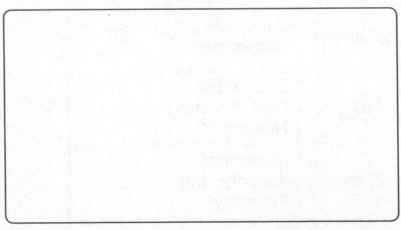

4. Use the clues to complete the table below.

- No kittens were born in December, January, and February.

- In March, 6 kittens were born.

- Three kittens were born in April and in September.

- In May, 4 kittens were born.

- Two kittens were born in October and in November.

Kittens Born at the Sunshine Farm		
Season	Months	Number of Kittens Born
Spring	March, April, and May	
Summer	June, July, and August	28
Fall	September, October, and November	
Winter	December, January, and February	

5. Joy says that more kittens were born in the summer than in all other seasons combined. Is she correct? Explain.

_____

_____

_____

_____

_____

6. How many more kittens were born in the spring than in the fall?

Show how to solve the problem with a subtraction equation.

© Pearson Education, Inc. 2

Work with Equal Groups

Essential Questions: How can you show even and odd numbers? How do arrays relate to repeated addition?

Digital Resources

Solve   Learn   Glossary
Tools   Assessment   Help   Games

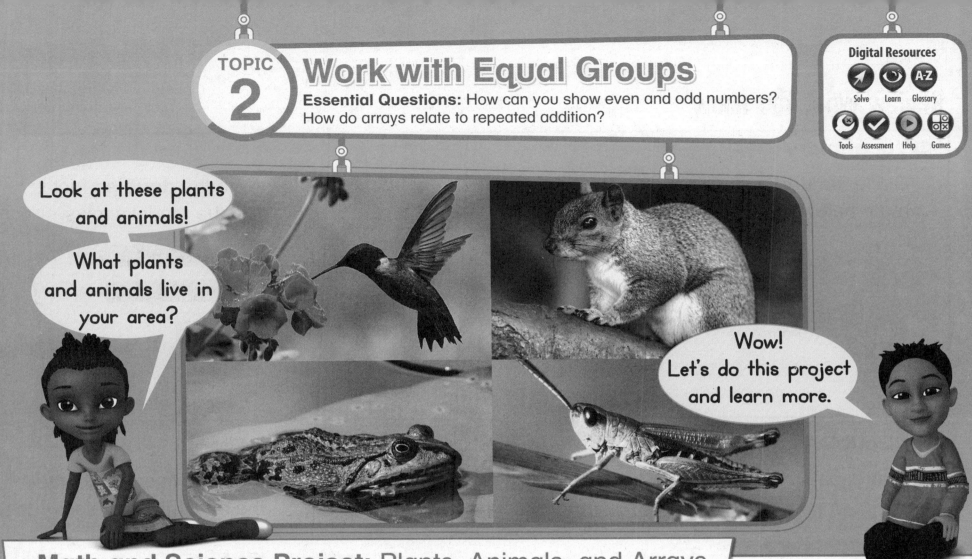

Look at these plants and animals!

What plants and animals live in your area?

Wow! Let's do this project and learn more.

Math and Science Project: Plants, Animals, and Arrays

Find Out Make lists of different types of plants and wild animals that you see. Look in your neighborhood or in a nearby park. Look at how the animals and plants come together.

Journal: Make a Book Show what you find out in a book. In your book, also:

• Tell about plants or animals that you see in groups. Look for patterns.

• Make an array of a group of plants and an array of a group of animals.

Name _____

Review What You Know

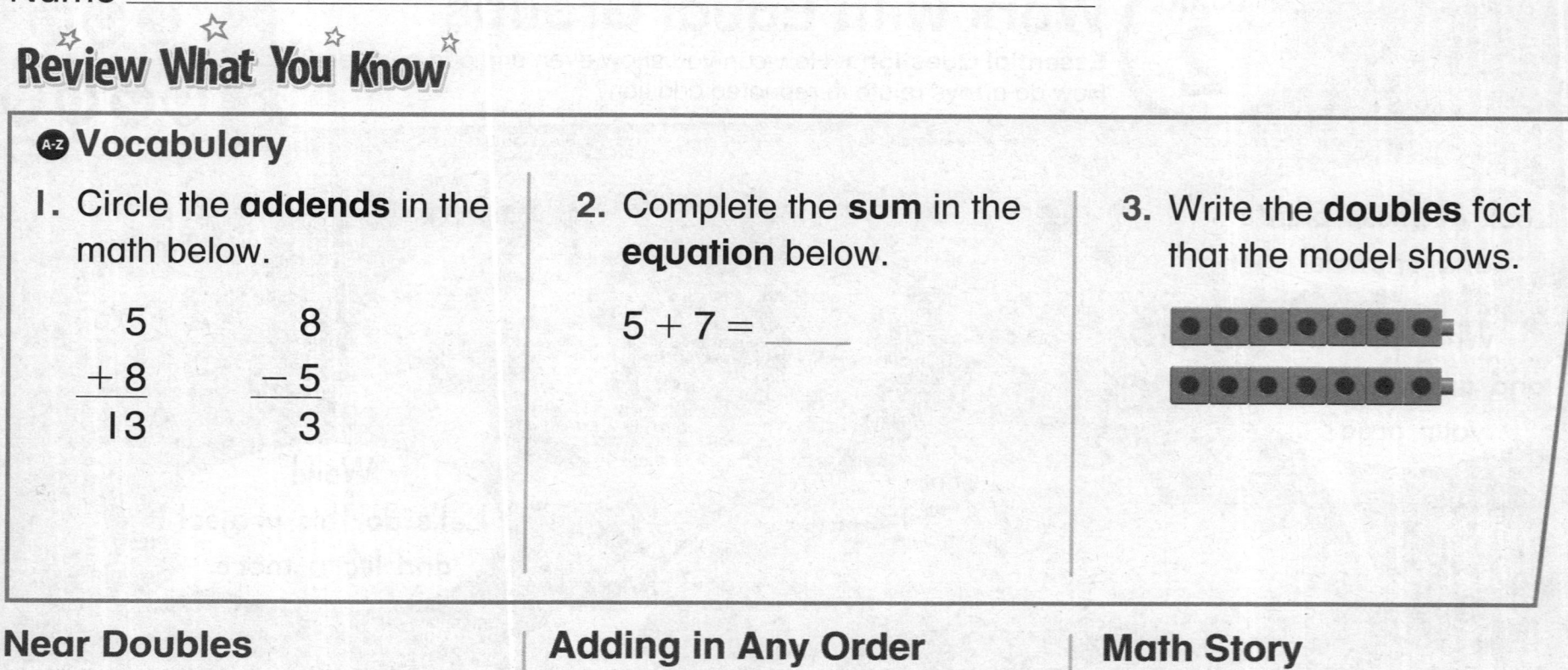

A-Z Vocabulary

1. Circle the **addends** in the math below.

$$5$$
$$\underline{+\ 8}$$
$$13$$

$$8$$
$$\underline{-\ 5}$$
$$3$$

2. Complete the **sum** in the **equation** below.

$$5 + 7 = \underline{}$$

3. Write the **doubles** fact that the model shows.

Near Doubles

4. Find each sum.

$$7$$
$$\underline{+\ 6}$$

$$4$$
$$\underline{+\ 5}$$

$$9$$
$$\underline{+\ 8}$$

Adding in Any Order

5. Change the order of the addends and complete both equations.

$$6 + 8 = \underline{}$$

$$\underline{} + \underline{} = \underline{}$$

Math Story

6. Five brown cows go into the barn. Then 8 black and white cows go into the barn. How many cows are now in the barn?

_____ cows

My Word Cards

Study the words on the front of the card.
Complete the activity on the back.

A-Z Glossary

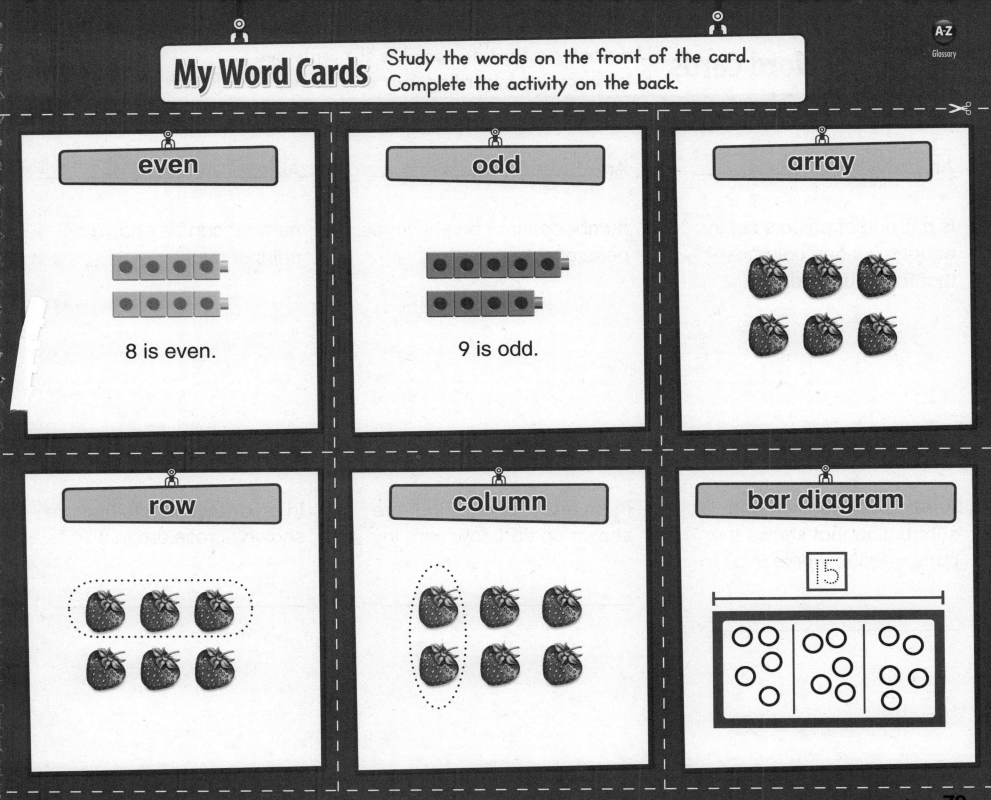

even

8 is even.

odd

9 is odd.

array

row

column

bar diagram

15

My Word Cards

Use what you know to complete the sentences.
Extend learning by writing your own sentence using each word.

An ______________________

is a group of objects set in equal rows and columns that forms a rectangle.

An ______________________

number cannot be shown as pairs of cubes.

An ______________________

number can be shown as pairs of cubes.

A model for addition and subtraction that shows the parts and the whole is a

______________________.

In an array, objects that are shown up and down are in a

______________________.

In an array, objects that are shown across are in a

______________________.

Name _____

Solve & Share

Use cubes to make the numbers below. Shade all the numbers that can be shown as two equal groups of cubes.

What do you notice about the numbers you shaded?

I can ...
tell if a group of objects is even or odd.

I can also use math tools correctly.

1	2	3	4	5	6	7	8	9	10
11	12	13	14	15	16	17	18	19	20

How can you tell if a number is **even** or **odd**?

Use cubes to find out.

8

9

An even number can be shown as two equal parts using cubes.

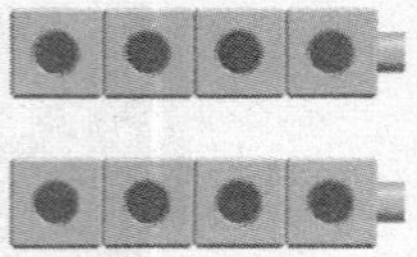

8 is even.
$4 + 4 = 8$

An odd number cannot be shown as two equal parts using cubes.

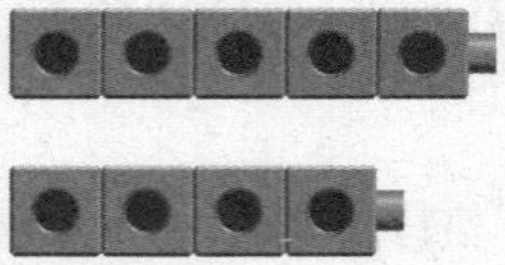

9 is odd.
$5 + 4 = 9$

The ones digit tells you if a number is even or odd.

18 is even.
19 is odd.

1	2	3	4	5	6	7	8	9	10
11	12	13	14	15	16	17	18	19	20

Do You Understand?

Show Me! You break apart a tower of cubes to make two equal parts, but there is one cube left over.
Is the number of cubes even or odd? Explain.

☆ **Guided Practice** ☆   Look at the number. Circle even or odd. Then write the equation.

1.

14

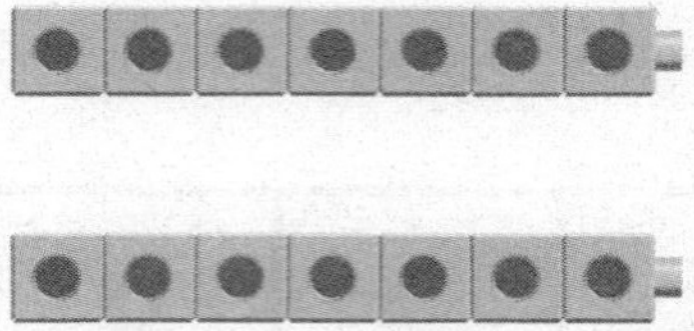

odd   (even)

$7 + 7 = 14$

2.

19

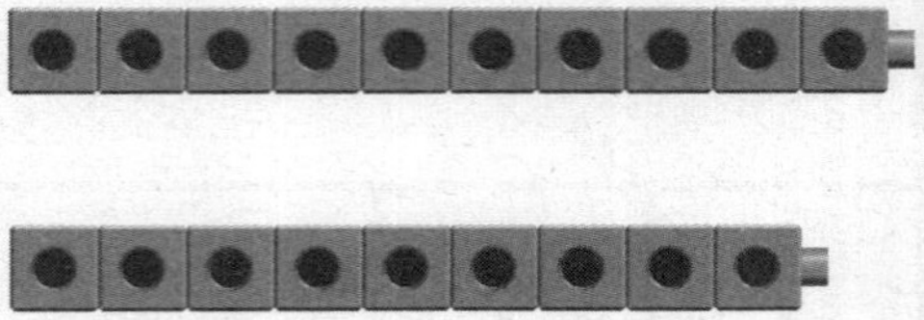

odd   even

___ + ___ = ___

Name _____

Independent Practice

Look at the number. Circle even or odd.
Then write the equation. Use cubes to help.

3. 20

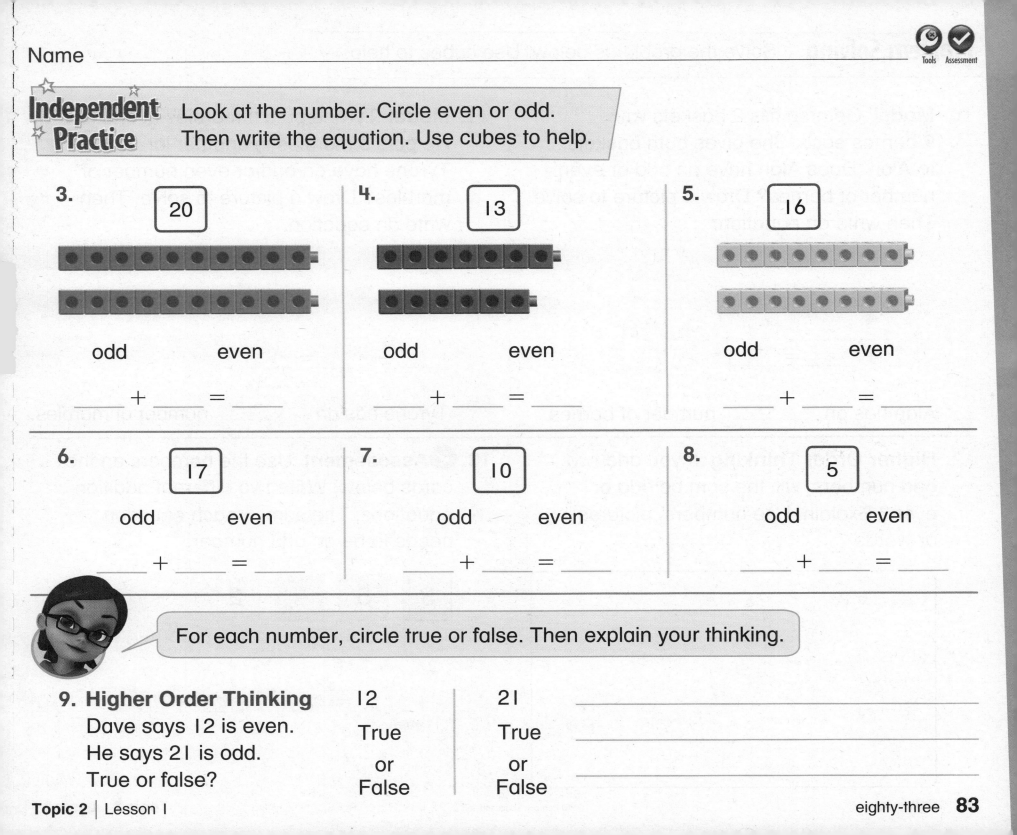

odd   even

___ + ___ = ___

4. 13

odd   even

___ + ___ = ___

5. 16

odd   even

___ + ___ = ___

6. 17

odd   even

___ + ___ = ___

7. 10

odd   even

___ + ___ = ___

8. 5

odd   even

___ + ___ = ___

For each number, circle true or false. Then explain your thinking.

9. Higher Order Thinking

Dave says 12 is even.
He says 21 is odd.
True or false?

12

True

or

False

21

True

or

False

_____

_____

10. **Model** Gemma fills 2 baskets with 9 berries each. She gives both baskets to Alan. Does Alan have an odd or even number of berries? Draw a picture to solve. Then write an equation.

_____ + _____ = _____

Alan has an _____ number of berries.

11. **Model** Tyrone puts 4 marbles in one jar. He puts 3 marbles in another jar. Does Tyrone have an odd or even number of marbles? Draw a picture to solve. Then write an equation.

_____ + _____ = _____

Tyrone has an _____ number of marbles.

12. **Higher Order Thinking** If you add two odd numbers, will the sum be odd or even? Explain. Use numbers, pictures, or words.

13. ✓**Assessment** Use the numbers on the cards below. Write two different addition equations. The sum in each equation needs to be an odd number.

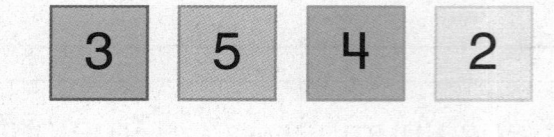

| 3 | 5 | 4 | 2 |

_____ + _____ = _____   _____ + _____ = _____

Name _____

Another Look!

An **even** number can be shown as two equal parts using cubes.
An **odd** number cannot be shown as two equal parts using cubes.

HOME ACTIVITY Choose a number from 2 to 20. Have your child tell if it is even or odd. If needed, he or she can use pennies to help solve.

There are 6 cubes.
Is 6 an even or odd number?
Draw lines to match the cubes.

The cubes can be shown as two equal parts.
$3 + 3 = 6$

6 is an <u>even</u> number.

There are 7 cubes.
Is 7 an even or odd number?
Draw lines to match the cubes.

The cubes cannot be shown as two equal parts.
$4 + 3 = 7$

7 is an <u>odd</u> number.

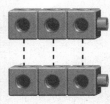

Draw lines to match the cubes.
Then tell if the number is even or odd.

1.

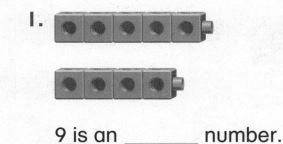

9 is an _____ number.

2.

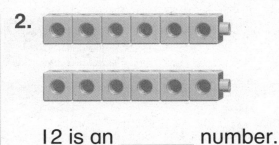

12 is an _____ number.

3.

15 is an _____ number.

4. 8 is an _____ number.

$4 + \underline{\quad} = 8$

5. 11 is an _____ number.

$6 + \underline{\quad} = 11$

6. 18 is an _____ number.

$\underline{\quad} + 9 = 18$

Number Sense Look at the pictures. Circle the number you will add or subtract. Then complete the equation.

7. The sum is an **odd** number.

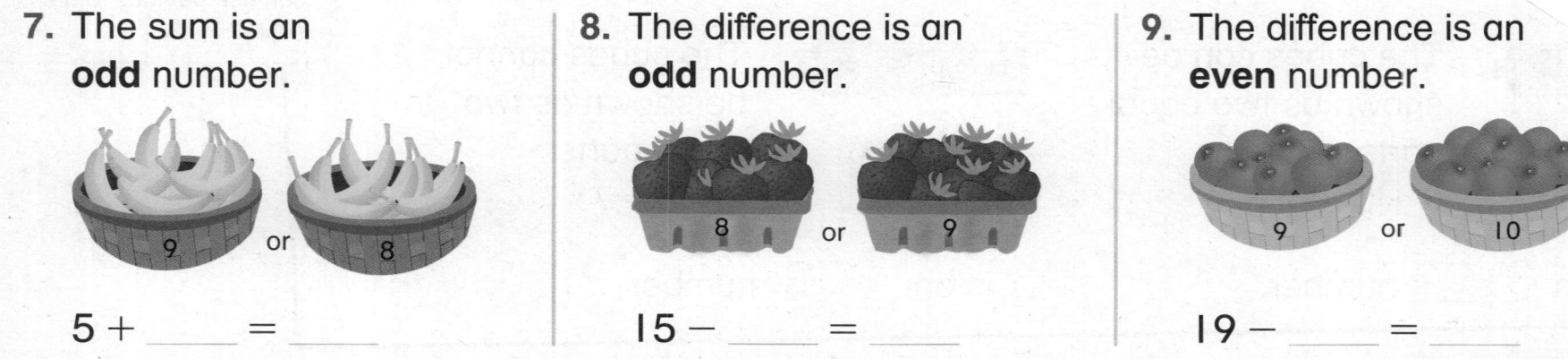

9 or 8

$5 + \underline{\quad} = \underline{\quad}$

8. The difference is an **odd** number.

8 or 9

$15 - \underline{\quad} = \underline{\quad}$

9. The difference is an **even** number.

9 or 10

$19 - \underline{\quad} = \underline{\quad}$

10. Higher Order Thinking Shailen is adding three numbers. He gets a sum that is an even number between 10 and 20. Show two addition equations Shailen could have written.

$\underline{\quad} + \underline{\quad} + \underline{\quad} = \underline{\quad}$

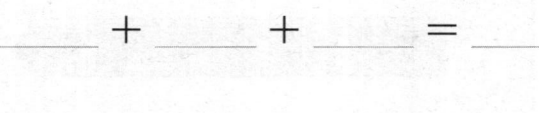

$\underline{\quad} + \underline{\quad} + \underline{\quad} = \underline{\quad}$

11. ✓**Assessment** Use the numbers on the cards below. Write two different addition equations. The sum in each equation needs to be an even number.

| 6 | 3 | 8 | 9 |

$\underline{\quad} + \underline{\quad} = \underline{\quad} \qquad \underline{\quad} + \underline{\quad} = \underline{\quad}$

Name _____

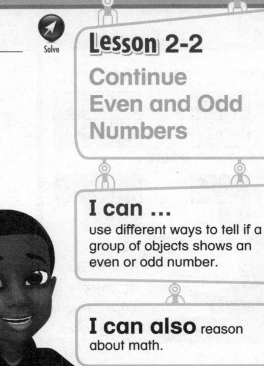

Lesson 2-2

Continue Even and Odd Numbers

I can ...
use different ways to tell if a group of objects shows an even or odd number.

I can also reason about math.

Solve & Share

Is the sum of 3 + 3 even or odd?
Circle **odd** or **even**. Explain. You can use cubes.

Write two more equations where the addends are the same. Is the sum even or odd? What patterns do you see? Use cubes to show each equation.

3   +   3   = _____   even   odd

_____ + _____ = _____   even   odd

_____ + _____ = _____   even   odd

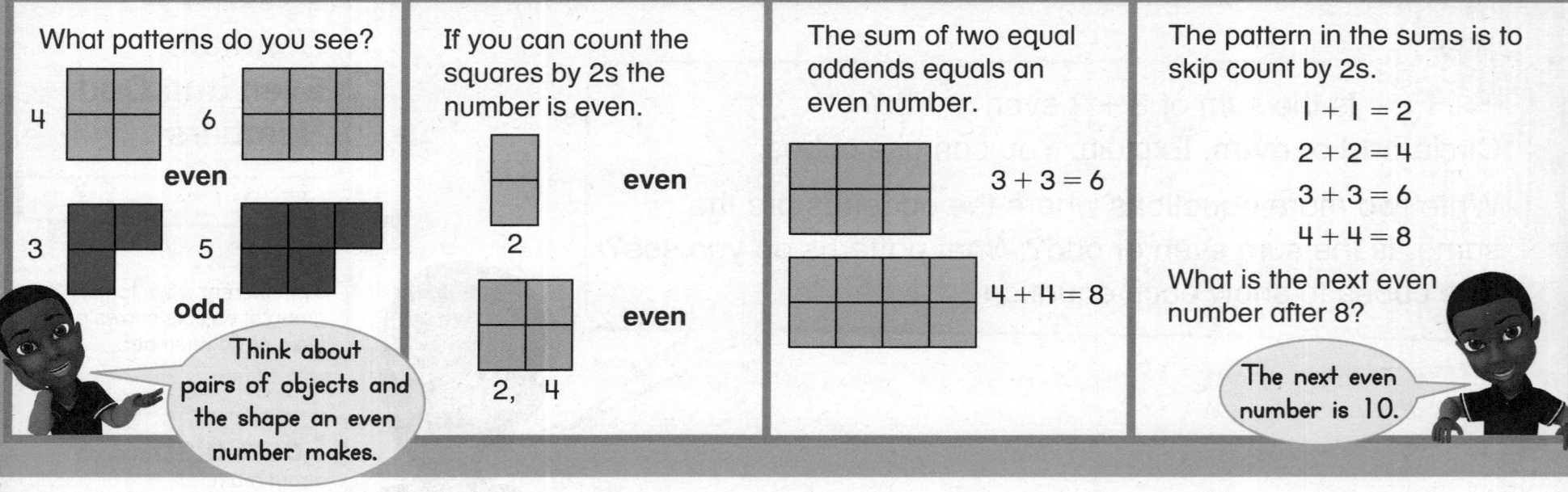

What patterns do you see?

4   6

even

3   5

odd

Think about pairs of objects and the shape an even number makes.

If you can count the squares by 2s the number is even.

2   **even**

even

2, 4

The sum of two equal addends equals an even number.

3 + 3 = 6

4 + 4 = 8

The pattern in the sums is to skip count by 2s.

$1 + 1 = 2$
$2 + 2 = 4$
$3 + 3 = 6$
$4 + 4 = 8$

What is the next even number after 8?

The next even number is 10.

Do You Understand?

Show Me! Is the number 10 even or odd? Draw a picture to show how you know.

☆ Guided ☆ Practice

Write the number for each model.
Circle even or odd. Then write the equation.

1.

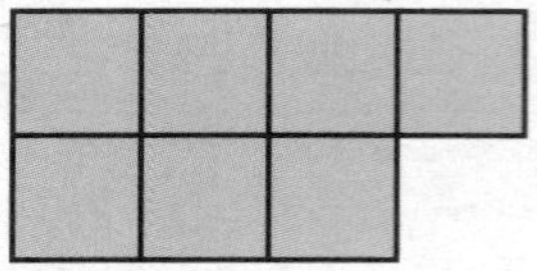

___7___   even   (odd)

4 + 3 = 7

2.

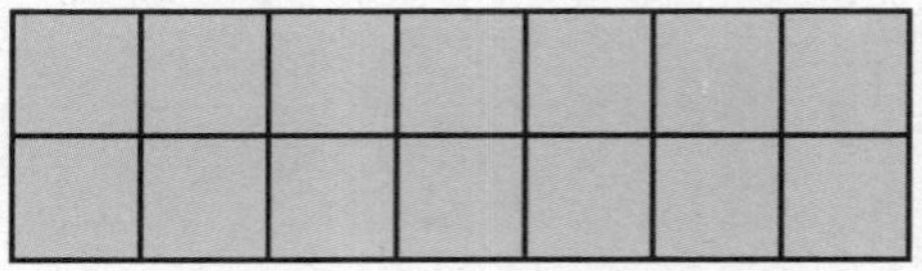

_____   even   odd

___ + ___ = ___

© Pearson Education, Inc. 2

Name _____

Independent Practice

Write the number for each model. Circle even or odd. Then write the equation.

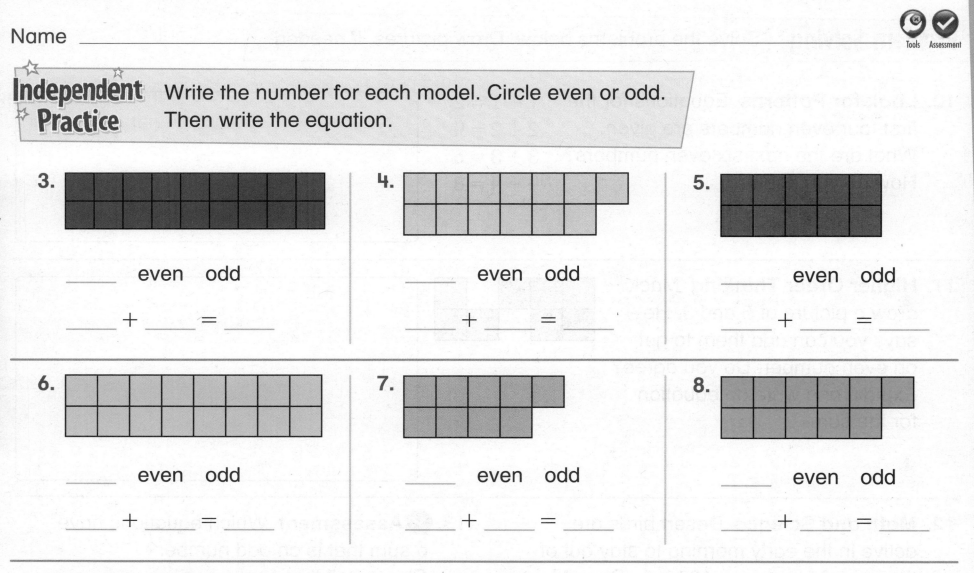

3. _____ even odd

_____ + _____ = _____

4. _____ even odd

_____ + _____ = _____

5. _____ even odd

_____ + _____ = _____

6. _____ even odd

_____ + _____ = _____

7. _____ even odd

_____ + _____ = _____

8. _____ even odd

_____ + _____ = _____

9. **Number Sense** How many squares are shown? Is this an even or odd amount? Draw a picture that shows how you know. Write an equation for your picture.

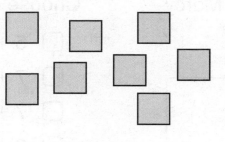

10. **Look for Patterns** Equations for the first four even numbers are given. What are the next six even numbers? How do you know?

$$1 + 1 = 2$$
$$2 + 2 = 4$$
$$3 + 3 = 6$$
$$4 + 4 = 8$$

11. **Higher Order Thinking** Mack drew a picture of 5 and 3. He says you can add them to get an even number. Do you agree? Explain and write an equation for the sum.

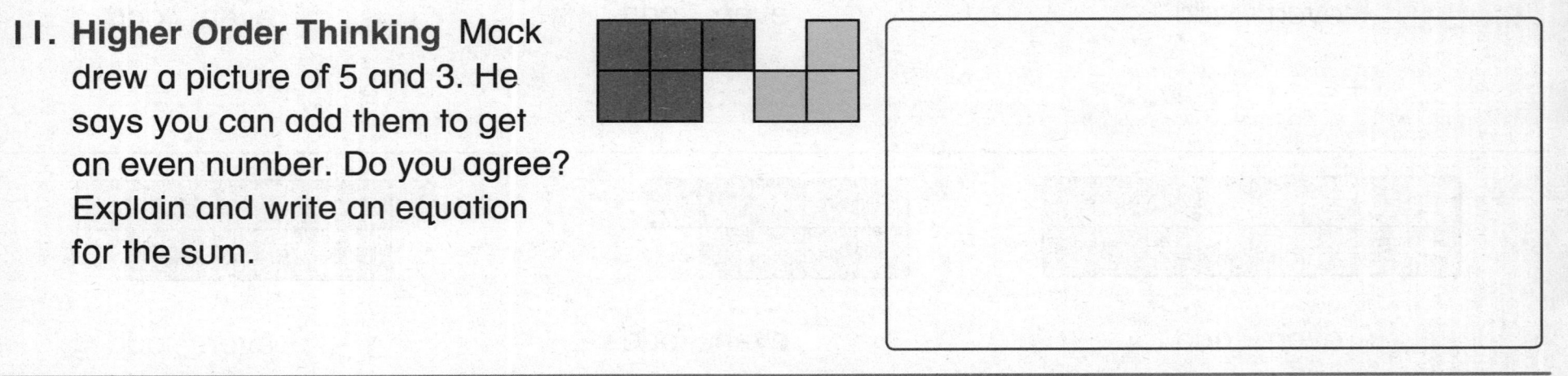

12. **Math and Science** Desert birds are active in the early morning to stay out of the heat. Marcy sees 19 birds. Does Marcy see an odd or even number of birds? Explain with a drawing and equation.

13. ✅ **Assessment** Which equations have a sum that is an odd number? Choose all that apply.

☐ $5 + 7 = 12$

☐ $7 + 7 = 14$

☐ $7 + 6 = 13$

☐ $8 + 7 = 15$

Name _____

Help Tools Games

Homework
& Practice 2-2
Continue
Even and Odd
Numbers

Another Look! The pictures show an even and an odd number.

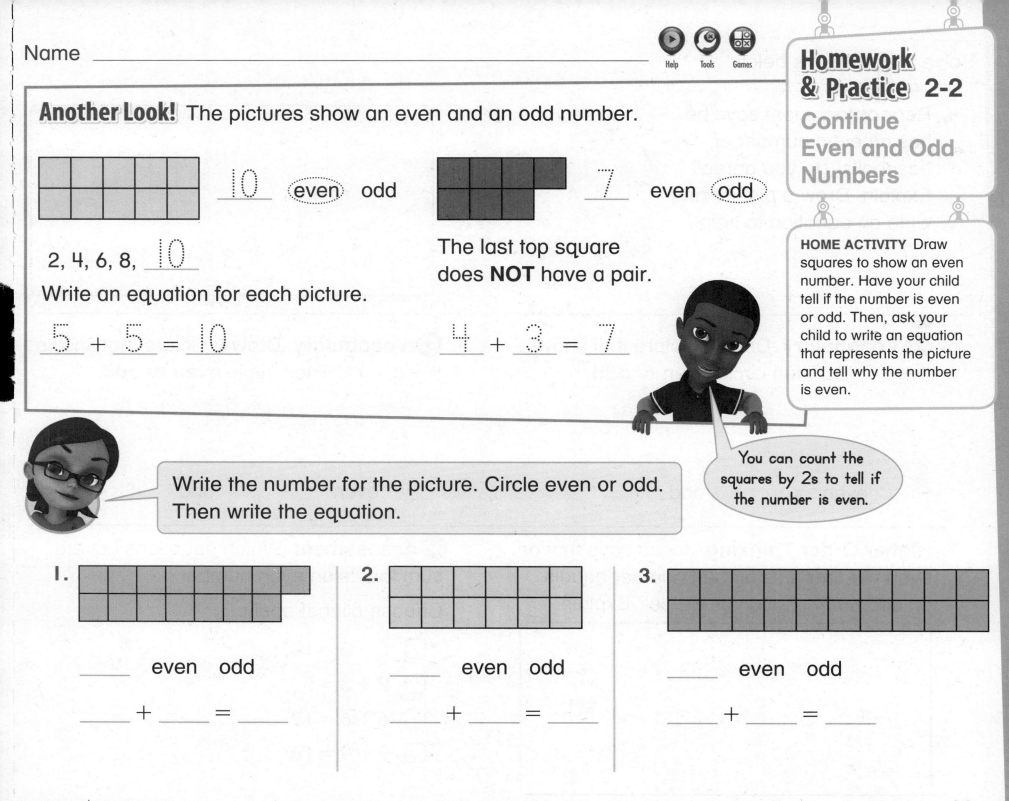

10 (even) odd

7 even (odd)

2, 4, 6, 8, __10__

Write an equation for each picture.

The last top square does **NOT** have a pair.

5 + 5 = 10

4 + 3 = 7

HOME ACTIVITY Draw squares to show an even number. Have your child tell if the number is even or odd. Then, ask your child to write an equation that represents the picture and tell why the number is even.

You can count the squares by 2s to tell if the number is even.

Write the number for the picture. Circle even or odd. Then write the equation.

1.
_____ even odd

___ + ___ = ___

2.
_____ even odd

___ + ___ = ___

3.
_____ even odd

___ + ___ = ___

Solve the problems below.

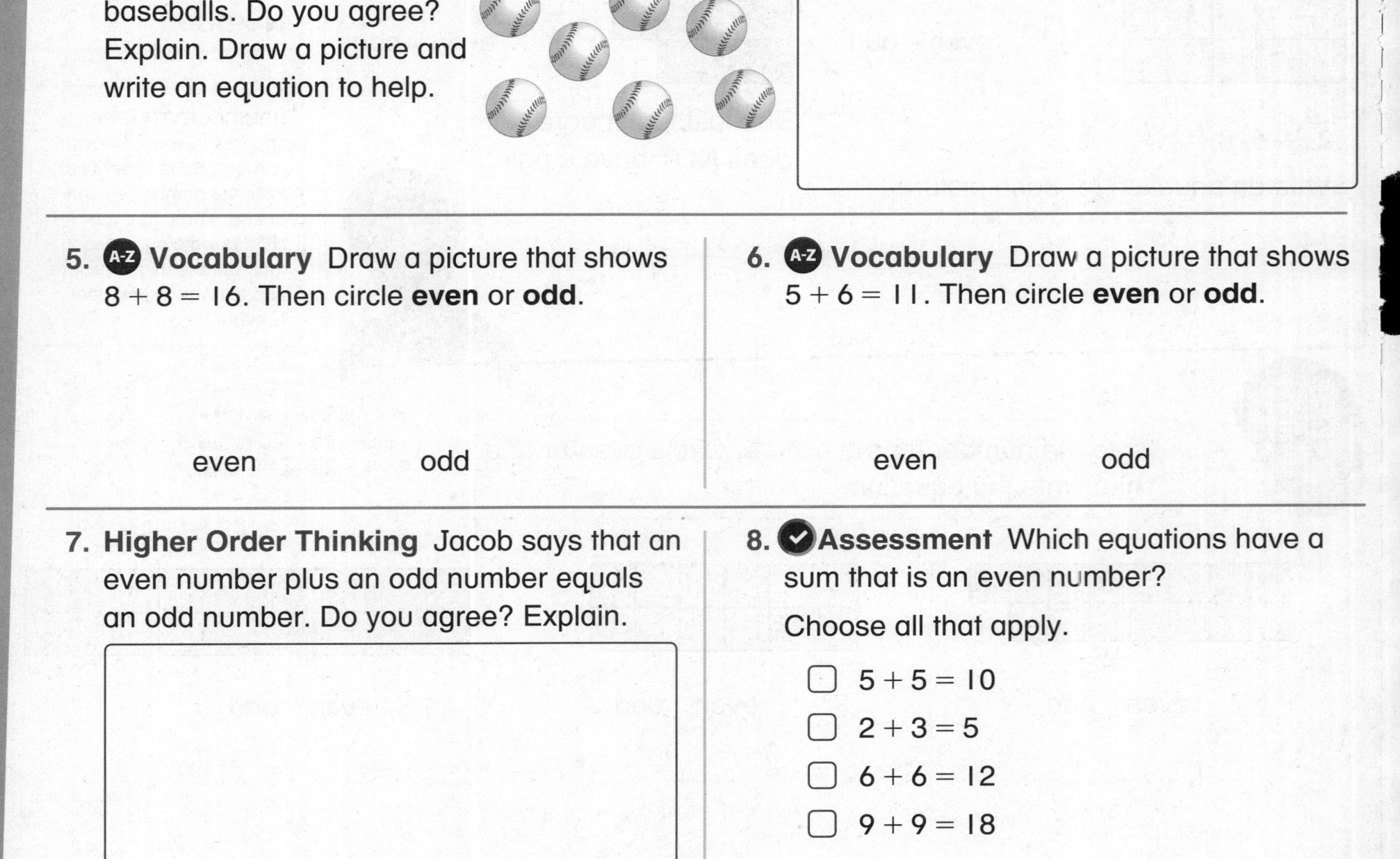

4. **Reasoning** Liam says he has an even number of baseballs. Do you agree? Explain. Draw a picture and write an equation to help.

5. 🄰🄯 **Vocabulary** Draw a picture that shows $8 + 8 = 16$. Then circle **even** or **odd**.

even   odd

6. 🄰🄯 **Vocabulary** Draw a picture that shows $5 + 6 = 11$. Then circle **even** or **odd**.

even   odd

7. **Higher Order Thinking** Jacob says that an even number plus an odd number equals an odd number. Do you agree? Explain.

8. ✓**Assessment** Which equations have a sum that is an even number?

Choose all that apply.

☐ $5 + 5 = 10$

☐ $2 + 3 = 5$

☐ $6 + 6 = 12$

☐ $9 + 9 = 18$

© Pearson Education, Inc. 2

Name _____

Solve & Share

Show and explain two different ways to find how many circles in all.

I can ...
find the total number of objects in a set of rows and columns.

I can also look for patterns.

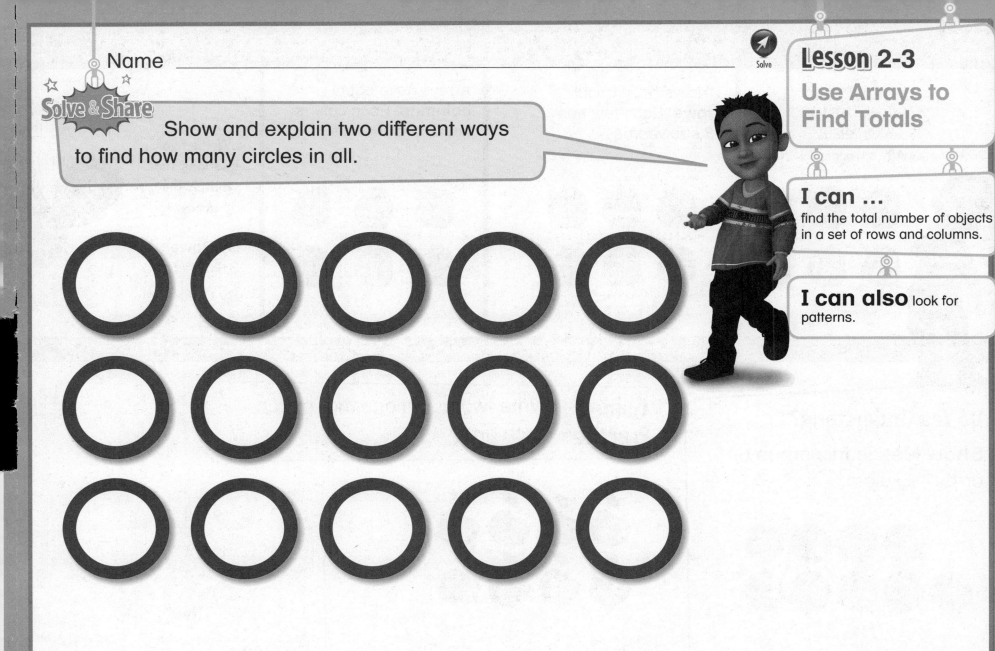

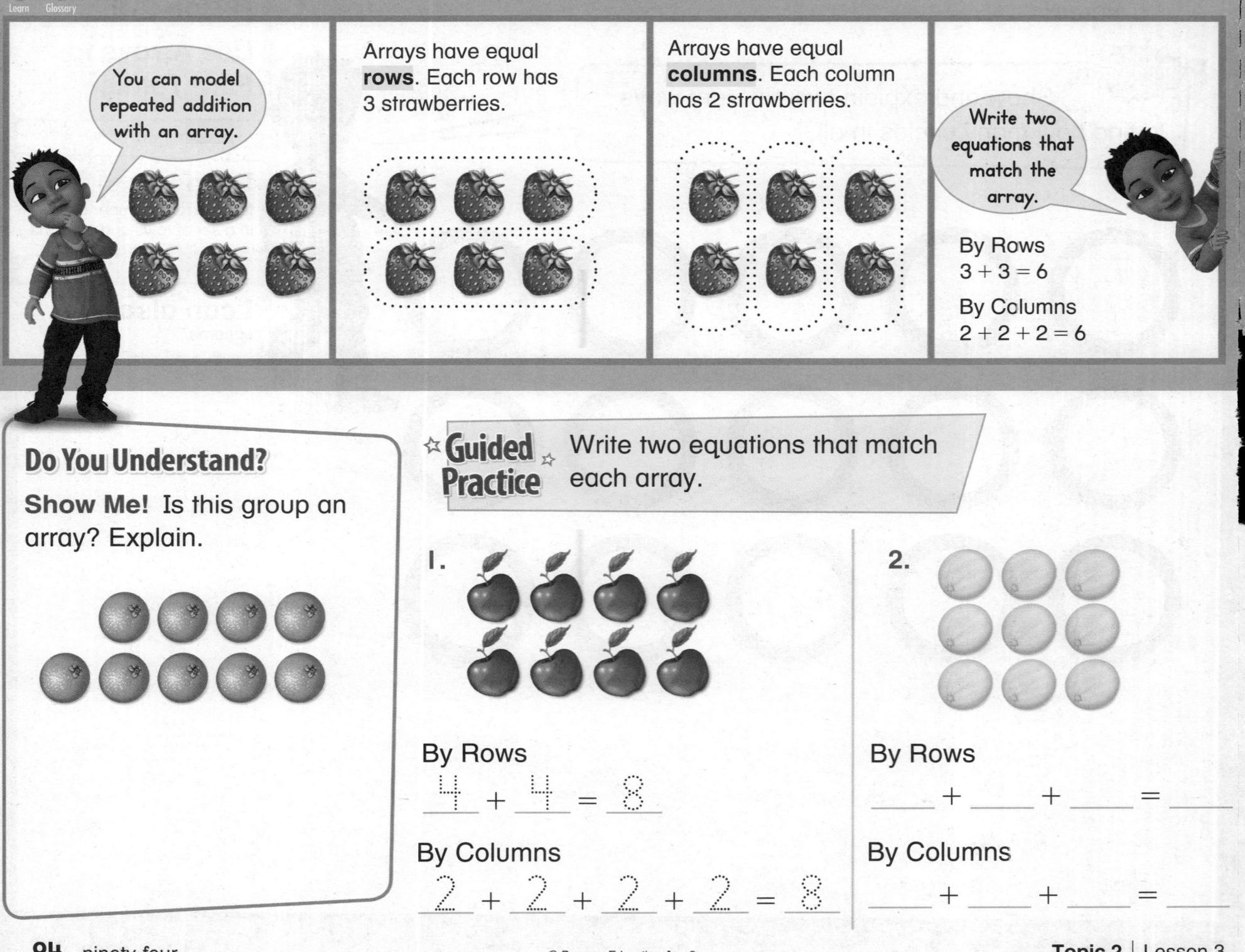

You can model repeated addition with an array.

Arrays have equal **rows**. Each row has 3 strawberries.

Arrays have equal **columns**. Each column has 2 strawberries.

Write two equations that match the array.

By Rows
$3 + 3 = 6$

By Columns
$2 + 2 + 2 = 6$

Do You Understand?

Show Me! Is this group an array? Explain.

☆ Guided ☆ Practice

Write two equations that match each array.

1.

By Rows

$\underline{4} + \underline{4} = \underline{8}$

By Columns

$\underline{2} + \underline{2} + \underline{2} + \underline{2} = \underline{8}$

2.

By Rows

$\underline{} + \underline{} + \underline{} = \underline{}$

By Columns

$\underline{} + \underline{} + \underline{} = \underline{}$

Tools Assessment

Independent Practice ☆ Write two equations that match each array.

3.

By Rows

_____ + _____ + _____ + _____ + _____ = _____

By Columns _____ + _____ + _____ = _____

4.

_____ + _____ + _____ = _____

_____ + _____ + _____ + _____ = _____

5.

By Rows _____ + _____ = _____

By Columns _____ + _____ = _____

6.

_____ + _____ + _____ + _____ + _____ = _____

_____ + _____ + _____ + _____ + _____ = _____

7. Algebra Use the array to find the missing number.

_____ + 5 = 10

8. Look for Patterns Ross places the berries in an array. Write two equations that match the array. How many berries are there in all?

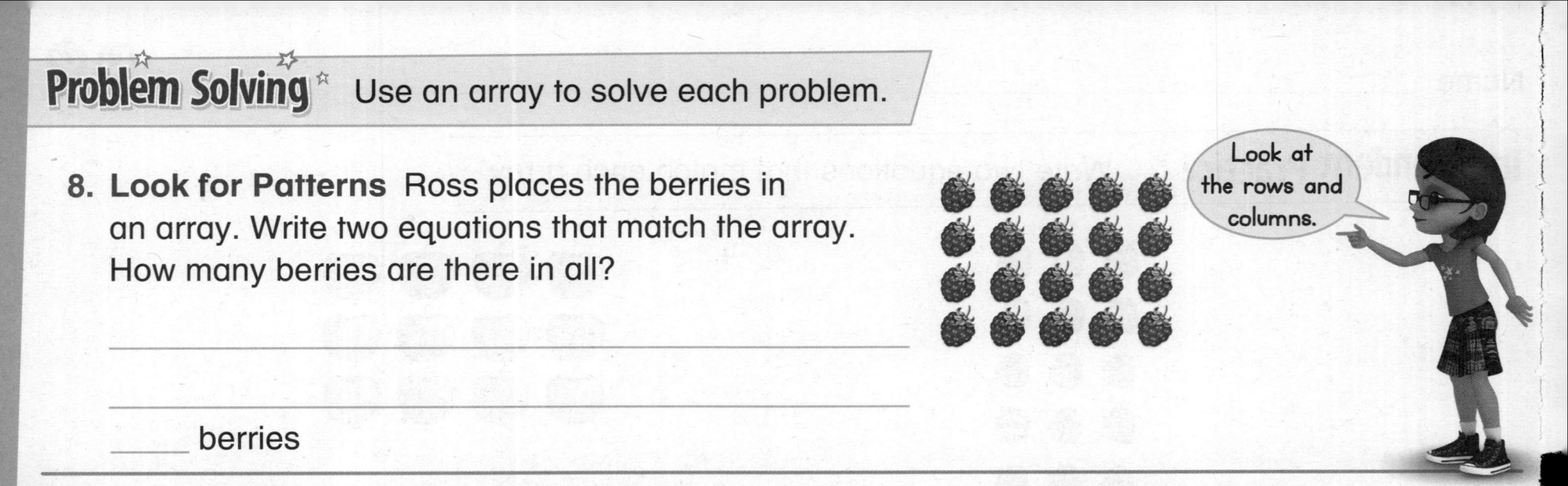

Look at the rows and columns.

_____

_____

_____ berries

9. The array shows cars in a parking lot. Can you write two different equations that match the array? Explain. How many cars are in the parking lot in all?

_____

_____

_____ cars

10. Higher Order Thinking Draw a garden with up to 5 rows and that has the same number of flowers in each row. Then write two equations that match your array.

11. ✔ **Assessment** Blake sets basketballs in an array. He has 4 rows of basketballs with 3 basketballs in each row. Which equation shows the array Blake made and how many basketballs in all?

Ⓐ $3 + 3 + 3 + 3 = 12$

Ⓑ $3 + 3 = 6$

Ⓒ $4 + 4 = 8$

Ⓓ $3 + 3 + 3 = 9$

Name _____

Another Look! You can use an array to show equal groups.

There are 3 rows.
There are
3 circles in
each row.

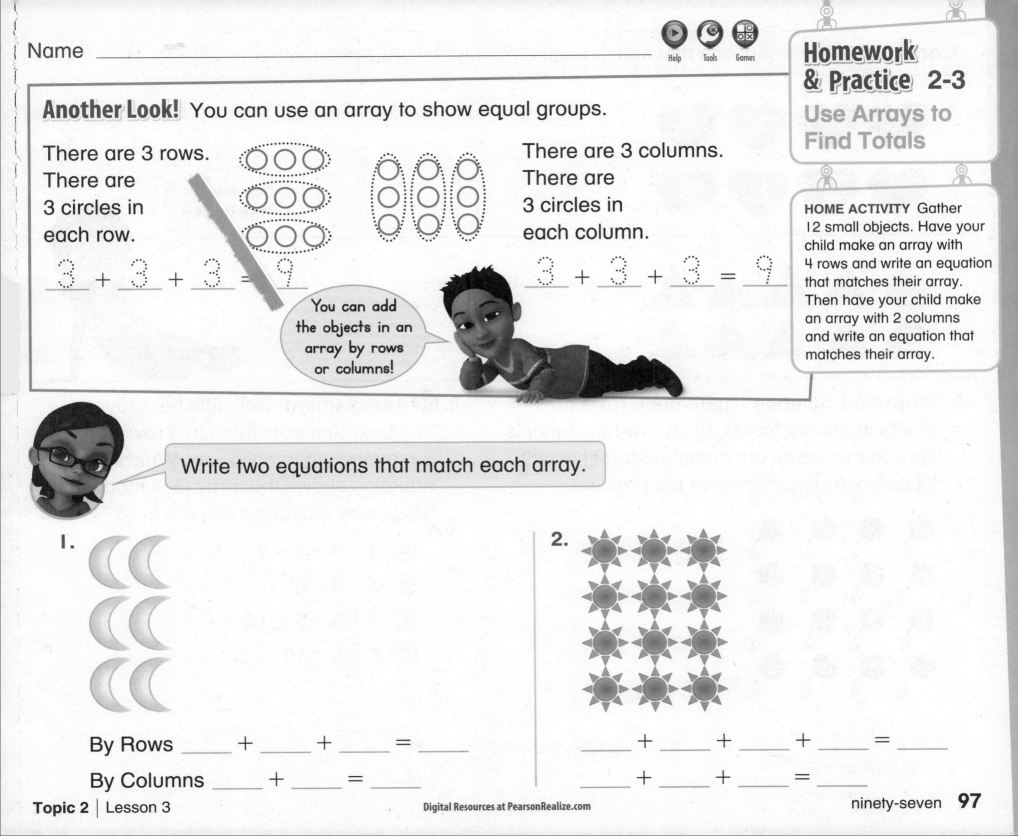

There are 3 columns.
There are
3 circles in
each column.

_3_ + _3_ + _3_ = _9_

You can add the objects in an array by rows or columns!

_3_ + _3_ + _3_ = _9_

HOME ACTIVITY Gather 12 small objects. Have your child make an array with 4 rows and write an equation that matches their array. Then have your child make an array with 2 columns and write an equation that matches their array.

Write two equations that match each array.

1.

By Rows ___ + ___ + ___ = ___

By Columns ___ + ___ = ___

2.

___ + ___ + ___ + ___ = ___

___ + ___ + ___ = ___

Model Write two equations that match each array and tell the total number of objects.

3.

_____

_____

Remember to write the sum.

4.

_____

_____

5. **Math and Science** There are 4 rows of plants in the rainforest. Each row has 4 plants. How many plants are in the rainforest in all? Write an equation to solve the problem.

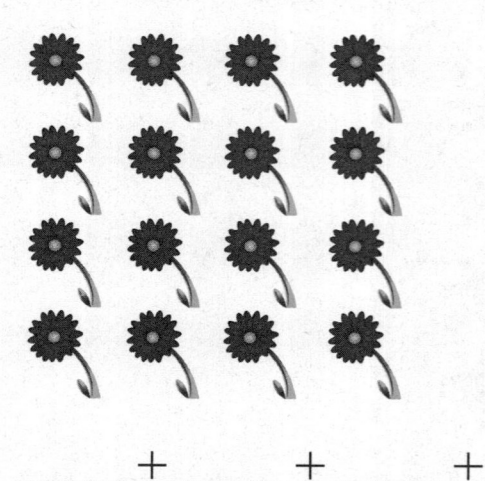

___ + ___ + ___ + ___ = ___

___ plants

6. ✓**Assessment** Gail puts her crayons in a box. She puts them in 3 rows. 5 crayons are in each row. Which equation shows the array Gail made and how many crayons there are in all?

Ⓐ $3 + 3 + 3 = 9$

Ⓑ $3 + 3 = 6$

Ⓒ $5 + 5 + 5 = 15$

Ⓓ $5 + 5 = 10$

Name _____

Solve & Share

Rusty places his toy trucks in 4 columns. He places 3 trucks in each column. How many trucks does Rusty have in all?

Show how you know with counters and an equation.

I can ...
make arrays with equal rows or equal columns.

I can also use math tools correctly.

Equation

_____

_____ trucks

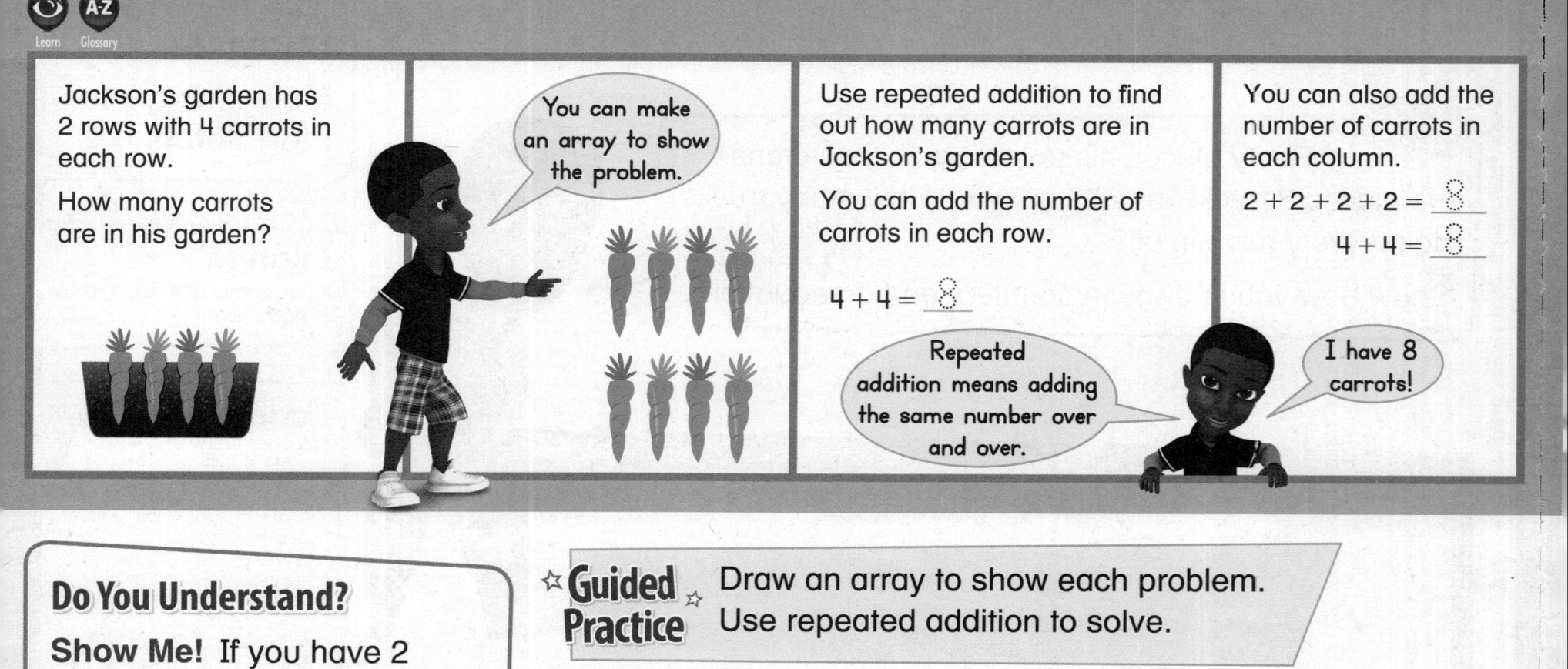

Jackson's garden has 2 rows with 4 carrots in each row.

How many carrots are in his garden?

You can make an array to show the problem.

Use repeated addition to find out how many carrots are in Jackson's garden.

You can add the number of carrots in each row.

$4 + 4 = \underline{8}$

Repeated addition means adding the same number over and over.

You can also add the number of carrots in each column.

$2 + 2 + 2 + 2 = \underline{8}$

$4 + 4 = \underline{8}$

I have 8 carrots!

Do You Understand?

Show Me! If you have 2 rows with different amounts in each row do you have an array? Explain.

☆ **Guided Practice** ☆ Draw an array to show each problem. Use repeated addition to solve.

1. Monica has 2 shelves in her pantry. She puts 3 cans of peas on each shelf. How many cans of peas does she have in all?

   $\underline{3} + \underline{3} = \underline{6}$ cans of peas

2. Dominick is organizing his stickers in columns. He has 4 columns with 4 stickers in each column. How many stickers does he have in all?

   $\underline{} + \underline{} + \underline{} + \underline{} = \underline{}$ stickers

© Pearson Education, Inc. 2

Independent Practice Draw an array to show each problem.
Use repeated addition to solve.

3. Sarah bakes loaves of bread. She places them in
3 rows with 5 loaves in each row. How many loaves
of bread does Sarah have in all?

_____ + _____ + _____ = _____ loaves of bread

4. Kristin has 5 shelves in her bookcase.
She puts 4 books on each shelf.
How many books does Kristin have in all?

_____ + _____ + _____ + _____ + _____ = _____ books

5. Malcolm puts his marbles in two columns.
He put 2 marbles in each column.
How many marbles does Malcolm have in all?

_____ + _____ = _____ marbles

6. **Algebra** Find the missing numbers.
Frank has 10 baseball cards. He places them in 2 equal rows.
Show how many baseball cards are in each row.

☐ + ☐ = 10 baseball cards

7. **Reasoning** Jenny has 5 rows on each page in her photo album. She puts 2 pictures in each row. How many pictures does she have on each page?

____ + ____ + ____ + ____ + ____ = ____ pictures

8. **Reasoning** Nina has a bookcase with 4 shelves. She places 5 dolls on each shelf. How many dolls does Nina have in all?

____ + ____ + ____ + ____ = ____ dolls

9. **Higher Order Thinking** Write a story problem using repeated addition. Draw an array to match your story.

10. ✔ **Assessment** Whitney has a muffin tin with 2 rows. Each row has 4 muffins. Write an equation that shows how many muffins Whitney has in all.

_____

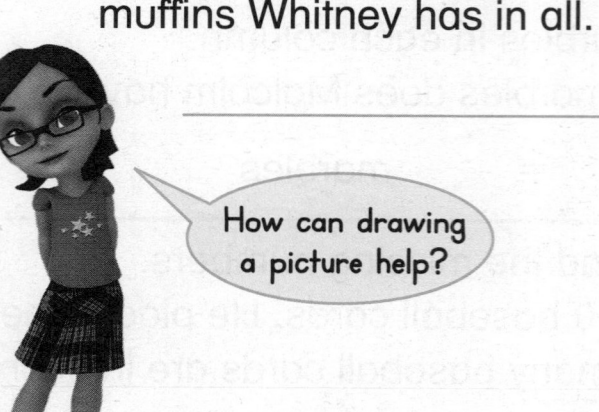

How can drawing a picture help?

Name _____

Another Look! Make an array and write an equation for the following problem.

Tia places bowls of soup on a tray in 3 columns with 2 bowls in each column. How many bowls of soup are on the tray?

"Arrays have equal rows and columns."

First, draw three columns with 2 bowls in each column.

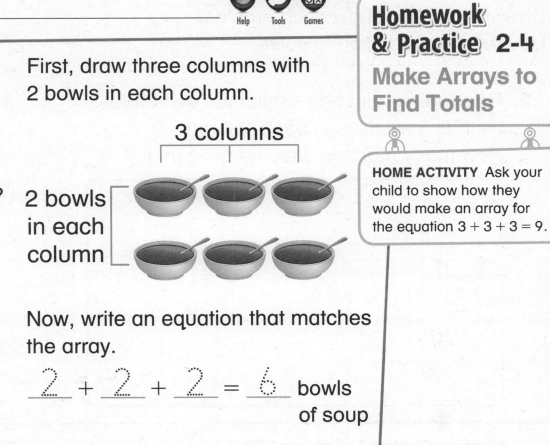

3 columns

2 bowls in each column

HOME ACTIVITY Ask your child to show how they would make an array for the equation $3 + 3 + 3 = 9$.

Now, write an equation that matches the array.

$\underline{2} + \underline{2} + \underline{2} = \underline{6}$ bowls of soup

Draw an array to show each problem. Use repeated addition to solve.

1. Mrs. Smith places the desks in her classroom in 5 columns. She puts 3 desks in each column. How many desks are in her classroom?

____ + ____ + ____ + ____ + ____ = ____ desks

Draw an array to show each problem.
Use repeated addition to solve.

2. **Reasoning** Jim has 4 columns of marbles. He has 3 marbles in each column. How many marbles does he have in all?

3. **Reasoning** Mike has 4 rows of crackers. He has 5 crackers in each row. How many crackers does he have in all?

4. **Higher Order Thinking** Jill has 10 teddy bears in all. If she has 2 columns, how many teddy bears are in each column? Draw an array and complete the equation.

_____ + _____ = 10

5. ✓**Assessment** Brian has 3 columns of bugs. Each column has 5 bugs. Write an equation that shows how many bugs Brian has in all.

Think about the meaning of the word column.

© Pearson Education, Inc. 2

Name _____

Solve & Share

There are 4 tables in a classroom. 3 children sit at each table. How many children are there in all?

Draw a picture and write an equation to model and solve the problem.

I can ...
model problems using equations, drawings, arrays, and bar diagrams.

I can also add correctly.

Thinking Habits
How can a picture and an equation help me model problems?

Does my answer make sense?

_____ + _____ + _____ + _____ = _____

_____ children

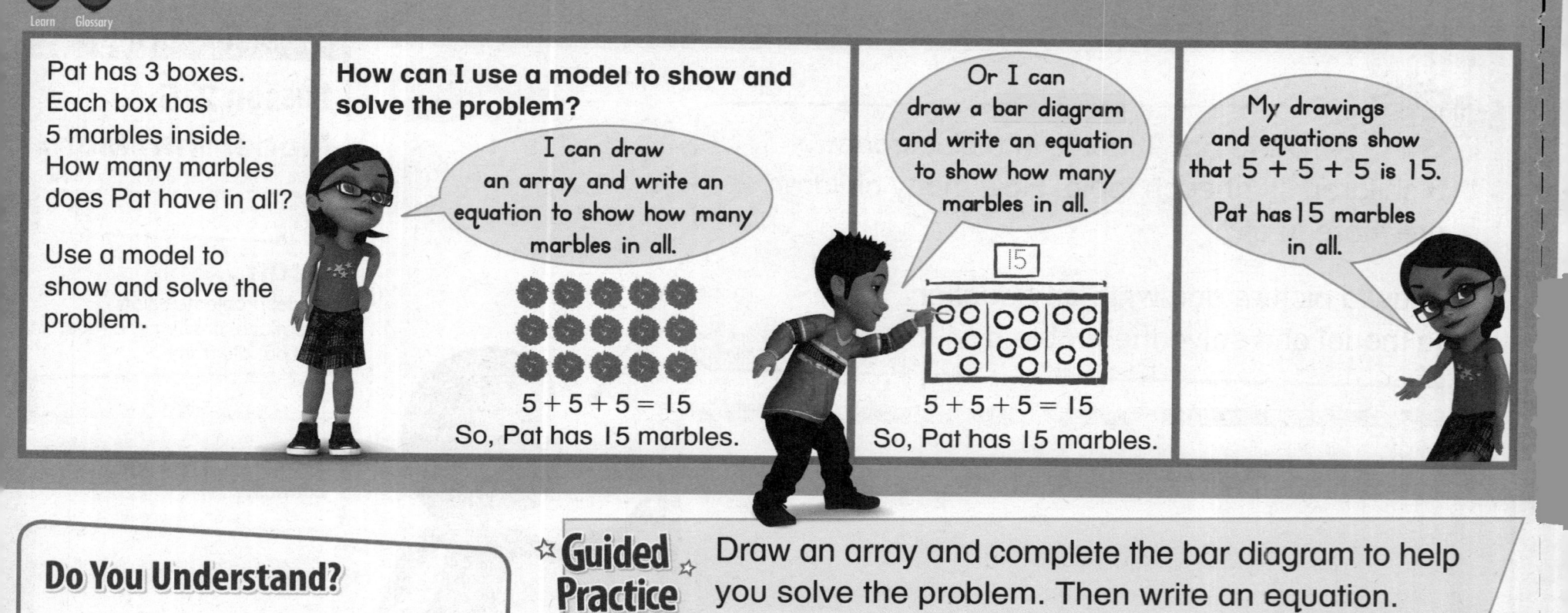

Pat has 3 boxes. Each box has 5 marbles inside. How many marbles does Pat have in all?

Use a model to show and solve the problem.

How can I use a model to show and solve the problem?

I can draw an array and write an equation to show how many marbles in all.

5 + 5 + 5 = 15
So, Pat has 15 marbles.

Or I can draw a bar diagram and write an equation to show how many marbles in all.

15

5 + 5 + 5 = 15
So, Pat has 15 marbles.

My drawings and equations show that 5 + 5 + 5 is 15.

Pat has 15 marbles in all.

Do You Understand?

Show Me! How does drawing a picture and writing an equation help you model a problem?

☆ Guided Practice ☆

Draw an array and complete the bar diagram to help you solve the problem. Then write an equation.

1. Ray has 2 bookshelves in his room.
He has 5 books on each shelf.
How many books does Ray have in all?

10

$\underline{5} + \underline{5} = \underline{}$ books

Tools Assessment

Independent Practice Draw an array or bar diagram to help you solve each problem. Then write an equation.

2. Mika has 4 groups of playing cards. If there are 4 playing cards in each group, how many cards does Mika have in all?

____ + ____ + ____ + ____ = ____

3. Anita has 3 packs of baseball cards. If there are 6 cards in each pack, how many baseball cards does Anita have in all?

____ + ____ + ____ = ____

4. Algebra Tina drew this bar diagram to show 2 equal groups can make 18. What are the missing numbers? Explain how you know.

Window Displays

Mr. Miller's Hobby Shop has 3 window displays. One is for posters, one is for paint cans, and one is for crayon boxes. The displays are described at the right.

Which display has the least number of items?

Posters	Paint Cans	Crayon Boxes
3 rows	4 rows	2 rows
6 posters in each row	3 paint cans in each row	8 crayon boxes in each row

5. **Make Sense** What are you asked to find?

_____

_____

_____

6. **Explain** Mr. Miller says he will add 3 + 6 to find the total number of posters in the posters display. Do you agree with his plan? Explain.

_____

_____

_____

7. **Model** Use a model to help you find which display has the least number of items. Be prepared to explain which model you used and why.

Name _____

Another Look! You can draw an array or bar diagram to model and help solve problems.

Terri has 3 baskets. Each basket has 2 toys.
How many toys does Terri have in all?

The equation 2 + 2 + 2 = 6 also models the problem.

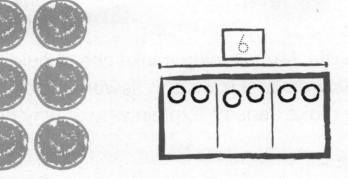

So, Terri has 6 toys in all.

HOME ACTIVITY Have your child draw an array and then write an equation to model this problem: Joel has 2 bags. Each bag has 3 apples. How many apples does Joel have in all?

Draw an array or bar diagram to help you solve each problem. Then write an equation.

1. Beth has 3 rows of sunflowers in her garden. Each row has 5 flowers. How many sunflowers does Beth have in all?

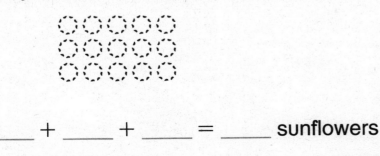

____ + ____ + ____ = ____ sunflowers

2. Curtis makes 2 books. Each book has 7 pages. How many pages does Curtis make in all?

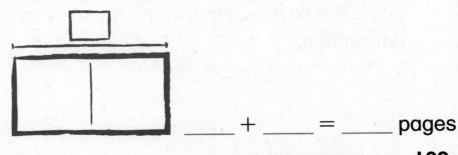

____ + ____ = ____ pages

Topic 2 | Lesson 5   Digital Resources at PearsonRealize.com   one hundred nine **109**

Planting Flowers

Mrs. Dunlap is planting some flowers in her garden. She has 10 tulips, 5 roses, and 10 daffodils. She wants to plant the flowers in an array, where each row has 5 flowers. How many rows of flowers will be in her garden?

Think about what a row means.

3. **Make Sense** What do you know? What are you asked to find?

_____

_____

_____

_____

4. **Explain** Mrs. Dunlap thinks she should plant the flowers in 4 rows of 5 flowers. Does her plan make sense? Explain why or why not.

_____

_____

_____

_____

5. **Model** Draw an array to show how Mrs. Dunlap should plant her flowers. Label the flowers. How many rows are in her garden?

Name _____

Follow the Path

Color a path from **Start** to **Finish**. Follow the sums and differences that are odd numbers. You can only move up, down, right, or left.

I can ... add and subtract within 20.

Start								
5 + 6	14 − 6	13 − 9	7 − 3	1 + 9	10 − 5	2 + 9	9 + 8	16 − 7
3 + 4	14 − 7	2 + 5	11 − 6	4 + 8	8 − 3	12 − 6	1 + 5	11 − 4
7 − 1	4 + 4	12 − 4	12 − 7	14 − 9	4 + 7	15 − 7	2 + 5	1 + 8
9 + 9	1 + 7	6 − 4	2 + 8	6 + 2	1 + 9	13 − 9	15 − 6	2 + 4
17 − 9	3 + 9	7 + 5	8 + 8	16 − 6	9 − 5	10 − 6	5 + 4	10 − 3

Finish

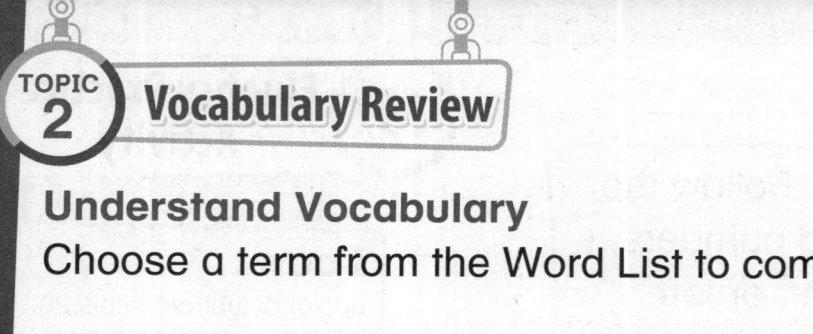

Word List
- addends
- array
- bar diagram
- column
- doubles
- equation
- even
- odd
- row
- sum

Understand Vocabulary

Choose a term from the Word List to complete each sentence.

1. An _____ number cannot be shown as pairs of cubes.

2. An _____ is a group of objects set in equal rows and columns.

3. In an array, objects that are shown across are in a _____.

4. A model for addition and subtraction that shows the parts and the whole is called a _____.

Write T for *true* or F for *false*.

5. _____ 9 is an even number.

6. _____ 13 is an odd number.

7. _____ You can model repeated addition with an array.

8. _____ In an array, objects that are shown up and down are in a column.

Use Vocabulary in Writing

9. Which model could you use to show 4 groups of 5 objects in each group? Use at least 1 term from the Word List.

© Pearson Education, Inc. 2

Set A

You can use cubes to tell if a number is even or odd.

12

The number of cubes is even if you can pair or count them by 2s.

odd   (even)

6 + 6 = 12

Circle even or odd. Then write the equation. Use cubes to help.

1.

11

(odd)   even

___ + ___ = ___

2.

18

odd   even

___ + ___ = ___

Set B

You can use repeated addition to find the total number of loaves.

Write two equations that match the array.

Rows: 3 + 3 = 6

Columns: 2 + 2 + 2 = 6

Write two equations that match the array.

3.

Rows: ___ + ___ + ___ + ___ = ___

Columns:

___ + ___ + ___ + ___ + ___ = ___

You can draw arrays and use repeated
addition to solve problems.

Alli has 3 shelves in her pantry.
She puts 4 cans of beans on each shelf.
How many cans of beans does Alli have in all?

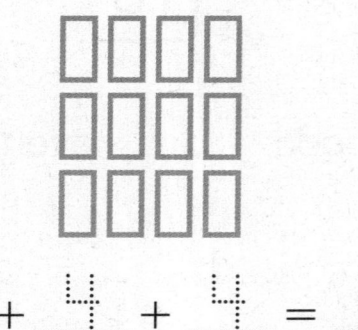

_4_ + _4_ + _4_ = _12_ cans

Thinking Habits

Model with Math

Can I use a drawing,
diagram, table, or graph
to model the problem?

Can I write an equation
to show the problem?

Draw an array to show the problem.
Use repeated addition to solve.

4. Steven puts 3 rows of apples on a table.
   Each row has 6 apples. How many
   apples does Steven put on the table?

____ + ____ + ____ = ____ apples

Draw a model and solve the problem.

5. There are 2 rows of cars.
   Each row has 8 cars.
   How many cars are in the parking lot?

____ + ____ = ____ cars

Name _____

 Assessment

1. José writes an equation.
The sum is an even number
greater than 14.

Which equation does José write?

Ⓐ $6 + 6 = ?$

Ⓑ $6 + 7 = ?$

Ⓒ $8 + 8 = ?$

Ⓓ $8 + 7 = ?$

2. Jen has 2 rows of apples
with 4 apples in each row.

Which equation shows how
many apples Jen has in all?

Ⓐ $4 + 2 = 6$

Ⓑ $2 + 2 + 2 = 6$

Ⓒ $4 + 4 = 8$

Ⓓ $4 + 4 + 4 = 12$

3. Choose Yes or No to tell if the sum in the equation is an even number.

$3 + 4 = 7$ $5 + 5 = 10$ $7 + 6 = 13$ $9 + 7 = 16$

○ Yes ○ No   ○ Yes ○ No   ○ Yes ○ No   ○ Yes ○ No

4. Will has 3 rows of trees in his yard.
Each row has 4 trees.
How many trees in all?

Draw a picture to show the array
of trees.

Then write an equation for your
picture.

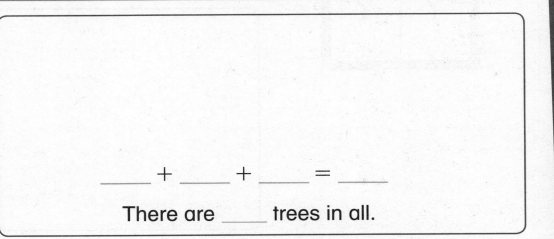

_____ + _____ + _____ = _____

There are _____ trees in all.

5. How many squares are shown? Is the number even or odd?

Draw a picture to show how you know.

6. Ben has 8 pennies. Look at each equation. Choose Yes or No to tell if Ben can use the equation to make an array with his pennies.

$2 + 2 + 2 + 2 = 8$ ○ Yes ○ No

$5 + 3 = 8$ ○ Yes ○ No

$4 + 4 = 8$ ○ Yes ○ No

$6 + 2 = 8$ ○ Yes ○ No

7. Becky drew this bar diagram to show 2 equal groups can make 14.

14

?	?

Part A
Draw a picture to show what the "?" stands for.

Part B
Change 14 to 16 in the bar diagram. What does the "?" stand for now? Tell how you know.

_____

_____

_____

© Pearson Education, Inc. 2

Topic 2 | Assessment

Name _____

School Garden
Students are planting a garden at school.
The pictures show the number of some plants
in the garden.

Number of Tomato Plants

Number of Corn Plants

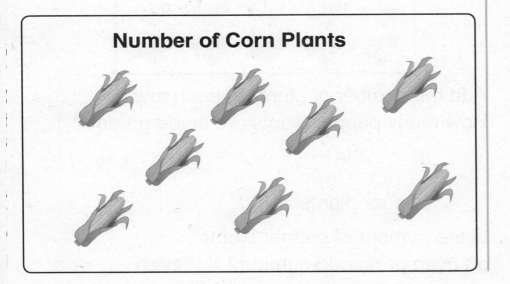

1. Is there an even or odd
number of tomato plants
in the garden?

Circle your answer.   **even**   **odd**

Show or tell how you know.

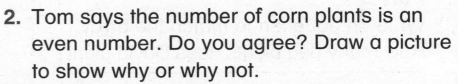

2. Tom says the number of corn plants is an
even number. Do you agree? Draw a picture
to show why or why not.

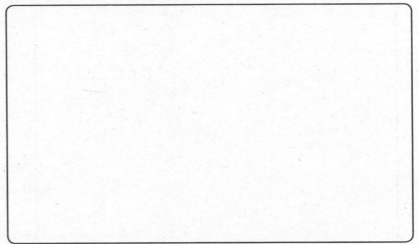

3. David plants peas in the school garden. He plants 4 rows of peas with 3 plants in each row.

Part A

Draw an array to show how David planted the peas.

Part B

Write an equation to match the array. How many pea plants does David plant?

4. Jesse says there are other ways to make an array of 12 plants. Show an array of 12 plants that is different from the array David used.

5. The array below shows the number of pepper plants in the garden.

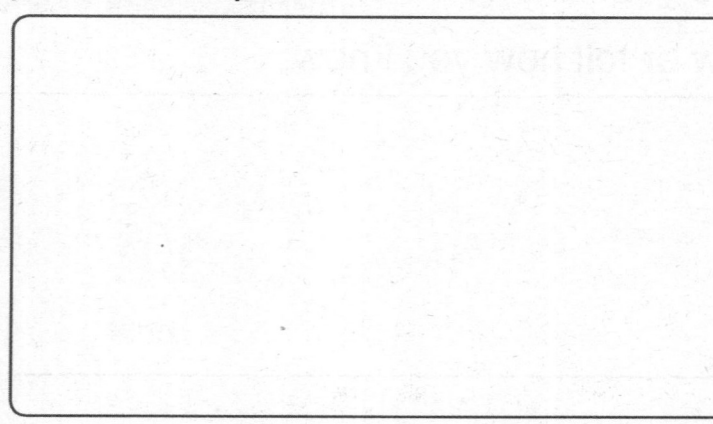

Number of Pepper Plants

Add the number of plants in each row. How many pepper plants are in the garden?

_____ + _____ + _____ + _____ + _____ = _____

_____ pepper plants

Is the number of pepper plants an even or an odd number?   **even**   **odd**

TOPIC 3

Add Within 100 Using Strategies

Essential Question: What are strategies for adding numbers to 100?

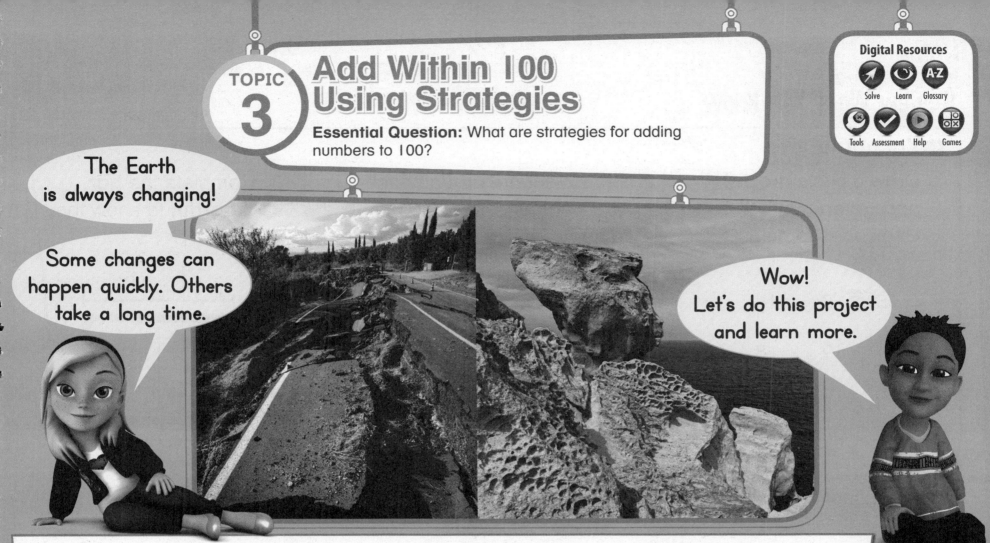

The Earth is always changing!

Some changes can happen quickly. Others take a long time.

Wow! Let's do this project and learn more.

Math and Science Project: Earth Changes and Addition Strategies

Find Out Find and share books about how the Earth changes. Talk about changes that people can see, hear, and feel. Talk about changes that people cannot see happening.

Journal: Make a Book Show what you learn in a book. In your book, also:

• Write new science words you learn. Draw pictures that help show what the words mean.

• Write new math words you learn. Draw pictures that help show what the words mean.

Name _____

A-Z Vocabulary

1. Draw a circle around each **even** number. Use cubes to help.

    15   7   14

    2   19   18

2. Draw a square around each **odd** number. Use cubes to help.

    12   3   6

    17   11   4

3. Complete the **bar diagram** to show the sum of 3 + 5.

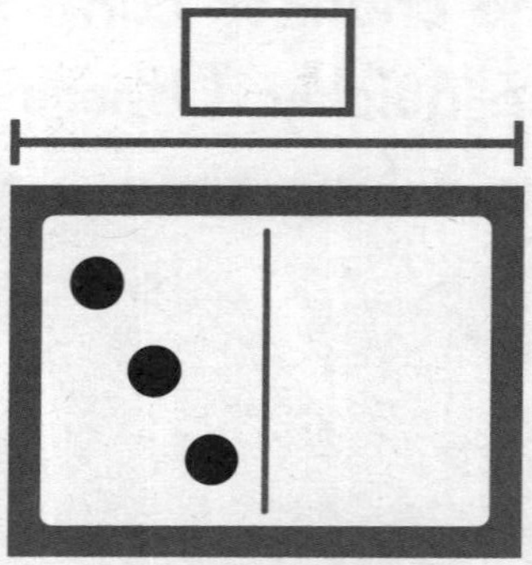

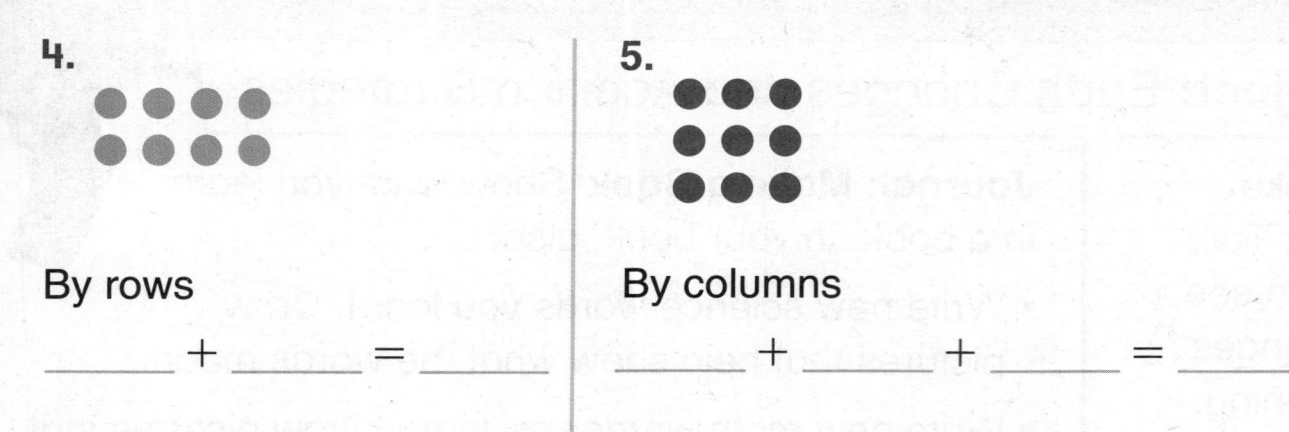

Arrays

Write an equation to show the number of circles in each array.

4.

By rows

_____ + _____ = _____

5.

By columns

_____ + _____ + _____ = _____

Math Story

6. Joe has 5 apples. He picks 3 more apples. How many apples does Joe have now?

    _____ apples

    Does Joe have an even or an odd number of apples?

    _____ number

© Pearson Education, Inc. 2

My Word Cards Study the words on the front of the card. Complete the activity on the back.

A-Z Glossary

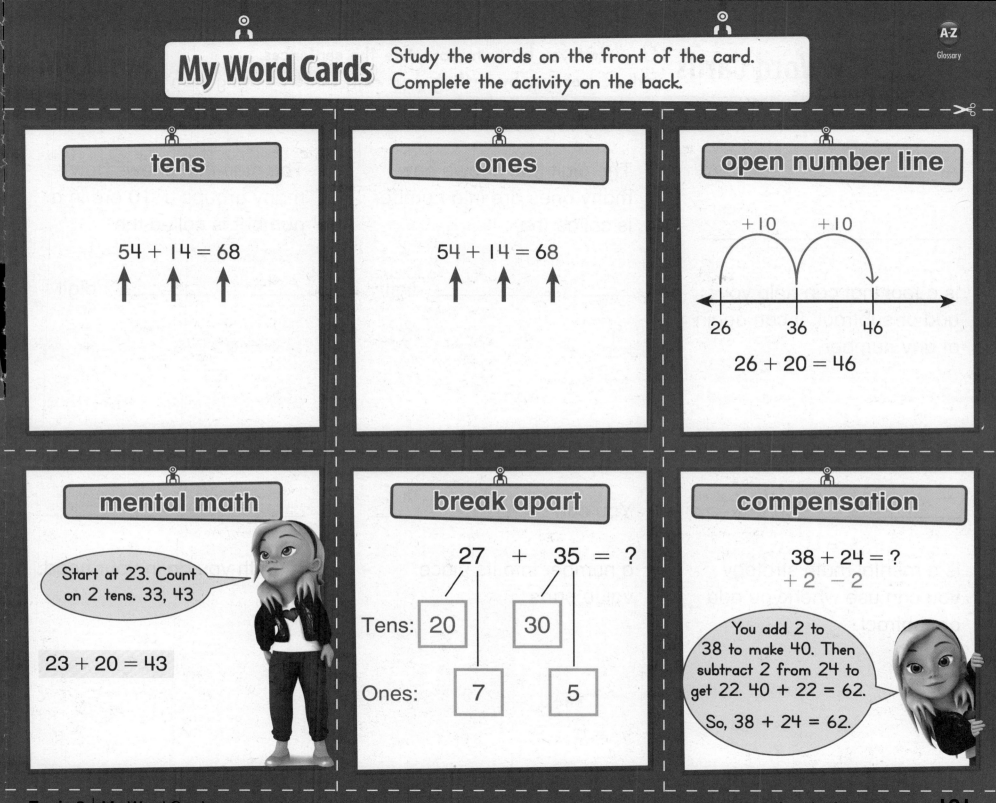

tens

$54 + 14 = 68$

ones

$54 + 14 = 68$

open number line

$+10$ $+10$

26   36   46

$26 + 20 = 46$

mental math

Start at 23. Count on 2 tens. 33, 43

$23 + 20 = 43$

break apart

$27 + 35 = ?$

Tens: 20   30

Ones: 7   5

compensation

$38 + 24 = ?$
$+2 \quad -2$

You add 2 to 38 to make 40. Then subtract 2 from 24 to get 22. $40 + 22 = 62$.

So, $38 + 24 = 62$.

My Word Cards

Use what you know to complete the sentences.
Extend learning by writing your own sentence using each word.

An _____

_____

is a tool that can help you add or subtract. It can begin at any number.

The digit that shows how many ones are in a number is called the

_____ digit.

The digit that shows how many groups of 10 are in a number is called the

_____ digit.

_____

is a mental math strategy you can use when you add or subtract.

You can _____

a number into its place value parts.

_____

is math you do in your head.

Name _____

Solve & Share

How can you use the hundred chart to help you find 32 + 43? Explain.

Write an equation to show the sum.

I can ...
add within 100 using place-value strategies.

I can also make math arguments.

1	2	3	4	5	6	7	8	9	10
11	12	13	14	15	16	17	18	19	20
21	22	23	24	25	26	27	28	29	30
31	32	33	34	35	36	37	38	39	40
41	42	43	44	45	46	47	48	49	50
51	52	53	54	55	56	57	58	59	60
61	62	63	64	65	66	67	68	69	70
71	72	73	74	75	76	77	78	79	80
81	82	83	84	85	86	87	88	89	90
91	92	93	94	95	96	97	98	99	100

____ + ____ = ____

You can add on a hundred chart. Find 54 + 18.

Start at 54. You need to add the tens from 18. Move down 1 row to show 1 ten.

51	52	53	54	55	56	57	58	59	60
61	62	63	64	65	66	67	68	69	70
71	72	73	74	75	76	77	78	79	80

Now add the **ones.**

You are already at 64. Now move ahead 8 to show 8 ones. You need to go to the next row to add them all. So, 54 + 18 = 72.

51	52	53	54	55	56	57	58	59	60
61	62	63	64	65	66	67	68	69	70
71	72	73	74	75	76	77	78	79	80

Do You Understand?

Show Me! How can you use a hundred chart to find 53 + 24?

☆ Guided Practice ☆

Add using the hundred chart. Draw arrows on the chart if needed.

11	12	13	14	15	16	17	18	19	20
21	22	23	24	25	26	27	28	29	30
31	32	33	34	35	36	37	38	39	40
41	42	43	44	45	46	47	48	49	50

1. 17 + 32 = __49__

2. 28 + 21 = _____

3. _____ = 19 + 20

4. 18 + 8 = _____

Tools   Assessment

Independent Practice ☆   Add using the hundred chart.

1	2	3	4	5	6	7	8	9	10
11	12	13	14	15	16	17	18	19	20
21	22	23	24	25	26	27	28	29	30
31	32	33	34	35	36	37	38	39	40
41	42	43	44	45	46	47	48	49	50
51	52	53	54	55	56	57	58	59	60
61	62	63	64	65	66	67	68	69	70
71	72	73	74	75	76	77	78	79	80
81	82	83	84	85	86	87	88	89	90
91	92	93	94	95	96	97	98	99	100

5. $33 + 9 =$ _____

6. _____ $= 12 + 73$

7. $38 + 21 =$ _____

8. $56 + 42 =$ _____

9. $47 + 28 =$ _____

10. $39 + 17 =$ _____

11. _____ $= 61 + 19$

12. **Higher Order Thinking** Write the digit that makes each equation true.

$\boxed{} + 83 = 90$ $34 + 2\boxed{} = 57$ $1\boxed{} + 51 = 67$ $62 + \boxed{}1 = 83$

Use Tools Use the hundred chart to solve the problems.

13. Sara has 48 buttons. Luis has 32 buttons. How many buttons do they have in all?

_____ buttons

31	32	33	34	35	36	37	38	39	40
41	42	43	44	45	46	47	48	49	50
51	52	53	54	55	56	57	58	59	60
61	62	63	64	65	66	67	68	69	70
71	72	73	74	75	76	77	78	79	80
81	82	83	84	85	86	87	88	89	90
91	92	93	94	95	96	97	98	99	100

14. Mika had 70 buttons. Then she found 19 more buttons. How many buttons does Mika have now?

_____ buttons

15. **Higher Order Thinking** Write the steps you take to add 43 and 39 on a hundred chart.

16. ✓**Assessment** Which weights will balance the weights already on the scale? Use a hundred chart to help.

Ⓐ 18, 20

Ⓑ 15, 20

Ⓒ 16, 30

Ⓓ 30, 17

© Pearson Education, Inc. 2

Name _____

Another Look!

Find 16 + 23.

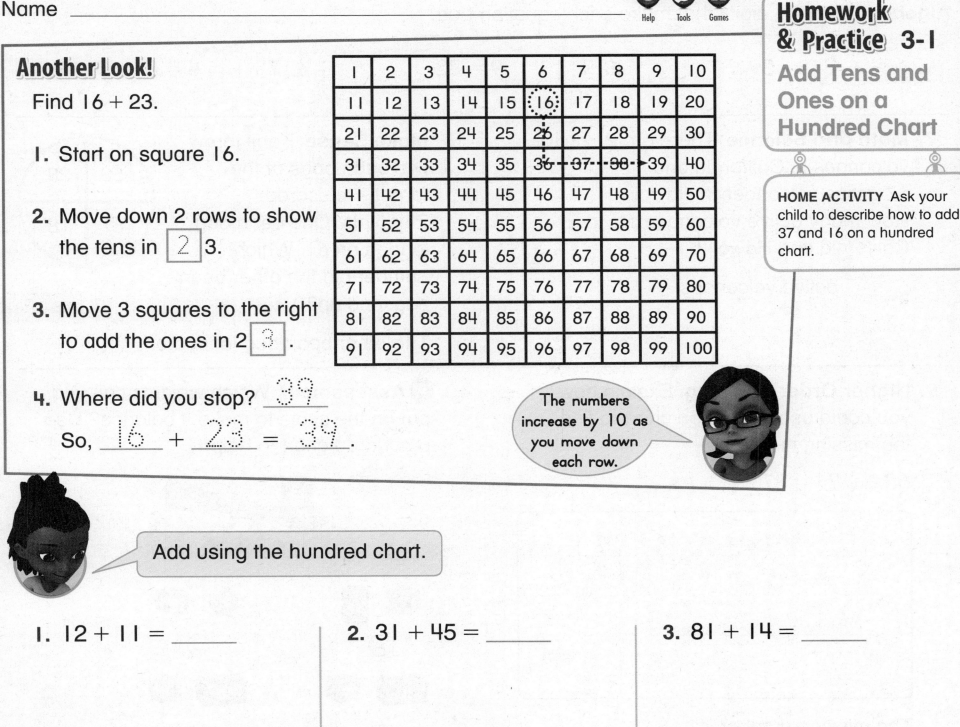

1	2	3	4	5	6	7	8	9	10
11	12	13	14	15	16	17	18	19	20
21	22	23	24	25	26	27	28	29	30
31	32	33	34	35	36	37	38	39	40
41	42	43	44	45	46	47	48	49	50
51	52	53	54	55	56	57	58	59	60
61	62	63	64	65	66	67	68	69	70
71	72	73	74	75	76	77	78	79	80
81	82	83	84	85	86	87	88	89	90
91	92	93	94	95	96	97	98	99	100

1. Start on square 16.

2. Move down 2 rows to show the tens in 2̲ 3.

3. Move 3 squares to the right to add the ones in 2 3̲.

4. Where did you stop? __39__

So, __16__ + __23__ = __39__.

The numbers increase by 10 as you move down each row.

HOME ACTIVITY Ask your child to describe how to add 37 and 16 on a hundred chart.

Add using the hundred chart.

1. 12 + 11 = _____

2. 31 + 45 = _____

3. 81 + 14 = _____

Algebra Write the digits that make each equation true.

4. $\boxed{}4 + 1\boxed{} = 39$

5. $4\boxed{} + \boxed{}9 = 82$

6. $74 + \boxed{}4 = 8\boxed{}$

---

7. **Math and Science** There are 21 active volcanoes in California and 17 active volcanoes in Hawaii. How many active volcanoes are in California and Hawaii?

_____ active volcanoes

8. **Make Sense** Kenji threw two bean bags at the target. He scored 79 points. One bean bag landed on 61. Which number did the other bean bag land on?

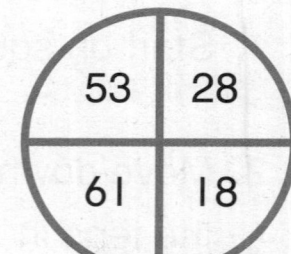

The other bean bag landed on _____.

---

9. **Higher Order Thinking** Explain how you could use a hundred chart to find the missing number.

$63 + \boxed{?} = 87$

The missing number is _____.

10. ✅**Assessment** Which weights can you put on the scale to make it balance? Use a hundred chart to help.

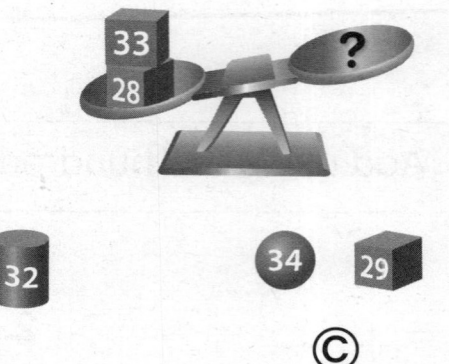

A. 29 32
B. 30 29
C. 34 29
D. 30 34

© Pearson Education, Inc. 2

Name _____

Solve & Share

How can you use the number line to help you find 30 + 40? Explain.

Write an equation to show the sum.

I can ...
add tens on an open number line.

I can also model with math.

_____ + _____ = _____

Find 36 + 30.

You can add tens on an **open number line**.

First, place 36 on the number line.

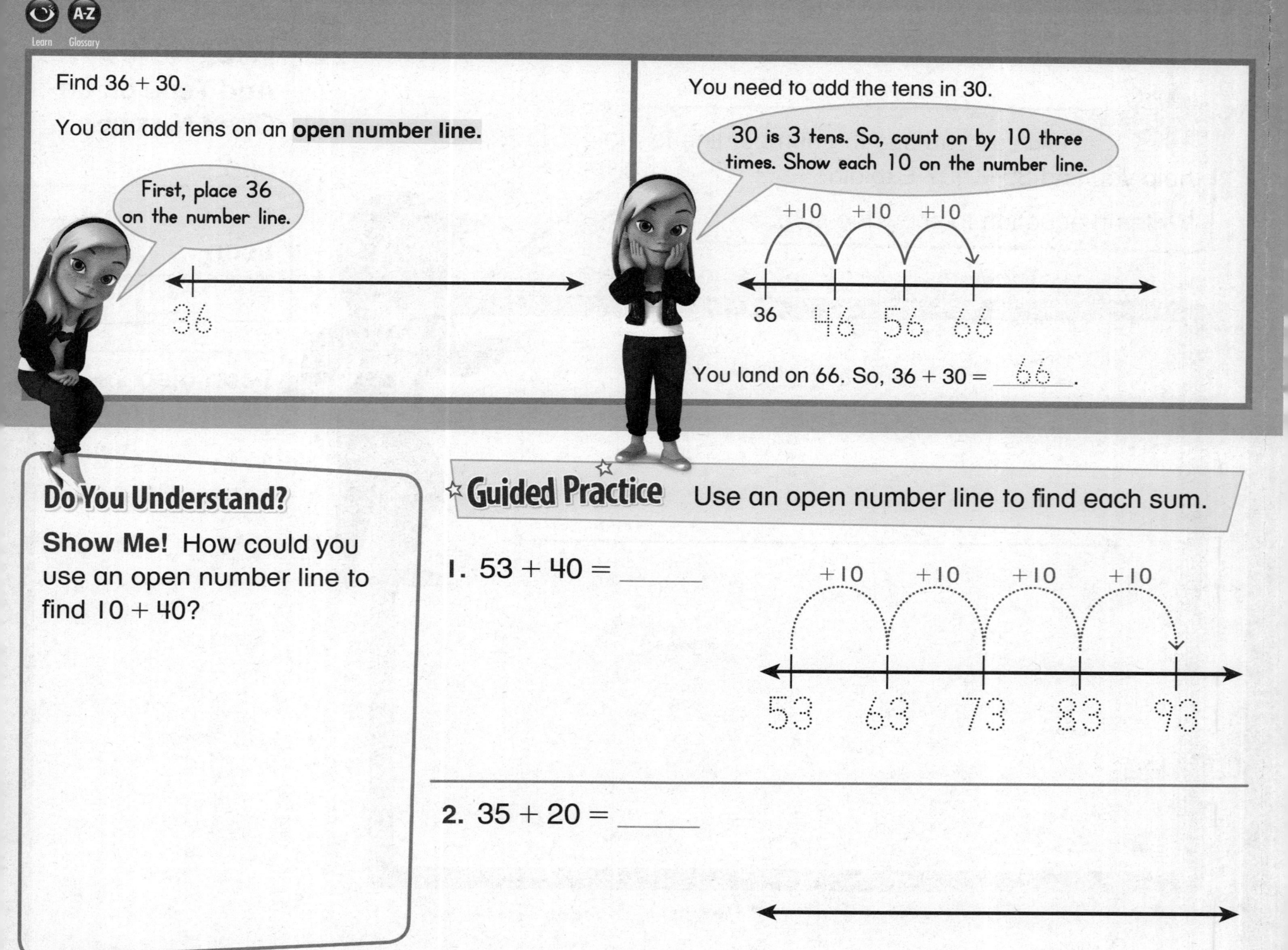

36

You need to add the tens in 30.

30 is 3 tens. So, count on by 10 three times. Show each 10 on the number line.

+10   +10   +10

36   46   56   66

You land on 66. So, 36 + 30 = __66__.

Do You Understand?

Show Me! How could you use an open number line to find 10 + 40?

⭐Guided Practice   Use an open number line to find each sum.

1. 53 + 40 = _____

+10   +10   +10   +10

53   63   73   83   93

2. 35 + 20 = _____

© Pearson Education, Inc. 2

Topic 3 | Lesson 2

Independent Practice Use an open number line to find each sum.

3. 30 + 10 = _____

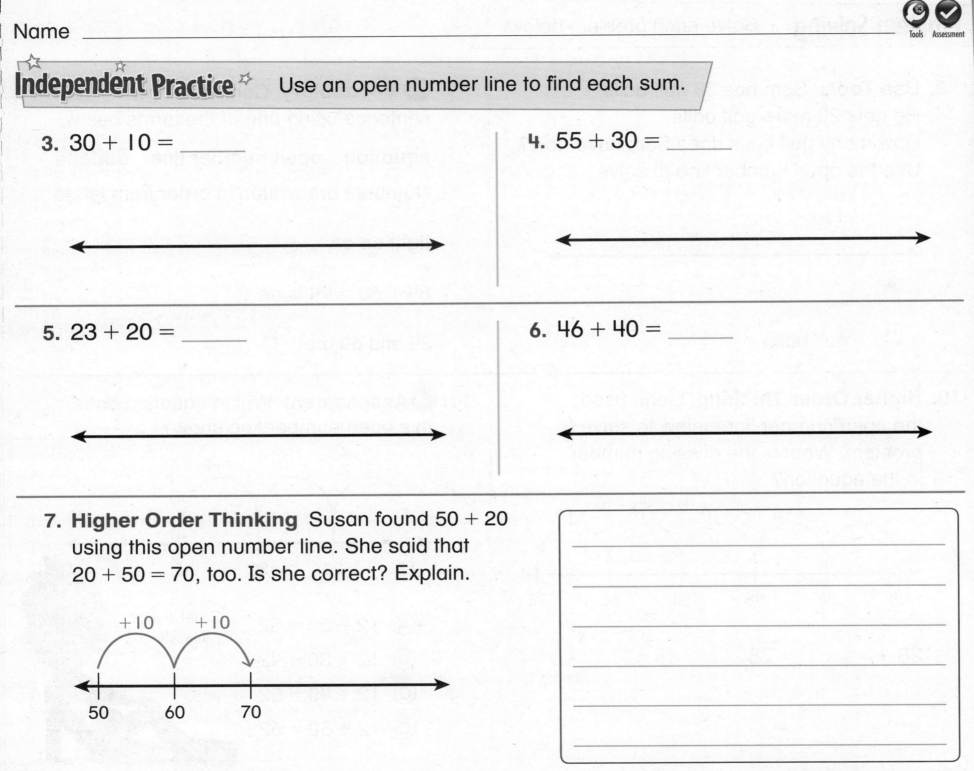

4. 55 + 30 = _____

5. 23 + 20 = _____

6. 46 + 40 = _____

7. Higher Order Thinking Susan found 50 + 20 using this open number line. She said that 20 + 50 = 70, too. Is she correct? Explain.

+10   +10

50   60   70

8. **Use Tools** Sam has 38 golf balls.
He gets 20 more golf balls.
How many golf balls does Sam have now?
Use the open number line to solve.

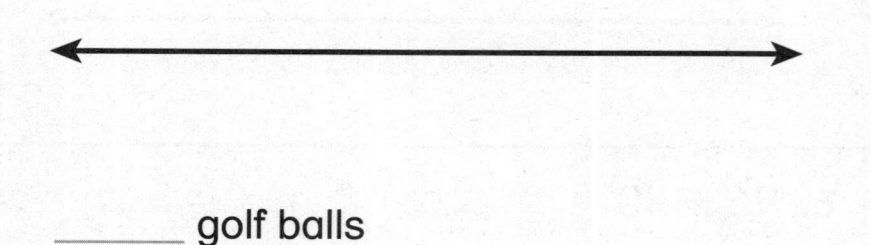

_____ golf balls

9. **A-Z Vocabulary** Complete each sentence using one of the terms below.

equation   open number line   addend

Numbers are written in order from left to

right on an _____.

$34 + 60 = 94$ is an _____.

34 and 60 are _____.

10. **Higher Order Thinking** Geno used the open number line below to solve a problem. What is the missing number in the equation?

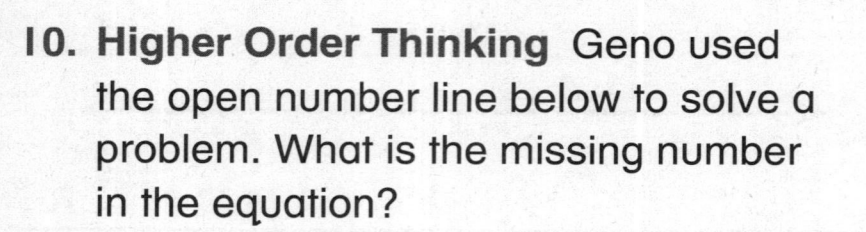

$28 + \underline{\quad} = 78$

11. ✓ **Assessment** Which equation does this open number line show?

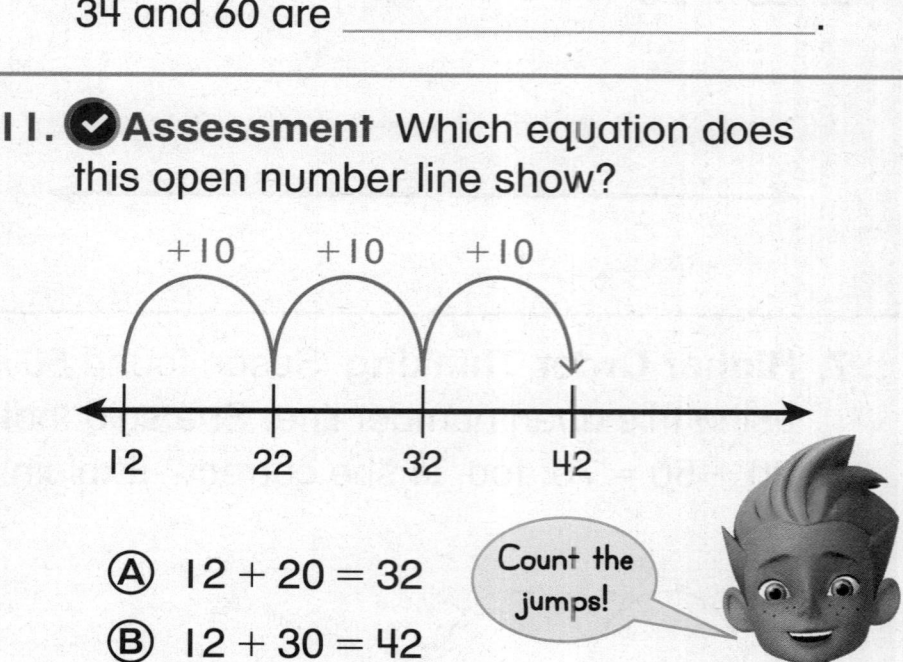

Ⓐ $12 + 20 = 32$

Ⓑ $12 + 30 = 42$

Ⓒ $12 + 40 = 52$

Ⓓ $12 + 50 = 62$

Count the jumps!

© Pearson Education, Inc. 2

Topic 3 | Lesson 2

Help Tools Games

Another Look! Find 64 + 20 using an open number line.

Place 64 on the number line. Then count on by 10 twice.

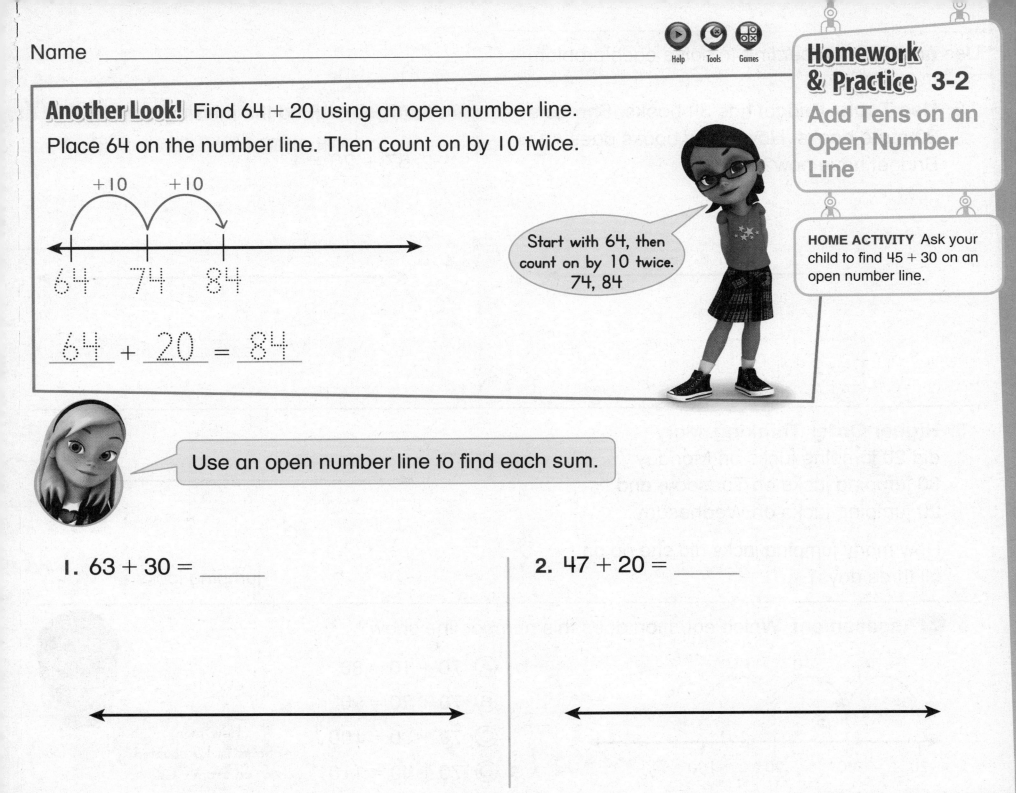

+10   +10

64   74   84

64 + 20 = 84

Start with 64, then count on by 10 twice. 74, 84

HOME ACTIVITY Ask your child to find 45 + 30 on an open number line.

Use an open number line to find each sum.

1. 63 + 30 = _____

2. 47 + 20 = _____

Digital Resources at PearsonRealize.com

3. **Use Tools** Bridget has 34 books. She gets 30 more books. How many books does Bridget have now?

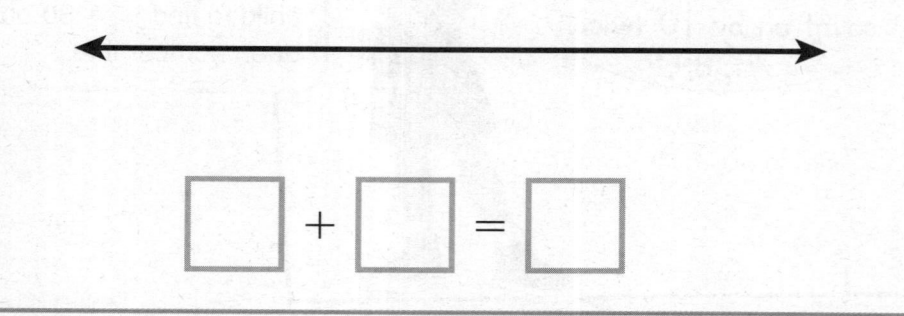

$$\boxed{} + \boxed{} = \boxed{}$$

4. **Algebra** Find the missing number.

$$57 + 20 = \boxed{}$$

5. **Higher Order Thinking** Mary did 20 jumping jacks on Monday, 30 jumping jacks on Tuesday, and 20 jumping jacks on Wednesday.

How many jumping jacks did she do on all three days?

_____ jumping jacks

6. ✓**Assessment** Which equation does this number line show?

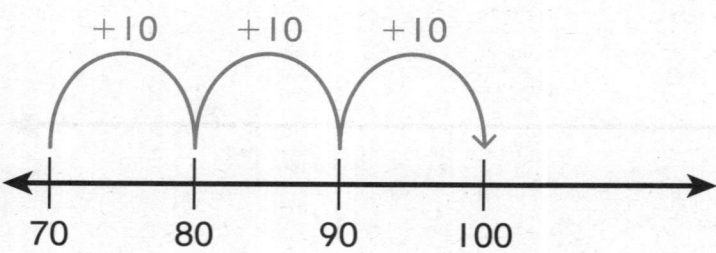

Ⓐ $70 + 10 = 80$

Ⓑ $70 + 20 = 90$

Ⓒ $70 + 30 = 100$

Ⓓ $70 + 40 = 110$

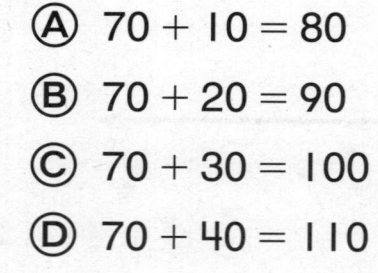

How many times is 10 counted on from 70?

© Pearson Education, Inc. 2

Topic 3 | Lesson 2

Name _____

How can you use the open number line to find 35 + 24?

Write an equation to show the sum. Explain your work.

I can ...
use an open number line to add tens and ones within 100.

I can also model with math.

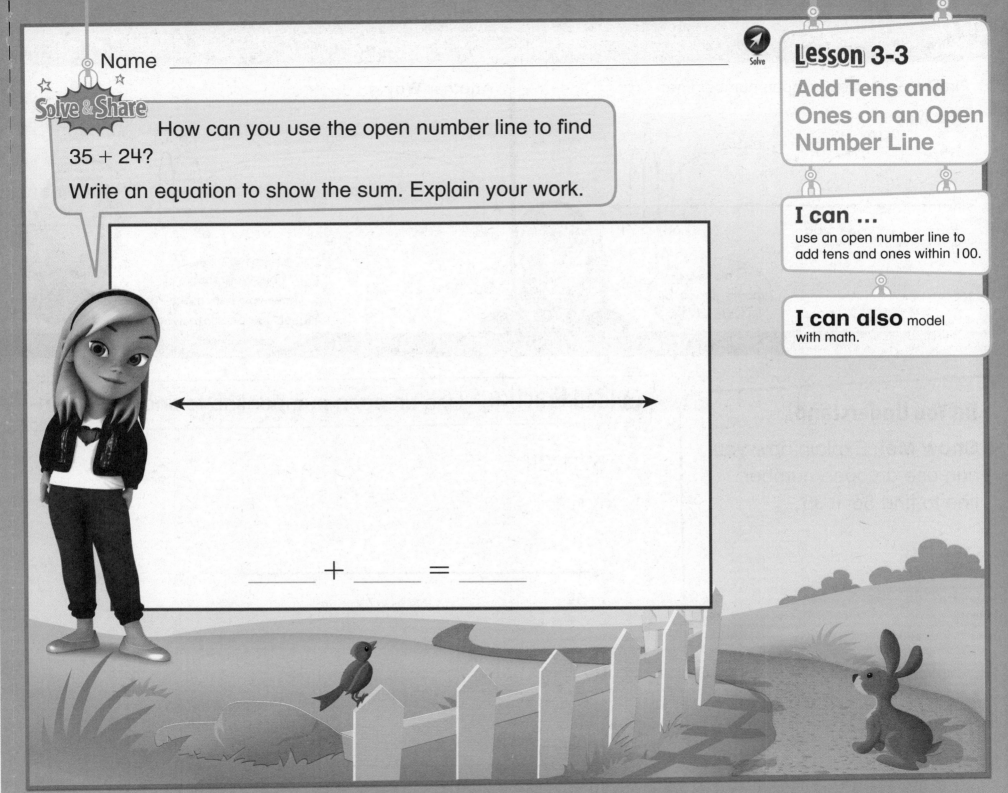

_____ + _____ = _____

Find 48 + 23. Use an open number line.

One Way

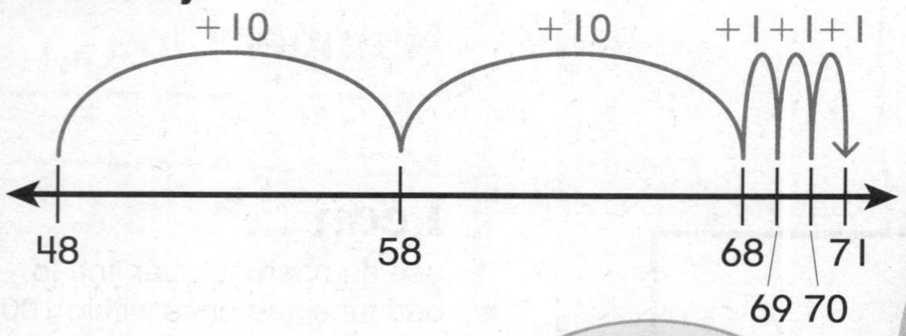

+10   +10   +1+1+1

48   58   68/ \71
                    69 70

This way shows jumps by 10s and 1s.

Another Way

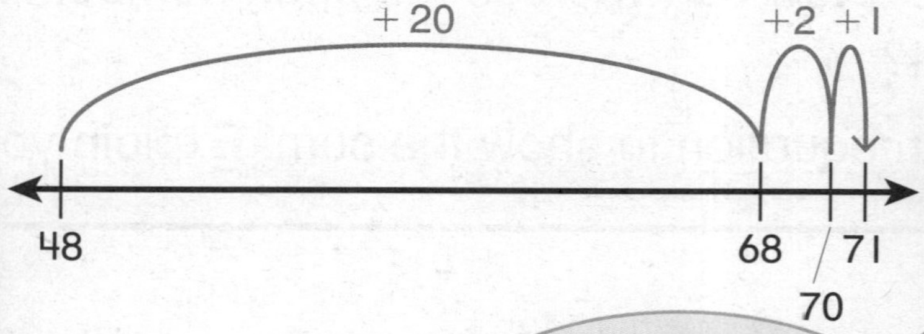

+ 20   +2 +1

48   68 /71
                        70

So, 48 + 23 = 71.

This way shows how you can make bigger jumps. Both ways are correct.

Do You Understand?

Show Me! Explain how you can use an open number line to find 56 + 35.

☆ Guided Practice   Use an open number line to find each sum.

1. 59 + 24 = _____

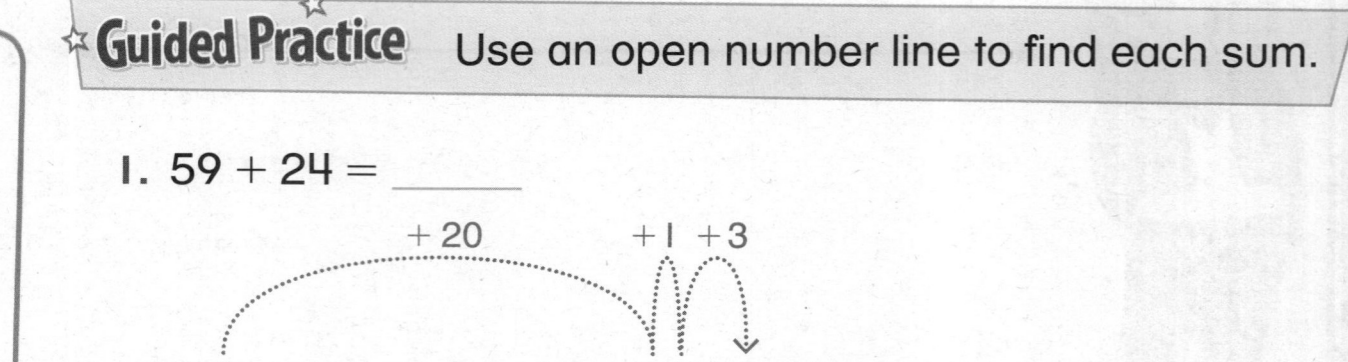

+ 20   +1 +3

59   79 \ 83
                  80

2. 47 + 25 = _____

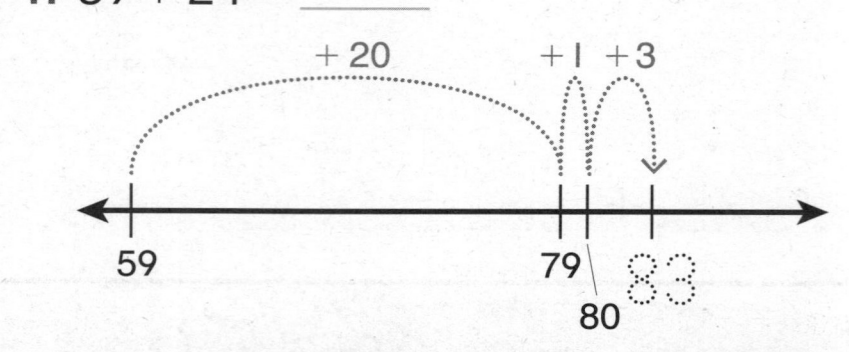

© Pearson Education, Inc. 2

Independent Practice ☆ Use an open number line to find each sum.

3. 34 + 15 = _____

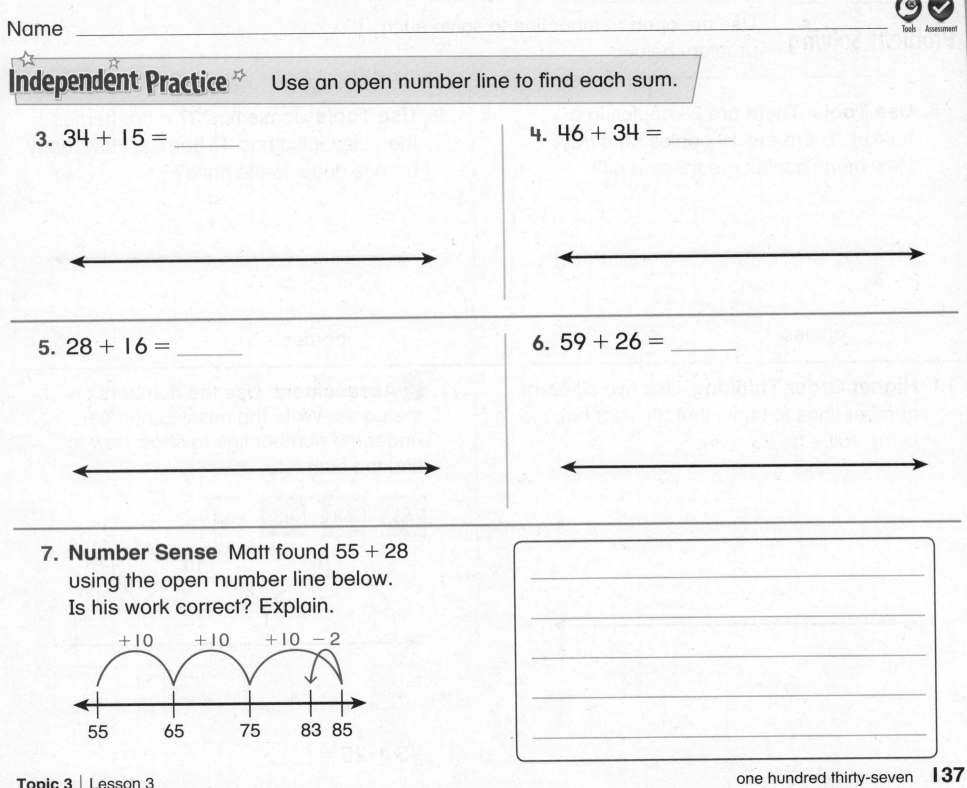

4. 46 + 34 = _____

5. 28 + 16 = _____

6. 59 + 26 = _____

7. Number Sense Matt found 55 + 28 using the open number line below. Is his work correct? Explain.

+10   +10   +10 −2

55   65   75   83 85

8. **Use Tools** There are 24 apples in a basket. There are 19 apples on a tray. How many apples are there in all?

_____ apples

9. **Use Tools** Jamie has 27 more berries than Lisa. Lisa has 37 berries. How many berries does Jamie have?

_____ berries

10. **Higher Order Thinking** Use two different number lines to show that 34 + 23 has the same value as 23 + 34.

11. ✅ **Assessment** Use the numbers on the cards. Write the missing numbers under the number line to show how to find the sum.

| 63 | 68 | 43 | 53 |

43 + 25 = _____

Name _____

Another Look! You can add two-digit numbers by counting on an open number line. 46 + 27 = ?

Place 46 on an open number line.

Count on 2 tens from 46.

I can use this strategy to add any numbers.

HOME ACTIVITY Ask your child to show how he or she would find 28 + 13 using an open number line.

Count on 7 ones from 66.

So, 46 + 27 = 73.

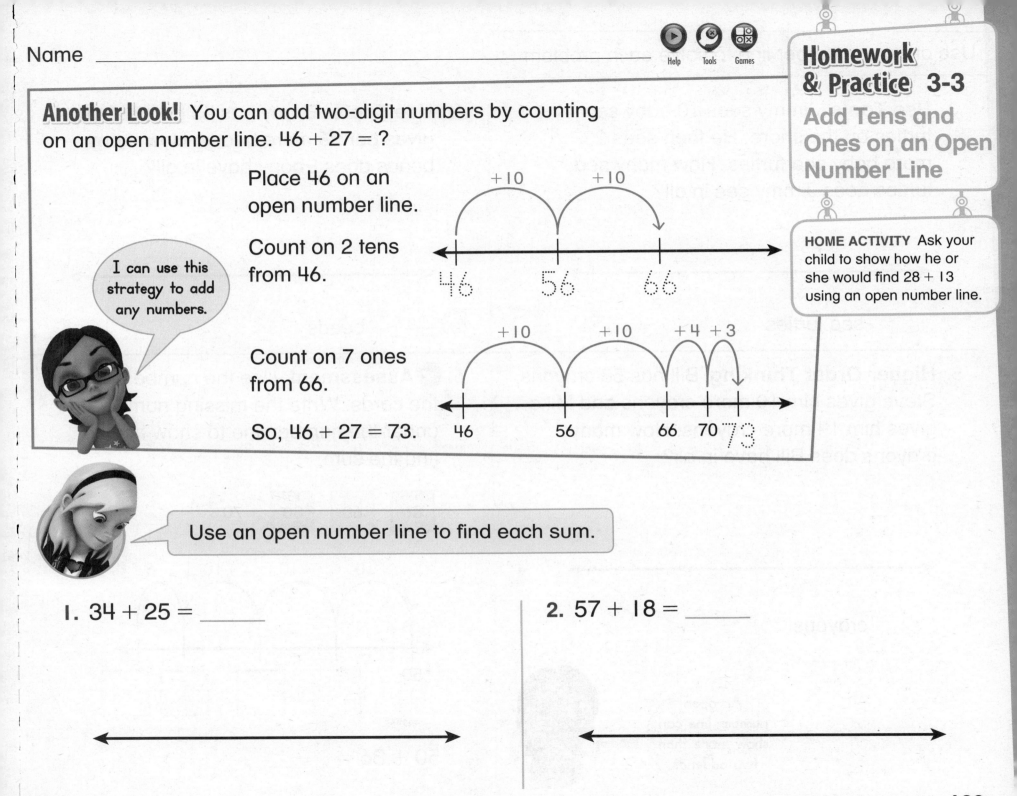

Use an open number line to find each sum.

1. 34 + 25 = _____

2. 57 + 18 = _____

3. **Use Tools** Jimmy sees 10 baby sea turtles on the shore. He then sees 23 more baby sea turtles. How many sea turtles does Jimmy see in all?

_____ sea turtles

4. **Use Tools** Ebony has 45 beads. Ivory gives her 26 more beads. How many beads does Ebony have in all?

_____ beads

5. **Higher Order Thinking** Bill has 58 crayons. Steve gives him 10 more crayons and Mika gives him 14 more crayons. How many crayons does Bill have in all?

_____ crayons

An open number line can show more than two addends.

6. ✅**Assessment** Use the numbers on the cards. Write the missing numbers under the number line to show how to find the sum.

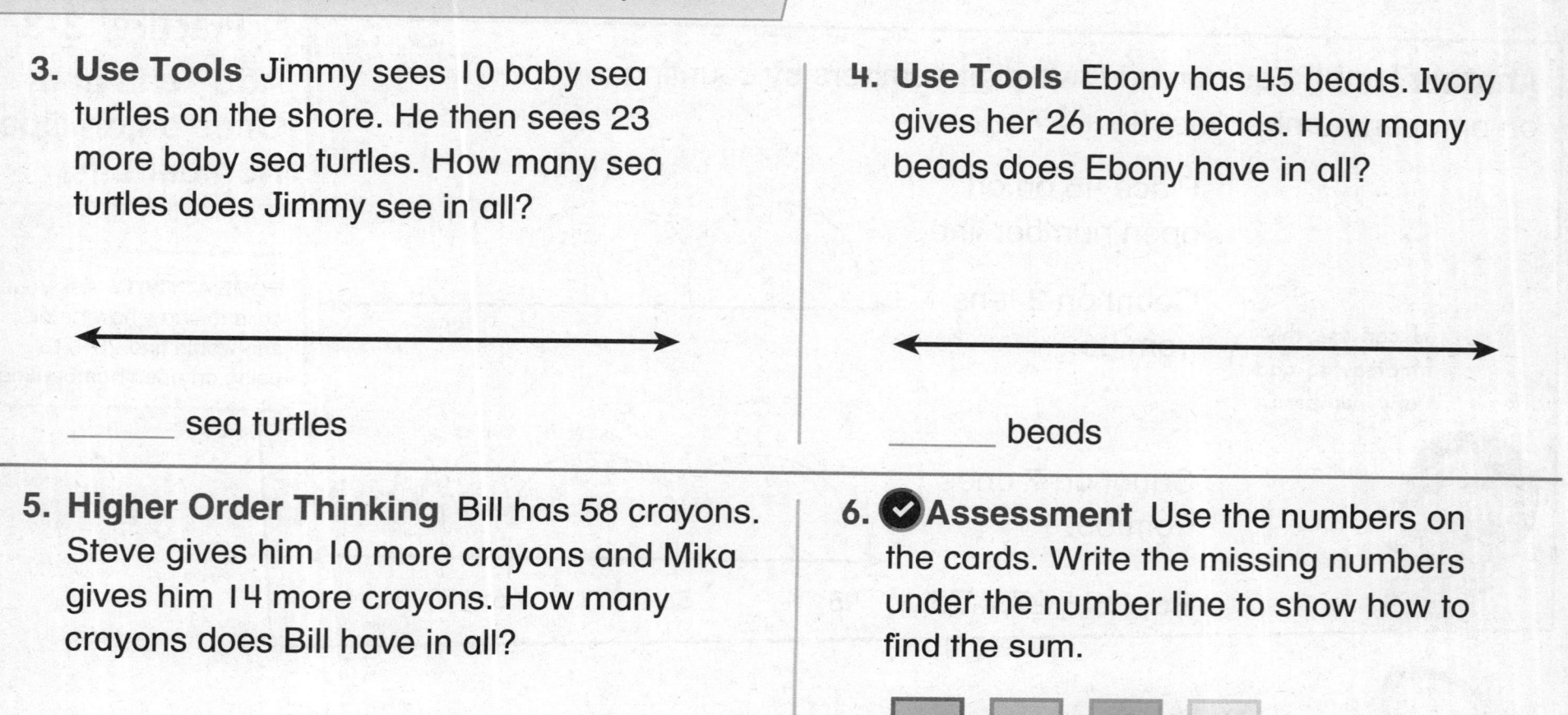

$$50 + 36 = \underline{\quad}$$

Name _____

Solve & Share

Monica has 24 crayons. Paul has 64 crayons. How many crayons do they have in all?

Solve any way you choose. Explain your work.

24 + 64 = _____

_____ crayons

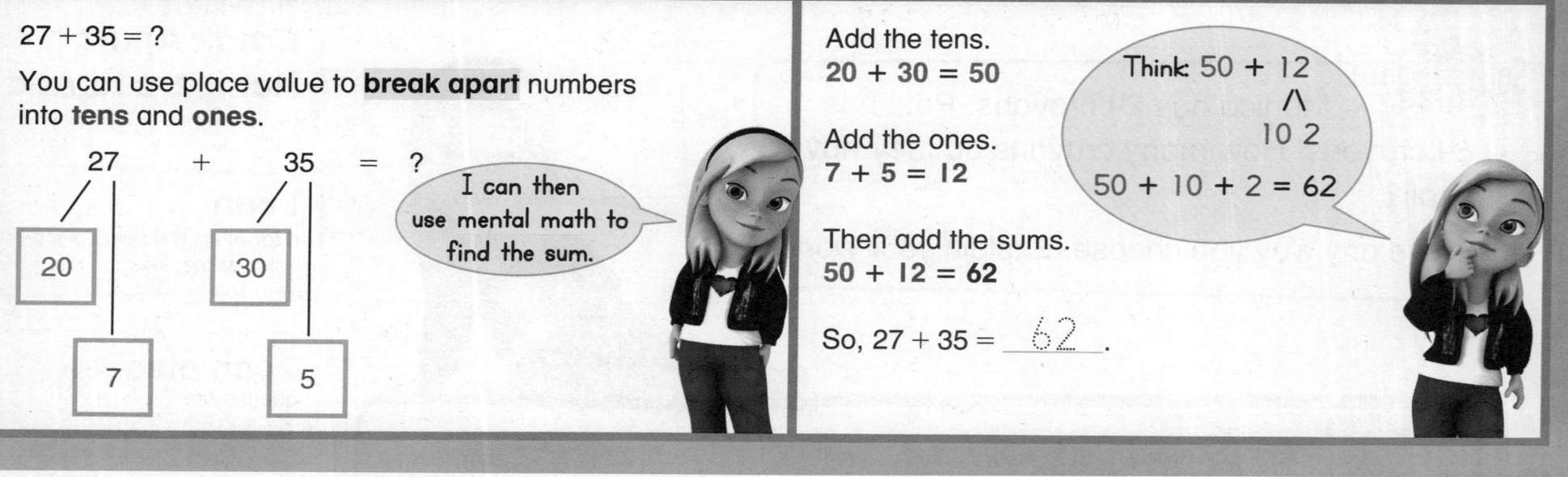

27 + 35 = ?

You can use place value to **break apart** numbers into **tens** and **ones**.

27   +   35   =   ?

20   30

7   5

I can then use mental math to find the sum.

Add the tens.
20 + 30 = 50

Add the ones.
7 + 5 = 12

Then add the sums.
50 + 12 = 62

So, 27 + 35 = __62__ .

Think: 50 + 12
         ∧
        10 2

50 + 10 + 2 = 62

Do You Understand?

Show Me! Explain how you can break apart numbers to find 14 + 32.

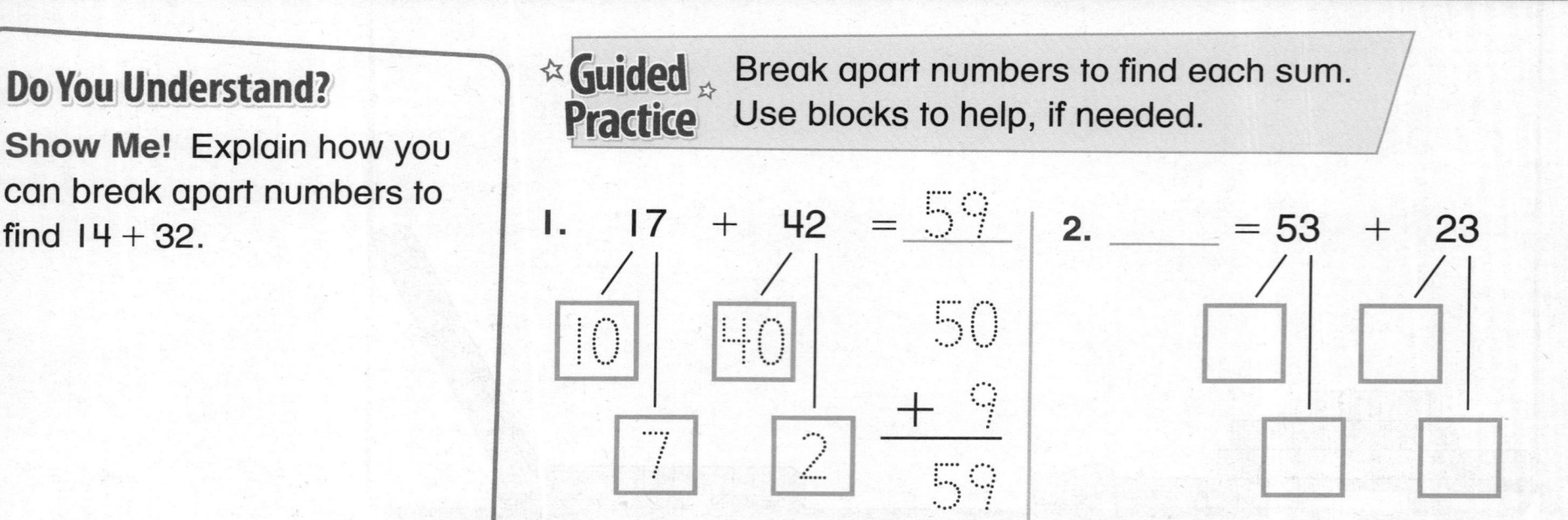

☆ **Guided Practice** ☆   Break apart numbers to find each sum. Use blocks to help, if needed.

1.   17   +   42   = __59__

10   40   50

7   2   + 9
                    ___
                    59

2.   ____ = 53   +   23

Topic 3 | Lesson 4

Tools Assessment

Independent Practice

Break apart numbers to find each sum.
Use blocks to help, if needed.

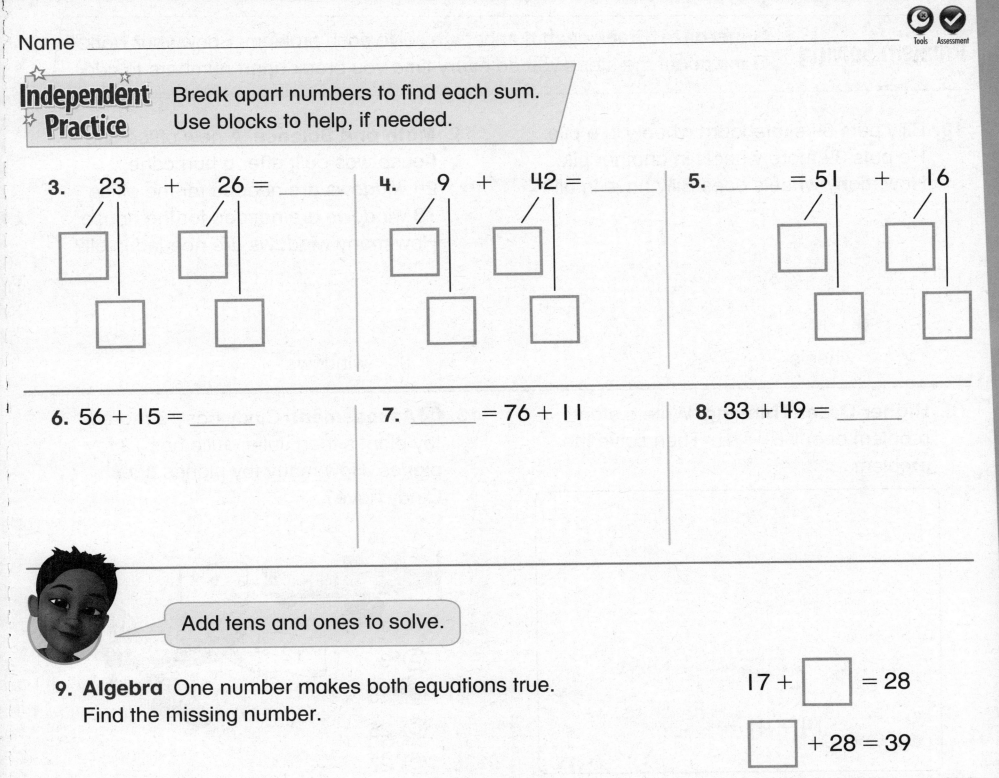

3.   23   +   26 = _____

4.   9   +   42 = _____

5. _____ = 51   +   16

6. 56 + 15 = _____

7. _____ = 76 + 11

8. 33 + 49 = _____

Add tens and ones to solve.

9. **Algebra** One number makes both equations true.
Find the missing number.

$$17 + \boxed{} = 28$$

$$\boxed{} + 28 = 39$$

Generalize Break apart numbers to solve each problem. Show your work. Think about the steps you do every time you break apart numbers to add.

10. Billy puts 34 skateboard wheels in a pile. He puts 34 more wheels in another pile. How many wheels does Billy have in all?

_____ wheels

11. **Math and Science** A new office and house was built after a hurricane. 24 windows are needed for the office. 18 windows are needed for the house. How many windows are needed in all?

_____ windows

12. **Higher Order Thinking** Write a story problem about $14 + 41$. Then solve the problem.

$14 + 41 =$ _____

13. ✔**Assessment** Cindy has 15 more toy planes than Julie. Julie has 12 toy planes. How many toy planes does Cindy have?

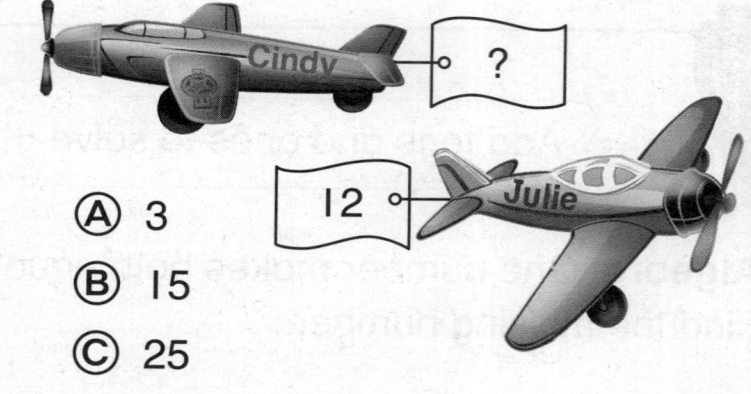

   Ⓐ 3

   Ⓑ 15

   Ⓒ 25

   Ⓓ 27

© Pearson Education, Inc. 2

Name _____

Another Look!
Find 34 + 24.

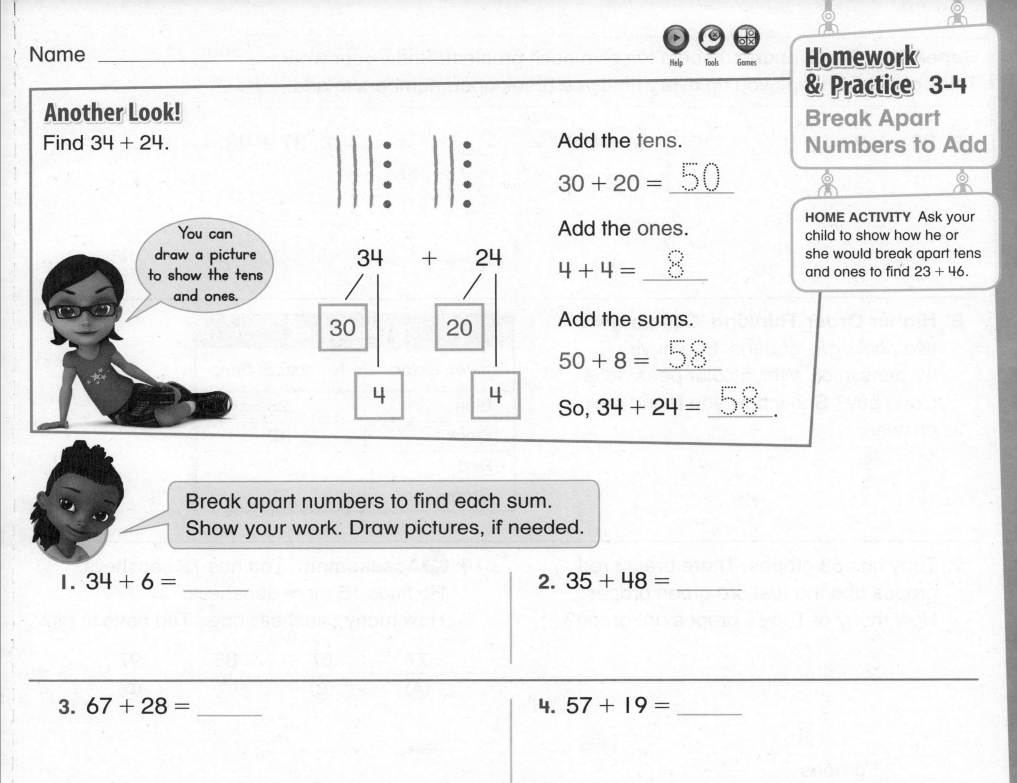

You can draw a picture to show the tens and ones.

34   +   24

30   20

4   4

Add the **tens**.

30 + 20 = __50__

Add the **ones**.

4 + 4 = __8__

Add the sums.

50 + 8 = __58__

So, 34 + 24 = __58__.

HOME ACTIVITY Ask your child to show how he or she would break apart tens and ones to find 23 + 46.

Break apart numbers to find each sum.
Show your work. Draw pictures, if needed.

1. 34 + 6 = _____

2. 35 + 48 = _____

3. 67 + 28 = _____

4. 57 + 19 = _____

Generalize Break apart numbers to solve each problem. Show your work. Think about the steps you do every time you break apart numbers to add.

5. $32 + 12 =$ _____

6. $54 + 7 =$ _____

7. $37 + 43 =$ _____

8. **Higher Order Thinking** Carla buys two packages of pens. She buys 49 pens in all. Which color pens does Carla buy? Show how you found the answer.

Pen Packages	
Pen Color	Number of Pens
Blue	25
Black	12
Red	24
Green	33

9. Toby has 63 grapes. There are 33 red grapes and the rest are green grapes. How many of Toby's grapes are green?

10. ✓ **Assessment** Tad has 72 seashells. He finds 15 more seashells. How many seashells does Tad have in all?

77   87   88   97
Ⓐ   Ⓑ   Ⓒ   Ⓓ

_____ grapes

Name _____

Solve & Share

Josh has 34 cans to recycle. Jill has 27 cans. How many cans do they have in all?

Solve any way you choose. Use drawings and equations to explain your work.

I can ...
break apart numbers into tens and ones to find their sum.

I can also make sense of problems.

_____ + _____ = _____ cans

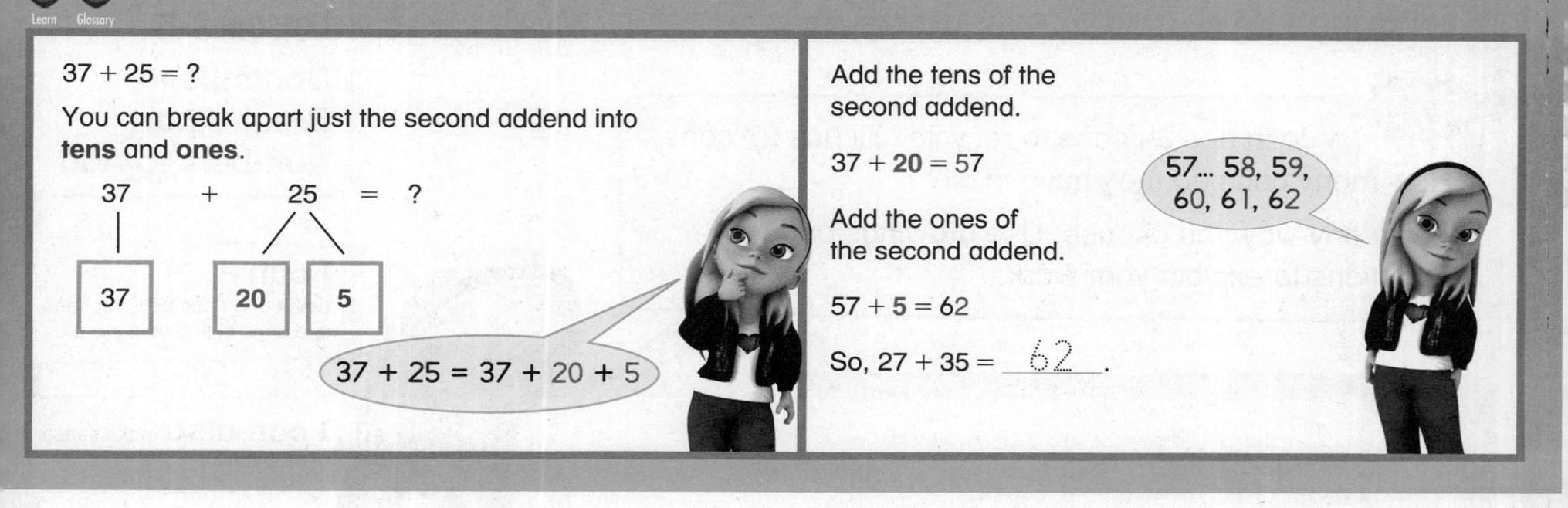

$37 + 25 = ?$

You can break apart just the second addend into **tens** and **ones**.

37   +   25   =   ?

| 37 | | 20 | 5 |

$37 + 25 = 37 + 20 + 5$

Add the tens of the second addend.

$37 + 20 = 57$

Add the ones of the second addend.

$57 + 5 = 62$

So, $27 + 35 = \underline{62}$.

57... 58, 59, 60, 61, 62

Do You Understand?

Show Me! Explain how you can break apart 28 to find $33 + 28$.

☆ **Guided Practice** ☆ Break apart the second addend to find the sum. Show your work. Use blocks to help, if needed.

1. 57   +   32 = _____

| 57 | | 30 | 2 |

$\underline{57} + \underline{30} = \underline{87}$

$\underline{87} + \underline{2} = \underline{89}$

2. 24   +   13 = _____

| | | | |

© Pearson Education, Inc. 2

Topic 3 | Lesson 5

Independent Practice Break apart the second addend to find the sum.
Show your work. Use blocks, if needed.

3. 42 + 16 = _____

$\square$ $\square\square$

4. 36 + 44 = _____

$\square$ $\square\square$

5. 41 + 37 = _____

$\square$ $\square\square$

6. 35 + 47 = _____

7. 32 + 28 = _____

8. 48 + 27 = _____

9. **Number Sense** Write the digit that makes each equation true.

3 $\square$ + 58 = 94

28 + 4 $\square$ = 75

1 $\square$ + 43 = 61

53 + 2 $\square$ = 82

It helps to break apart the numbers.

10. Amir planted 35 trees.
Juan planted 27 trees.
How many trees did they plant in all?

_____ trees

11. Carmen has 18 pennies.
Patrick has 12 more pennies than Carmen.
How many pennies does Patrick have?

_____ pennies

12. Higher Order Thinking Use the numbers on the cards. Use each number once to write a true equation.

| 3 | 2 | 8 |

5☐ + ☐4 = ☐6

13. ✓Assessment Which has a sum of 67? Choose all that apply.

☐ 15 + 52
☐ 15 + 62
☐ 38 + 29
☐ 11 + 55

Remember, you can add numbers in any order.

© Pearson Education, Inc. 2

Name _____

Another Look!

Find 25 + 34.

Think 25 plus 3 tens and 4 ones.

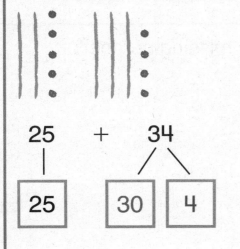

```
  25    +    34
   |          / \
 ┌────┐   ┌────┐ ┌────┐
 │ 25 │   │ 30 │ │ 4  │
 └────┘   └────┘ └────┘
```

Count on by tens to add 3 tens.

25, <u>35</u>, <u>45</u>, <u>55</u>

Then count on by ones to add 4 ones.

55, <u>56</u>, <u>57</u>, <u>58</u>, <u>59</u>

So, 25 + 34 = 59.

You can break apart the second addend to find the sum.

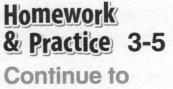

HOME ACTIVITY Ask your child to explain how to add 43 + 26 in his or her head.

Break apart numbers to find the sums. Show your work. Draw pictures, if needed.

1. 16 + 22 = _____

2. 47 + 29 = _____

3. 56 + 35 = _____

Break apart numbers to find each sum. Show your work. Draw pictures, if needed.

4. $14 + 28 =$ _____

5. $26 + 48 =$ _____

6. $43 + 17 =$ _____

---

7. Look for Patterns Break apart numbers to solve. Show your work.

Lily has 46 songs on her music player. Tonya has 53 songs on her music player. How many songs do they have in all?

_____ songs

8. Algebra Write the missing number.

$50 +$ ▲ $= 75$

▲ $+\ 25\ =\ 50$

▲ $=$ _____

■ $+ 38 = 80$

$30 +$ ■ $= 72$

■ $=$ _____

---

9. Higher Order Thinking Use the numbers on the cards. Use each number once to write a true equation.

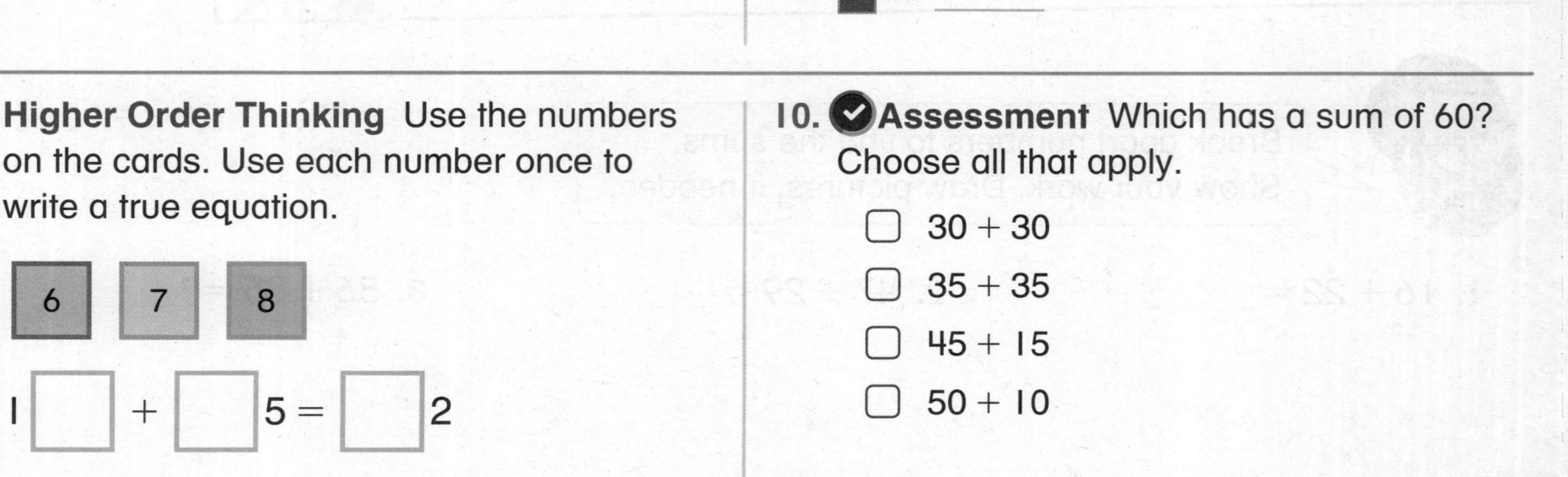

| 6 | 7 | 8 |

1 ☐ $+$ ☐ $5 =$ ☐ 2

10. ✓**Assessment** Which has a sum of 60? Choose all that apply.

☐ $30 + 30$

☐ $35 + 35$

☐ $45 + 15$

☐ $50 + 10$

© Pearson Education, Inc. 2

Solve & Share

35 + 8 = _____

Solve the problem by changing the 8 so that it is easier to find the sum of 35 + 8.

Explain your work.

Lesson 3-6
Add Using Compensation

I can ...
break apart addends and combine them in different ways to make numbers that are easy to add mentally.

I can also reason about math.

35 + 8 = ____

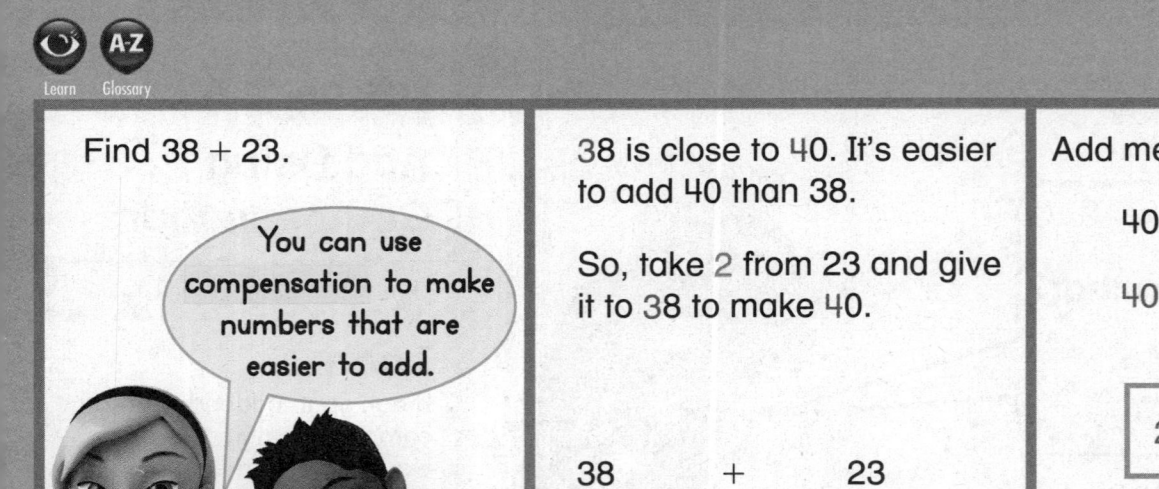

Find 38 + 23.

You can use compensation to make numbers that are easier to add.

40   21

38 is close to 40. It's easier to add 40 than 38.

So, take 2 from 23 and give it to 38 to make 40.

38	+	23
+ 2		− 2
40	+	21 = ?

Add mentally.

40 + 21 = ?

40 + 21

20   1

40 + 20 + 1 = 60 + 1 = 61

So, 40 + 21 = 61.

If you give an amount to one addend, you must take away the same amount from the other addend, so the sum stays the same.

40 + 21 = 38 + 23

So, 38 + 23 = 61.

Do You Understand?

Show Me! Solve.

$19 + 26 =$ ☐

Explain how you can change the addends to make them easier to add.

☆ **Guided Practice** ☆ Use compensation to make numbers that are easier to add. Then solve. Show your work.

1. $17 + 9 =$ _____
    $+ 3 \quad - 3$
    $20 + 6 = 26$

2. $23 \bigcirc \quad + \quad 12 \bigcirc =$ _____
    ___ + ___ = ___

3. $25 \bigcirc \quad + \quad 47 \bigcirc =$ _____
    ___ + ___ = ___

© Pearson Education, Inc. 2   **Topic 3** | Lesson 6

Independent Practice

Use compensation to make numbers that are easier to add.
Then solve. Show your work.

4.   33   +   19   = _____
○_____   ○_____

_____ + _____ = _____

5.   28   +   8   = _____
○_____   ○_____

_____ + _____ = _____

6.   27   +   36   = _____
○_____   ○_____

_____ + _____ = _____

7. **Number Sense** Explain how you can use compensation to make numbers that are easy to add. Solve. Show your work.

28   +   37   = ☐

_____ + _____ = ☐

8. **Higher Order Thinking** Show two different ways you could use compensation to make numbers that are easy to add. Solve. Show your work.

17 + 26 = ☐

9. **Explain** Bella said there is only one way to rewrite this problem to make the numbers easier to add. Is she correct? Explain. Then solve.

   $42 + 29 = \boxed{}$

   _____

   _____

   _____

   _____

10. **A-Z Vocabulary** Show two different ways to use **compensation** to find the sum. Then solve.

    $46 + 47 = \boxed{}$

    What number is close to 46 or 47?

11. **Higher Order Thinking** Show two different ways to use compensation to find the sum. Then solve.

    $37 + 16 + 5 = \boxed{}$

12. **✓ Assessment** Is the amount equal to $42 + 4 + 8$? Choose Yes or No.

$50 + 4$	◯ Yes	◯ No
$40 + 4 + 10$	◯ Yes	◯ No
54	◯ Yes	◯ No
$40 + 12$	◯ Yes	◯ No

© Pearson Education, Inc. 2

Topic 3 | Lesson 6

Name _____

Another Look! You can use compensation to make numbers that are easy to add mentally.

Use compensation to find $47 + 28$.

- Give 3 to 47 to make 50.
  Give 2 to 28 to make 30.

  $47 + 28$
  $+ 3 \quad + 2$

- Then it is easy to add in your head.

  $50 + 30 = 80$

- You added $3 + 2 = 5$. So subtract 5 from 80 to find the answer.
  You can count back 5 from 80 to check your answer.

  $80 - 5 = 75$

  80, 79, 78, 77, 76, 75

Compensation is a way to make numbers that are easy to add in your head!

So, $47 + 28 = 75$.

Use compensation to make numbers that are easier to add. Then solve. Show your work.

1. $26 + 6 =$ _____
   ◯ ◯
   ____ ____
   ____ + ____ = ____

2. $17 + 19 =$ _____
   ◯ ◯
   ____ ____
   ____ + ____ = ____

3. $39 + 54 =$ _____
   ◯ ◯
   ____ ____
   ____ + ____ = ____

Use compensation to make numbers that are easier to add.
Then solve. Show your work.

4. $24 + 18 =$ _____
○ _____ ○ _____

_____ + _____ = _____

5. $25 + 27 =$ _____
○ _____ ○ _____

_____ + _____ = _____

6. $43 + 32 =$ _____
○ _____ ○ _____

_____ + _____ = _____

7. **Reasoning** Use compensation to solve.
Show your work.

Wendy found 13 bugs and Wally found
27 bugs. How many bugs did they find in all?

_____ bugs

8. **Higher Order Thinking** Use compensation
to write 3 different equations with the same
sum as $38 + 16$. Then solve.

$38 + 16 =$ _____

A. _____ + _____ = _____

B. _____ + _____ = _____

C. _____ + _____ + _____ = _____

9. ✓ **Assessment** Which is equal to
$14 + 8$? Choose all that apply.

☐ $12 + 6$

☐ $12 + 10$

☐ $10 + 12$

☐ $10 + 4 + 8$

10. ✓ **Assessment** Is the amount equal to
$26 + 16$? Choose Yes or No.

$30 + 10 + 2$ ○ Yes ○ No

$30 + 12$ ○ Yes ○ No

$25 + 20$ ○ Yes ○ No

$20 + 22$ ○ Yes ○ No

Name _____

Tameka has 39 blocks. Kim has 43 blocks.
How many blocks do they have in all?

Choose any strategy. Solve. Show and explain your work.

I can ...
choose a strategy to help me
add two-digit numbers.

I can also model
with math.

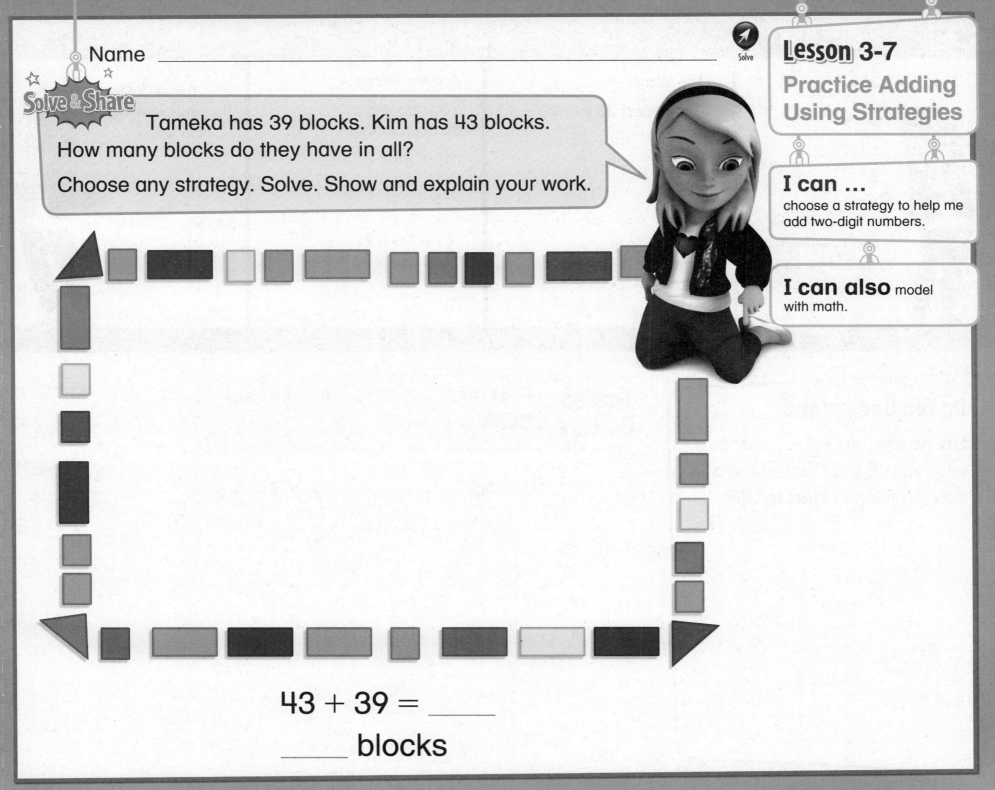

$43 + 39 =$ _____

_____ blocks

Find 66 + 25.

You can break apart numbers or use compensation.

One Way

Break apart 25 into 20 + 5.

66 + 25

66 + 20 + 5

86 + 5 = 91

Another Way

You can use compensation.

66 + 25
− 5   + 5
61 + 30 = 91

You get the same answer both ways!

So, 66 + 25 = 91.

Do You Understand?

Show Me! In 66 + 25 above, why was 5 subtracted from 66 and then added to 25?

☆ **Guided Practice** ☆ Find each sum. Use any strategy. Show your work.

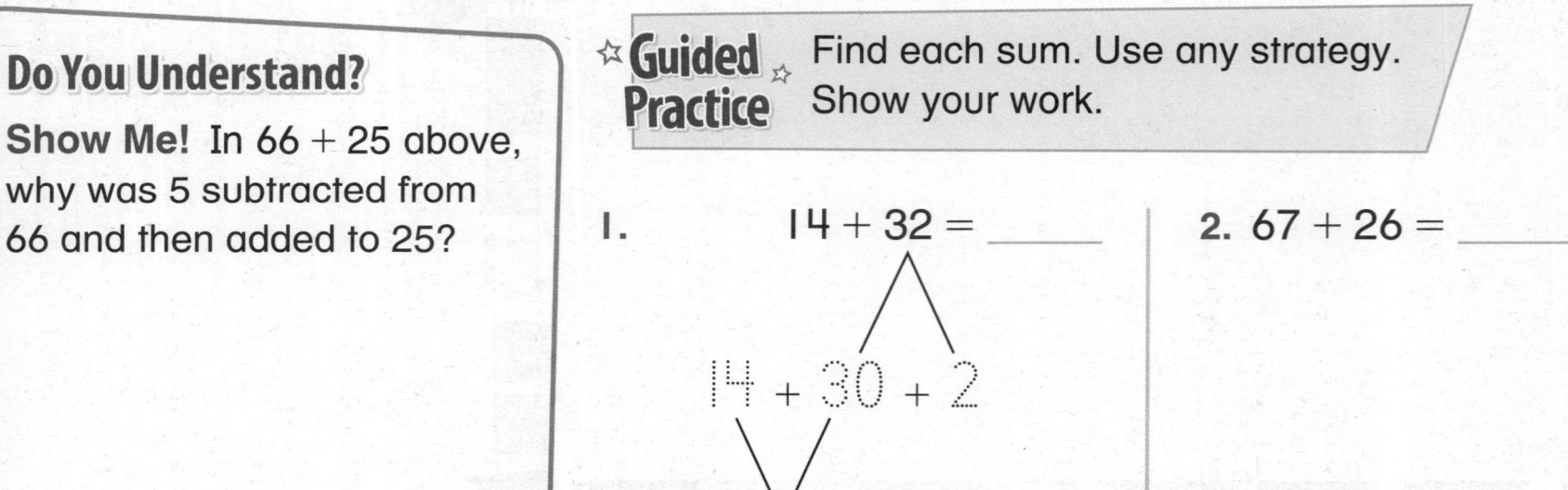

1.   14 + 32 = _____

14 + 30 + 2

44 + 2 = 46

2. 67 + 26 = _____

© Pearson Education, Inc. 2

Name _____

Independent Practice ☆ Find each sum. Use any strategy. Show your work.

3. 33 + 52 = _____

4. 27 + 6 = _____

5. _____ = 49 + 45

6. 57 + 12 = _____

7. _____ = 63 + 20

8. 14 + 58 = _____

9. 45 + 55 = _____

10. 87 + 9 = _____

11. 19 + 61 = _____

Number Sense Write the digit that makes each equation true.

12. $45 + 1\boxed{} = 61$

13. $84 = \boxed{}8 + 56$

14. $3\boxed{} + 19 = 56$

15. Reasoning Martin has 44 marbles. Carol has 39 marbles. Steve has 90 marbles. How many marbles do Martin and Carol have in all? Do they have more or fewer marbles than Steve?

_____ marbles

Circle: more   fewer

31	32	33	34	35	36	37	38	39	40
41	42	43	44	45	46	47	48	49	50
51	52	53	54	55	56	57	58	59	60
61	62	63	64	65	66	67	68	69	70
71	72	73	74	75	76	77	78	79	80
81	82	83	84	85	86	87	88	89	90
91	92	93	94	95	96	97	98	99	100

16. Higher Order Thinking José collected 32 leaves on Saturday. On Sunday, he collected 14 more leaves than he did on Saturday. How many leaves did José collect in all?

_____ leaves

Move down one row to show adding tens. Move ahead to show adding ones.

17. ✓**Assessment** Lucita wants to use an open number line to find $53 + 18$. Show and explain how Lucita can use an open number line to find $53 + 18$.

Help   Tools   Games

Another Look!

Find 24 + 56.

Step 1: Remember, 24 + 56 = 56 + 24.

Step 2: Place __56__ on an open number line.

Step 3: Count on __2__ tens from 56 to get to __76__.

Step 4: Then, count on __4__ ones from 76 to get to __80__.

So, 24 + 56 = __80__.

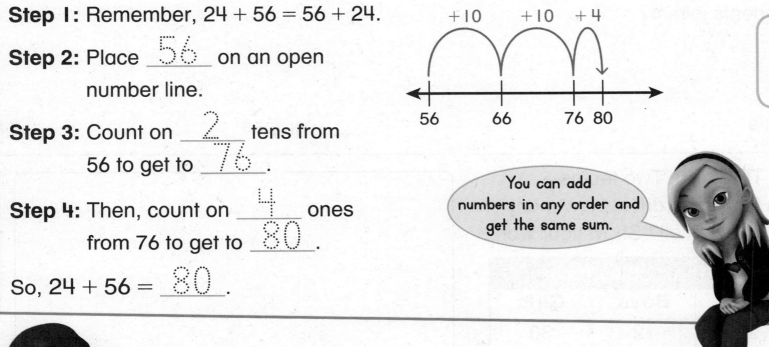

+10   +10   +4

56   66   76 80

You can add numbers in any order and get the same sum.

HOME ACTIVITY Ask your child to show and describe how to find 46 + 27 using an open number line.

Add using an open number line or another strategy. Show your work.

1. 38 + 6 = _____

2. 29 + 67 = _____

3. 48 + 34 = _____

4. **Reasoning** There were 43 students on the playground. Some more students joined them. Now there are 63 students on the playground. How many students joined?

_____ students

5. Roger has 14 grapes. Lisa has 49 grapes. How many grapes do Roger and Lisa have in all?

_____ grapes

6. **Higher Order Thinking** Two teams collected cans for a food drive. How many cans did they collect in all? Show your work.

Red Team		Blue Team	
Boys	**Girls**	**Boys**	**Girls**
23	28	12	30

7. ✓**Assessment** Ali wrote this first step in how to add 27 + 12 on a hundred chart.

Start at 27 on the chart.

Write the other steps.

© Pearson Education, Inc. 2

Name _____

Solve

Lesson 3-8

Solve One-Step and Two-Step Problems

I can ...
use drawings and equations to solve one-step and two-step problems.

I can also model with math.

Solve & Share

The Red Team has 15 more points than the Blue team. The Blue Team has 36 points. How many points does the Red Team have?

Solve and explain your answer using counters, drawings, or equations.

Matt sold 17 tickets.
Jenn sold 8 fewer tickets than Matt.
Amy sold 3 more tickets than Jenn.

How many tickets did each person sell?

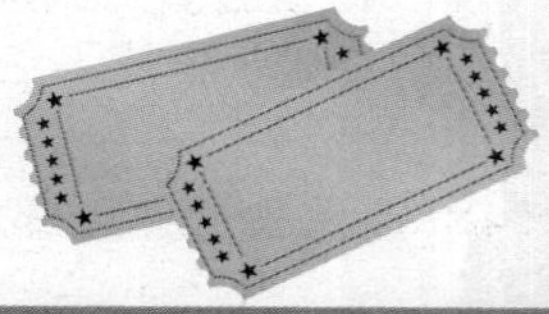

Step 1

tickets Matt sold

17

8	9

fewer   tickets
tickets   Jenn sold

$17 - 8 = 9$
Jenn sold 9 tickets.

Step 2

tickets Amy sold

12

9	3

tickets   more
Jenn sold   tickets

$9 + 3 = 12$
Amy sold 12 tickets.

Matt:	17 tickets
Jenn:	9 tickets
Amy:	12 tickets

Look back! Does your answer make sense?

Do You Understand?

Show Me! What steps did you take to find the number of tickets Amy sold? Explain.

⭐ **Guided Practice**   Solve the two-step problem. Show your work.

1. Steve read 15 books. Sam read 9 fewer books than Steve. Dixon read 8 more books than Sam.

How many books did Sam read?

$\underline{15} - \underline{9} = \underline{}$

How many books did Dixon read?

$\underline{6} + \underline{8} = \underline{}$

15

_____	9

Sam read _____ books.

_____

6	8

Dixon read _____ books.

© Pearson Education, Inc. 2

Topic 3 | Lesson 8

Tools Assessment

Independent Practice ☆ Solve the problems below. Show your work.

2. Brian has 17 fewer marbles than Kyle. Brian has 21 marbles. How many marbles does Kyle have?

_____ marbles

3. Clint catches 7 frogs. 3 frogs hop away. Then Clint catches 6 more frogs. How many frogs does Clint have now?

_____ frogs

4. Erwin sees 23 birds in a tree. Then 18 more birds come. How many birds does Erwin see now?

_____ birds

5. There are 31 blue fish in a pond. There are also 8 gold fish and 3 red fish in the pond. How many fish are in the pond?

_____ fish

6. Higher Order Thinking Mr. Leu buys 6 bananas. Then he buys 8 more bananas. He gives some bananas to Mr. Shen. Now Mr. Leu has 5 bananas. How many bananas did Mr. Leu give to Mr. Shen?

_____ bananas

7. There are 21 more green crayons than blue crayons. There are 14 blue crayons. How many green crayons are there?

_____ green crayons

8. **Make Sense** Dan swims 4 laps on Monday. He swims 5 laps on Tuesday. Then he swims 9 laps on Wednesday. How many laps does Dan swim in all?

_____ + _____ = _____

_____ + _____ = _____

_____ laps

9. **Higher Order Thinking** Robert has 20 blueberries. He has 10 more blueberries than Janessa. He has 14 fewer blueberries than Amari. How many blueberries does Janessa have? How many blueberries does Amari have?

_____ − _____ = _____

_____ + _____ = _____

Janessa has _____ blueberries.

Amari has _____ blueberries.

10. ✅ **Assessment** Billy saw 19 animals at Grayson Zoo in the morning. He saw 17 more animals after lunch. How many animals did Billy see in all?

_____ + _____ = _____ animals

Taylor saw 41 animals at Richmond Zoo. How many animals did Billy and Taylor see in all?

_____ + _____ = _____

Billy and Taylor saw _____ animals in all.

Name _____

Help Tools Games

Homework
& Practice 3-8
Solve One-
and Two-Step
Problems

Another Look! Write equations to solve two-step problems.

Allison collected 23 rocks.
Jason collected 15 more rocks than Allison.
Phil collected 3 fewer rocks than Allison.

How many rocks does Jason have?
How many rocks does Phil have?

Number of Rocks Jason has: $23 + 15 = ?$

$23 + 10 = 33$ and $33 + 5 = 38$

So, Jason has ___38___ rocks.

You can count back 3 from 23 to find the number of rocks Phil has.

23, __22__, __21__, __20__ So, Phil has __20__ rocks.

Be sure to solve
each part of the
problem!

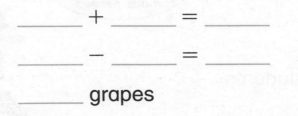

HOME ACTIVITY Make up
story problems that take
two questions, or steps,
to solve. Ask your child to
solve both steps of each
problem.

Write equations to solve the problems.

1. There are 4 fewer students in Ms. Jagger's class than Mr. Curley's class. Mr. Curley's class has 20 students. How many students are in Ms. Jagger's class?

_____ − _____ = _____

_____ students

2. There are 13 green grapes and 7 red grapes in a bowl. Joe ate 5 of the grapes. How many grapes are in the bowl now?

_____ + _____ = _____

_____ − _____ = _____

_____ grapes

Algebra Find the missing numbers.

3. ■ $+ 42 = 58$

■ $=$ _____

4. $33 + 49 =$ ▲

▲ $=$ _____

5. $76 +$ ◯ $= 89$

◯ $=$ _____

Write equations to solve each problem.

6. **Make Sense** There are 6 girls at a park. 6 boys join them. Then 4 girls go home. How many children are at the park now?

_____ $+$ _____ $=$ _____

_____ $-$ _____ $=$ _____

_____ children.

7. **Higher Order Thinking** Mr. Villa's class has 23 students. Ms. Anderson's class has 3 more students than Mr. Villa's class. How many students are there in all?

Check your work. Does your answer make sense?

_____ students

8. ✓**Assessment** Mike used 27 nails to build a chair. He used 14 more nails to build a table than he used to build the chair. How many nails did Mike use to build the table? Use any strategy to solve. Explain your solution.

_____ nails

© Pearson Education, Inc. 2

Name _____

Solve & Share

There are 23 red balloons in a bag. There are 38 blue balloons in the same bag. How many balloons are in the bag?

Use a tool to solve the problem. Be ready to explain which tool you used and why.

I can ...
choose a tool and use it to solve a problem.

I can also add and subtract.

Thinking Habits

Which of these tools can I use?

Tools

Cubes   Paper and
Counters   pencil
Hundred chart   Place-value
Technology   blocks

Is there a different tool I can use?

Ted's puzzle has 37 more pieces than Mia's puzzle. Mia's puzzle has 48 pieces. How many pieces does Ted's puzzle have?

Which tool can I use?

Tools
• cubes
• counters
• hundred chart
• technology
• paper and pencil
• place-value blocks

Which tool is a good choice?

Ted has 37 more pieces than Mia. I can use place-value blocks to find 48 + 37.

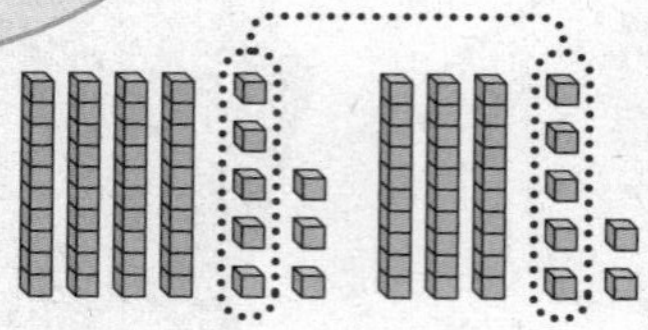

$48 + 37 = \underline{85}$
Ted's puzzle has 85 pieces.

If I used counters, I'd need to count each one.

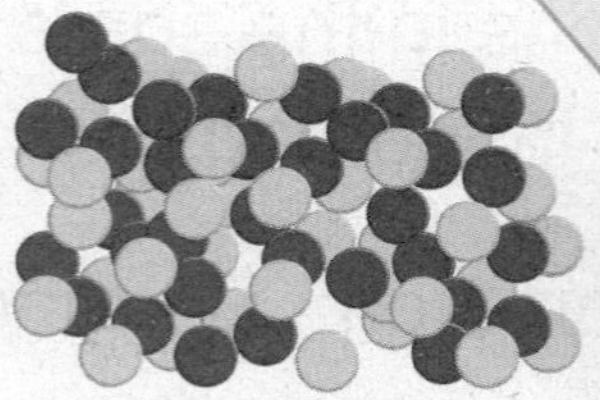

With place-value blocks, I can add the tens quicker.

I can break apart 37 and add each part to 48 to check.
$48 + 30 = 78$
$78 + 7 =$
$78 + 2 + 5 = 85$
My answer makes sense.

Do You Understand?

Show Me! Explain why a ten-frame is not the best tool to use to solve the problem above.

☆ Guided Practice ☆

Choose a tool to help you solve the problem. Show your work. Explain why you chose that tool and how you solved the problem.

1. There are 16 chickens in the yard. There are 19 chickens in the barn. How many chickens are there in all?

   Will you use place-value blocks or counters to solve the problem? Explain.

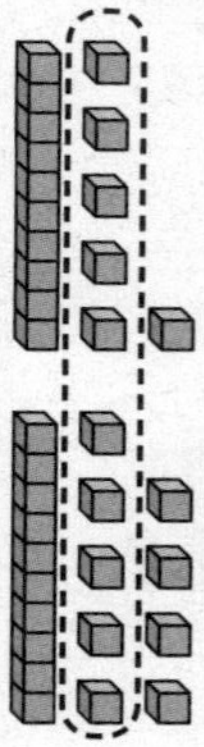

$16 \;\oplus\; 19 \;\ominus\; \underline{\quad}$
_____ chickens

© Pearson Education, Inc. 2
Topic 3 | Lesson 9

Independent Practice   Choose a tool to help solve each problem. Show your work. Explain your tool choice and how you solved the problem.

2. Greg had 45 sports cards. Jamal gives him 26 more cards. How many sports cards does Greg have now?

_____ ◯ _____ ◯ _____

_____ sports cards

3. Denise drew 8 stars with crayons. Then she drew 6 more stars. Trina drew 5 stars. How many fewer stars did Trina draw than Denise?

_____ ◯ _____ ◯ _____

_____ ◯ _____ ◯ _____

_____ fewer stars

Bean Bag Toss

Evan and Pam want to choose the best tool to solve this problem.

Evan and Pam each throw two bean bags. Points are added for a score. Pam's total score is 100. Which two numbers did Pam's bean bags land on?

| 24 | 56 |
| 44 | 33 |

Bean Bag Toss Game Board

4. Make Sense What information is given? What do you need to find?

_____

_____

_____

5. Explain Which numbers did Pam's bags land on? Explain how you know.

_____

_____

_____

6. Use Tools Which tool did you use? How could you use a hundred chart to solve the problem? Explain.

_____

_____

_____

1	2	3	4	5	6	7	8	9	10
11	12	13	14	15	16	17	18	19	20
21	22	23	24	25	26	27	28	29	30
31	32	33	34	35	36	37	38	39	40
41	42	43	44	45	46	47	48	49	50
51	52	53	54	55	56	57	58	59	60
61	62	63	64	65	66	67	68	69	70
71	72	73	74	75	76	77	78	79	80
81	82	83	84	85	86	87	88	89	90
91	92	93	94	95	96	97	98	99	100

Name _____

Another Look! What tool would you use to solve this problem?

Jamie read 23 pages of a book last week.
This week, she read 26 more pages.
How many pages did Jamie read in all?

㉓	24	25	26	27	28	29
33	34	35	36	37	38	39
㊸	44	45	46	47	48	㊾

A hundred chart is a good tool to use. You can start at 23 and count on 2 tens, and then 6 ones. You land on 49. So, 23 + 26 = 49.

23 + 26 = 49 pages. Jamie read 49 pages in all.

HOME ACTIVITY Take turns adding two 2-digit numbers. Use drawings of tens and ones to show how you found each sum.

Choose a tool to help you solve the problem. Show your work.
Explain your tool choice and how you solved the problem.

1. A year ago, Maggie's puppy weighed 16 pounds. Now her puppy weighs 37 pounds more. How much does Maggie's puppy weigh now?

_____ ○ _____ ○ _____ pounds

Rubber Bands

Juan is trying to find the best tool to solve this problem.

Juan wants to buy 1 large bag and 1 small bag of rubber bands. How many rubber bands will he buy?

Number of Rubber Bands

Small	Medium	Large
25	45	70

2. **Make Sense** What information is given? What do you need to find?

_____

_____

_____

3. **Reasoning** Juan wants to use counters to solve the problem. Do you think Juan's tool choice is a good one? Why or why not?

_____

_____

_____

4. **Use Tools** Use a tool to solve the problem. Which tool did you use? Is there a different tool you could have used to solve the problem? Explain.

_____

_____

_____

_____

Name _____

Find a Match

Find a partner. Point to a clue. Read the clue.

Look below the clues to find a match. Write the clue letter in the box next to the match.

Find a match for every clue.

I can ...
subtract within 20.

Clues

A Every difference equals 3.

B Every difference is less than 2.

C Every difference equals 11 − 5.

D Exactly two differences are equal.

E Every difference is greater than 8.

F Exactly three differences are odd.

G Every difference equals 16 − 8.

H Exactly three differences are even.

6 − 5 8 − 8 10 − 10 9 − 9	8 − 6 12 − 8 15 − 8 4 − 0	18 − 9 16 − 7 11 − 2 10 − 1	10 − 8 9 − 4 6 − 2 14 − 9
17 − 9 9 − 1 13 − 5 12 − 4	14 − 8 12 − 6 8 − 2 13 − 7	11 − 6 5 − 3 14 − 7 12 − 3	12 − 9 9 − 6 11 − 8 10 − 7

Word List
- bar diagram
- break apart
- compensation
- mental math
- ones
- open number line
- tens

Understand Vocabulary

1. Circle the numbers that have a 3 in the ones place.

33   45   13   38

2. Cross out the numbers that do **NOT** have an 8 in the tens place.

80   18   78   89

3. Write an equation to show how to break apart 54 by place value.

_____

4. Use the open number line to find $38 + 23$. Add the tens and then add the ones.

$\longleftrightarrow$

Use Vocabulary in Writing

5. Describe a way to find $47 + 18$. Use terms from the Word List.

_____
_____
_____

Name _____

Set A

You can use a hundred chart to help you add. Find 62 + 12.

Start at 62.
Move down
1 row to add
the one ten
in 12.

51	52	53	54	55	56	57	58	59	60
61	62	63	64	65	66	67	68	69	70
71	72	73	74	75	76	77	78	79	80
81	82	83	84	85	86	87	88	89	90
91	92	93	94	95	96	97	98	99	100

Then move over
2 columns to add
the 2 ones in 12. So, 62 + 12 = __74__.

Use a hundred chart to find each sum.

1. 85 + 15 = _____

2. 60 + 23 = _____

Set B

You can use an open number line to find 64 + 20.

Place 64 on the number line.

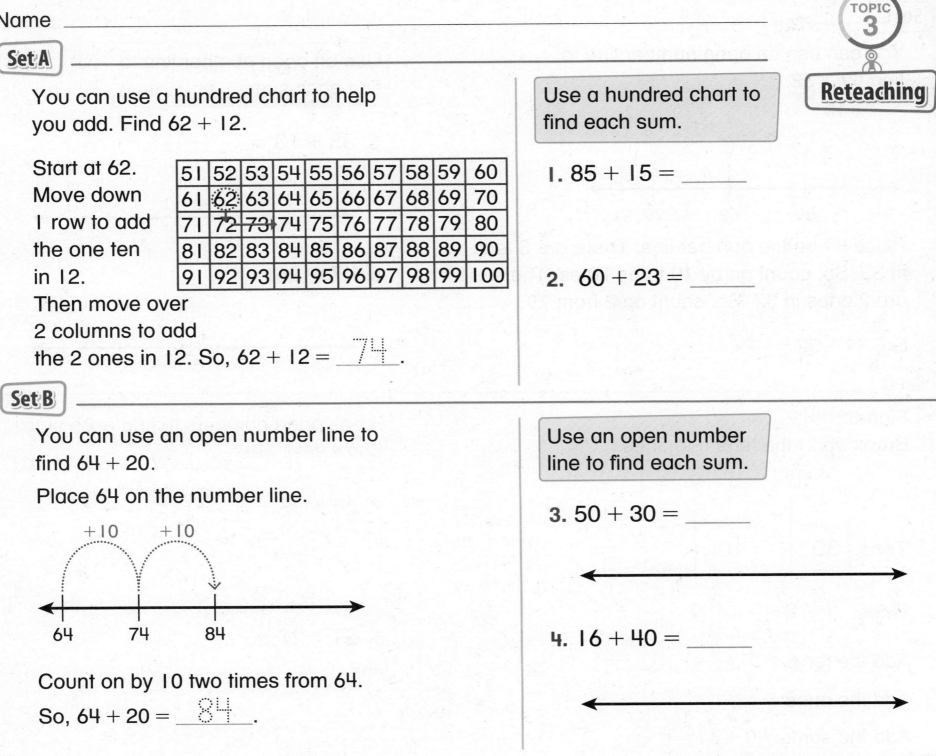

Count on by 10 two times from 64.

So, 64 + 20 = __84__.

Use an open number line to find each sum.

3. 50 + 30 = _____

4. 16 + 40 = _____

You can use an open number line to find 49 + 32.

+10   +10   +10   +2

49   59   69   79 81

Place 49 on the number line. There are 3 tens in 33. So, count on by 10 three times. There are 2 ones in 32. So, count on 2 from 79.

So, 49 + 32 = __81__ .

Find 32 + 19.
Break apart the tens and ones.

32 + 19 = __51__

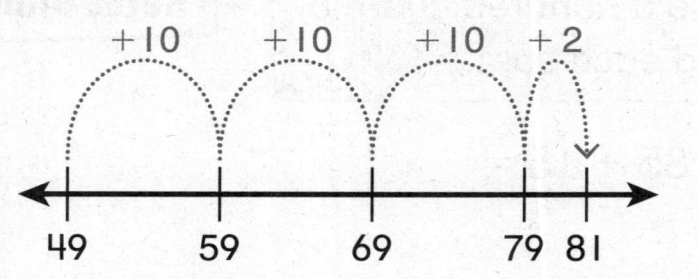

Tens | 30 | | 10 |

Ones | 2 | | 9 |

Add the tens: __30__ + __10__ = __40__

Add the ones: __2__ + __9__ = __11__

Add the sums: 40 + 11 = __51__

Use an open number line to find each sum.

5. 35 + 13 = _____

6. 47 + 26 = _____

Break apart numbers to find each sum. Show your work.

7. 24 + 55 = _____

8. 64 + 27 = _____

© Pearson Education, Inc. 2

Name _____

Set E _____

Find 55 + 17.
Break apart 17 into 10 + 7.

55   +   17 = ?

| 55 | | 10 | 7 |

Add tens: 55 + 10 = 65

Add ones: 65 + 7 = 72

So, 55 + 17 = __72__ .

Break apart the second addend to find the sum. Show your work.

9. 53 + 28 = _____

10. 78 + 19 = _____

Set F _____

Find 48 + 27.

48 is close to 50. So, take 2 from 27 and give it to 48 to make 50.

48 + 27 = ?
+2   −2

50 + 25 = ?

| 20 | 5 |

__50__ + __20__ + __5__ = __75__

So, 48 + 27 = __75__

Use compensation to make numbers that are easier to add. Then solve. Show your work.

11. 17 + 46 = _____

12. 29 + 57 = _____

Marla walks 12 blocks on Monday.
On Tuesday she walks 4 fewer blocks.
How many blocks does Marla walk in all?

Blocks Marla walks on Tuesday:

$$\underline{12} - \underline{4} = \underline{8}$$

Blocks Marla walks on Monday and Tuesday:

$$\underline{12} + \underline{8} = \underline{20}$$

$\underline{20}$ blocks

Solve the two-step problem.

13. Wyatt has 16 crayons.
His father buys him 24 new crayons.
Then Wyatt's sister gives him 7 more crayons.
How many crayons does Wyatt have now?

$$\underline{} + \underline{} = \underline{}$$

$$\underline{} + \underline{} = \underline{}$$

$\underline{}$ crayons

Thinking Habits

Use Tools

Which of these tools can I use?

Cubes   Paper and
Counters   pencil
Hundred chart   Place-value
Technology   blocks

Is there a different tool
I can use?

Choose a tool to help solve the problem. Show your work.
Explain your tool choice.

14. 42 people are at a park before lunch. 29 people join those people after lunch.
How many people are at the park in all?

1. Use mental math. Which weights can you put on the scale to make it balance?

Ⓐ  10 40   Ⓒ 40 33

Ⓑ 10 21   Ⓓ 33 10

2. Terry has 63 crayons.
She gets 25 more crayons.
How many crayons does Terry have in all? Show your work.

_____ crayons

3. Which equation does this number line show?

Ⓐ $50 + 30 = 80$ Ⓒ $50 + 50 = 100$

Ⓑ $50 + 40 = 90$ Ⓓ $50 + 90 = 140$

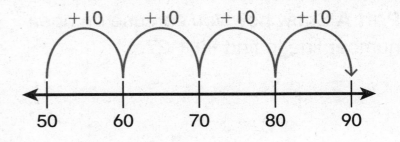

+10   +10   +10   +10

50   60   70   80   90

4. Use the numbers on the cards. Write the missing numbers under the number line to show how to find the sum of $40 + 35$.

75   60   50   70

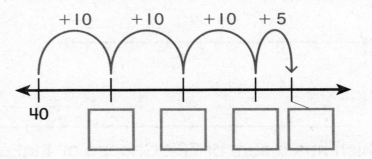

+10   +10   +10   +5

40

5. Colin has 54 pennies and 28 nickels. How many coins does Colin have?

Break apart the numbers to solve.
Show your work.

_____ coins

6. Show how to add 68 + 16 using the open number line.

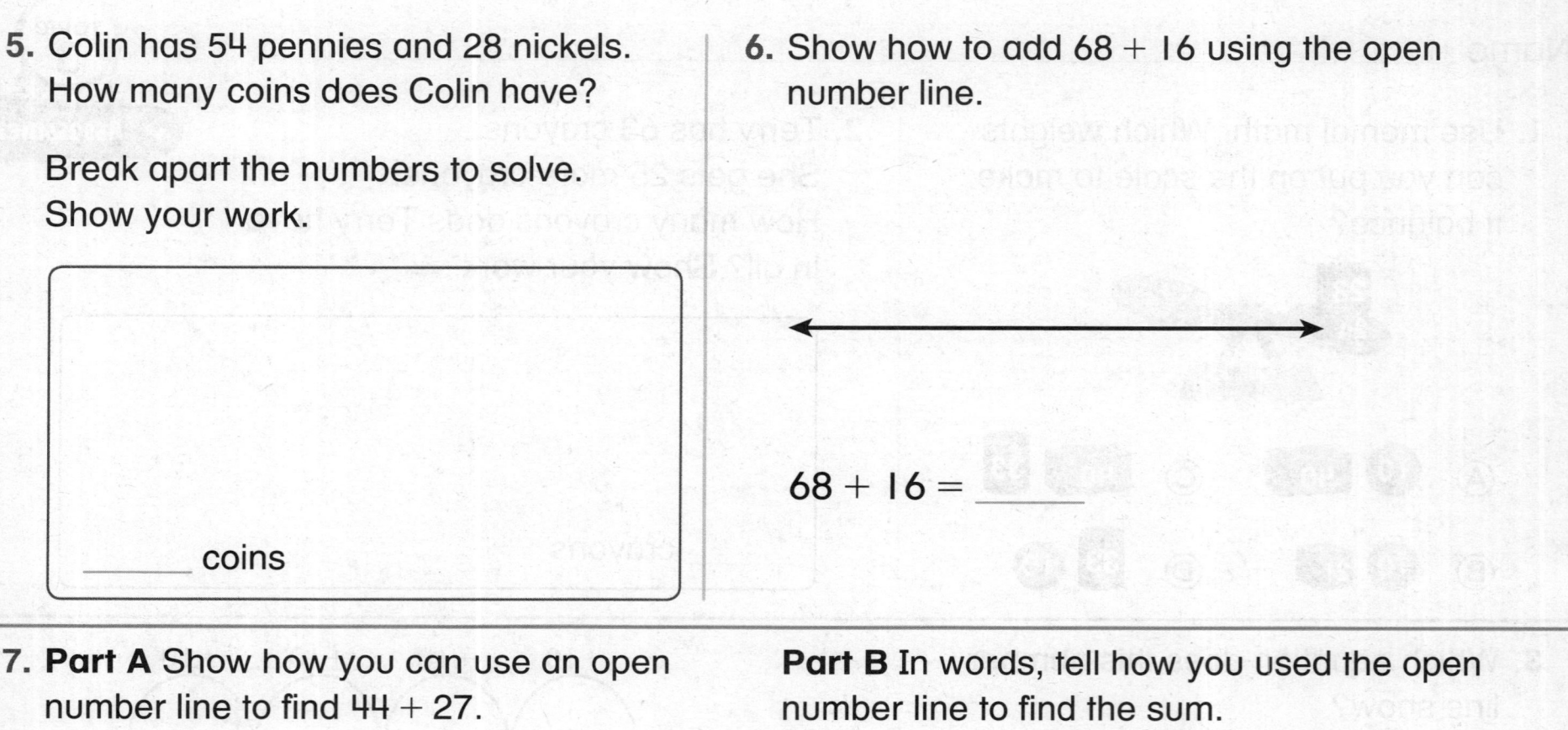

68 + 16 = _____

7. Part A Show how you can use an open number line to find 44 + 27.

44 + 27 = _____

Part B In words, tell how you used the open number line to find the sum.

_____

_____

_____

_____

8. Which has a sum of 70? Choose all that apply.

☐ 35 + 35   ☐ 40 + 30   ☐ 45 + 45   ☐ 50 + 20

9. Lisa has 18 markers.
Adam has 22 markers.
How many markers are there in all?

Choose a tool to solve the problem.

_____ markers

10. Ted has 52 cards in a box.
Tyrone has 48 more cards
than Ted. How many cards
does Tyrone have?

_____ cards

11. Which is equal to 47 + 25? Choose all that apply.

☐ 40 + 20 + 7 + 5   ☐ 40 + 20 + 12   ☐ 50 + 12   ☐ 50 + 22

12. Emma has 46 rocks.
She gets 25 more rocks from Gus.
How many rocks does Emma
have now?

_____ ◯ _____ = _____

_____ rocks

41	42	43	44	45	46	47	48	49	50
51	52	53	54	55	56	57	58	59	60
61	62	63	64	65	66	67	68	69	70
71	72	73	74	75	76	77	78	79	80

13. Is each sum 64? Choose Yes or No.

22 + 34 + 8   ○ Yes   ○ No

32 + 32   ○ Yes   ○ No

28 + 34 + 2   ○ Yes   ○ No

42 + 14 + 8   ○ Yes   ○ No

14. Break apart numbers to find 56 + 38.
Show your work.

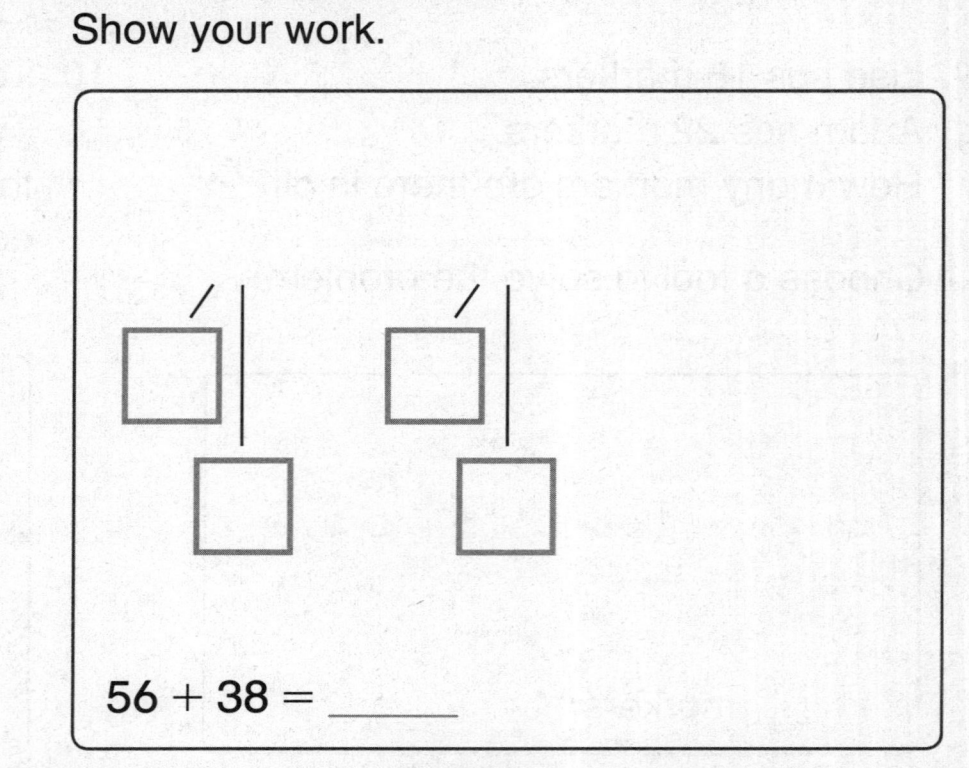

56 + 38 = _____

15. Write an equation to solve each part
of the two-step problem.

Ken has 45 stamps.
He uses 20 stamps.
Then he buys 7 more stamps.
How many stamps does he have now?

_____ ○ _____ = _____

_____ ○ _____ = _____

Ken has _____ stamps.

16. Show two different ways
to find 28 + 49.

Way 1

Way 2

Name _____

Popcorn Sales

A second-grade class is selling popcorn to help pay for a field trip.
This table shows how many boxes some students have sold.

Number of Popcorn Boxes Sold	
Ted	21
Nancy	19
Darnell	28
Mary	34
Elena	43

1. How many boxes of popcorn did Ted and Mary sell in all? Use the open number line to solve. Show your work.

←————————————————→

_____ boxes

2. James says that Mary and Nancy sold more boxes in all than Darnell and Ted sold in all. Do you agree with him?

Circle   **yes**   **no**

Explain your answer.

_____

_____

_____

_____

3. Which two students sold a total of 55 boxes? Use any strategy to solve. Show your work.

Circle the names of the two students.

Ted   Nancy   Darnell

Mary   Elena

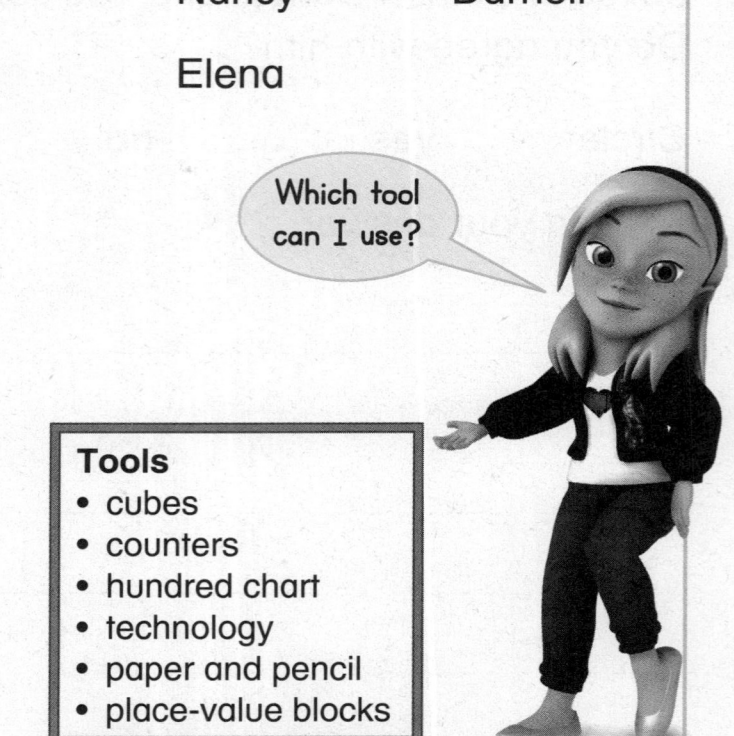

Which tool can I use?

Tools
- cubes
- counters
- hundred chart
- technology
- paper and pencil
- place-value blocks

4. Nancy sold 18 fewer boxes than Lucas. How many boxes did Lucas sell?

Part A Solve the problem. Show your work and explain your thinking.

_____ boxes

Part B Emily wants to use a tool to solve the problem. Look at the list of tools at the left. Which tool would be a good choice? Which tool would **NOT** be a good choice? Explain.

© Pearson Education, Inc. 2

Fluently Add Within 100

Essential Question: What are strategies for adding numbers to 100?

Digital Resources

Solve Learn Glossary

Tools Assessment Help Games

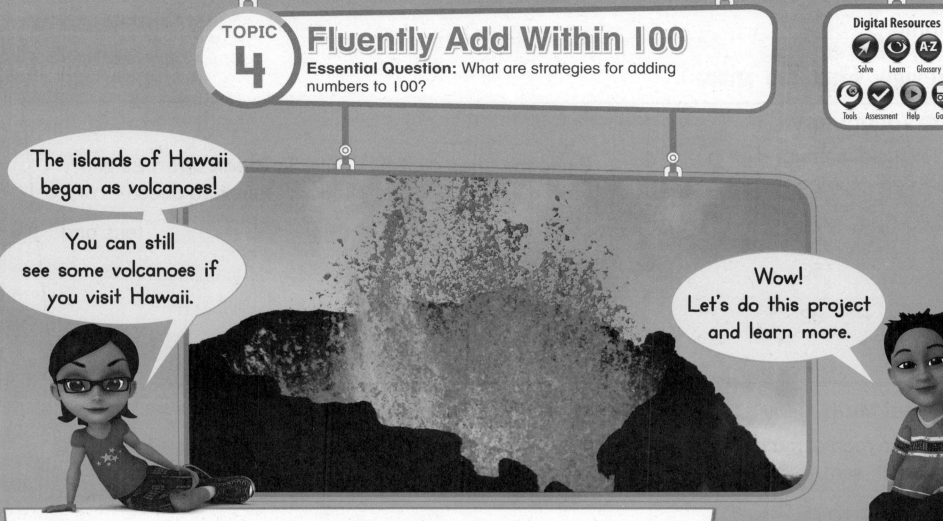

The islands of Hawaii began as volcanoes!

You can still see some volcanoes if you visit Hawaii.

Wow! Let's do this project and learn more.

Math and Science Project: Making and Using Models

Find Out Find and share books about Hawaii and volcanoes. Make a model of a volcano that becomes an island. Tell about how the island can change over a long time.

Journal: Make a Book Show what you learn in a book. In your book, also:

• Draw pictures to show how volcanoes can become islands.

• Show how you can use models to help you add numbers to 100.

Name _____

Review What You Know

A-Z Vocabulary

1. Circle the **tens** digit in each number.

    73

    53

    82

2. Circle the **ones** digit in each number.

    34

    43

    97

3. **Break apart** 23 into tens and ones.

    23 = _____ tens and

    _____ ones

Mental Math

4. Use mental math to find each sum.

    $34 + 10 =$ _____

    $50 + 5 =$ _____

    $20 + 40 =$ _____

Open Number Line

5. Use the open number line to find $39 + 15$.

    ⟷

    $39 + 15 =$ _____

Math Story

6. Stacy has 17 marbles. Diana gives her 22 marbles. How many marbles does Stacy have now?

    _____ marbles

My Word Cards

Study the words on the front of the card.
Complete the activity on the back.

partial sum

Tens	Ones
5	7
+ 2	8
7	0	← partial sum
+ 1	5	← partial sum
8	5	← sum

regroup

Tens	Ones

compatible numbers

$8 + 2$
$20 + 7$
$53 + 10$

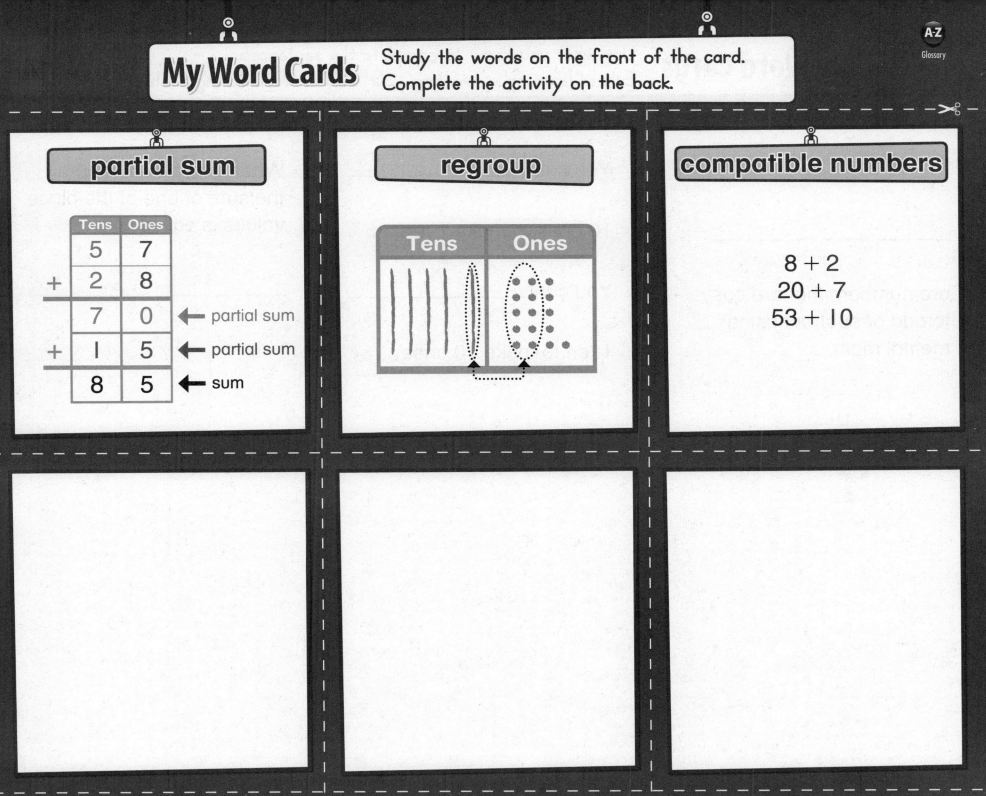

My Word Cards

Use what you know to complete the sentences.
Extend learning by writing your own sentence using each word.

_____

_____

are numbers that are easy
to add or subtract using
mental math.

You can _____

10 ones to make 1 ten.

You can _____

1 ten to make 10 ones.

When you add numbers,
the sum of one of the place
values is called a

_____.

Name _____

Solve & Share

Use place-value blocks to find 47 + 22. Then draw a picture to show your work.

I can ...
add using place value and partial sums.

I can also use math tools correctly.

47 + 22 = _____

Find 57 + 28.

I can use place-value blocks to check my work.

Tens	Ones
5	7
+ 2	8

First, add the tens.

That's one **partial sum**.

	Tens	Ones
	5	7
+	2	8
50 + 20 =	7	0

Then add the ones.

That's another partial sum.

	Tens	Ones
	5	7
+	2	8
50 + 20 =	7	0
7 + 8 =	1	5

Then add the partial sums to find the sum.

	Tens	Ones
	5	7
+	2	8
50 + 20 =	7	0
7 + 8 =	1	5
Sum =	8	5

So, 57 + 28 = 85.

Do You Understand?

Show Me! How can you use partial sums to add 23 + 8? Explain.

☆ Guided Practice ☆

Add. Use partial sums. Show your work. Use place-value blocks, if needed.

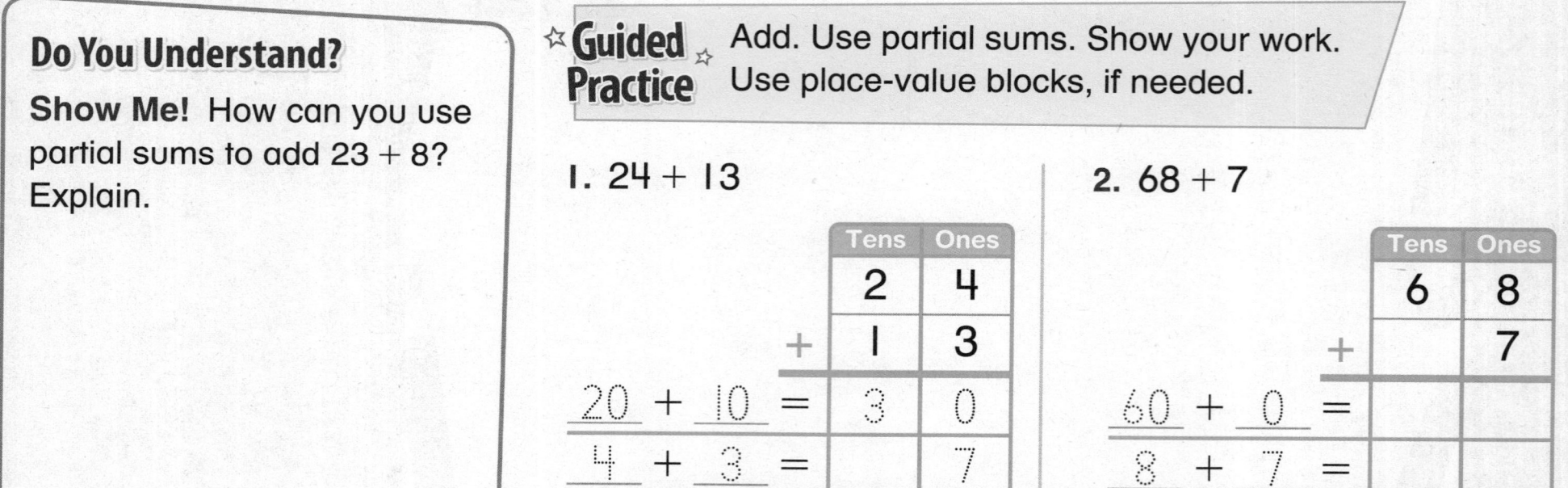

1. 24 + 13

	Tens	Ones
	2	4
+	1	3
20 + 10 =	3	0
4 + 3 =		7
Sum =		

2. 68 + 7

	Tens	Ones
	6	8
+		7
60 + 0 =		
8 + 7 =		
Sum =		

© Pearson Education, Inc. 2

Independent Practice   Add. Use partial sums. Use place-value blocks, if needed.

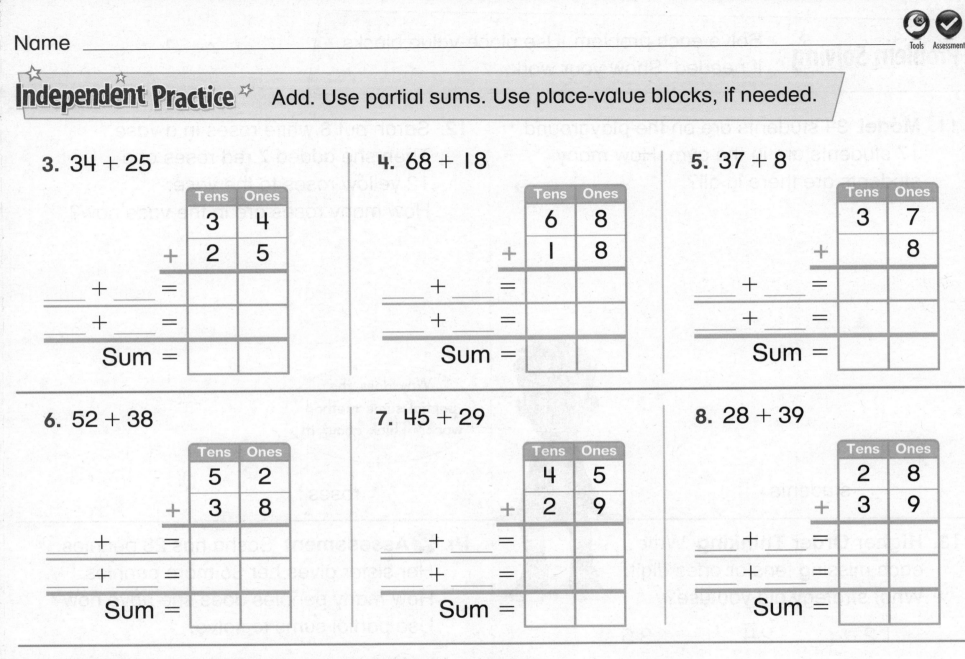

3. $34 + 25$

Tens	Ones
3	4
+ 2	5

+ ___ = ___
+ ___ = ___
Sum = ___

4. $68 + 18$

Tens	Ones
6	8
+ 1	8

+ ___ = ___
+ ___ = ___
Sum = ___

5. $37 + 8$

Tens	Ones
3	7
+	8

+ ___ = ___
+ ___ = ___
Sum = ___

6. $52 + 38$

Tens	Ones
5	2
+ 3	8

+ ___ = ___
+ ___ = ___
Sum = ___

7. $45 + 29$

Tens	Ones
4	5
+ 2	9

+ ___ = ___
+ ___ = ___
Sum = ___

8. $28 + 39$

Tens	Ones
2	8
+ 3	9

+ ___ = ___
+ ___ = ___
Sum = ___

Number Sense Write each missing tens or ones digit.

9. $23 + 1\boxed{} = 37$

10. $59 = \boxed{}8 + 31$

Solve each problem. Use place-value blocks, if needed. Show your work.

11. Model 34 students are on the playground. 17 students are in the gym. How many students are there in all?

_____ students

12. Sarah put 8 white roses in a vase. Then she added 7 red roses and 12 yellow roses to the vase. How many roses are in the vase now?

Why does the partial sums method work? Think about it!

_____ roses

13. Higher Order Thinking Write each missing tens or ones digit. What strategy did you use?

$$
\begin{array}{r}
1\,2 \\
+\,3\,\square \\
\hline
5\,0
\end{array}
\qquad
\begin{array}{r}
2\,4 \\
+\,3\,\square \\
\hline
6\,0
\end{array}
\qquad
\begin{array}{r}
3\,5 \\
+\,3\,\square \\
\hline
7\,0
\end{array}
$$

14. ✓Assessment Sasha has 28 pennies. Her sister gives her 36 more pennies. How many pennies does she have now? Use partial sums to solve.

Ⓐ 8

Ⓑ 12

Ⓒ 54

Ⓓ 64

© Pearson Education, Inc. 2

Name _____

Another Look! Use partial sums to find 32 + 45.

Break apart the numbers into tens and ones.

Write the problem this way.   32 + 45 = ?

Step 1: Add the tens   30 + 40 = 70

Step 2: Add the ones.   2 + 5 = 7

Step 3: Add the
           partial sums.   70 + 7 = 77

So, 32 + 45 = _77_.

HOME ACTIVITY Ask your child to show you how to add 24 + 33 using partial sums.

Add. Use partial sums. Show your work.

1. 23 + 16 = _____

Add the tens.

_____ + _____ = _____

Add the ones.

_____ + _____ = _____

Add the partial sums.

_____ + _____ = _____

2. 37 + 61 = _____

Add the tens.

_____ + _____ = _____

Add the ones.

_____ + _____ = _____

Add the partial sums.

_____ + _____ = _____

3. 35 + 29 = _____

Add the tens.

_____ + _____ = _____

Add the ones.

_____ + _____ = _____

Add the partial sums.

_____ + _____ = _____

Solve each problem. Show your work.

4. Make Sense 28 leaves fell from a tree. Then 32 more leaves fell. How many leaves fell in all?

5. Liam put 6 cars on his empty toy racetrack. Then Joe put 8 cars on the track. Then Kim put 4 cars on the track. How many cars are on the track now?

_____ leaves

_____ cars

6. Higher Order Thinking Write each missing number. What pattern do you see?

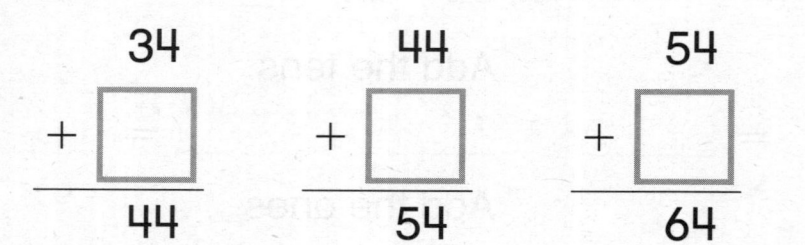

7. ✔**Assessment** Amir had 37 stamps. Then Tim gave him 16 more stamps. How many stamps does Amir have now? Use partial sums to solve.

Ⓐ 16
Ⓑ 21
Ⓒ 43
Ⓓ 53

© Pearson Education, Inc. 2

Topic 4 | Lesson 1

Solve & Share

Wendy picked 37 pears. Toni picked 46 pears. How many pears did they pick in all?

Solve the problem using partial sums.
Draw place-value blocks to help explain your work.

I can ...
add numbers using partial sums.

I can also reason about math.

	Tens	Ones
+		
___ + ___ =		
___ + ___ =		
Sum =		

_____ pears

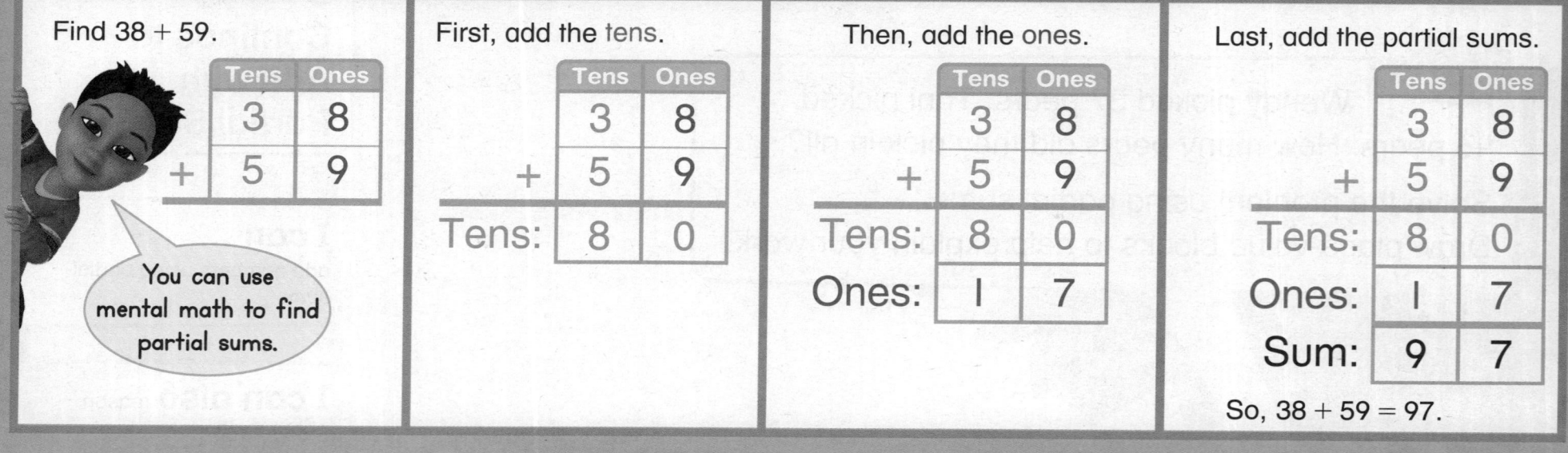

Find 38 + 59.

You can use mental math to find partial sums.

Tens	Ones
3	8
+ 5	9

First, add the tens.

Tens	Ones
3	8
+ 5	9
Tens: 8	0

Then, add the ones.

Tens	Ones
3	8
+ 5	9
Tens: 8	0
Ones: 1	7

Last, add the partial sums.

Tens	Ones
3	8
+ 5	9
Tens: 8	0
Ones: 1	7
Sum: 9	7

So, 38 + 59 = 97.

Do You Understand?

Show Me! Ken adds 43 + 27. His sum is 60. Is he correct? Explain.

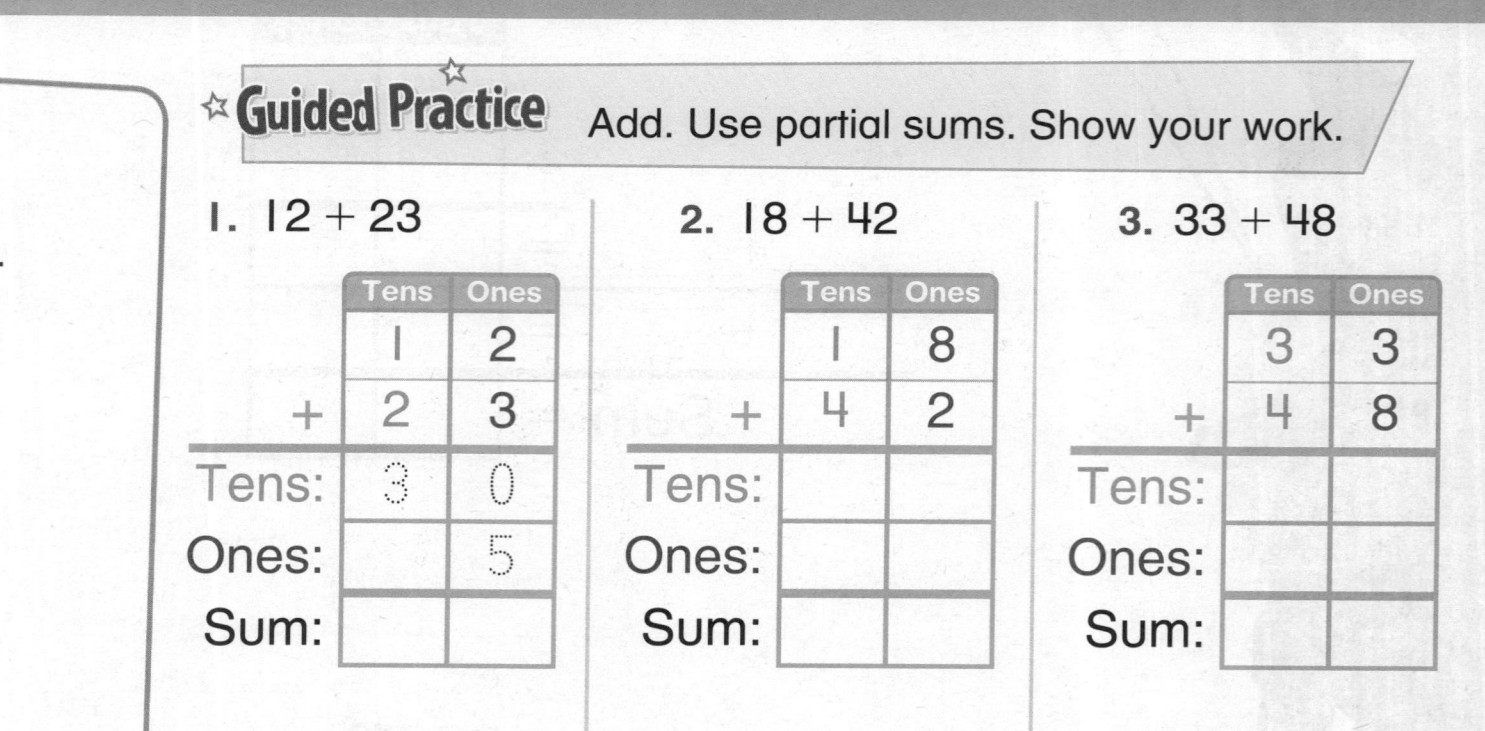

☆Guided Practice   Add. Use partial sums. Show your work.

1. 12 + 23

Tens	Ones
1	2
+ 2	3
Tens: 3	0
Ones:	5
Sum:	

2. 18 + 42

Tens	Ones
1	8
+ 4	2
Tens:	
Ones:	
Sum:	

3. 33 + 48

Tens	Ones
3	3
+ 4	8
Tens:	
Ones:	
Sum:	

Topic 4 | Lesson 2

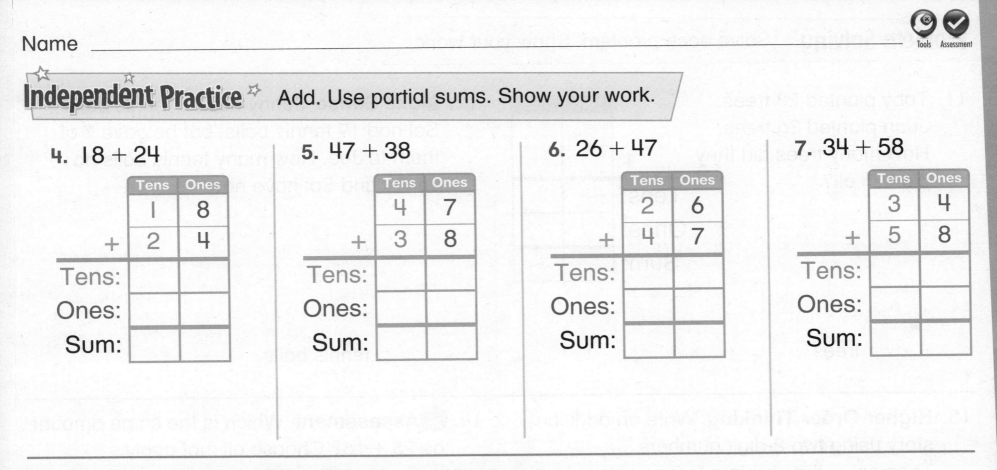

Independent Practice   Add. Use partial sums. Show your work.

4. 18 + 24

Tens	Ones
1	8
+ 2	4

Tens:
Ones:
Sum:

5. 47 + 38

Tens	Ones
4	7
+ 3	8

Tens:
Ones:
Sum:

6. 26 + 47

Tens	Ones
2	6
+ 4	7

Tens:
Ones:
Sum:

7. 34 + 58

Tens	Ones
3	4
+ 5	8

Tens:
Ones:
Sum:

Higher Order Thinking Read the sum above each box.
Circle all the pairs of numbers in the box that match the sum.

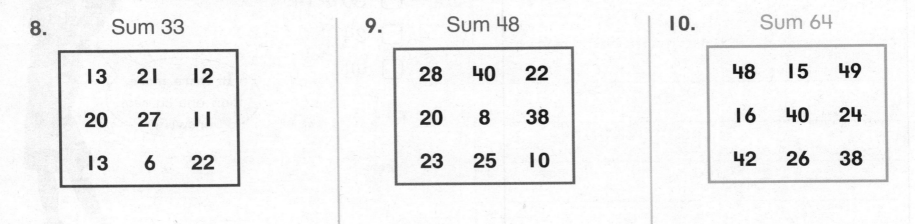

8.   Sum 33

13	21	12
20	27	11
13	6	22

9.   Sum 48

28	40	22
20	8	38
23	25	10

10.   Sum 64

48	15	49
16	40	24
42	26	38

11. Toby planted 28 trees. Juan planted 36 trees. How many trees did they plant in all?

Tens	Ones
+	
Tens:	
Ones:	
Sum:	

_____ trees

12. Make Sense Jenny has 13 tennis balls. Sal had 19 tennis balls, but he gave 7 of them to Joe. How many tennis balls do Jenny and Sal have now?

_____ tennis balls

13. Higher Order Thinking Write an addition story using two 2-digit numbers. Then solve the problem for your story.

_____

_____

_____

_____

14. ✓**Assessment** Which is the same amount as 28 + 16? Choose all that apply.

☐ 20 + 10 + 8 + 6

☐ 30 + 14

☐ 34

☐ 44

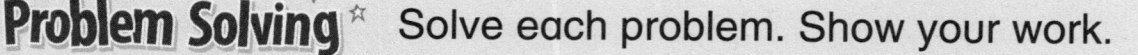

Is there more than one correct answer?

© Pearson Education, Inc. 2

Name _____

Another Look! Find 36 + 28.

Step 1
Add the tens.
3 tens + 2 tens
30 + 20 = 50

Tens	Ones
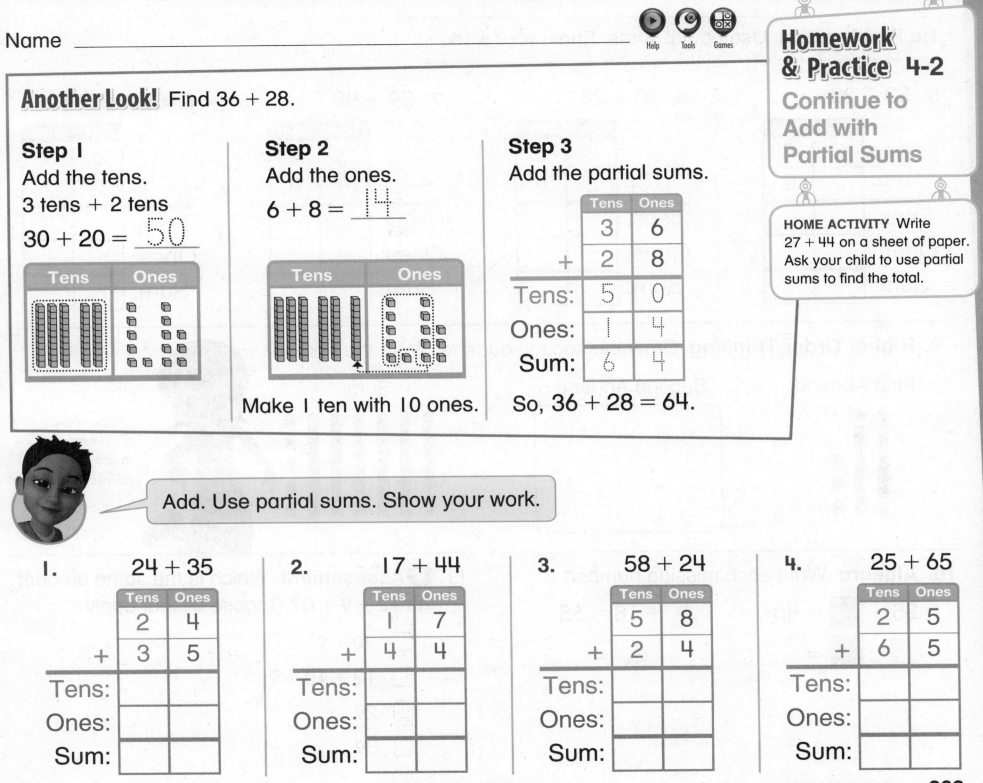	

Step 2
Add the ones.
6 + 8 = 14

Tens	Ones

Make 1 ten with 10 ones.

Step 3
Add the partial sums.

	Tens	Ones
	3	6
+	2	8
Tens:	5	0
Ones:	1	4
Sum:	6	4

So, 36 + 28 = 64.

HOME ACTIVITY Write 27 + 44 on a sheet of paper. Ask your child to use partial sums to find the total.

Add. Use partial sums. Show your work.

1. 24 + 35

	Tens	Ones
	2	4
+	3	5
Tens:		
Ones:		
Sum:		

2. 17 + 44

	Tens	Ones
	1	7
+	4	4
Tens:		
Ones:		
Sum:		

3. 58 + 24

	Tens	Ones
	5	8
+	2	4
Tens:		
Ones:		
Sum:		

4. 25 + 65

	Tens	Ones
	2	5
+	6	5
Tens:		
Ones:		
Sum:		

Be Precise Add. Use partial sums. Show your work.

5. 53 + 23

Tens	Ones
5	3
+ 2	3

Tens:
Ones:
Sum:

6. 35 + 28

Tens	Ones
3	5
+ 2	8

Tens:
Ones:
Sum:

7. 39 + 48

Tens	Ones
3	9
+ 4	8

Tens:
Ones:
Sum:

8. 69 + 27

Tens	Ones
6	9
+ 2	7

Tens:
Ones:
Sum:

9. Higher Order Thinking Draw the second addend. Write the number.

First Addend   Second Addend   Sum

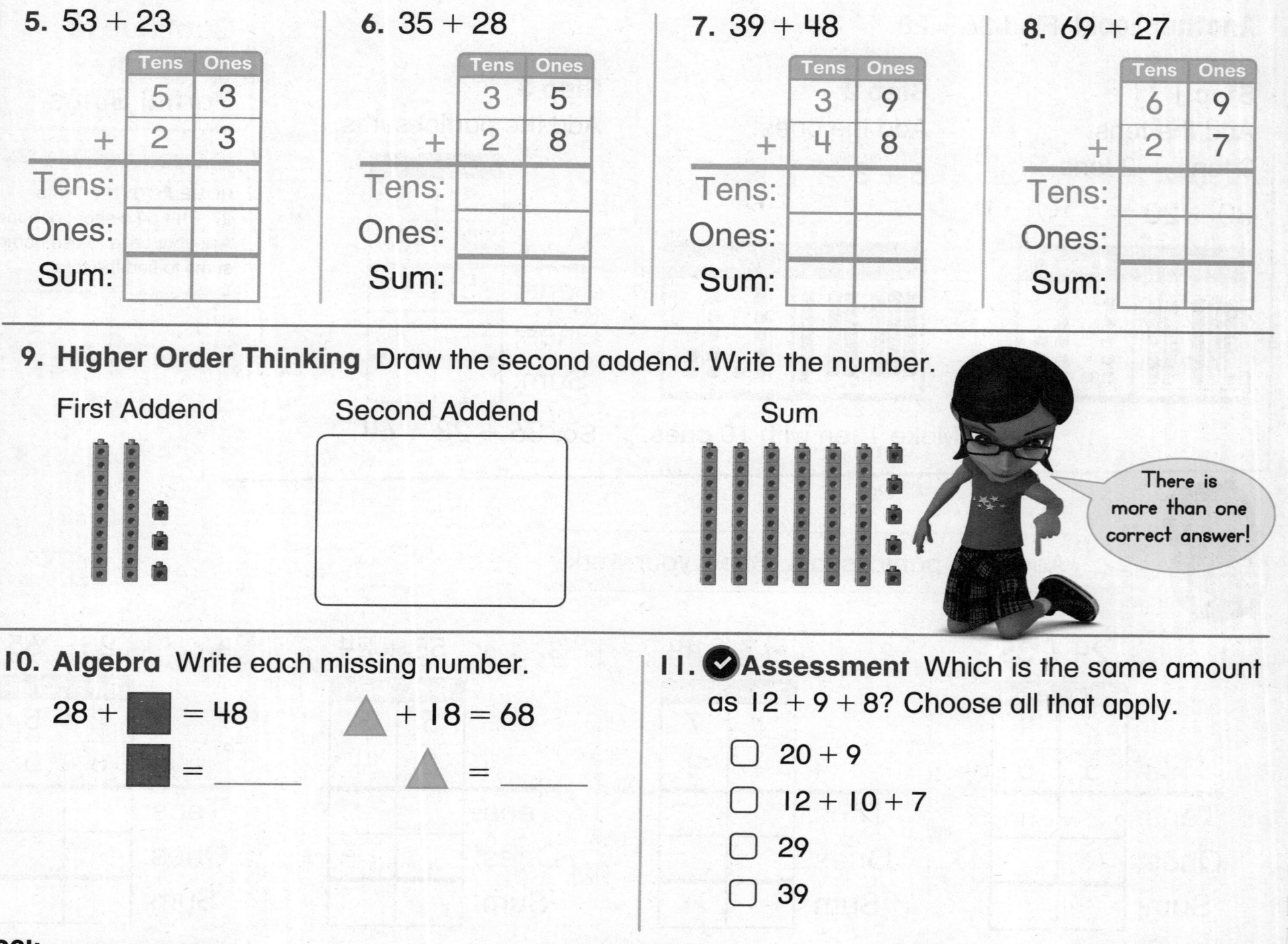

There is more than one correct answer!

10. Algebra Write each missing number.

28 + ■ = 48   ▲ + 18 = 68

■ = _____   ▲ = _____

11. ✓Assessment Which is the same amount as 12 + 9 + 8? Choose all that apply.

☐ 20 + 9

☐ 12 + 10 + 7

☐ 29

☐ 39

© Pearson Education, Inc. 2

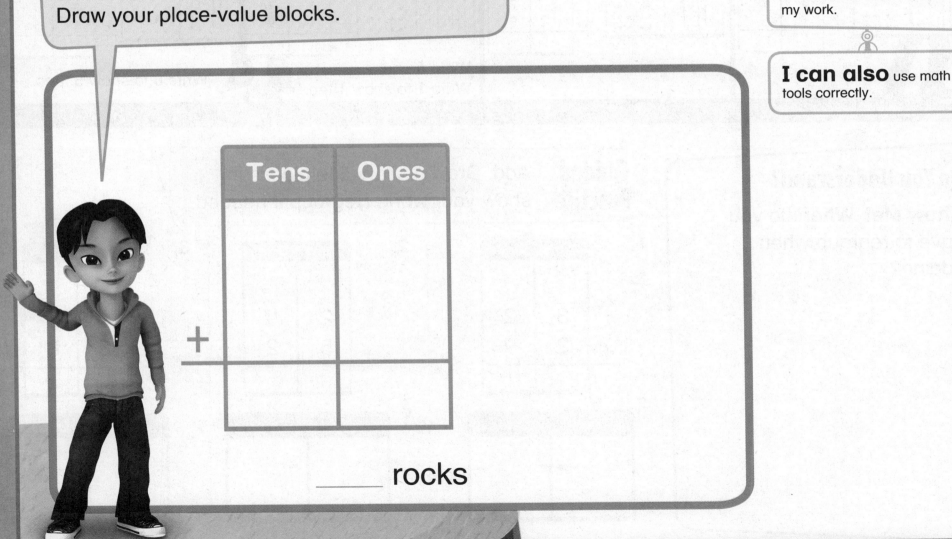

Solve

Lesson 4-3
Models to Add 2-Digit Numbers

I can ...
use models to add 2-digit numbers and then explain my work.

I can also use math tools correctly.

Name _____

Solve & Share

Leslie collects 36 rocks. Her brother collects 27 rocks. How many rocks do they collect in all?

Use place-value blocks to help you solve. Draw your place-value blocks.

Tens	Ones

\+

_____ rocks

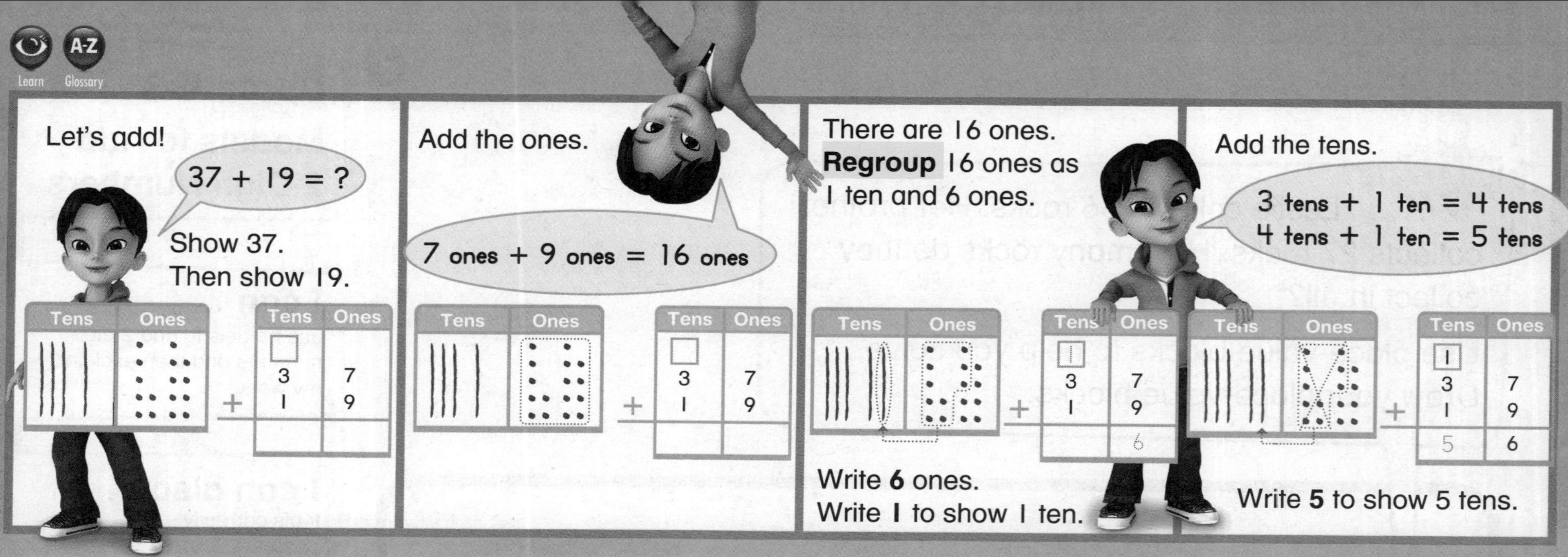

Learn Glossary

Let's add!

37 + 19 = ?

Show 37.
Then show 19.

Tens	Ones
	3	7
+	1	9

Add the ones.

7 ones + 9 ones = 16 ones

Tens	Ones
	3	7
+	1	9

There are 16 ones.
Regroup 16 ones as
1 ten and 6 ones.

Tens	Ones
	3	7
+	1	9
		6

Write **6** ones.
Write **1** to show 1 ten.

Add the tens.

3 tens + 1 ten = 4 tens
4 tens + 1 ten = 5 tens

Tens	Ones
1	3	7
+	1	9
	5	6

Write **5** to show 5 tens.

Do You Understand?

Show Me! When do you have to regroup when adding?

☆ Guided Practice ☆

Add. Draw place-value blocks to show your work. Regroup if needed.

1.

Tens	Ones
1	
3	2
+ 2	9
6	1

Tens	Ones

2.

Tens	Ones
☐	
2	4
+ 5	2

Tens	Ones

3.

Tens	Ones
☐	
1	5
+ 3	8

Tens	Ones

206 two hundred six

© Pearson Education, Inc. 2

Topic 4 | Lesson 3

Tools Assessment

Independent Practice Add. Draw place-value blocks to show your work. Regroup if needed.

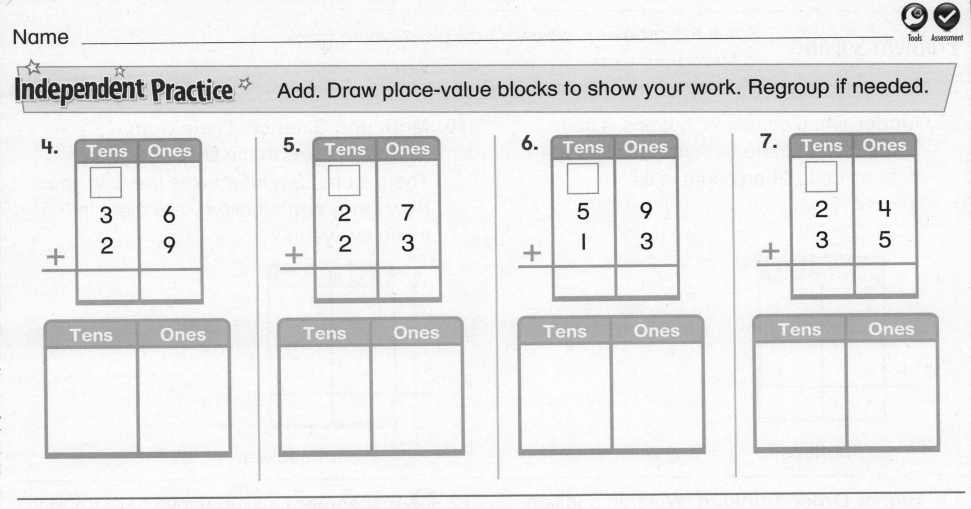

4.
Tens	Ones
□	
3	6
2	9
+	

Tens	Ones

5.
Tens	Ones
□	
2	7
2	3
+	

Tens	Ones

6.
Tens	Ones
□	
5	9
1	3
+	

Tens	Ones

7.
Tens	Ones
□	
2	4
3	5
+	

Tens	Ones

8. **Higher Order Thinking** Draw the second addend.

First Addend   Second Addend   Sum

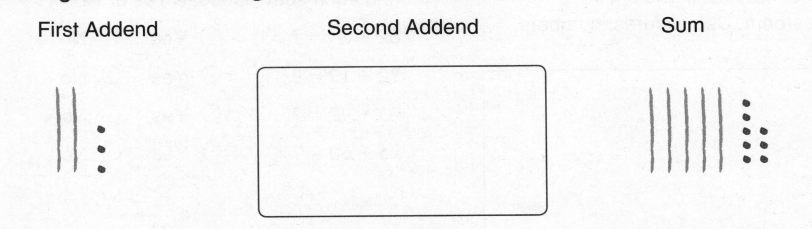

9. **Model** Chen counts 47 buttons. Then he counts 20 more buttons. How many buttons does Chen count in all?

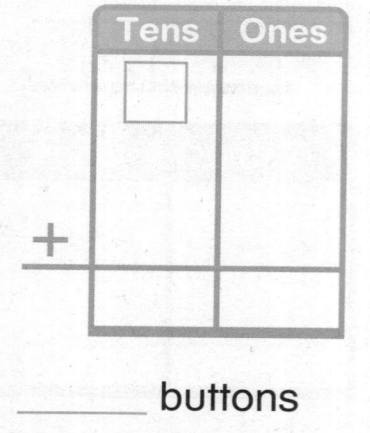

_____ buttons

10. **Math and Science** There were 24 earthquakes in the U.S. one year. There were 23 earthquakes the next year. How many earthquakes were there in those two years?

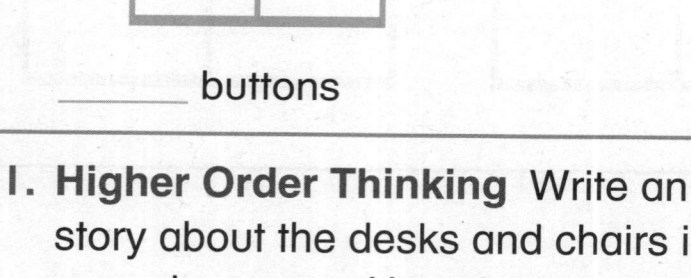

_____ earthquakes

11. **Higher Order Thinking** Write an addition story about the desks and chairs in your classroom. Use pictures, numbers, or words.

12. ✓ **Assessment** Do you have to regroup to find each sum? Choose Yes or No.

$62 + 34 = ?$ ○ Yes   ○ No

$72 + 19 = ?$ ○ Yes   ○ No

$43 + 49 = ?$ ○ Yes   ○ No

$26 + 60 = ?$ ○ Yes   ○ No

© Pearson Education, Inc. 2

Name _____

Another Look! You can use these steps to add. Add 46 + 18.

Way 1:

Step 1: Draw the tens and ones.
Make 1 ten with 10 ones.

Tens	Ones
|||| |	(dotted X)

Step 2: Count the tens. Count the ones.

Tens	Ones
||||| |	. .

Way 2:

	Tens	Ones
	1	
	4	6
+	1	8
	6	4

$46 + 18 = \underline{64}$

HOME ACTIVITY Ask your child to show you how to add 27 + 34. Have your child explain each step of the addition.

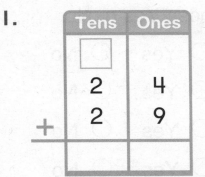

Follow the steps to add. Draw place-value blocks to show your work. Regroup if needed.

1.

	Tens	Ones
	☐	
	2	4
+	2	9

2.

	Tens	Ones
	☐	
	3	8
+	4	5

Topic 4 | Lesson 3
Digital Resources at PearsonRealize.com
two hundred nine **209**

Higher Order Thinking Write the missing numbers.
Draw place-value blocks if you need to.

3.

Tens	Ones
□	
5	7
+ 2	7

4.

Tens	Ones
□	
6	2
+ 1	5

5.

Tens	Ones
□	
1	9
+ 3	3

Remember to write the regrouped numbers.

6.

Tens	Ones
□	
2	7
+ ○	8
4	5

7.

Tens	Ones
□	
2	○
+ 5	7
8	0

8.

Tens	Ones
□	
3	8
+ ○	4
6	2

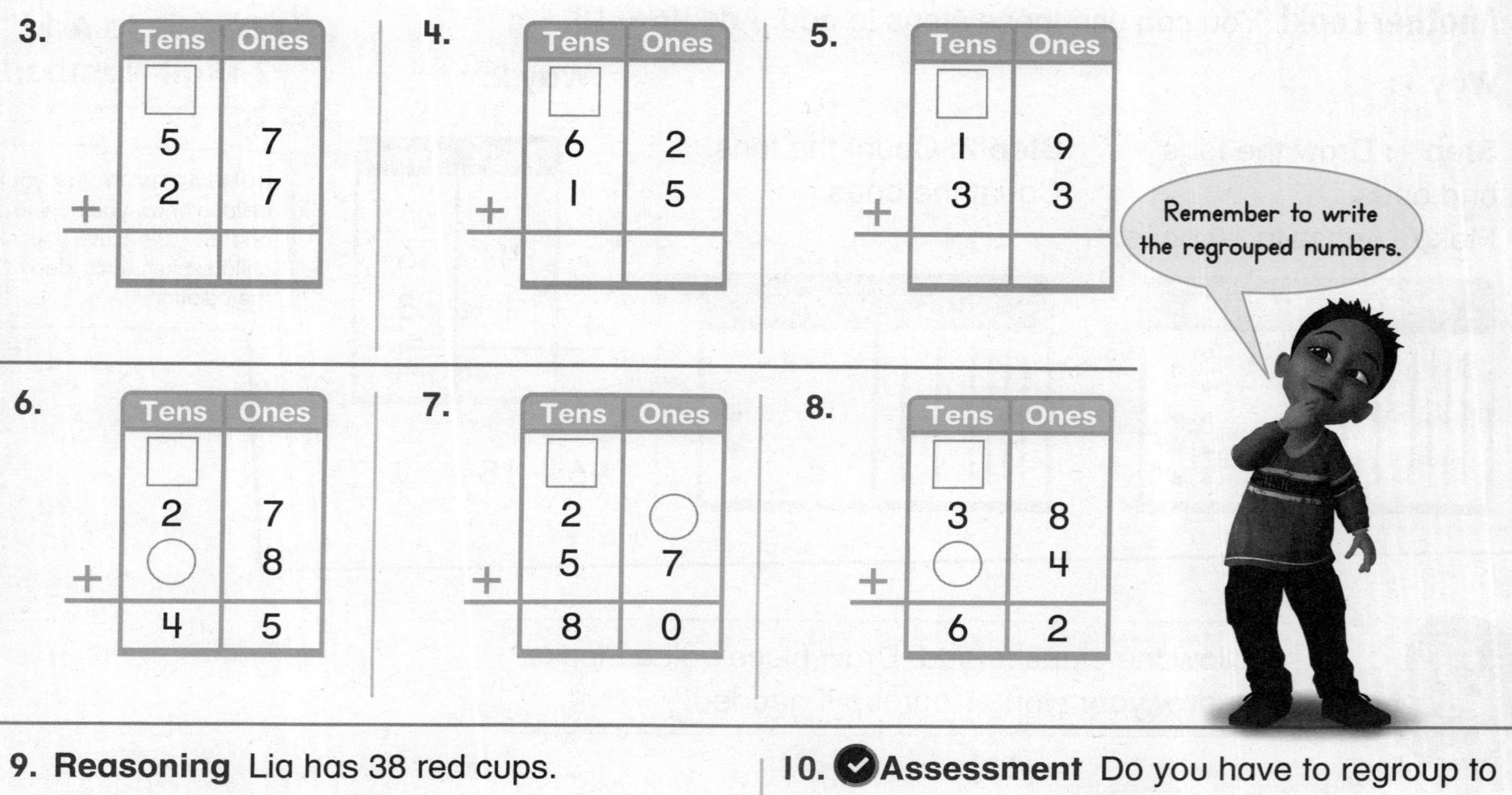

9. Reasoning Lia has 38 red cups.
She has 25 blue cups.
How many cups does Lia have in all?

_____ cups

10. ✅**Assessment** Do you have to regroup to find each sum? Choose Yes or No.

$22 + 41 = ?$ ○ Yes ○ No

$19 + 60 = ?$ ○ Yes ○ No

$64 + 28 = ?$ ○ Yes ○ No

$39 + 52 = ?$ ○ Yes ○ No

© Pearson Education, Inc. 2

Topic 4 | Lesson 3

Name _____

Solve & Share

Add 46 + 26.

Draw place-value blocks, if needed. Explain how you solved the problem.

I can ...
add 2-digit numbers and then explain my work.

I can also model with math.

Tens	Ones

+

_____

_____

_____

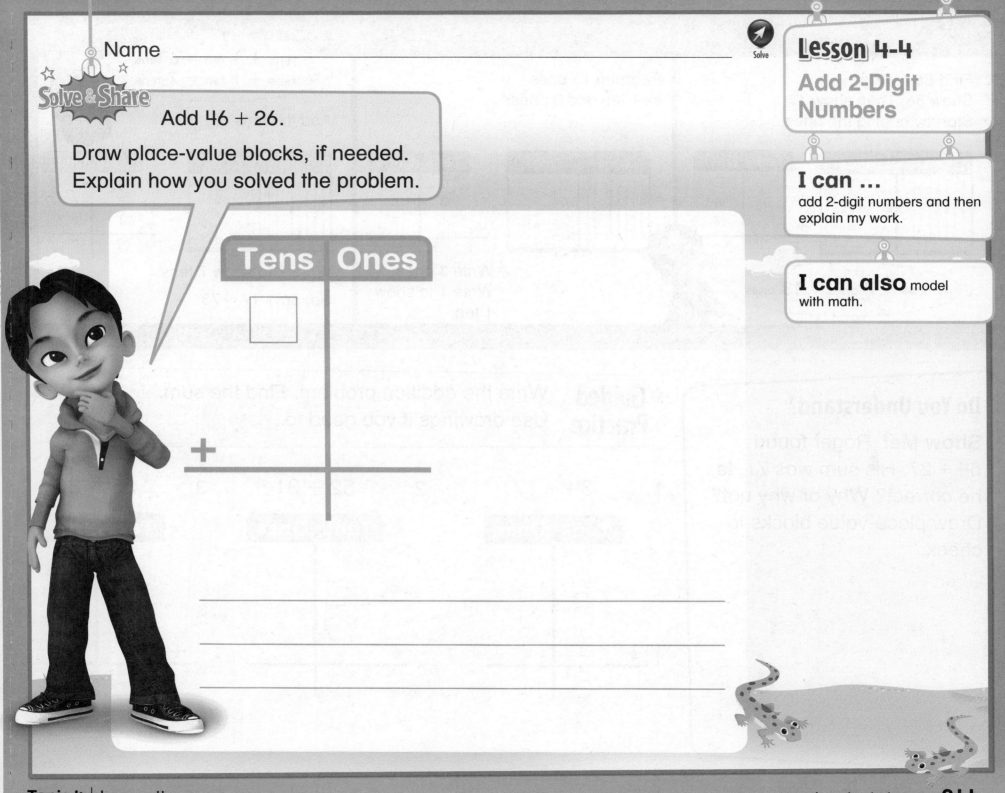

Find 56 + 17.
Show 56. Then show 17.
Start by adding the ones.

6 ones + 7 ones = 13 ones

Regroup 13 ones
as 1 ten and 3 ones.

Write **3** ones.
Write **1** to show
1 ten.

5 tens + 1 ten = 6 tens
6 tens + 1 ten = 7 tens

Add the tens.

Write **7** to show 7 tens.
So, 56 + 17 = 73.

Do You Understand?

Show Me! Roger found
54 + 27. His sum was 71. Is
he correct? Why or why not?
Draw place-value blocks to
check.

☆ **Guided Practice** ☆ Write the addition problem. Find the sum.
Use drawings if you need to.

1.   34 + 17

Tens	Ones
1	
3	4
1	7
5	1

2.   52 + 31

Tens	Ones

3.   35 + 26

Tens	Ones

Topic 4 | Lesson 4

Tools Assessment

Independent Practice Write the addition problem. Find the sum.
Use drawings if you need to.

4. 15 + 28

Tens	Ones
□	

+

5. 29 + 20

Tens	Ones
□	

+

6. 63 + 29

Tens	Ones
□	

+

7. 37 + 48

Tens	Ones
□	

+

8. 67 + 17

Tens	Ones
□	

+

9. 15 + 18

Tens	Ones
□	

+

10. 43 + 49

Tens	Ones
□	

+

11. 62 + 28

Tens	Ones
□	

+

Higher Order Thinking Write the missing ones or tens digits.

12. 27 + 2 □ = 50

13. 3 □ + 16 = 48

14. □ 4 + 49 = 93

15. Make Sense
Amir plants 25 trees.
Juan plants 27 trees.
How many trees do
they plant in all?

Tens	Ones
□	
+	

_____ trees

16. On Monday, Sasha
puts 32 pennies in her
bank. On Tuesday, she
puts 57 more pennies
in her bank. How many
pennies does she put in
her bank on both days?

Tens	Ones
□	
+	

_____ pennies

17. Higher Order Thinking Write an addition
story using 2 two-digit numbers. Then
solve the problem for your story.

_____
_____
_____
_____
_____
_____

Tens	Ones
□	
+	

18. ✓**Assessment** 52 acorns fall from a
tree. Then 37 more acorns fall. How
many acorns in all fall from the tree?
Show how you solved the problem.

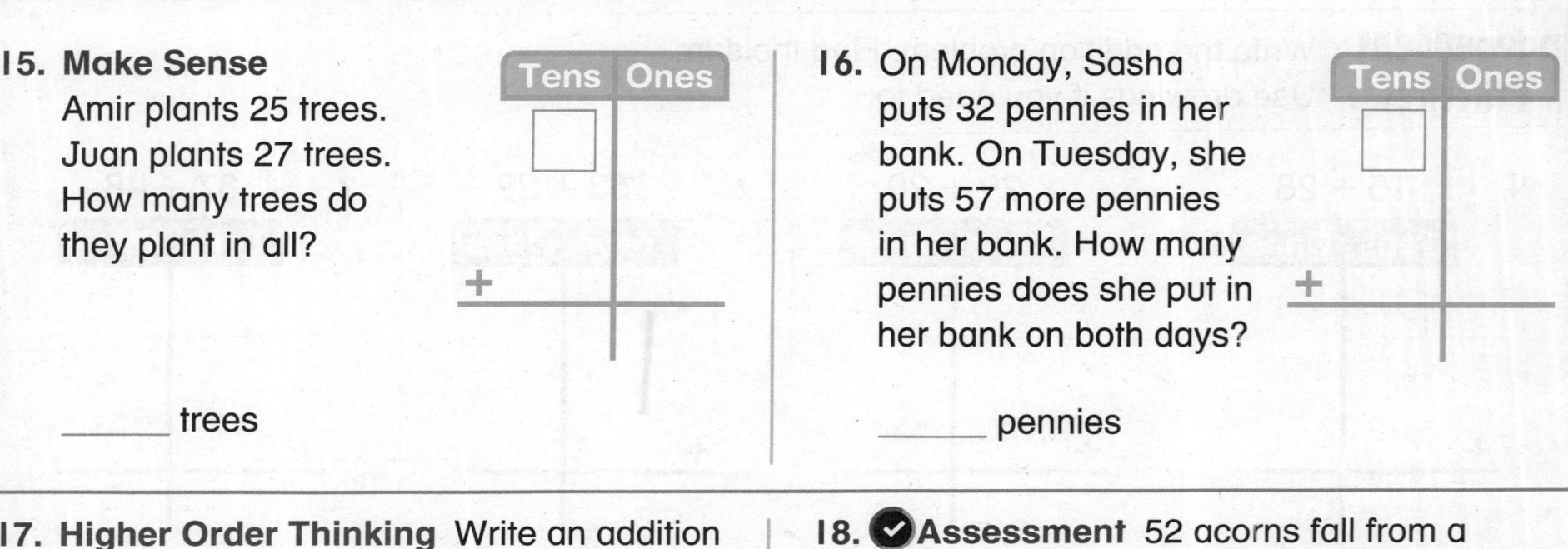

37

52

_____ acorns

Name _____

Another Look! Remember these steps for adding.

Step 1:	Step 2:	Step 3:
Add the ones.	Regroup if you need to.	Add the tens.

$34 + 27 = ?$
Regroup
11 ones as
1 ten and
1 one.

Tens	Ones
1	
3	4
+ 2	7
6	1

$12 + 36 = ?$
You do
not need
to regroup
8 ones.

Tens	Ones
1	2
+ 3	6
4	8

HOME ACTIVITY Write 28 + 45 on a sheet of paper. Have your child find the sum using paper and pencil. Once finished, have your child explain why regrouping was needed.

Write the addition problem. Find the sum. Use drawings, if needed.

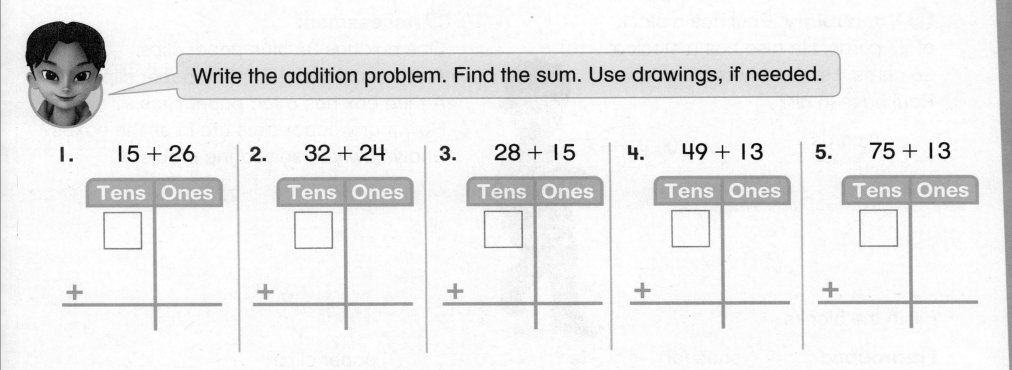

1. $15 + 26$

Tens	Ones
+	

2. $32 + 24$

Tens	Ones
+	

3. $28 + 15$

Tens	Ones
+	

4. $49 + 13$

Tens	Ones
+	

5. $75 + 13$

Tens	Ones
+	

Higher Order Thinking Read the sum. Circle all of the number pairs in the box that match that sum.

6. Sum 22

10	4	18
12	15	14
20	21	13

7. Sum 55

25	30	14
18	14	45
15	21	10

8. Sum 83

30	45	30
56	19	64
27	29	20

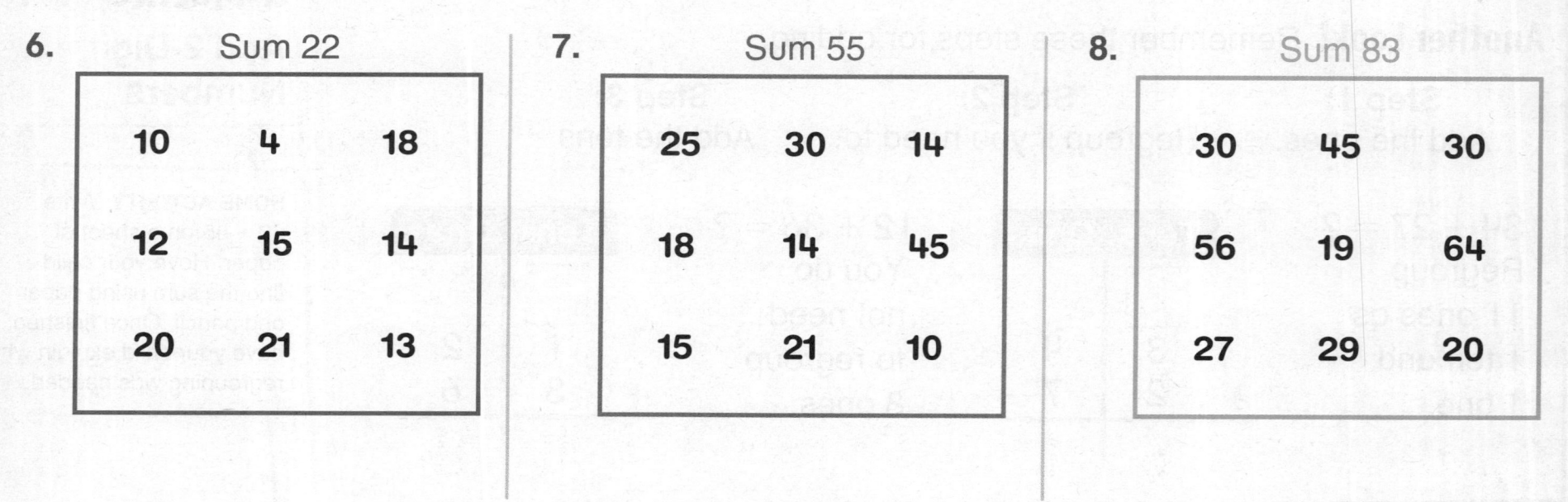

9. 🔤 **Vocabulary** Paul has a stack of 47 cards. He also has a stack of 36 cards. How many cards does Paul have in all?

_____ cards

Be precise.

10. ✅ **Assessment**
One box has 38 blue paper clips.
Another box has 43 green paper clips.
A third box has 6 red paper clips.
How many paper clips are in all the boxes?
Show how you solved the problem.

Fill in the blanks.

I **regrouped** _____ ones for _____ ten.

_____ paper clips

Name _____

Solve & Share

Make three 2-digit numbers. The tens digit for each number is shown below. Toss a number cube three times to find the ones digit for each number.

How can you add your three numbers? Explain.

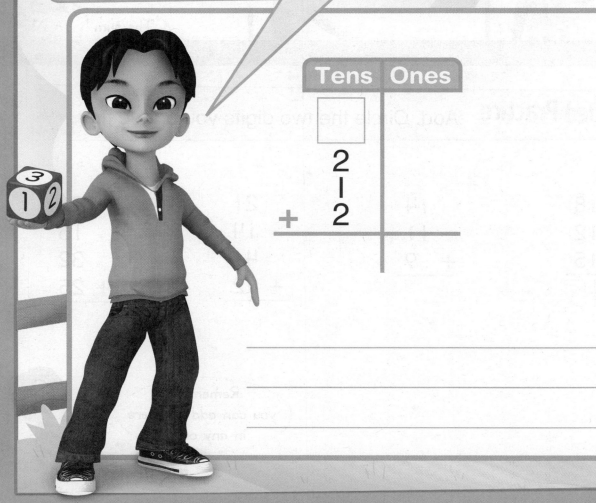

Tens	Ones
2	
1	
+ 2	

_____

_____

_____

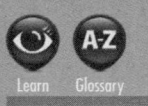
Start by adding the ones. Add in any order.	You can use doubles.	Or you can make 10.	Then add the tens.
2 4 1 6 1 4 + 1 5	2 ④ 1 6 1 ④ + 1 5 —— 9	2 4 1 ⑥ 1 ④ + 1 5 —— 9	2 4 1 6 1 4 + 1 5 —— 6 9

4 + 4 = 8
6 + 5 = 11
11 + 8 = 19

6 + 4 = 10
4 + 5 = 9
10 + 9 = 19

The sum is 69!

Do You Understand?

Show Me! When you add more than three numbers, can you always make 10 to help you add the ones digits? Explain.

★ **Guided Practice** Add. Circle the two digits you added first.

1.
```
 1⑧
 1②
+ 15
————
 45
```

2.
```
 14
 11
+  9
```

3.
```
 21
 14
 41
+  2
```

4.
```
 21
 15
 32
+ 25
```

Remember, you can add numbers in any order.

© Pearson Education, Inc. 2

Name _____

Independent Practice ☆ Add. Circle the two digits you added first.

5.　22
　　14
　+ 22

6.　16
　　23
　+ 26

7.　27
　　13
　+ 21

8.　13
　　33
　+ 25

9.　25
　　21
　+ 32

10.　55
　　　7
　　24
　+　2

11.　32
　　16
　　18
　+ 31

12.　16
　　42
　　12
　+ 22

13.　17
　　41
　　27
　+ 13

14.　37
　　11
　　15
　+ 28

Algebra Find the missing numbers.

15. $8 + 3 + \boxed{} + 2 = 18$

16. $5 + \boxed{} + 6 + 5 = 19$

17. $7 + 27 + 23 + \boxed{} = 61$

18. $\boxed{} + 24 + 18 + 4 = 52$

19. Generalize

28 trucks are blue.
32 trucks are yellow.
17 trucks are green.
11 trucks are pink.
How many trucks are
there in all?

28   32

17   11

Are there shortcuts
you can take to
solve the problems?

_____ trucks

20. Higher Order Thinking Henry is adding
the numbers 24, 36, and 18. He makes a
ten to add. Which ones digits does Henry
add first? Explain.

_____

_____

_____

21. ✓ Assessment Find the sum.
Explain your work.

$$\begin{array}{r} 25 \\ 16 \\ 15 \\ +\ 8 \\ \hline \end{array}$$

_____

_____

_____

_____

_____

_____

_____

© Pearson Education, Inc. 2

Name _____

Another Look! You can add three or four numbers in any order. Remember to add the ones first. Then, add the tens.

Look for doubles.

$$\begin{array}{r} 14 \\ 35 \\ + 24 \\ \hline 73 \end{array}$$

$4 + 4 = 8$
$8 + 5 = 13$

Make a ten.

$$\begin{array}{r} 13 \\ 26 \\ 24 \\ + 12 \\ \hline 75 \end{array}$$

$6 + 4 = 10$
$3 + 2 = 5$
$10 + 5 = 15$

Count on.

$$\begin{array}{r} 53 \\ 19 \\ + 22 \\ \hline 94 \end{array}$$

Count on from 12.
13, 14

$9 + 3 = 12$

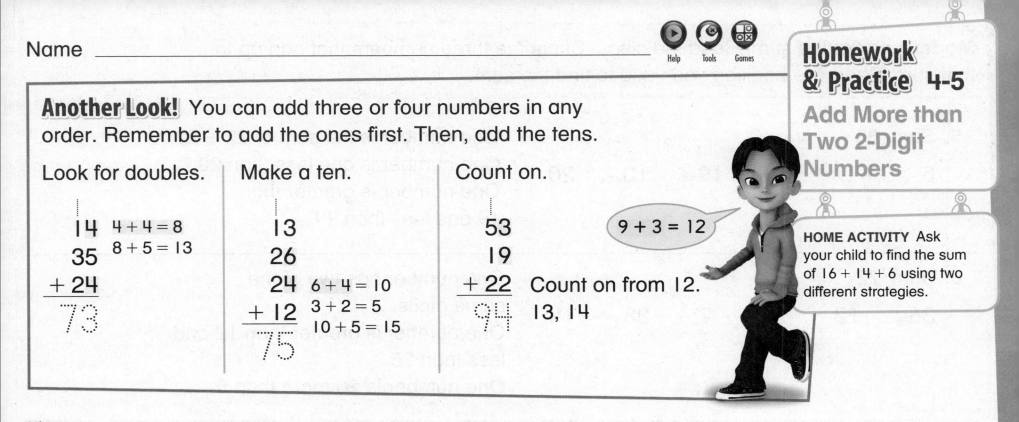

HOME ACTIVITY Ask your child to find the sum of $16 + 14 + 6$ using two different strategies.

Add. Circle the two digits you added first.

1. Look for doubles.

$$\begin{array}{r} 21 \\ 10 \\ 34 \\ + 24 \\ \hline \end{array}$$

2. Count on.

$$\begin{array}{r} 12 \\ 17 \\ + 24 \\ \hline \end{array}$$

3. Make a ten.

$$\begin{array}{r} 15 \\ 28 \\ + 22 \\ \hline \end{array}$$

4. Choose a way to add.

$$\begin{array}{r} 26 \\ 22 \\ + 36 \\ \hline \end{array}$$

Model Look at the sum. Read the clues. Circle the three numbers that add up to that sum. Show the addition you used to find the sum.

5. Sum: 83

    5   44   12   19   10   20

One number is the sum of 22 + 22.
One number is one less than 20.
One number is greater than 19 and less than 44.

---

6. Sum: 72

    36   12   25   7   33   14

One number has two of the same digits.
One number is greater than 12 and less than 25.
One number is 20 more than 5.

---

7. **Higher Order Thinking** Mac's family donates clothes to charity. Mac donates 16 shirts. His brother donates 14 shirts, and his mother donates 9 more shirts than Mac. How many shirts does Mac's family give to charity?

_____ shirts

8. ✅ **Assessment** There are 37 ants, 39 worms, 12 moths, and 11 beetles living in a big garden. Find the sum. Explain your work.

$$\begin{array}{r} 37 \\ 39 \\ 12 \\ +\ 11 \\ \hline \end{array}$$

Name _____

Solve & Share

Maria has 39 stickers. Sally has 28 stickers. They found 14 more stickers. How many stickers do they have in all?

Show your work. Explain how you found the answer.

I can ...
use mental math strategies and models to add more than two numbers.

I can also model with math.

_____ stickers

Find 27 + 38 + 12 + 3.
One Way: Use partial sums.

Tens	Ones
2	(7)
3	8
1	2
+	(3)
Tens: 6	0
Ones: 2	0
Sum: 8	0

Look for compatible numbers to make tens.
7 + 3 = 10
8 + 2 = 10
10 + 10 = 20

Another Way: Add the ones. Regroup, if needed. Then add the tens.

I get the same sum either way!

Tens	Ones
2	
2	(7)
3	8
1	2
	(3)
8	0

Check your work.

You can add the numbers in a different order to check your work.

30
27 + 38 + 12 + 3 =
50
30 + 50 = 80
So, 27 + 38 + 12 + 3 = 80.

Do You Understand?

Show Me! Find the sum of 14 + 28 + 33 + 22. Explain.

Guided Practice Add.

1.
```
 18
 43
+12
 73
```

How can you check your work?

2.
```
 29
+47
```

3.
```
  9
 34
+21
```

4.
```
 33
 27
 18
+13
```

© Pearson Education, Inc. 2

Independent Practice Add.

5.
```
  28
+  8
```

6.
```
   8
+ 17
```

7.
```
   5
  31
+ 29
```

8.
```
  36
   4
+ 28
```

9.
```
  20
  16
+ 16
```

10.
```
  27
  13
  12
+  5
```

11.
```
   9
  29
   5
+ 35
```

12.
```
  18
  23
   7
+ 42
```

13.
```
  27
  15
  33
+ 24
```

14.
```
  13
   7
  20
+ 55
```

Number Sense Solve each problem. In which order did you add the numbers? Explain.

15. $22 + 17 + 8 + 3 =$ _____

16. $5 + 12 + 15 + 3 =$ _____

17. Model Kim has 38 seashells. Mike has 27 seashells. Use **partial sums** to find how many shells they have in all. Then check your answer by adding another way.

_____ seashells

18. Math and Science Fossils form slowly over millions of years. Many fossils come from the sea. Kyle has 9 fossils, Jorie has 12 fossils, Leah has 6 fossils, and Joshua has 8 fossils. How many fossils did they have in all?

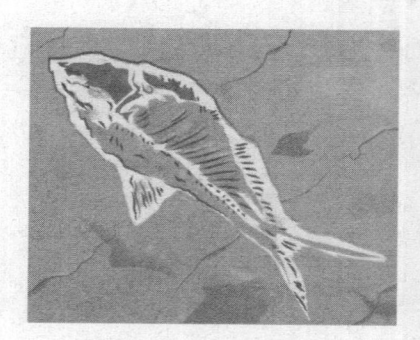

_____ fossils

19. Higher Order Thinking Find the sum. Explain why your strategy works.

$$
\begin{array}{r}
22 \\
13 \\
18 \\
+\ 7 \\
\end{array}
$$

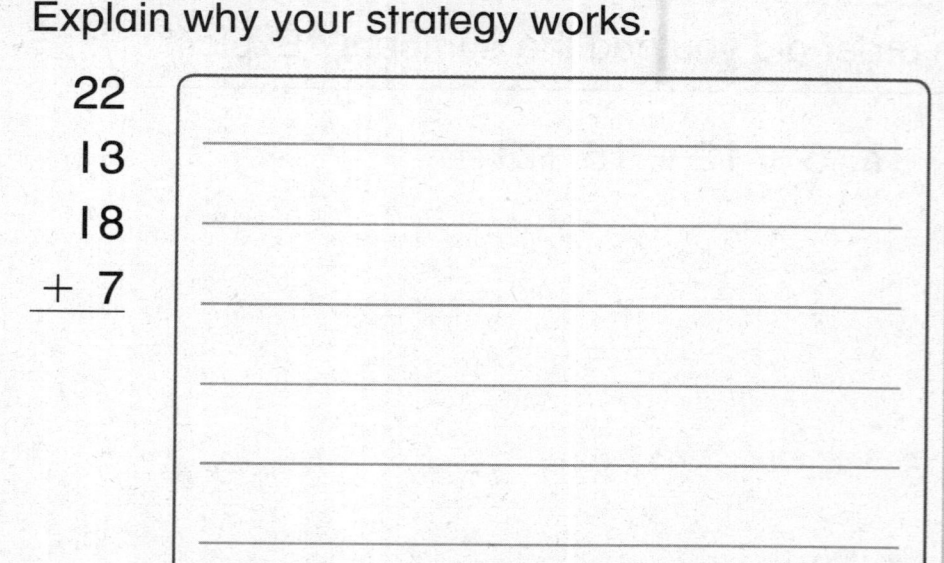

20. ✓**Assessment** Kate has 7 balloons. Claire has 9 balloons. Billy has 6 balloons. How many balloons do they have in all? Show your work.

_____ balloons

Another Look! Find the sum.

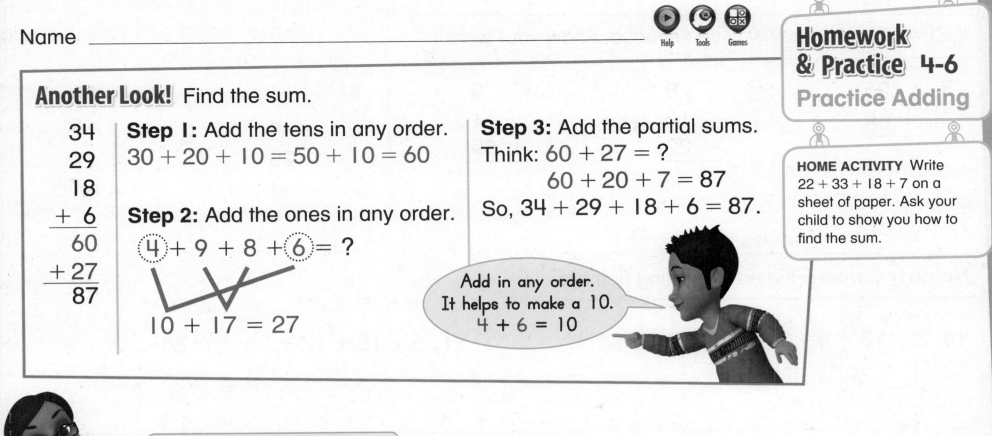

```
  34
  29
  18
+  6
────
  60
+ 27
────
  87
```

Step 1: Add the tens in any order.
$30 + 20 + 10 = 50 + 10 = 60$

Step 2: Add the ones in any order.
$④ + 9 + 8 + ⑥ = ?$

$10 + 17 = 27$

Step 3: Add the partial sums.
Think: $60 + 27 = ?$
$60 + 20 + 7 = 87$
So, $34 + 29 + 18 + 6 = 87$.

Add in any order.
It helps to make a 10.
$4 + 6 = 10$

HOME ACTIVITY Write $22 + 33 + 18 + 7$ on a sheet of paper. Ask your child to show you how to find the sum.

Add using partial sums.

1.

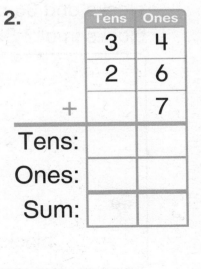

Tens	Ones
2	8
1	③
+	⑦
Tens: 3	0
Ones: 1	8
Sum:	

2.

Tens	Ones
3	4
2	6
+	7
Tens:	
Ones:	
Sum:	

3.

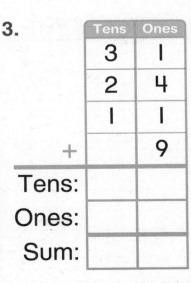

Tens	Ones
3	1
2	4
1	1
+	9
Tens:	
Ones:	
Sum:	

4.

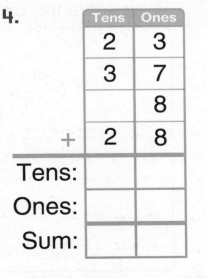

Tens	Ones
2	3
3	7
	8
+ 2	8
Tens:	
Ones:	
Sum:	

Be Precise Add any way you choose. Show your work.

5. 26
  + 48

6.   8
    13
  + 22

7.   5
    11
  + 59

8. 16
     4
    28
  + 48

9. 20
     6
    17
  + 46

Number Sense Find each missing number.

10. $6 + 13 + 4 + 7 = \boxed{}$

11. $5 + 15 + 12 + \boxed{} = 38$

12. **Higher Order Thinking** Write an addition story problem with 3 or more addends. Then solve the problem. Show your work.

13. ✅**Assessment** Ricky is building a toy. He uses 27 red blocks. He uses 10 blue blocks and 36 brown blocks. How many blocks in all? Show your work.

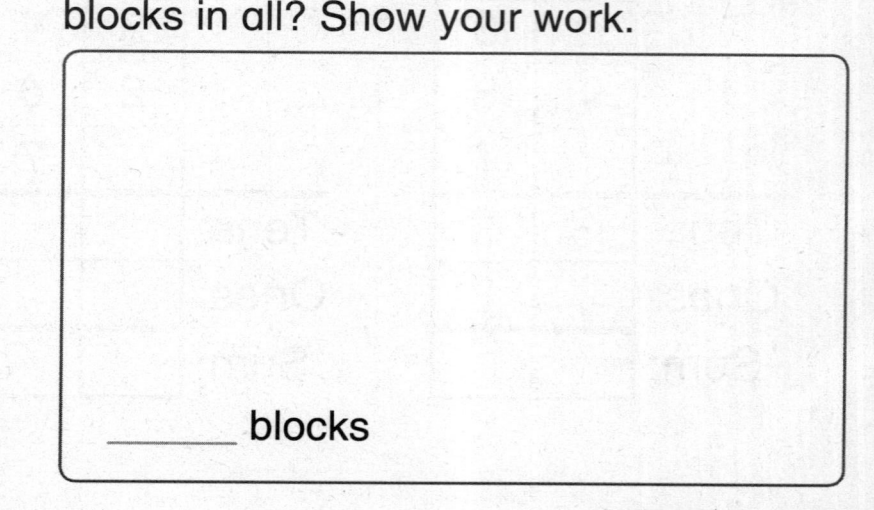

_____ blocks

© Pearson Education, Inc. 2

Name _____

Solve & Share

The second graders take a trip to a nature center. The Green Class sees 23 animals. The Blue Class sees 14 animals. The Yellow Class sees 32 animals. How many animals do they see in all?

Solve using drawings, models, or an equation. Be prepared to explain your work.

I can ...
use drawings, models, and equations to solve one- and two-step problems.

I can also model with math.

_____ animals

Aimee and Devin count 36 butterflies. Suddenly, more butterflies join them. Now, there are 53 butterflies.

How many new butterflies join them?

53

| 36 | ? |

$36 + ? = 53$

The total is 53. The first group has 36 butterflies. I will use a bar diagram to model the problem.

I can use mental math to find $36 + ? = 53$.

Think: $36 + 10 = 46$
$46 + 4 = 50$
$50 + 3 = 53$

$10 + 4 + 3 = 17$

So, $36 + \underline{17} = 53$.

So, 17 butterfiles join them.

Check your work.

$$\begin{array}{r} 3\;6 \\ +\;1\;7 \\ \hline 5\;3 \end{array}$$

The answer makes sense.

$36 + 17 = 53$

Do You Understand?

Show Me! Suppose you count 28 butterflies. Then suddenly there are 54. How could you use mental math to find how many join?

☆ **Guided Practice** ☆ Use the bar diagram and mental math to solve each problem. Then check your work.

1. There are 29 red marbles, 7 green marbles, and 11 blue marbles in a bag.

   How many marbles are in the bag?

   $\underline{29} + \underline{7} + \underline{11} = \underline{}$

   $\underline{}$ marbles

   | 29 | 7 | 11 |

   □

   $$\begin{array}{r} 2\;9 \\ 7 \\ +\;1\;1 \\ \hline \end{array}$$

© Pearson Education, Inc. 2

Name _____

Independent Practice

Use the bar diagram and mental math to solve each problem. Then check your work.

2. 29 students are on the bus.
Then some more students get on the bus.
Now, there are 46 students on the bus.
How many students got on the bus?

Check:

+

___ + ___ = ___

___ students

3. Ella has 34 more buttons than Julio.
Julio has 49 buttons. How many buttons does Ella have?

Check:

+

___ + ___ = ___

___ buttons

4. Wendy has 14 more crayons than Oscar.
Oscar has 54 crayons.
How many crayons does Wendy have?

The bar diagram helps you see how the numbers are related.

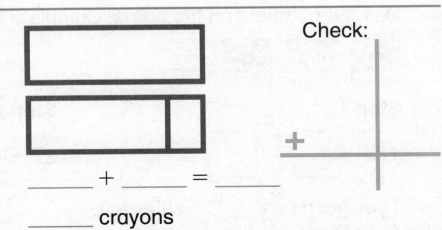

Check:

+

___ + ___ = ___

___ crayons

Topic 4 | Lesson 7

two hundred thirty-one **231**

5. **Make Sense** Mariah has 17 figs. Kendra has 20 more figs than Mariah. Toby has 33 more figs than Kendra. How many figs do Kendra and Toby each have?

Step 1:

How many figs does Kendra have?

_____ ◯ _____ = _____ _____ figs

Step 2:

How many figs does Toby have?

_____ ◯ _____ = _____ _____ figs

6. **Higher Order Thinking** 8 girls and some boys are in the pool. In all, 17 children are in the pool. Then some more boys jump in the pool. Now there are 13 boys in the pool. How many more boys jumped in the pool?

Step 1:

_____ ◯ _____ = _____

Step 2:

_____ ◯ _____ = _____

_____ more boys jumped in the pool

Solve one step at a time.

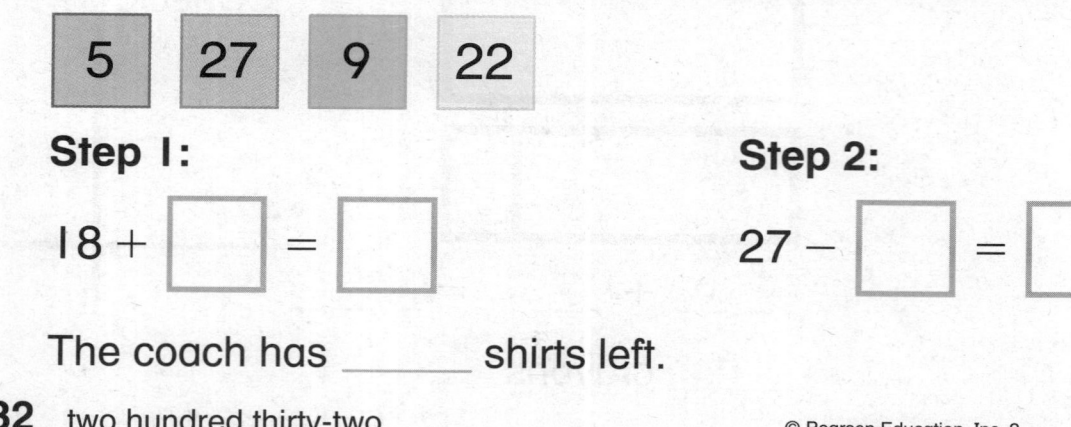

7. ✓ **Assessment** The soccer coach has 18 shirts. Then she gets 9 more shirts. There are 22 players on her team. She gives a shirt to each player. How many shirts does the coach have left?

Use the numbers on the cards. Complete both equations to solve the problem.

| 5 | 27 | 9 | 22 |

Step 1:

$18 + \square = \square$

Step 2:

$27 - \square = \square$

The coach has _____ shirts left.

© Pearson Education, Inc. 2

Name _____

Another Look! You can write the numbers in a chart to solve the problem.

There are 33 red cars, 27 gray cars, and 25 tan cars in the parking lot. How many cars in all?

Tens	Ones
3	③
2	⑦
+ 2	5

	Tens	Ones
Tens:	7	0
Ones:	1	5
Sum:	8	5

85

33	27	25

_____ cars

Add in any order. It helps to make a 10.
3 + 7 = 10
10 + 5 = 15

HOME ACTIVITY Write 39 + 14 + 11 on a sheet of paper. Ask your child to show you how to find the sum.

Solve the problem. Show your work.

1. On Monday, Matt puts 32 cents in his bank. On Tuesday, he puts in 25 cents. On Wednesday, he puts in 18 cents. How much money does Matt put in his bank on those three days?

Tens	Ones
+	

	Tens	Ones
Tens:		
Ones:		
Sum:		

_____ cents

Solve each problem. Show your work.

2. **Generalize** Alexis has 16 peaches, 18 apples, and 12 pears to bring to school for the class snack. How many pieces of fruit does Alexis have in all?

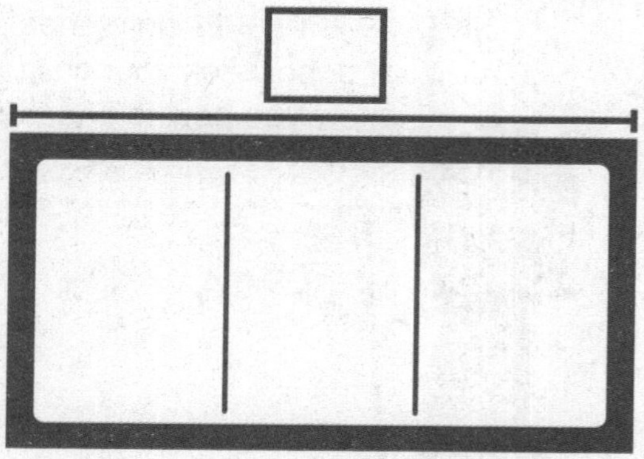

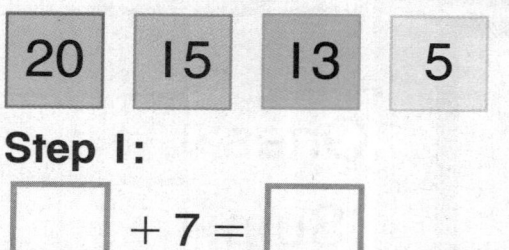

_____ + _____ + _____ = _____

_____ pieces of fruit

3. **Higher Order Thinking** Chris has 16 party hats. Then he gets 27 more hats. He gives away 20 hats at his birthday party. How many hats are left?

Step 1:

_____ ◯ _____ = _____

Step 2:

_____ ◯ _____ = _____

_____ hats

4. ✓**Assessment** The dance team has 13 dancers. Then 7 more dancers join. The next week 5 dancers quit. How many dancers are now on the team?

Use the numbers on the cards. Complete both equations to solve the problem.

| 20 | 15 | 13 | 5 |

Step 1:

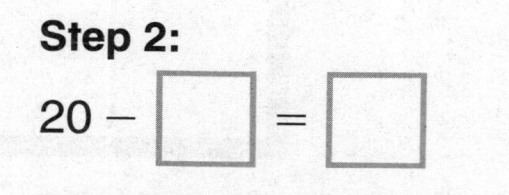

☐ + 7 = ☐

Step 2:

20 − ☐ = ☐

The team now has _____ dancers.

Name _____

Solve & Share

Kim puts 25 toys into an empty toy box.
Then she puts 17 more toys in the toy box.
How many toys are in the box in all?

Use a model to show the problem. Be ready to explain
how your model helps you solve the problem.

I can ...
make models to help solve
math problems.

I can also add two-digit
numbers.

Thinking Habits
Can I use a drawing,
diagram, table,
graph, or objects to
show the problem?

Can I write an
equation to show
the problem?

_____ toys

Eric has 29 crayons. He buys a box of 16 crayons. How many crayons does Eric have in all?

Here are some models you can use or make.

Models
arrays
bar diagrams
drawings
equations

Which model can I use to show this problem?

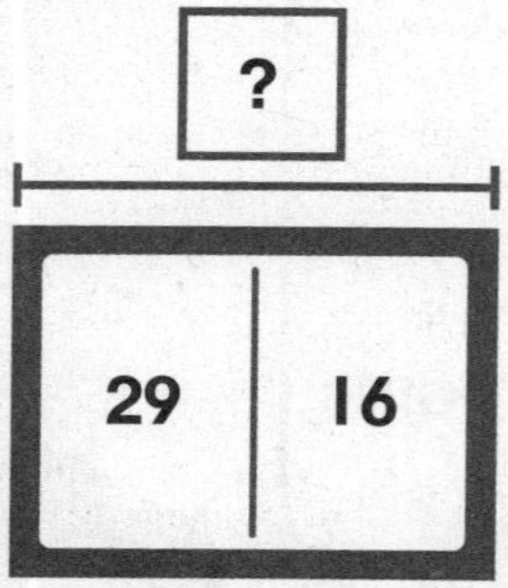

?

| 29 | 16 |

29 + 16 = ?

I can also model the problem with an equation. An equation uses numbers and symbols.

I can show parts and a whole with a bar diagram.

$$\begin{array}{r} 1 \\ 29 \\ + 16 \\ \hline 45 \end{array}$$

I can regroup to find 29 + 16. My answer makes sense.

So, Eric has 45 crayons in all.

Do You Understand?

Show Me! How does drawing a bar diagram or writing an equation model a problem? Is there another way to model the problem?

☆ **Guided Practice** ☆ Complete the bar diagram and write an equation to model and solve each problem.

1. Flora has 24 books about birds. She has 18 books about bugs. How many books is that?

   __24__ + __18__ = __?__ books

   ?

   | 24 | 18 |

   $$\begin{array}{r} 1 \\ 2\;4 \\ + 1\;8 \\ \hline 4\;2 \end{array}$$

2. Barb saw 14 cars on one street. She saw 15 cars on another street. How many cars did Barb see on both streets?

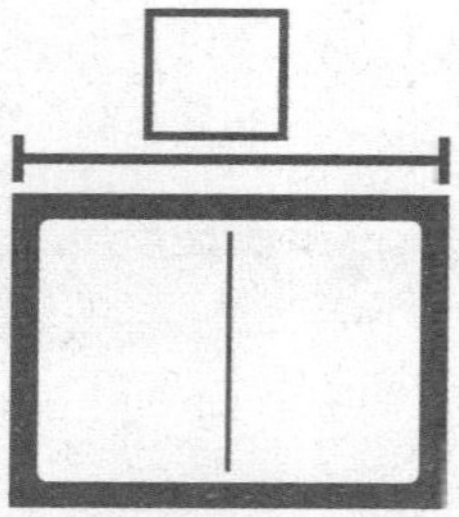

   _____ + _____ = _____ cars

© Pearson Education, Inc. 2

Tools   Assessment

Independent Practice

Make a model to show each problem. Then use the model to solve.
Show your work.

3. Avi takes 16 pictures.
   Then he takes 17 more pictures.
   How many pictures does Avi take?

Remember, you can use different models. Be ready to explain how your model shows the problem!

4. Tina picks 55 blueberries.
   Then she picks 27 more.
   How many blueberries does Tina pick?

5. Raj finds 47 acorns in his front yard.
   He finds 29 acorns in his back yard.
   How many acorns does Raj find in all?

African Safari

The Santos family are on an African safari. The chart at the right shows the number of animals they see.

How many animals do they see?

Number of Animals	
Giraffes	15
Elephants	9
Lions	16
Zebras	11

6. **Make Sense** What do you know? What are you asked to find?

_____

_____

_____

7. **Reasoning** Make a model to help you find the number of animals they see. Be ready to explain why you chose the model you did.

8. **Model** What other model could you use to show the problem? Make another model. Explain which model you think is better.

_____

_____

Name _____

Another Look! Complete the bar diagram and equation to model and solve the problem.

Paul has 23 counters.
He gets 27 more counters.
How many counters does Paul have in all?

You can show pictures or numbers in a bar diagram.

HOME ACTIVITY Ask your child to model and find $14 + 19$ by drawing a bar diagram and writing an equation.

?

$$\underline{23} + \underline{27} = \underline{?}$$

$$\begin{array}{r} 2\ 3 \\ +\ 2\ 7 \\ \hline 5\ 0 \end{array}$$

Paul has 50 counters in all.

Make a model to show the problem. Then use the model to solve. Show your work.

Be ready to explain how your model shows the problem!

1. There were 38 yo-yos at a toy store.
Then the store got 12 more yo-yos.
How many yo-yos are at the store now?

On the Path

The diagram shows the distances, in feet, of paths between each farm animal.
What is the total distance of the paths from the cow to the chicken, to the horse, to the pig, to the cow?

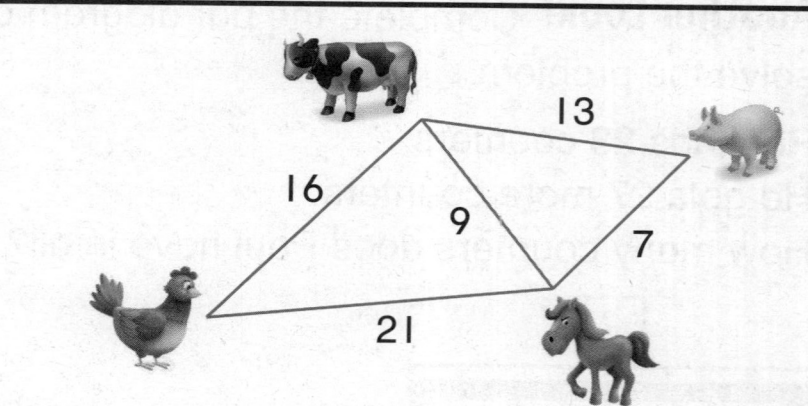

2. **Make Sense** What do you know? What are you asked to find?

_____

_____

_____

_____

3. **Reasoning** Make a model to help you find the total distance in the problem.
Be ready to explain why you chose the model you did.

4. **Model** What other model could you use to show the problem? Make another model. Explain which model you think is better.

Point & Tally

Find a partner. Get paper and a pencil.
Each partner chooses a different color: light blue or dark blue.

Partner 1 and Partner 2 each point to a black number at the same time. Both partners add those numbers.

If the answer is on your color, you get a tally mark.
Work until one partner gets twelve tally marks.

I can …
add within 20.

Partner 1		Partner 2
7		8
4		6
9		5
6		4
8		7
5		9

13	17	14	10	9	12
15	11	8	18	13	16

Tally Marks for Partner 1

Tally Marks for Partner 2

A-Z Glossary

Word List
- compatible numbers
- ones
- partial sum
- regroup
- sum
- tens

Understand Vocabulary

Use the problem at the right.
Write *partial sum* or *sum* for each.

1. 70 is a _____.

2. 17 is a _____.

3. 87 is the _____.

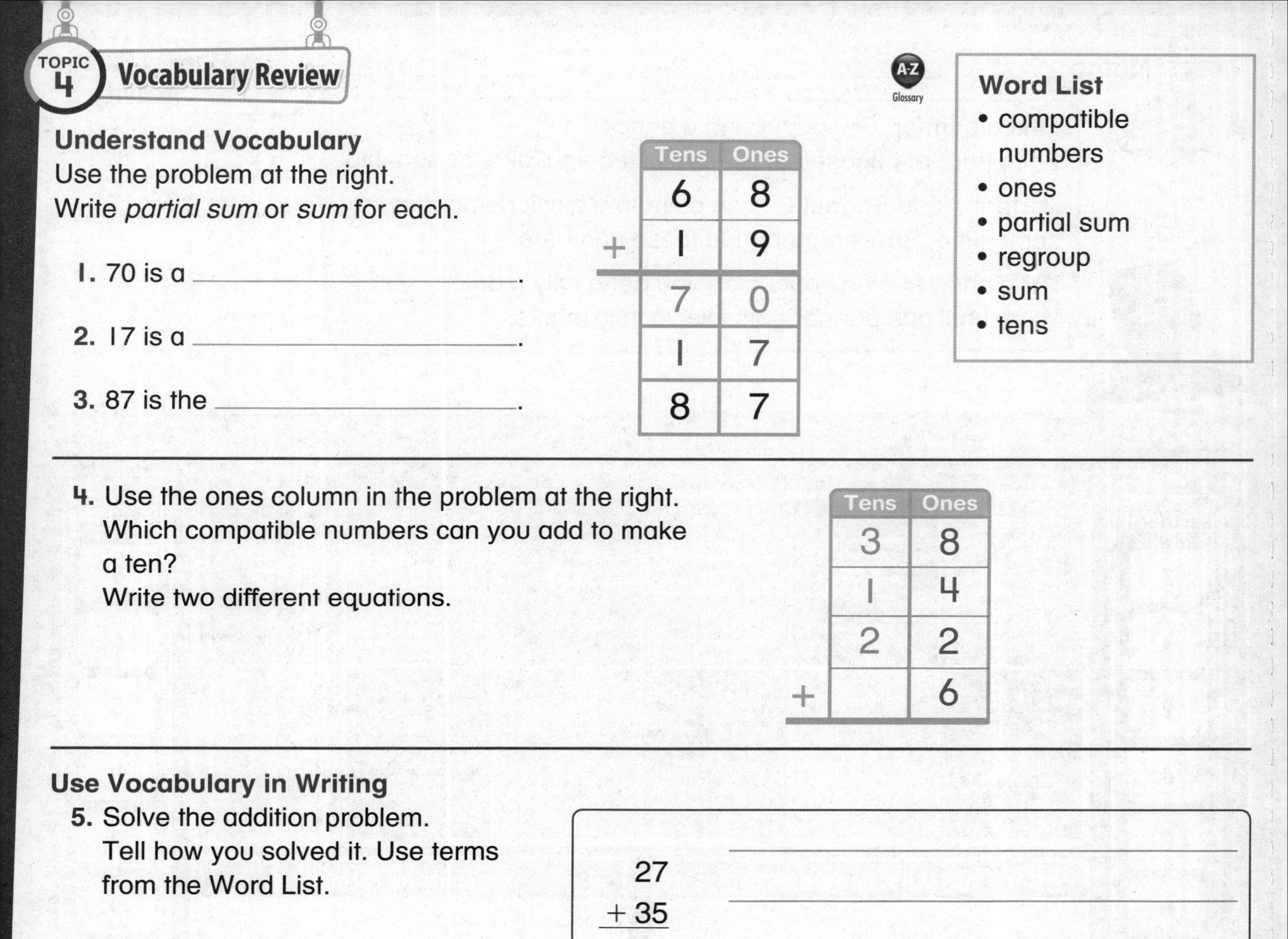

Tens	Ones
6	8
+ 1	9
7	0
1	7
8	7

4. Use the ones column in the problem at the right.
Which compatible numbers can you add to make a ten?
Write two different equations.

Tens	Ones
3	8
1	4
2	2
+	6

Use Vocabulary in Writing

5. Solve the addition problem.
Tell how you solved it. Use terms from the Word List.

```
  27
+ 35
```

_____
_____
_____

Set A

You can use partial sums to find the sum. Find 46 + 37.

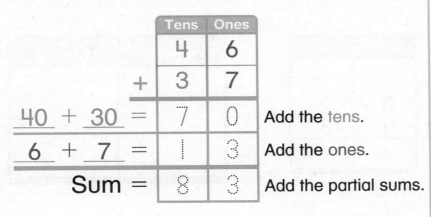

	Tens	Ones
	4	6
+	3	7
40 + 30 =	7	0
6 + 7 =	1	3
Sum =	8	3

40 + 30 = Add the tens.
6 + 7 = Add the ones.
Sum = Add the partial sums.

Reteaching

Add. Use partial sums. Use place-value blocks, if needed.

1.

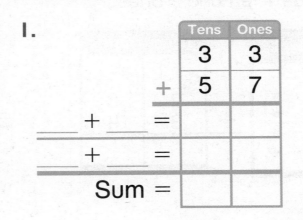

	Tens	Ones
	3	3
+	5	7
+ ___ =		
+ ___ =		
Sum =		

Set B

You can show partial sums another way. Find 29 + 63.

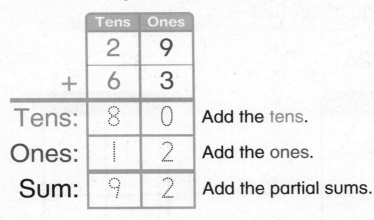

	Tens	Ones
	2	9
+	6	3
Tens:	8	0
Ones:	1	2
Sum:	9	2

Tens: Add the tens.
Ones: Add the ones.
Sum: Add the partial sums.

Add. Use partial sums. Show your work.

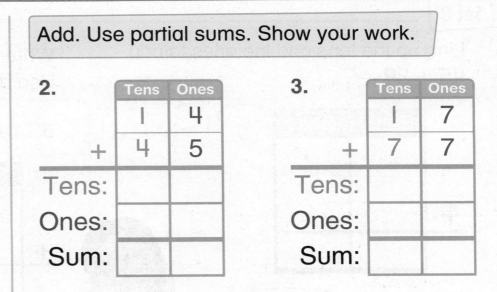

2.

	Tens	Ones
	1	4
+	4	5
Tens:		
Ones:		
Sum:		

3.

	Tens	Ones
	1	7
+	7	7
Tens:		
Ones:		
Sum:		

You can regroup to find a sum.
Find 28 + 34.

8 ones + 4 ones = 12 ones.
So regroup 12 as 1 ten and 2 ones.

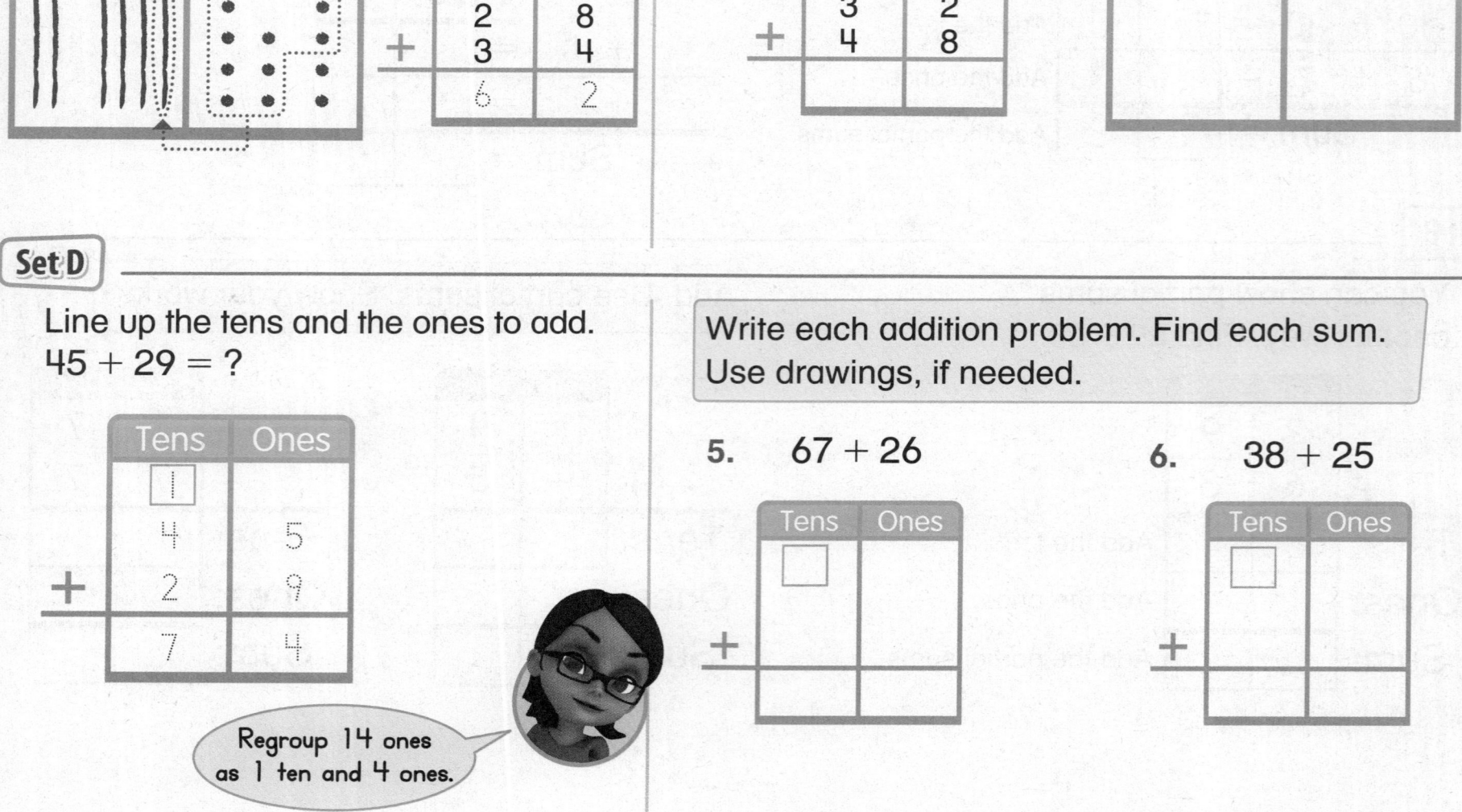

Tens	Ones
1	
2	8
+ 3	4
6	2

Add. Draw place-value blocks to show your work. Regroup if needed.

4.

Tens	Ones
☐	
3	2
+ 4	8

Tens	Ones

Line up the tens and the ones to add.
45 + 29 = ?

Tens	Ones
1	
4	5
+ 2	9
7	4

Regroup 14 ones as 1 ten and 4 ones.

Write each addition problem. Find each sum.
Use drawings, if needed.

5.   67 + 26

Tens	Ones
☐	
+	

6.   38 + 25

Tens	Ones
☐	
+	

© Pearson Education, Inc. 2

Set E

You can add more than two 2-digit numbers. Add the ones in any order. Make a 10 to help. Then add the tens.

```
  1 5
  3 7
  2 2
+ 2 3
-----
  8 7
```

Add. Circle the two digits you added first.

7.
```
    15
     9
+   21
------
```

8.
```
    33
    46
     2
+   14
------
```

Set F

Use partial sums to find $45 + 7 + 21 + 13$.

Tens	Ones
4	5
	7
2	1
+ 1	3
Tens: 7	0
Ones: 1	6
Sum: 8	6

Look for compatible numbers to make tens. $7 + 3 = 10$

So, $45 + 7 + 21 + 13 = \underline{86}$

Add using partial sums.

9.

Tens	Ones
2	2
2	1
	9
+ 1	8
Tens:	
Ones:	
Sum:	

27 students are eating lunch.
More students join them.
Now 63 students are eating lunch.
How many students joined them?

Write an equation: $27 + ? = 63$
Count on to find the missing addend:

$27 + 30 = 57$	$30 + 3 + 3 = \underline{36}$
$57 + 3 = 60$	$27 + \underline{36} = 63$
$60 + 3 = 63$	

So, 36 students joined them.

Complete the bar diagram and solve.

10. Lana has 24 crayons.
Then she gets some
more crayons.
Now she has 42 crayons.
How many crayons does
Lana get?

$24 + ? = 42$

Thinking Habits

Model with Math

Can I use a drawing,
diagram, table, graph, or
objects to show the problem?

Can I write an equation to
show the problem?

Make a model and solve the problem.

11. Students ride buses to the museum.
28 students ride in Bus A.
27 students ride in Bus B.
How many students ride in both buses?

Name _____

✔ Assessment

1. Kelly has 46 beads.
Her sister gives her 28 more beads.
How many beads does Kelly have now?

Ⓐ 18

Ⓑ 22

Ⓒ 64

Ⓓ 74

2. Which is the same amount as 45 + 38? Choose all that apply.

☐ 40 + 30 + 5 + 8

☐ 70 + 13

☐ 83

☐ 93

3. Do you have to regroup to find each sum? Choose Yes or No.

42 + 56 = ?   ○ Yes ○ No

52 + 29 = ?   ○ Yes ○ No

37 + 50 = ?   ○ Yes ○ No

63 + 19 = ?   ○ Yes ○ No

4. Circle the addition problem that you can use regrouping to solve.
Then explain how you know.

30 + 29   54 + 38   43 + 44

5. Ryan has 57 stones in his collection. Joy gives him 15 more stones. How many stones does Ryan have now?

Ⓐ 82

Ⓑ 72

Ⓒ 62

Ⓓ 42

6. Which is the same amount as $13 + 8 + 7$? Choose all that apply.

☐ $20 + 8$

☐ $10 + 10 + 8$

☐ 18

☐ 28

7. One zoo has 26 dolphins. Another zoo has 53 dolphins. A third zoo has 7 dolphins. How many dolphins in all?

Show your work.

_____ dolphins

8. Faith has 23 shells. Then she finds 19 more shells. Faith gives 10 of the shells to a friend. How many shells does Faith have now?

Show your work.

_____ shells

Name _____

9. Part A Find the sum.
Show your work.

```
   25
   37
   15
 +  8
```

Part B
Tell how you found the sum.

_____

_____

_____

_____

_____

---

10. Ms. Wise has 12 tablets.
Then she gets 9 more tablets.
Ms. Wise has 20 students in her class.
She gives each student one tablet.
How many tablets does she have left?

Use the numbers on the cards below.
Complete both equations to solve the problem.

| 1 | 9 | 20 | 21 |

Step 1: 12 + ☐ = ☐

Step 2: 21 − ☐ = ☐

_____ tablet

11. Pearl has 8 medals.
Grace has 9 medals.
Timmy has 6 medals.
How many medals do they have in all?

Solve and show your work in the blue box at the right.

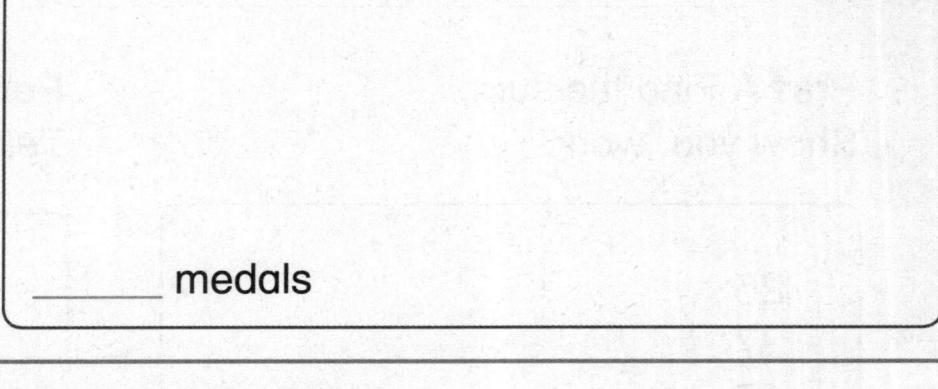

_____ medals

12. Match each number card to an equation to find the missing addend.
Draw lines to match. Then write the missing addend in the gray box.

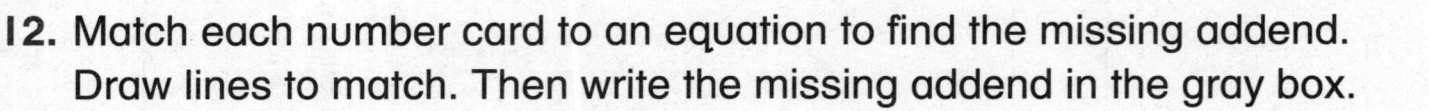

| 5 | ○ 6 + 14 + ☐ + 3 = 30 |

| 6 | ○ 3 + 32 + 7 + ☐ = 50 |

| 7 | ○ 25 + 25 + ☐ + 5 = 60 |

| 8 | ○ 5 + ☐ + 15 + 14 = 40 |

13. Corey has 17 more marbles than Tony.
Tony has 64 marbles.
How many marbles does Corey have?

Use the bar diagram to model and solve the problem. Show your work.

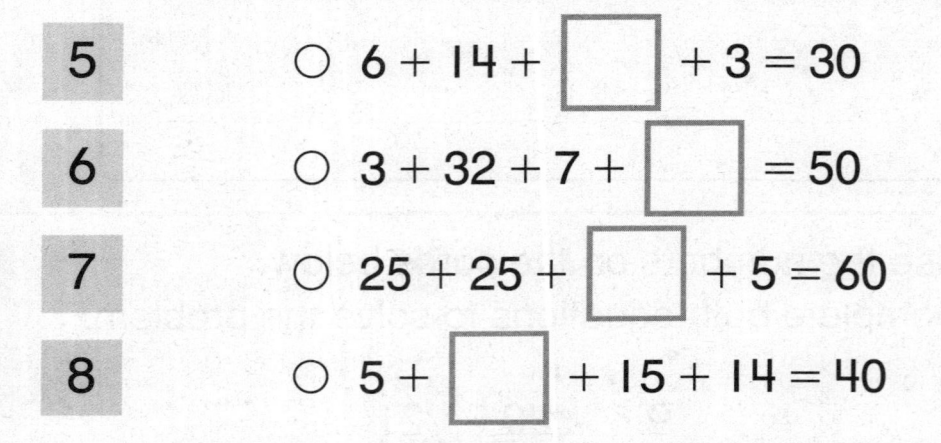

_____ marbles

© Pearson Education, Inc. 2

Topic 4 | Assessment

Name _____

Our Pets

Students draw pictures of their pets. The chart shows the number of pets the students have.

Number of Pets	
Dogs 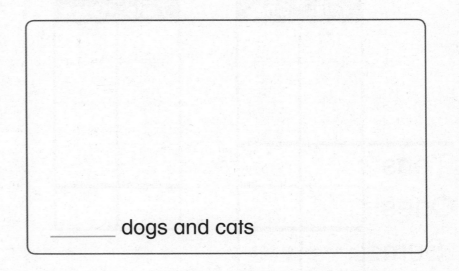	41
Cats	29
Rabbits	6
Fish	24

1. How many dogs and cats do the students have?
Show your work.

_____ dogs and cats

2. How many cats and fish do the students have?
Show your work.

_____ cats and fish

3. Use partial sums to find how many cats, rabbits, and fish the students have. Then use regrouping to check your work.

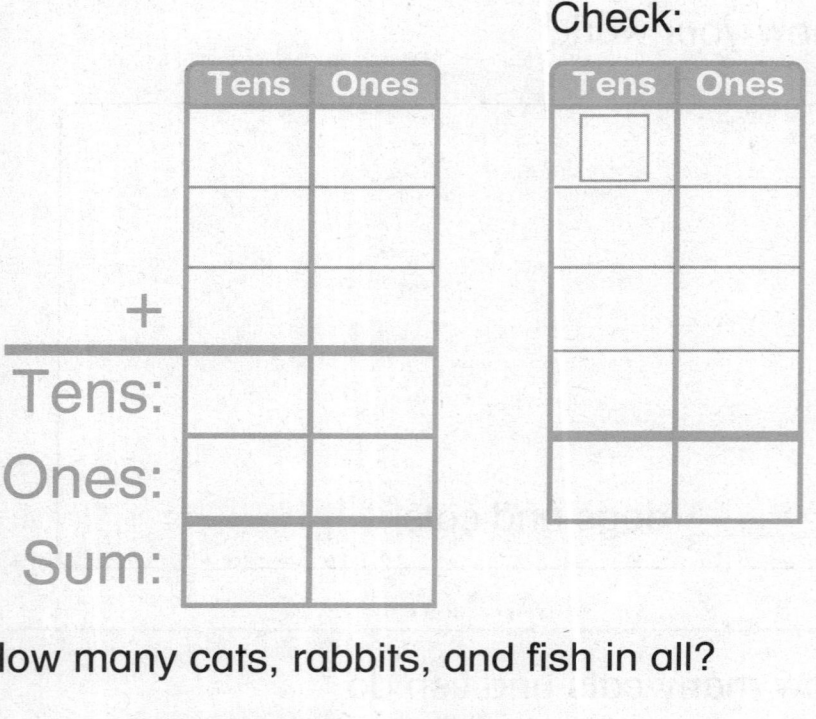

Check:

Tens	Ones
+	

Tens:

Ones:

Sum:

Tens	Ones
☐	

How many cats, rabbits, and fish in all?

_____ cats, rabbits, and fish

---

4. Explain why you can use regrouping when you add.

_____

_____

_____

---

5. The students also draw pictures of 10 hamsters, 19 birds, and 5 mice.

Part A

Complete the model to show how to find the total number of hamsters, birds, and mice.

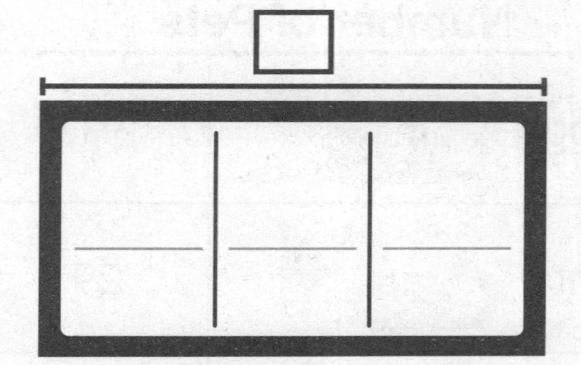

Part B

Complete the equation to show how many hamsters, birds and mice they draw. Then write the total.

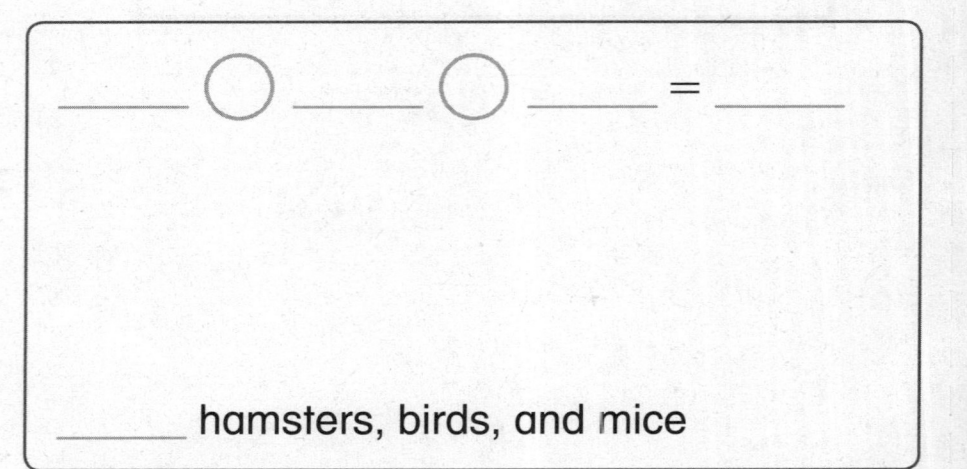

____ ◯ ____ ◯ ____ = ____

_____ hamsters, birds, and mice

© Pearson Education, Inc. 2

Subtract Within 100 Using Strategies

Essential Question: What are strategies for subtracting numbers to 100?

Digital Resources

Solve Learn Glossary

Tools Assessment Help Games

Look at the big pieces of ice in the water!

How can heating and cooling change water and ice?

Wow! Let's do this project and learn more.

Math and Science Project: Heating, Cooling, and Subtraction

Find Out Have an adult help you heat and cool water and other materials. Find out if water and ice can change back and forth. Find out if heating and cooling an egg can change it back and forth.

Journal: Make a Book Show what you learn in a book. In your book, also:

• Tell about how heating and cooling are related.

• Tell about how addition and subtraction are related.

Name _____

A-Z Vocabulary

1. Circle each **difference** in the math problems shown below.

$$15 - 5 = 10$$

```
  23          14
+ 32         - 7
----         ---
  55           7
```

2. Circle the statement if it describes **mental math**.

Math that is done with paper and pencil.

Math that you can do in your head.

3. Circle the statement if it describes **compatible numbers**.

Numbers that are close to numbers that you want to add or subtract.

Numbers that you can add or subtract using mental math.

Addition and Subtraction Facts

4. Complete the related addition and subtraction facts below.

$$6 + \boxed{} = 13$$

$$13 - \boxed{} = 6$$

5. Write each sum or difference.

```
   4      12       9      16
 + 7     - 3     + 6     - 8
```

You can use addition facts to help you subtract.

Math Story

6. Tim has 25 stamps. Roy gives him 51 more stamps. How many stamps does Tim have now?

_____ stamps

How can you use the hundred chart to help you find 57 − 23? Explain. Write an equation.

I can ...
use a hundred chart to subtract tens and ones.

I can also make sense of problems.

1	2	3	4	5	6	7	8	9	10
11	12	13	14	15	16	17	18	19	20
21	22	23	24	25	26	27	28	29	30
31	32	33	34	35	36	37	38	39	40
41	42	43	44	45	46	47	48	49	50
51	52	53	54	55	56	57	58	59	60
61	62	63	64	65	66	67	68	69	70
71	72	73	74	75	76	77	78	79	80
81	82	83	84	85	86	87	88	89	90
91	92	93	94	95	96	97	98	99	100

____ ◯ ____ = ____

Find 43 − 28 using a hundred chart.

I need to find the difference between 28 and 43.

Start at 28. Count to the next number that matches the ones in 43.

Count by ones! I counted 5 ones to get from 28 to 33.

Count by tens to 43.

That's 1 ten, or 10 more.

I added 5 and 10. That makes 15.

28 + 15 = 43
So, 43 − 28 = 15.

Do You Understand?

Show Me! How can you use a hundred chart to find 60 − 18?

☆ Guided Practice ☆

Subtract using the hundred chart. Draw arrows if you need to.

21	22	23	24	25	26	27	28	29	30
31	32	33	34	35	36	37	38	39	40
41	42	43	44	45	46	47	48	49	50
51	52	53	54	55	56	57	58	59	60
61	62	63	64	65	66	67	68	69	70

1. 69 − 36 = 33

2. 54 − 24 = _____

3. _____ = 65 − 34

4. 47 − 22 = _____

Topic 5 | Lesson 1

Name _____

Tools Assessment

Independent Practice ☆ Subtract using the hundred chart. Draw arrows if you need to.

1	2	3	4	5	6	7	8	9	10
11	12	13	14	15	16	17	18	19	20
21	22	23	24	25	26	27	28	29	30
31	32	33	34	35	36	37	38	39	40
41	42	43	44	45	46	47	48	49	50
51	52	53	54	55	56	57	58	59	60
61	62	63	64	65	66	67	68	69	70
71	72	73	74	75	76	77	78	79	80
81	82	83	84	85	86	87	88	89	90
91	92	93	94	95	96	97	98	99	100

5. $54 - 7 =$ _____

6. _____ $= 96 - 63$

7. $45 - 22 =$ _____

8. $82 - 61 =$ _____

9. $65 - 21 =$ _____

10. _____ $= 79 - 47$

11. $84 - 6 =$ _____

Algebra Write the digit that makes each equation true.

12. $73 - \boxed{}2 = 41$

$5\boxed{} - 32 = 26$

13. $46 - \boxed{}1 = 15$

$78 - 36 = \boxed{}2$

14. $53 - \boxed{}2 = 31$

$99 - \boxed{}3 = 16$

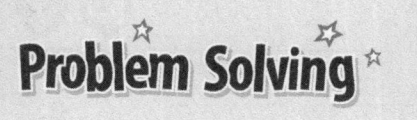

Problem Solving Use Tools Use the hundred chart to solve the problems below.

15. Darren's puzzle has 98 pieces. Darren fits 55 pieces together. How many more pieces does Darren still need to fit to complete the puzzle?

_____ − _____ = _____ pieces

16. A test has 86 questions. Glenda needs to answer 23 more questions to finish the test. How many test questions has Glenda answered already?

_____ questions

The hundred chart is a good tool to use. Count by ones and tens to subtract.

41	42	43	44	45	46	47	48	49	50
51	52	53	54	55	56	57	58	59	60
61	62	63	64	65	66	67	68	69	70
71	72	73	74	75	76	77	78	79	80
81	82	83	84	85	86	87	88	89	90
91	92	93	94	95	96	97	98	99	100

17. **Higher Order Thinking** Chris wants to subtract 76 − 42. Write the steps he can take to subtract 42 from 76 on the hundred chart.

_____

_____

_____

18. ✓**Assessment** Lu has 75 buttons. 49 of the buttons are green. The rest of the buttons are red. How many of the buttons are red?

Ⓐ 16   Ⓑ 20   Ⓒ 26   Ⓓ 36

© Pearson Education, Inc. 2

Name _____

Help Tools Games

Homework
& Practice 5-1
Subtract Tens
and Ones on a
Hundred Chart

Another Look! Here is another way to subtract on a hundred chart.

Find 36 − 24.

1. Start at 36.

2. Move up 2 rows to subtract
   __2__ tens.

3. Move left 4 columns to subtract
   __4__ ones.

So 36 − 24 = 12.

1	2	3	4	5	6	7	8	9	10
11	12	13	14	15	16	17	18	19	20
21	22	23	24	25	26	27	28	29	30
31	32	33	34	35	36	37	38	39	40
41	42	43	44	45	46	47	48	49	50
51	52	53	54	55	56	57	58	59	60
61	62	63	64	65	66	67	68	69	70
71	72	73	74	75	76	77	78	79	80
81	82	83	84	85	86	87	88	89	90
91	92	93	94	95	96	97	98	99	100

HOME ACTIVITY Ask your child to subtract 58 − 23 on a hundred chart and explain how he or she subtracted.

Subtract using the hundred chart.

1. 87 − 7 = _____

2. 79 − 48 = _____

3. 65 − 41 = _____

4. 99 − 52 = _____

5. 35 − 13 = _____

6. _____ = 84 − 33

7. ☐3 − 2☐ = 71

8. 5☐ − ☐1 = 14

9. 78 − ☐5 = 4☐

10. **Look for Patterns** A treasure is hidden under one of the rocks. Follow the clues to find the treasure. Color each rock you land on.

A. Start at 55.	**B.** Subtract 20.
C. Add 5.	**D.** Add 20.
E. Add 10.	**F.** Subtract 5.
G. Subtract 20.	**H.** Add 5.
I. Subtract 20.	**J.** Subtract 5.

```
 1   2   3   4   5   6   7   8   9  10
11  12  13  14  15  16  17  18  19  20
21  22  23  24  25  26  27  28  29  30
31  32  33  34  35  36  37  38  39  40
41  42  43  44  45  46  47  48  49  50
51  52  53  54  55  56  57  58  59  60
61  62  63  64  65  66  67  68  69  70
71  72  73  74  75  76  77  78  79  80
81  82  83  84  85  86  87  88  89  90
91  92  93  94  95  96  97  98  99 100
```

The treasure is hidden under the last rock that you colored. What is the number of that rock? _____
Describe the pattern you see in the numbers you colored.

_____

11. ✓**Assessment** A pan holds 36 biscuits. Kiana put 12 biscuits on the pan. How many more biscuits will fit on the pan?

　Ⓐ 24　　Ⓑ 23　　Ⓒ 22　　Ⓓ 21

12. ✓**Assessment** A garden has room for 22 flowers. Dan needs to plant 11 more flowers to fill the garden. How many flowers did Dan already plant?

　Ⓐ 10　　Ⓑ 11　　Ⓒ 12　　Ⓓ 13

Name _____

Solve & Share

Jesse had 50 balloons at the fair.
A strong wind blew away 30 balloons.
How many balloons does Jesse have left?
Use the number line below to show your work.

I can ...
use an open number line to subtract tens.

I can also reason about math.

POPCORN

_____ ◯ _____ = _____

Find 56 – 20.

You can subtract tens on an open number line. First, place 56 on the number line.

56

One Way

20 is 2 tens. So, count back by 10 two times. Show each 10 on the number line as you count.

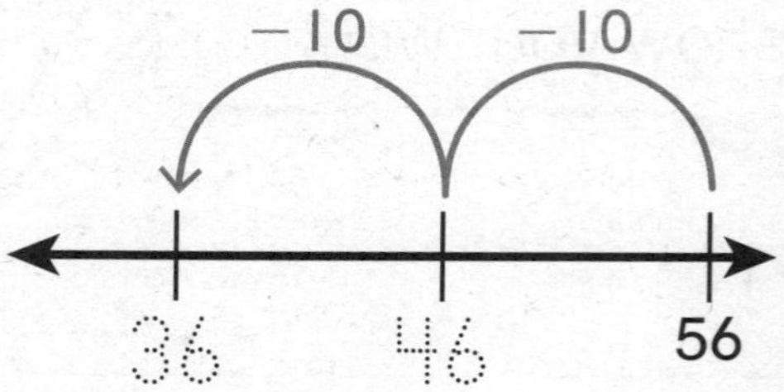

–10   –10

36   46   56

Another Way
Moving back 2 tens from 56 is the same as 56 – 20.

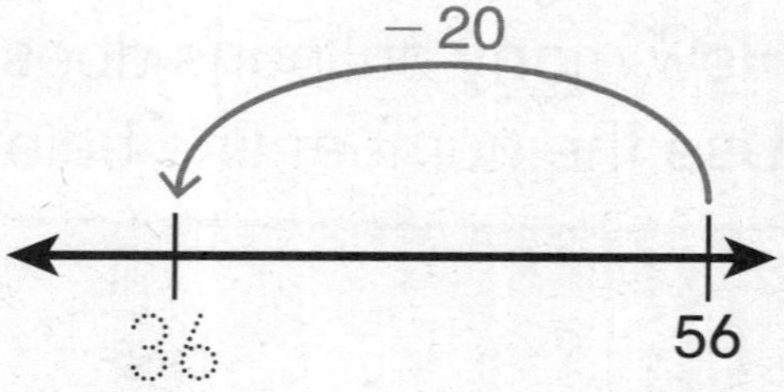

– 20

36   56

You land on 36. So, 56 – 20 = 36.

Do You Understand?

Show Me! How can an open number line help you subtract numbers?

☆ Guided Practice ☆

Use an open number line to find each difference.

1. 70 – 20 = _____

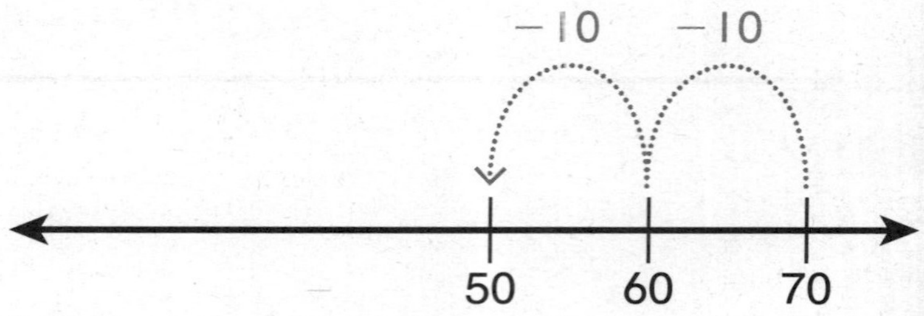

–10   –10

50   60   70

2. 67 – 30 = _____

© Pearson Education, Inc. 2

☆ **Independent Practice** ☆   Use an open number line to find each difference.

3. 60 − 40 = _____

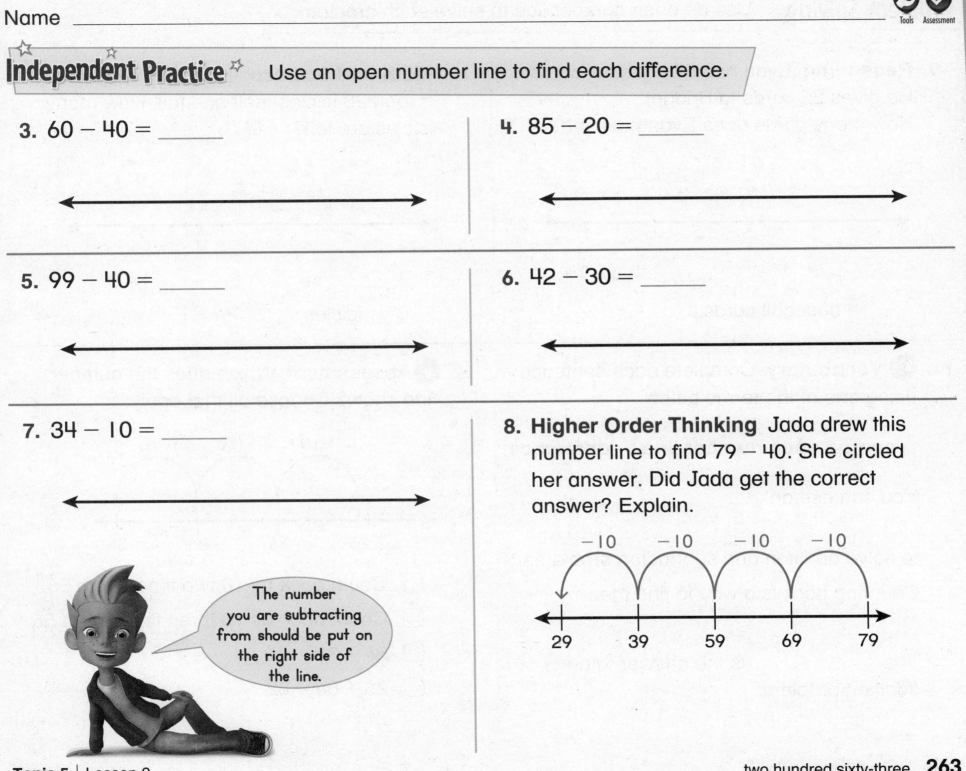

4. 85 − 20 = _____

5. 99 − 40 = _____

6. 42 − 30 = _____

7. 34 − 10 = _____

The number you are subtracting from should be put on the right side of the line.

8. Higher Order Thinking Jada drew this number line to find 79 − 40. She circled her answer. Did Jada get the correct answer? Explain.

−10   −10   −10   −10

29   39   59   69   79

9. **Reasoning** Evan has 62 baseball cards. He gives 30 cards to Bridget. How many cards does Evan have left?

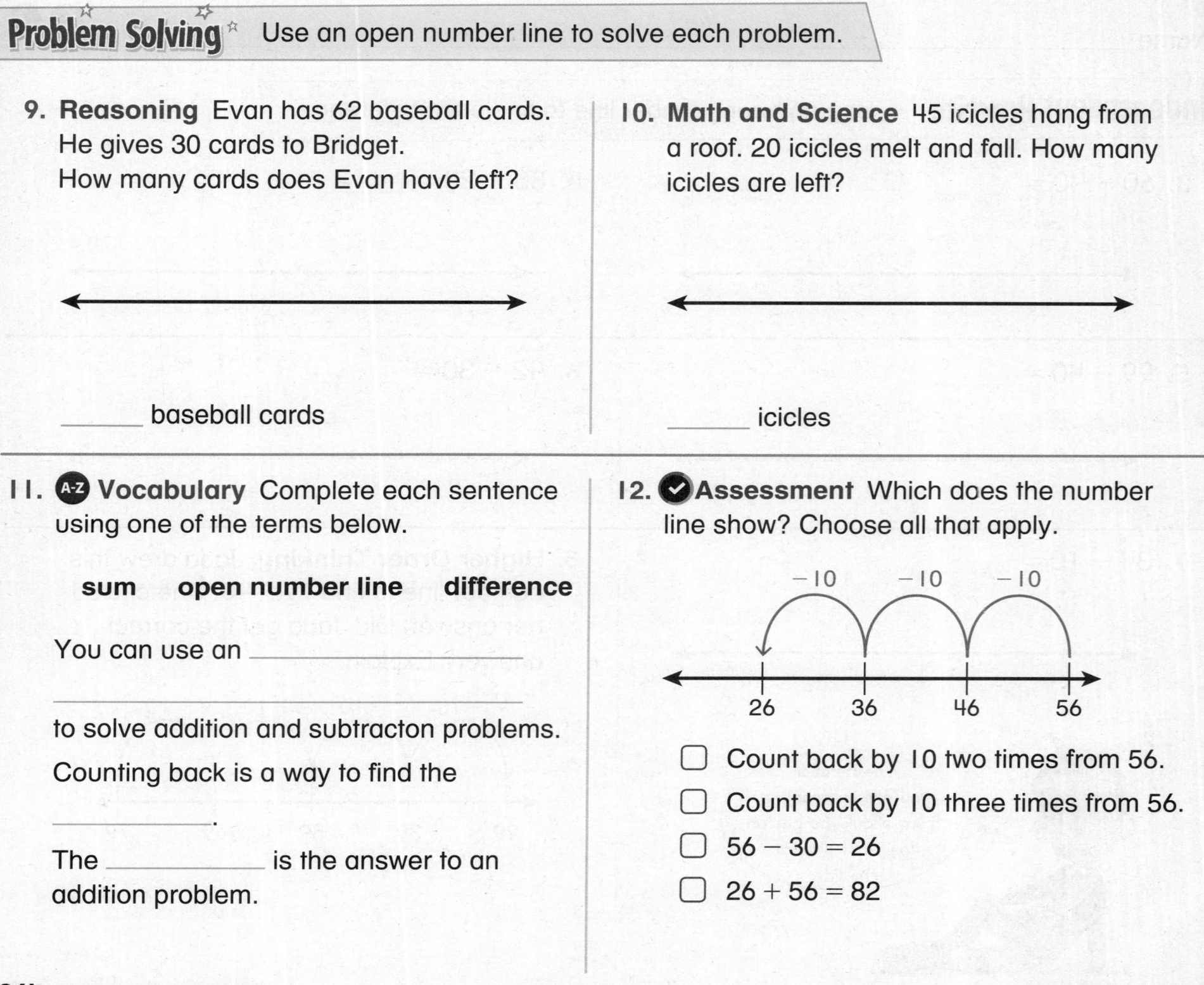

_____ baseball cards

10. **Math and Science** 45 icicles hang from a roof. 20 icicles melt and fall. How many icicles are left?

_____ icicles

11. 🅰🅩 **Vocabulary** Complete each sentence using one of the terms below.

sum   open number line   difference

You can use an _____

_____

to solve addition and subtracton problems.

Counting back is a way to find the

_____.

The _____ is the answer to an addition problem.

12. ✅**Assessment** Which does the number line show? Choose all that apply.

☐ Count back by 10 two times from 56.

☐ Count back by 10 three times from 56.

☐ $56 - 30 = 26$

☐ $26 + 56 = 82$

Name _____

Another Look! Find 45 − 20 using an open number line.

You can use an open number line to make subtracting tens easier.

Place 45 on the number line. Then count back by 10 twice to subtract 20.

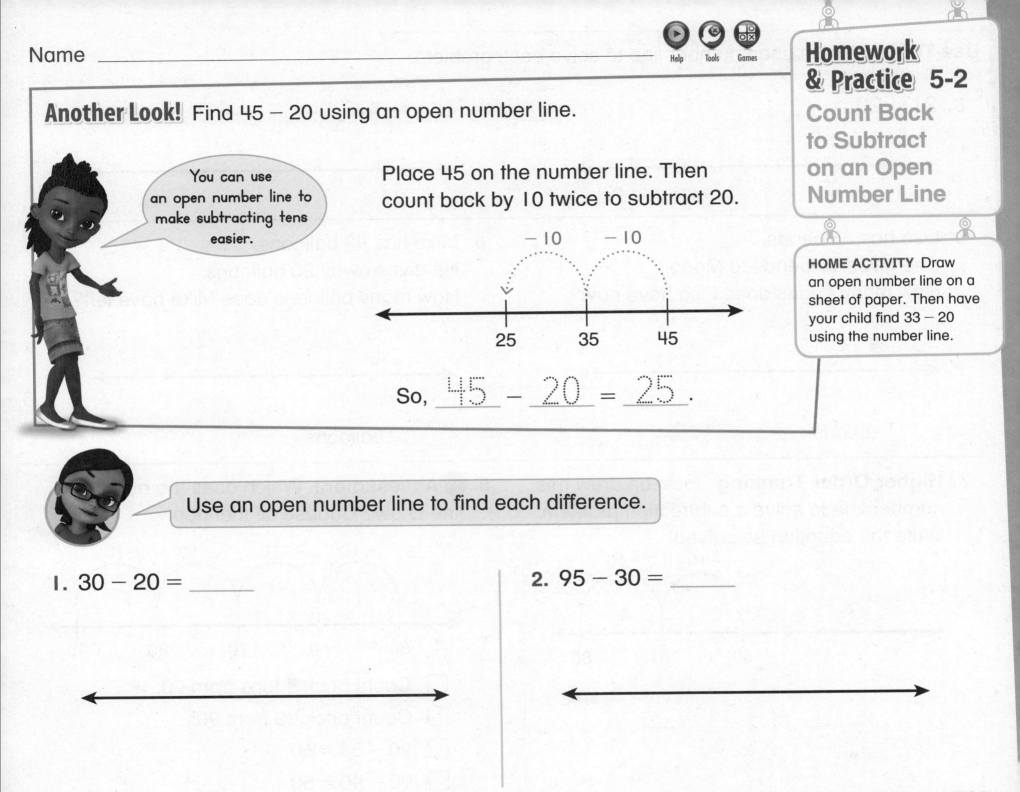

-10 -10

25   35   45

So, 45 − 20 = 25.

HOME ACTIVITY Draw an open number line on a sheet of paper. Then have your child find 33 − 20 using the number line.

Use an open number line to find each difference.

1. 30 − 20 = _____

2. 95 − 30 = _____

Use Tools Use an open number line to solve each problem.

3. 21 − 20 = _____

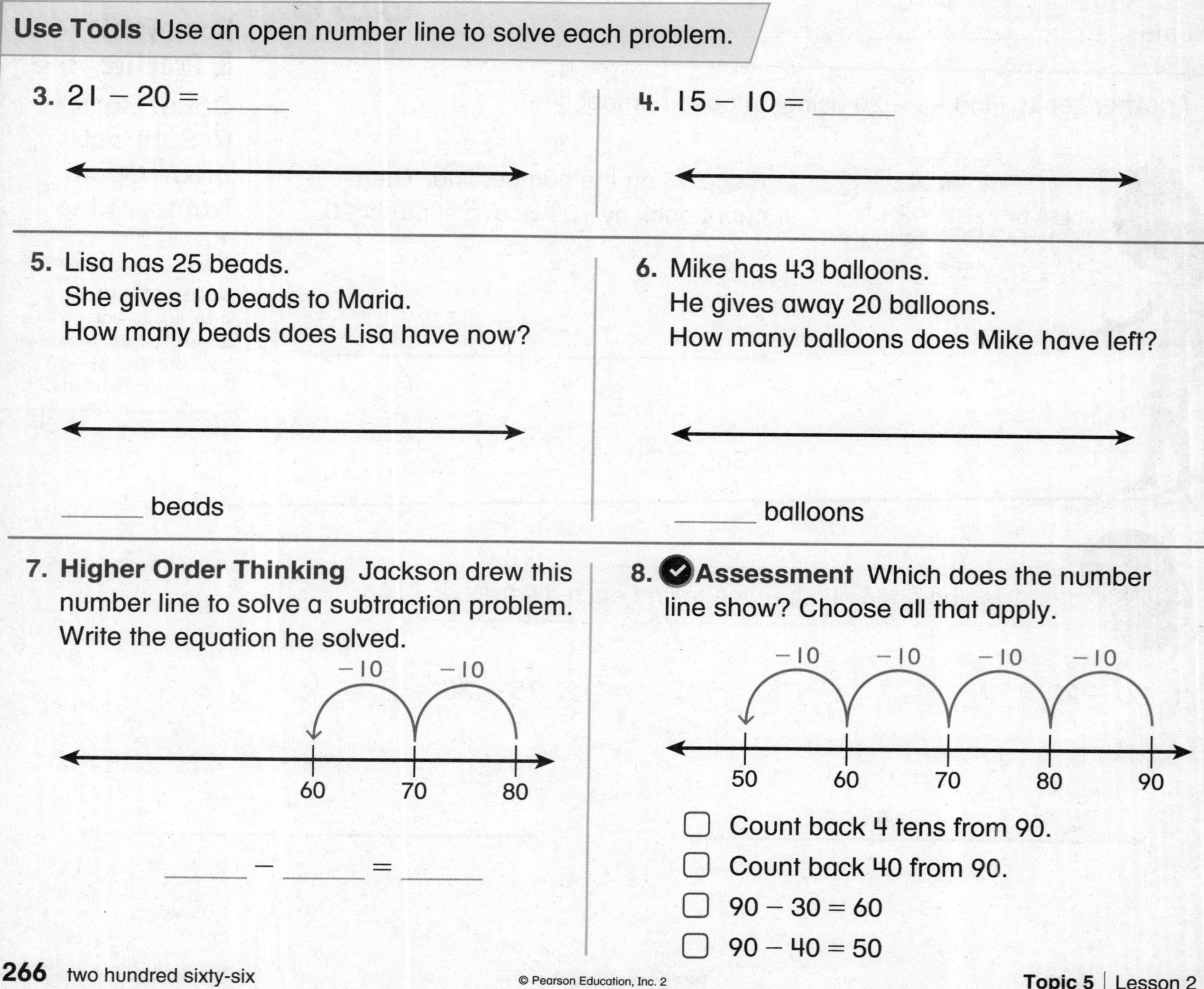

4. 15 − 10 = _____

5. Lisa has 25 beads.
She gives 10 beads to Maria.
How many beads does Lisa have now?

_____ beads

6. Mike has 43 balloons.
He gives away 20 balloons.
How many balloons does Mike have left?

_____ balloons

7. Higher Order Thinking Jackson drew this number line to solve a subtraction problem. Write the equation he solved.

−10   −10

60   70   80

_____ − _____ = _____

8. ✓ **Assessment** Which does the number line show? Choose all that apply.

−10   −10   −10   −10

50   60   70   80   90

☐ Count back 4 tens from 90.
☐ Count back 40 from 90.
☐ 90 − 30 = 60
☐ 90 − 40 = 50

© Pearson Education, Inc. 2

Name _____

Solve & Share

Jeremy had 56 bug stickers.
He gave 24 stickers to Eric.
How many bug stickers does Jeremy have left?
Use the open number line below to show your work.

I can ...
use an open number line to subtract tens and ones.

I can also model with math.

_____ − _____ = _____

Find 68 − 23.

Let's use an open number line and count back. First, place 68 on the line.

68

One Way

23 is 2 tens and 3 ones.
So, count back 2 tens from 68.
58, 48
Then, count back 3 ones from 48.
47, 46, 45

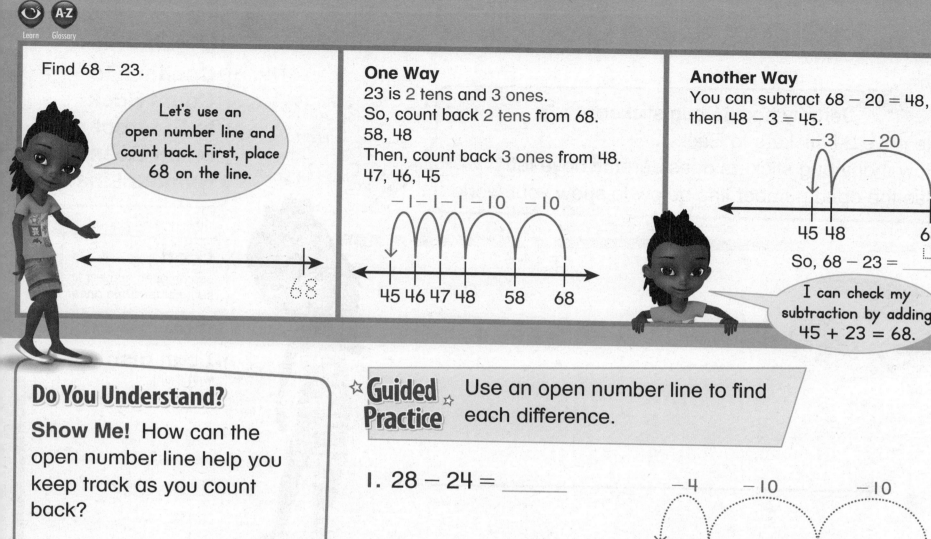

−1 −1 −1 −10 −10

45 46 47 48   58   68

Another Way

You can subtract 68 − 20 = 48,
then 48 − 3 = 45.

−3   −20

45 48   68

So, 68 − 23 = __45__.

I can check my subtraction by adding 45 + 23 = 68.

Do You Understand?

Show Me! How can the open number line help you keep track as you count back?

☆ **Guided Practice** ☆   Use an open number line to find each difference.

1. 28 − 24 = _____

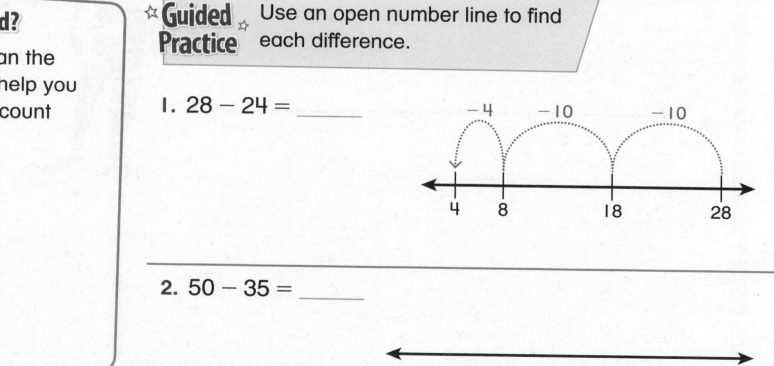

−4   −10   −10

4   8   18   28

2. 50 − 35 = _____

© Pearson Education, Inc. 2

Topic 5 | Lesson 3

Name _____

Independent Practice ✩ Use an open number line to find each difference.

3. 45 − 13 = _____

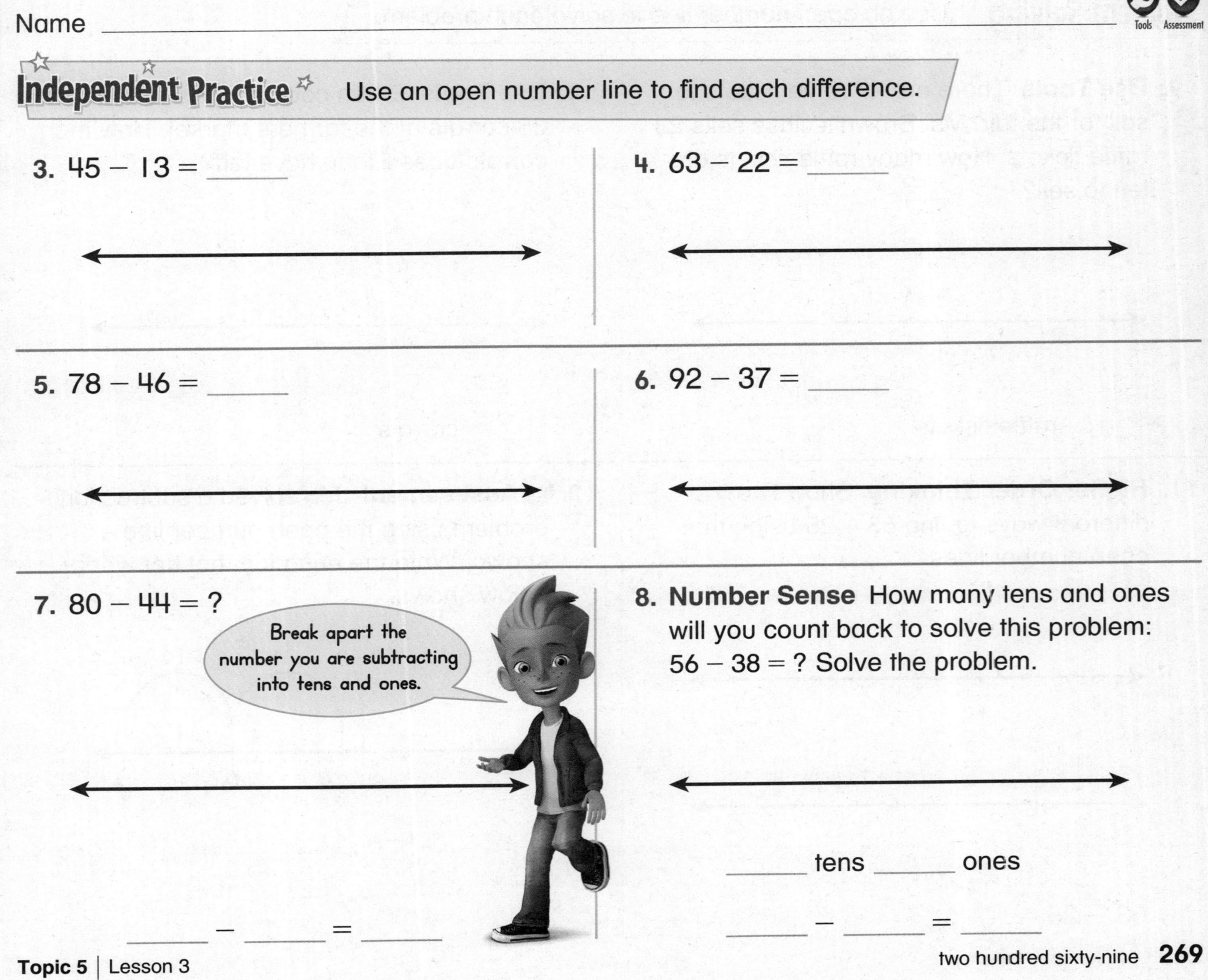

4. 63 − 22 = _____

5. 78 − 46 = _____

6. 92 − 37 = _____

7. 80 − 44 = ?

> Break apart the number you are subtracting into tens and ones.

_____ − _____ = _____

8. Number Sense How many tens and ones will you count back to solve this problem: 56 − 38 = ? Solve the problem.

_____ tens _____ ones

_____ − _____ = _____

9. **Use Tools** There are 47 raffle tickets to sell for the fair. Ms. Brown's class sells 23 raffle tickets. How many raffle tickets are left to sell?

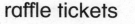

_____ raffle tickets

10. **Use Tools** Ethan counts 78 carrots. He sells 35 carrots at the farmers market. How many carrots does Ethan have left?

_____ carrots

11. **Higher Order Thinking** Show two different ways to find 63 − 25 using the open number lines.

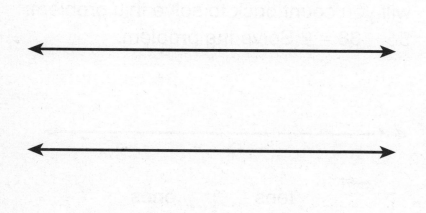

63 − 25 = _____

12. ✅**Assessment** Jen solved a subtraction problem using the open number line shown. Write the equation that her work below shows.

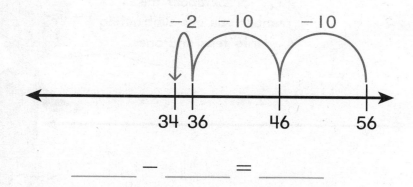

_____ − _____ = _____

© Pearson Education, Inc. 2

Name _____

Another Look! Find 83 − 35.

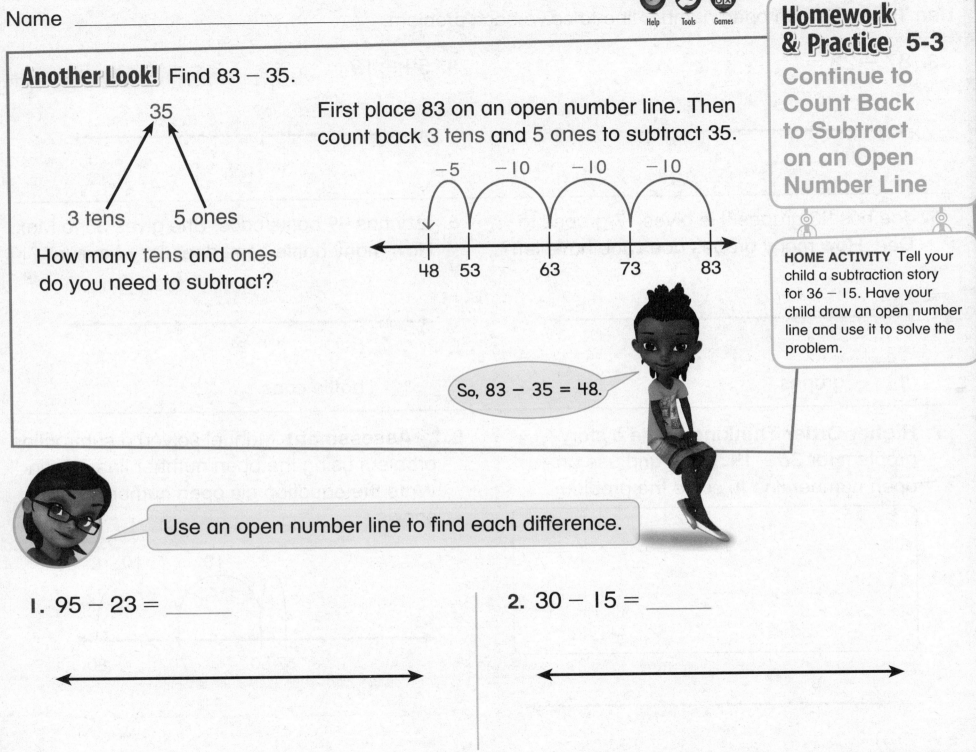

35

3 tens   5 ones

How many tens and ones do you need to subtract?

First place 83 on an open number line. Then count back 3 tens and 5 ones to subtract 35.

−5   −10   −10   −10

48   53   63   73   83

So, 83 − 35 = 48.

HOME ACTIVITY Tell your child a subtraction story for 36 − 15. Have your child draw an open number line and use it to solve the problem.

Use an open number line to find each difference.

1. 95 − 23 = _____

2. 30 − 15 = _____

Use Tools Use an open number line to solve each problem.

3. 87 − 23 = _____

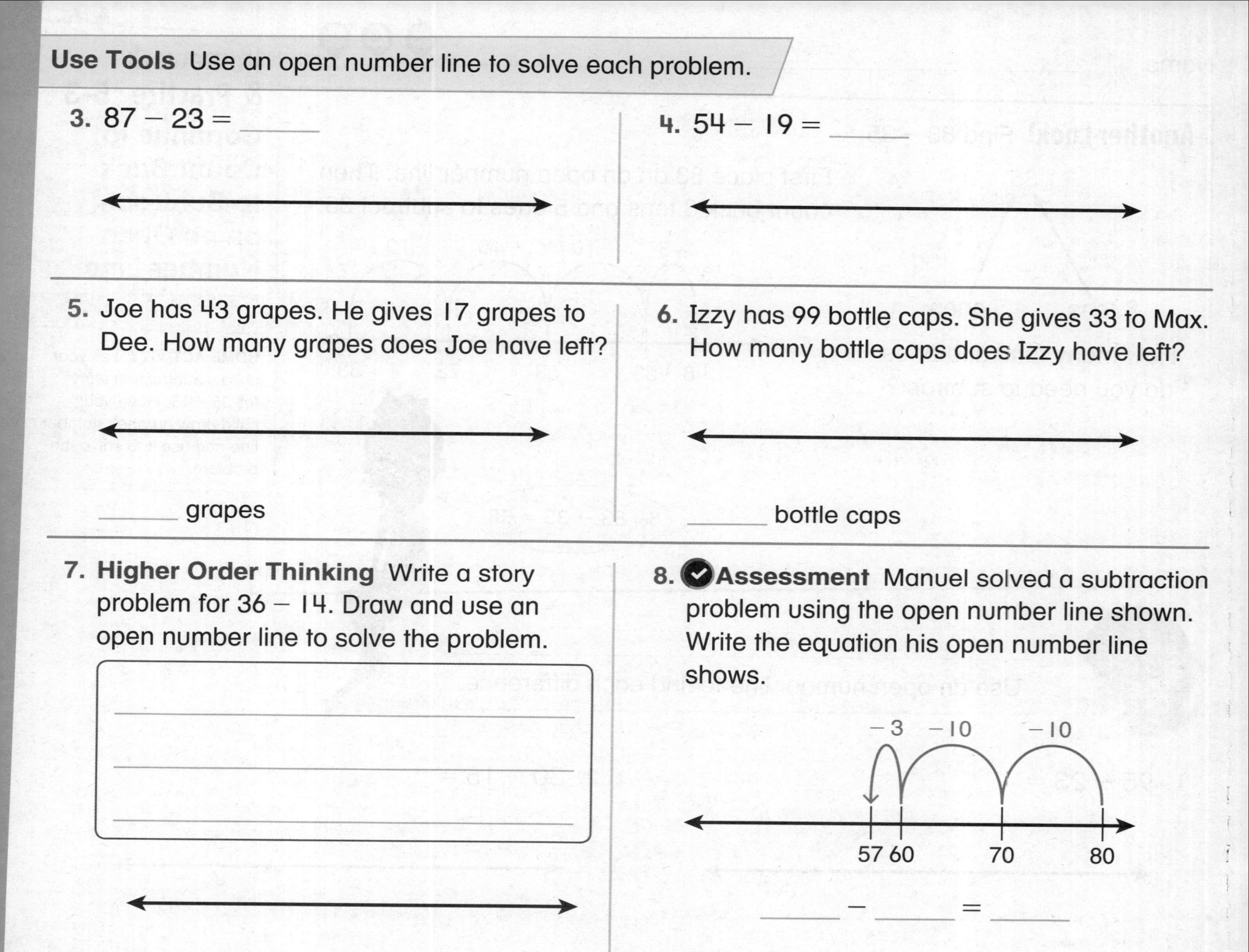

4. 54 − 19 = _____

5. Joe has 43 grapes. He gives 17 grapes to Dee. How many grapes does Joe have left?

_____ grapes

6. Izzy has 99 bottle caps. She gives 33 to Max. How many bottle caps does Izzy have left?

_____ bottle caps

7. Higher Order Thinking Write a story problem for 36 − 14. Draw and use an open number line to solve the problem.

8. ✓**Assessment** Manuel solved a subtraction problem using the open number line shown. Write the equation his open number line shows.

− 3   − 10   − 10

57 60   70   80

_____ − _____ = _____

© Pearson Education, Inc. 2

Name _____

Solve & Share

There are 50 children at the park. 28 are boys and the rest are girls. How many girls are at the park?

Use the open number line to solve. Show your work.

I can ...
add up to subtract using an open number line.

I can also use math tools correctly.

⟵————————————————————⟶

_____ ◯ _____ = _____

Find 57 − 28.

You can add up from 28 to subtract. Place 28 on the number line first.

28

You can add 2 to get to 30.

Then add 10, and 10 again, to get to 50.

Then add 7 to land on 57.

+2 +10 +10 +7

28 30 40 50 57

Add the tens and ones.

$2 + 10 + 10 + 7 = 29$

So, $57 − 28 = 29$.

I can check by adding!
$28 + 29 = 57$

Do You Understand?

Show Me! How can you add up to find 42 − 17?

☆ Guided Practice ☆ Add up to find each difference. Use an open number line.

1. 45 − 27 = _____

+3 +10 +5

27 30 40 45

2. 66 − 39 = _____

© Pearson Education, Inc. 2

Independent Practice — Add up to find each difference. Use an open number line.

3. 41 − 19 = _____

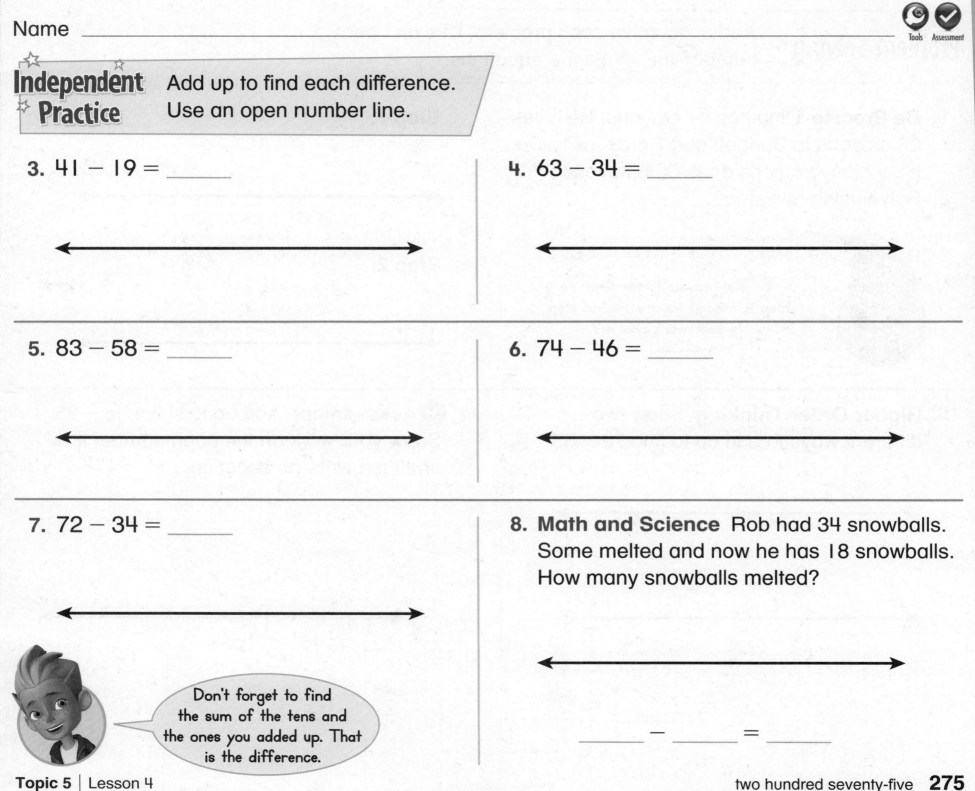

4. 63 − 34 = _____

5. 83 − 58 = _____

6. 74 − 46 = _____

7. 72 − 34 = _____

8. Math and Science Rob had 34 snowballs. Some melted and now he has 18 snowballs. How many snowballs melted?

_____ − _____ = _____

Don't forget to find the sum of the tens and the ones you added up. That is the difference.

9. **Be Precise** Dino has 41 crayons. He gives 23 crayons to Bridget, and 7 crayons to Dan. How many crayons does Dino have left? Solve using two steps.

The answer to the first step is needed for the second step. Is your work precise?

Step 1: _____ ◯ _____ = _____

Step 2: _____ ◯ _____ = _____

---

10. **Higher Order Thinking** Show two different ways to add up to find 72 − 35.

_____ − _____ = _____

11. ✔**Assessment** Add up to solve 46 − 25. Show your work on the open number line and then write an equation.

_____ − _____ = _____

© Pearson Education, Inc. 2

Name _____

Help Tools Games

Homework & Practice 5-4

Add Up
to Subtract
Using an Open
Number Line

Another Look!

You can add up on an open number line to subtract 73 − 45.

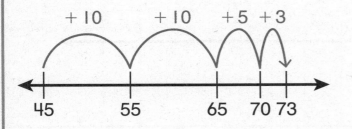

So, 73 − 45 = 28.

You can start at 45. Add 10, and 10 again, to get to 65.
Then add 5 to get to 70. Then add 3 to get to 73.

Add tens and ones to find the difference:

<u>10</u> + <u>10</u> + <u>5</u> + <u>3</u> = <u>28</u>

HOME ACTIVITY Have your child tell a story about 52 − 34. Tell your child to solve the problem by adding up on an open number line. Then, have your child write an equation to show the answer.

Add up to find each difference. Use an open number line.

1. 93 − 65 = _____

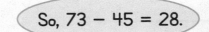

2. 84 − 67 = _____

Add up to solve each problem. Use an open number line. Write the equations.

3. **Use Tools** Misha has 36 bows. She gives 19 bows to Alice. How many bows does Misha have left?

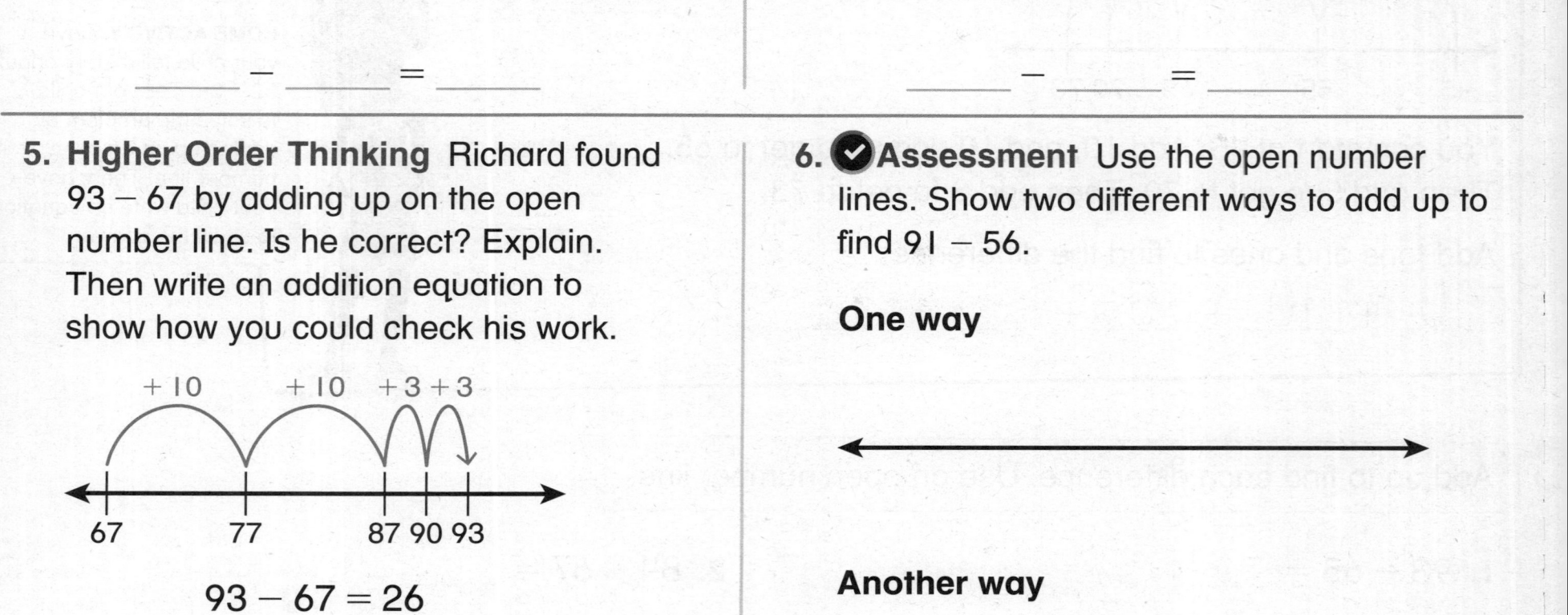

_____ – _____ = _____

4. **Use Tools** Remi has 80 golf balls. He hits 53 of them. How many golf balls does Remi have left?

_____ – _____ = _____

5. **Higher Order Thinking** Richard found 93 – 67 by adding up on the open number line. Is he correct? Explain. Then write an addition equation to show how you could check his work.

+10   +10   +3 +3

67   77   87 90 93

93 – 67 = 26

_____ ◯ _____ = _____

6. ✅**Assessment** Use the open number lines. Show two different ways to add up to find 91 – 56.

One way

Another way

91 – 56 = _____

Name _____

Solve & Share

Don wants to find 42 − 7 by breaking apart the 7 into two numbers. Use and draw place-value blocks to show how Don could find the difference.

I can ...
break apart 1-digit numbers to help me subtract mentally.

I can also 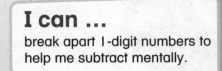 break apart problems.

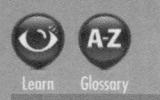

$33 - 6 = ?$

You can break apart the number you are subtracting to find the difference.

Here are 3 ways to break apart 6. Which is best for subtracting 6 from 33?

$$\underset{1 + 5}{6} \qquad \underset{2 + 4}{6} \qquad \underset{3 + 3}{6}$$

$33 - 6 = \underline{\hspace{2cm}} ?$

$$\underset{3 \qquad 3}{33 - 6}$$

Start at 33. Subtract 3 to get to 30. Then subtract 3 more.

11	12	13	14	15	16	17	18	19	20
21	22	23	24	25	26	27	28	29	30
31	32	33	34	35	36	37	38	39	40

$33 - 6 = \underline{27}$

Do You Understand?

Show Me! Look at the problem above. Why wasn't the 6 broken apart into $1 + 5$ to find $33 - 6$?

☆ Guided Practice ☆

Subtract. Break apart the number you are subtracting. Show your work.

1. $43 - 9 = \underline{\hspace{1.5cm}}$

   [ ]   [ ]

2. $\underline{\hspace{1.5cm}} = 24 - 6$

   [ ]   [ ]

11	12	13	14	15	16	17	18	19	20
21	22	23	24	25	26	27	28	29	30
31	32	33	34	35	36	37	38	39	40
41	42	43	44	45	46	47	48	49	50

© Pearson Education, Inc. 2
Topic 5 | Lesson 5

Independent Practice

Subtract. Break apart the number you are subtracting.
Show your work. Use a hundred chart if needed.

3. $35 - 8 =$ _____

☐ ☐

4. $41 - 5 =$ _____

☐ ☐

5. _____ $= 82 - 7$

☐ ☐

6. $53 - 7 =$ _____

☐ ☐

7. $97 - 8 =$ _____

☐ ☐

8. $64 - 9 =$ _____

☐ ☐

9. $86 - 8 =$ _____

10. _____ $= 32 - 9$

11. $93 - 6 =$ _____

12. **Algebra** One number makes both equations true.
Find the missing number.

$48 +$ ☐ $= 56$ $56 -$ ☐ $= 48$

The missing number is _____.

Think about how addition and subtraction are related.

13. Explain Karen has 7 pencils. Karen's teacher has 45 pencils. How many fewer pencils does Karen have than her teacher? Explain how you solved the problem.

_____

_____

_____

_____ fewer pencils

Is your explanation clear?

14. Higher Order Thinking Write a story problem about $63 - 8$. Then solve.

_____

_____

_____

_____

$63 - 8 = $ _____

15. ✓**Assessment** Duane has 24 seashells. He gives 9 shells to his cousin Rob. How many seashells does Duane have now?

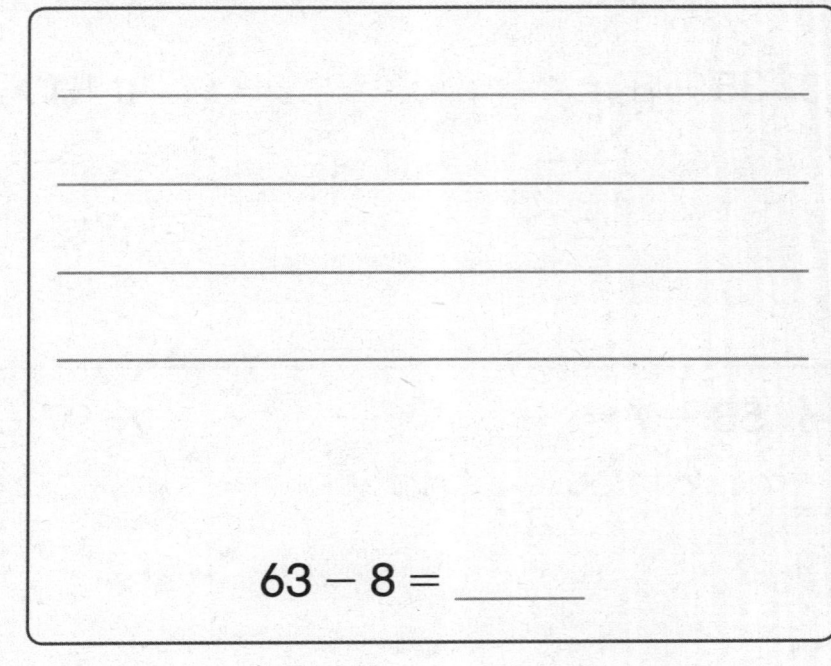

$24 - 9 = ?$

Ⓐ 16   Ⓒ 14

Ⓑ 15   Ⓓ 13

© Pearson Education, Inc. 2

Name _____

Another Look! Find $55 - 8$.

You can break apart 8 to find $55 - 8$.

One way is $8 = 5 + 3$.

There is a 5 in the ones place in 55. It's easy to subtract $55 - 5$.

$$55 - 5 = 50$$

Next, subtract $50 - 3$. You can count back 3 from 50.

$$50 - 3 = 47$$

So, $55 - 8 = 47$.

HOME ACTIVITY Ask your child to show you how to break apart the 5 in $43 - 5$ to find the difference.

Subtract. Break apart the number you are subtracting. Show your work.

1. $65 - 9 =$ _____

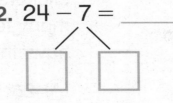

2. $24 - 7 =$ _____

3. _____ $= 84 - 8$

Explain Subtract. Break apart the number you are subtracting. Show your work to explain your thinking.

4. $41 - 5 = $ _____

5. _____ $= 94 - 8$

6. $25 - 9 = $ _____

7. **Higher Order Thinking** The table shows how many spools of thread Smith's Fabric Store sold on Monday.

Before the sale, there were 34 red spools and 53 black spools. How many red spools were left at the end of Monday? How many black spools were left?

_____ red spools   _____ black spools

Spools of Thread Sold	
Thread Color	Number of Spools
Red	8
Blue	7
Black	6

8. ✓**Assessment** Ron has 21 comic books. He sells 6 of them to a friend. How many comic books does Ron have now?

Ⓐ 17
Ⓑ 16
Ⓒ 15
Ⓓ 14

9. ✓**Assessment** Yelena has 5 animal stickers. Vera has 41 animal stickers. How many fewer animal stickers does Yelena have than Vera?

Ⓐ 26
Ⓑ 34
Ⓒ 35
Ⓓ 36

© Pearson Education, Inc. 2

Name _____

Solve & Share

Gina wants to find 53 − 28 by breaking apart 28 into two numbers. Use place-value blocks and the hundred chart to show how Gina could find the difference.

I can ...
break apart 2-digit numbers to help me subtract.

I can also break apart problems.

21	22	23	24	25	26	27	28	29	30
31	32	33	34	35	36	37	38	39	40
41	42	43	44	45	46	47	48	49	50
51	52	53	54	55	56	57	58	59	60
61	62	63	64	65	66	67	68	69	70

$81 - 27 = ?$

You can use place value to break apart the number you are subtracting.

Break apart 27 into tens and ones. Then break apart the ones.

27
20 + 7

1 + 6

$81 - 27 = $ ___ ?

20   7

1   6

Start at 81.
Subtract 20 to get to 61.
Then subtract 1 to get to 60.
Then subtract 6 more.

51	52	53	54	55	56	57	58	59	60
61	62	63	64	65	66	67	68	69	70
71	72	73	74	75	76	77	78	79	80
81	82	83	84	85	86	87	88	89	90

So, $81 - 27 = $ 54.

Do You Understand?

Show Me! How do you decide how to break apart the ones?

☆ **Guided Practice** ☆ Subtract. Break apart the number you are subtracting. Show your work.

1. $54 - 26 = $ _____

2. $43 - 18 = $ _____

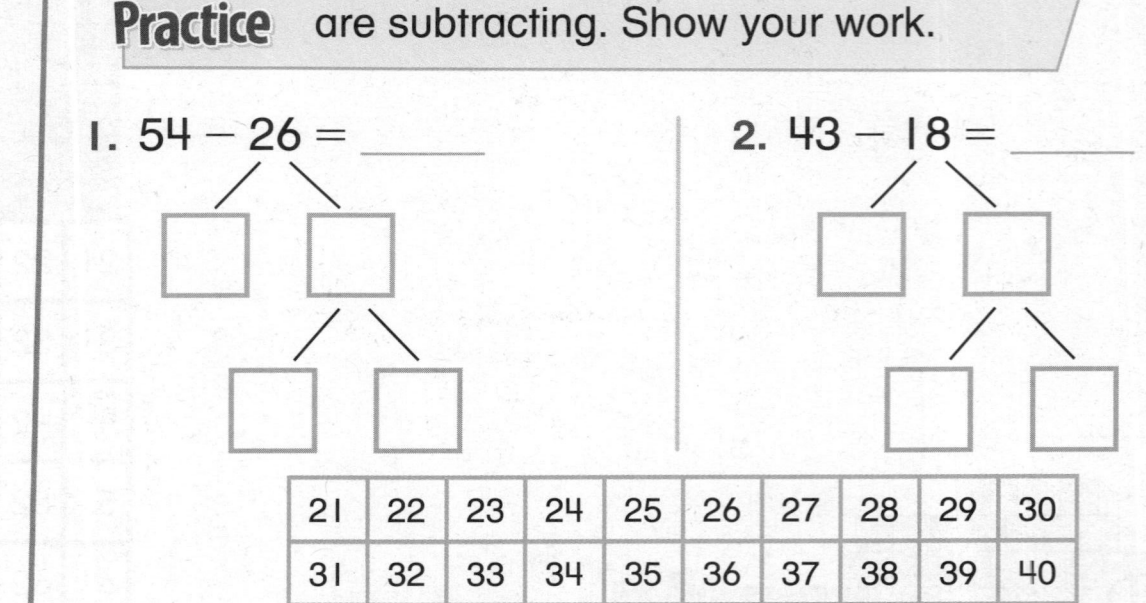

21	22	23	24	25	26	27	28	29	30
31	32	33	34	35	36	37	38	39	40
41	42	43	44	45	46	47	48	49	50
51	52	53	54	55	56	57	58	59	60

Independent Practice

Subtract. Break apart the number you are subtracting. Show your work. Use a hundred chart if needed.

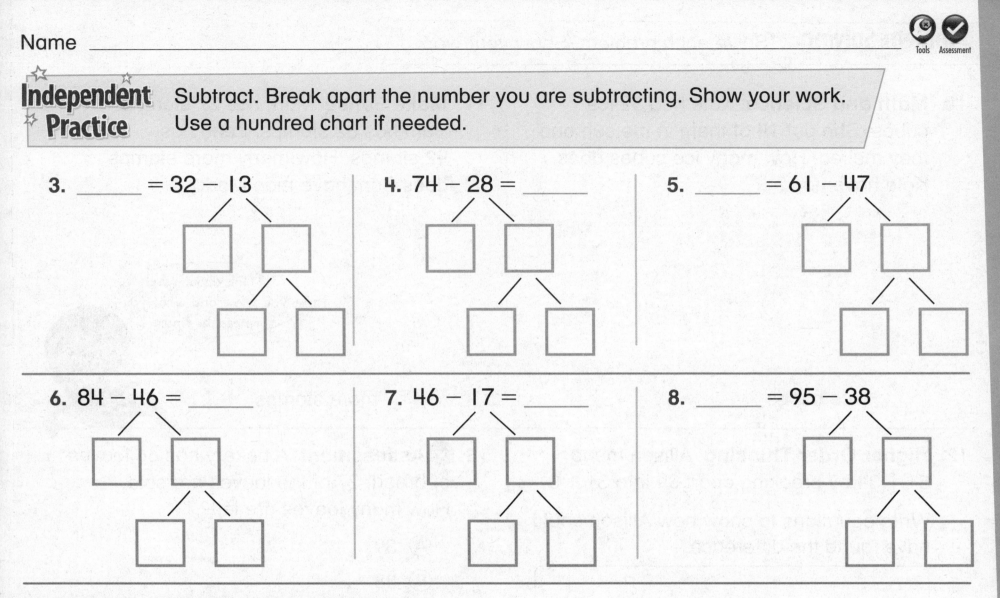

3. _____ = 32 − 13

4. 74 − 28 = _____

5. _____ = 61 − 47

6. 84 − 46 = _____

7. 46 − 17 = _____

8. _____ = 95 − 38

9. **Higher Order Thinking** Tina found 53 − 27 by breaking apart 27 into 23 and 4. Does Tina's way work?

Show another way you could break apart 27 to find 53 − 27. Then find the difference.

10. **Math and Science** Kate had 32 ice cubes. She put 14 of them in the sun and they melted. How many ice cubes does Kate have now?

_____ ice cubes

11. **Make Sense** Mark has 27 stamps. Sam has 82 stamps. Lena has 42 stamps. How many more stamps does Sam have than Mark?

> Think about what you know and what you need to find.

_____ more stamps

12. **Higher Order Thinking** Allison found 51 − 34 by breaking apart 34 into 31 + 3.

Write equations to show how Allison could have found the difference.

13. ✅**Assessment** A bakery has 66 loaves of bread. 27 of the loaves are sold. How many loaves are left?

Ⓐ 39

Ⓑ 38

Ⓒ 37

Ⓓ 36

Name _____

Another Look! Find 43 − 27.

To find 43 − 27, you can break apart 27. One way is 20 + 7.

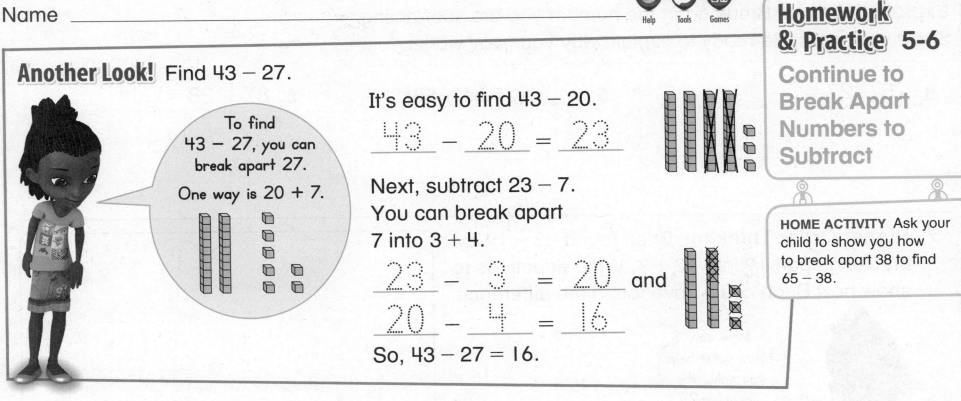

It's easy to find 43 − 20.

43 − 20 = 23

Next, subtract 23 − 7. You can break apart 7 into 3 + 4.

23 − 3 = 20 and

20 − 4 = 16

So, 43 − 27 = 16.

HOME ACTIVITY Ask your child to show you how to break apart 38 to find 65 − 38.

Subtract. Break apart the number you are subtracting. Show your work to explain your thinking.

1. 76 − 29 = _____

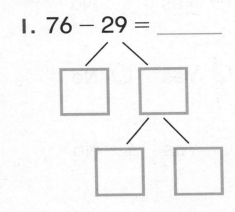

2. _____ = 82 − 39

3. 92 − 16 = _____

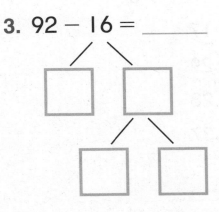

4. 75 − 27 = _____

5. _____ = 61 − 34

6. 87 − 28 = _____

7. **Higher Order Thinking** Brian found 42 − 19 by breaking apart 19 into 12 + 7. Write equations to show how Brian could have found the difference.

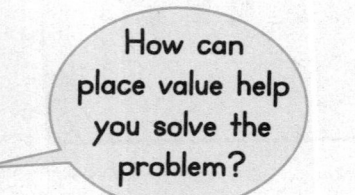

How can place value help you solve the problem?

8. ✔**Assessment** Rosita has 55 grapes. She gives a friend 26 of her grapes. How many grapes does Rosita have now?

Ⓐ 17

Ⓑ 29

Ⓒ 28

Ⓓ 37

9. ✔**Assessment** Can you use the equations to find 86 − 27? Choose Yes or No.

86 − 20 = 66   ○ Yes   ○ No
66 − 7 = 59

26 − 10 = 16   ○ Yes   ○ No
16 − 6 = 10

86 − 20 = 66   ○ Yes   ○ No
66 − 6 = 60
60 − 1 = 59

Name _____

Solve & Share

Yuri found 86 − 29 using mental math.
He changed 29 so it would be easier to find the difference.

Show how Yuri could have found the difference.
Explain how he could have used mental math.

Lesson 5-7
Subtract Using Compensation

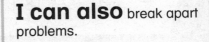

I can ...
make numbers that are easier to subtract, then use mental math to find the difference.

I can also break apart problems.

43 − 18 = ?

You can use compensation to make numbers that are easier to subtract.

It is easier to subtract 20, than 18.

One Way Add 2 to both numbers. Then subtract using mental math.

$$43 \quad - \quad 18 \quad = \quad ?$$
$$\downarrow +2 \qquad \downarrow +2$$
$$45 \quad - \quad 20 \quad = \quad 25$$

So, 43 − 18 = 25.

Another Way Add 2 to 18. Then subtract using mental math. Then add 2 to find the answer.

$$43 - 18 = ?$$
$$\downarrow +2$$
$$43 - 20 = 23$$
$$\qquad\qquad \downarrow +2$$
So, 43 − 18 = 25.

I subtracted 2 more than 18, so I need to add 2 to 23 to find the answer.

Do You Understand?

Show Me! Marc says to find 61 − 13, it's easier to subtract 10 instead of 13. He says if you subtract 3 from 13 to get 10, you must subtract 3 more from your answer. Do you agree? Explain.

☆ Guided Practice ☆

Use compensation to make numbers that are easier to subtract. Then solve. Show your work.

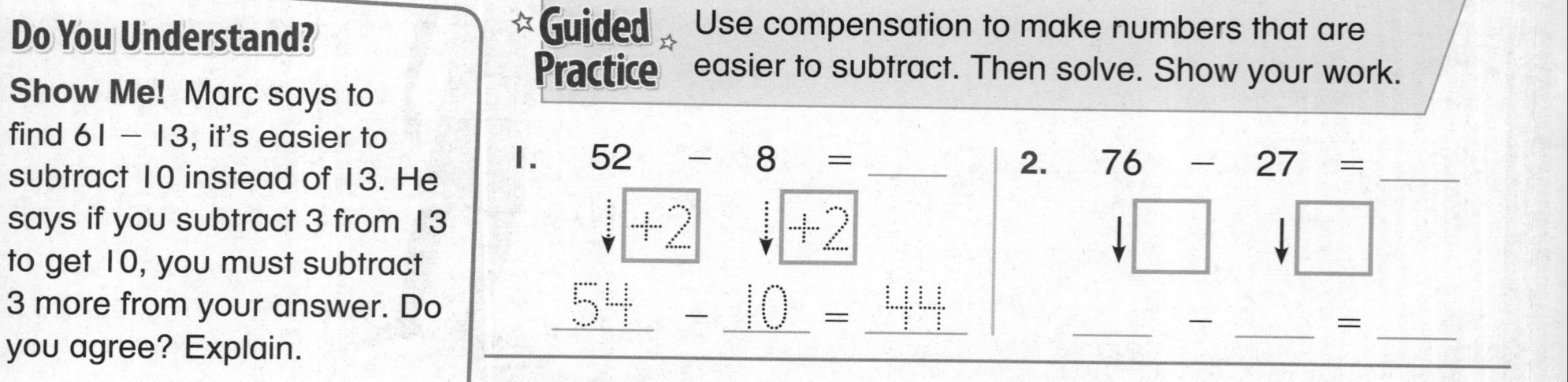

1. 52 − 8 = _____
    $\downarrow$ +2 $\downarrow$ +2
    54 − 10 = 44

2. 76 − 27 = _____
    $\downarrow$ ☐ $\downarrow$ ☐
    _____ − _____ = _____

3. 52 − 15 = _____
    $\downarrow$ +5
    52 − 20 = 32 ──▸ 37
    +5

4. 93 − 39 = _____
    $\downarrow$ ☐
    _____ ○ _____ = _____ ──▸ 54
    ☐

© Pearson Education, Inc. 2
Topic 5 | Lesson 7

Name _____

Independent Practice

Use compensation to make numbers that are easier to subtract. Then solve. Show your work.

5. 73 − 9 = ____

□

____ ○ ____ = ____ → 64

□

6. 35 − 16 = ____

□

____ ○ ____ = → 19

□

7. 43 − 28 = ____

□

____ ○ ____ = ____ → 15

□

8. 51 − 27 = ____

□   □

____ − ____ = ____

9. 74 − 35 = ____

□   □

____ − ____ = ____

10. 99 − 21 = ____

□   □

____ − ____ = ____

11. **Higher Order Thinking** Yoshi says that to find 91 − 32, she can subtract 2 from both numbers. Then subtract using mental math. She says the answer is 59. Do you agree?

Problem Solving ☆ Solve each problem. Show your thinking.

12. **Make Sense** There were some buttons in a jar. Mrs. Kim puts 19 more buttons in the same jar. Now there are 45 buttons in the jar. How many buttons were in the jar to begin with?

_____ buttons

13. Romi has 42 cards. Lisa has 75 cards. How many more cards does Lisa have than Romi?

_____ more cards

Think about what you are trying to find.

14. **Higher Order Thinking** Greg found $72 - 24$. First he subtracted 20 because he thinks it is easier. Use words and numbers to explain how Greg could have found the difference.

15. ✅ **Assessment** Use the numbers on the cards. Write the missing numbers to solve the problem.

| 2 | 25 | 30 | 55 |

$$53 \quad - \quad 28 \quad = \text{\_\_\_\_\_}$$

$$+\ 2 \qquad +\ \boxed{}$$

$$\text{\_\_\_\_\_} \quad - \quad \text{\_\_\_\_\_} \quad = \text{\_\_\_\_\_}$$

© Pearson Education, Inc. 2

Topic 5 | Lesson 7

Name _____

Another Look! You can use compensation to find $64 - 27$.

27 is close to ___30___.

$27 + $ __3__ $ = $ __30__

It's easy to find $64 - 30$.

$64 - 27 = ?$

$\downarrow + 3$

$64 - 30 = 34 \rightarrow 37$

$+ 3$

So, $64 - 27 = $ __37__.

Since I subtracted 30, I subtracted 3 more than 27.

So, I need to add 3 to 34 to find the answer.

HOME ACTIVITY Ask your child to show you how to use compensation to find $82 - 49$.

Use compensation to make numbers that are easier to subtract. Then solve. Show your thinking.

1.
$65 \quad - \quad 48 = $ _____

$\downarrow$ ☐

___ ◯ ___ = ___ $\rightarrow 17$

☐

2.
$96 \quad - \quad 37 = $ _____

$\downarrow$ ☐

___ ◯ ___ = ___ $\rightarrow 59$

☐

3.
$24 \quad - \quad 18 = $ _____

$\downarrow$ ☐

___ ◯ ___ = ___ $\rightarrow 6$

☐

Solve each problem. Show your work.

4. **Make Sense** A store had 45 hats for sale. On Friday, 26 of the hats were still for sale. How many hats sold? Think about what you are trying to find.

_____ hats

5. **A-Z Vocabulary** Complete each sentence using one of the terms below.

regroup   **subtract**

To find 56 + 38, you can _____ 14 ones as 1 ten and 4 ones.

You can use compensation to help you add and _____ mentally.

6. **Higher Order Thinking** Use compensation to find 93 − 78. Use words, pictures, or numbers to explain how you found the difference.

7. **✓ Assessment** Use the numbers on the cards. Write the missing numbers to solve the problem.

| 2 | 29 | 31 | 50 |

81 − 52 = _____

$\downarrow$ − 2

81 ◯ ☐ = ☐ → ☐

☐

Name _____

Solve & Share

Some frogs were sitting on a pond.
16 more frogs joined them.
Now there are 49 frogs on the pond.
How many frogs were on the pond at first?
Show how you know.

I can ...
solve one- and two-step problems using addition or subtraction.

I can also use math tools correctly.

_____ frogs

Brian had some baseball cards. Eric gave Brian 6 more cards. Now Brian has 15 cards. How many baseball cards did Brian have at first?

You can use a model to keep track of the numbers.

You know the whole and one part.

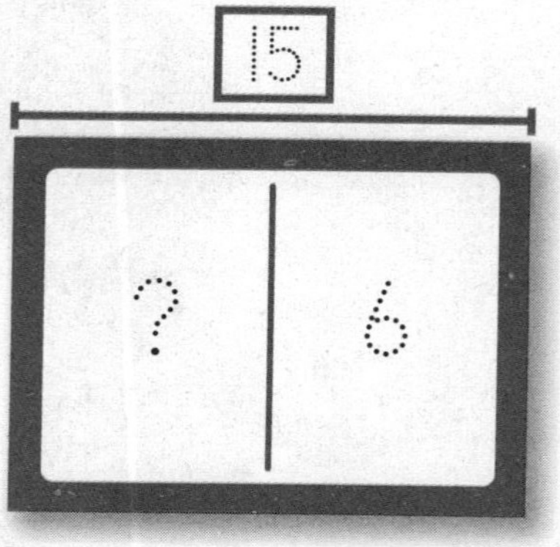

15

? | 6

You can use addition or subtraction to solve the problem.

$\underline{9} + 6 = 15$

or

$15 - 6 = \underline{9}$

So, Brian had $\underline{9}$ cards at first.

Check that your answer makes sense.

Brian had 9 cards. Then Eric gave him 6 more cards. Now he has 15 cards.

$9 + 6 = 15$

My answer makes sense!

Do You Understand?

Show Me! Cory scored some points. Then he scored 8 more points. He scored 14 points in all. How many points did Cory score at first? How can you solve the problem?

☆ Guided Practice ☆

Complete both equations to solve the problem. Use the model to help you.

1. Some people got on the bus at the first stop.
9 more people got on the bus at the second stop.
There are 21 people on the bus now.
How many people got on the bus at the first stop?

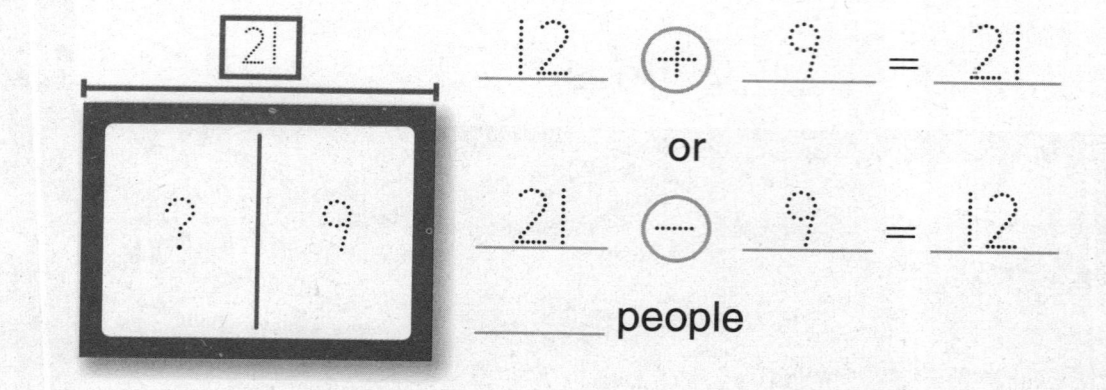

21

? | 9

$\underline{12} \oplus \underline{9} = \underline{21}$

or

$\underline{21} \ominus \underline{9} = \underline{12}$

_____ people

Independent Practice ☆ Solve each problem. Show your work.

2. Mr. Wing's class collected some cans to recycle on Tuesday. They collected 18 more cans on Wednesday. The class collected 44 cans in all. How many cans did the class collect on Tuesday?

You can use addition or subtraction to solve this problem.

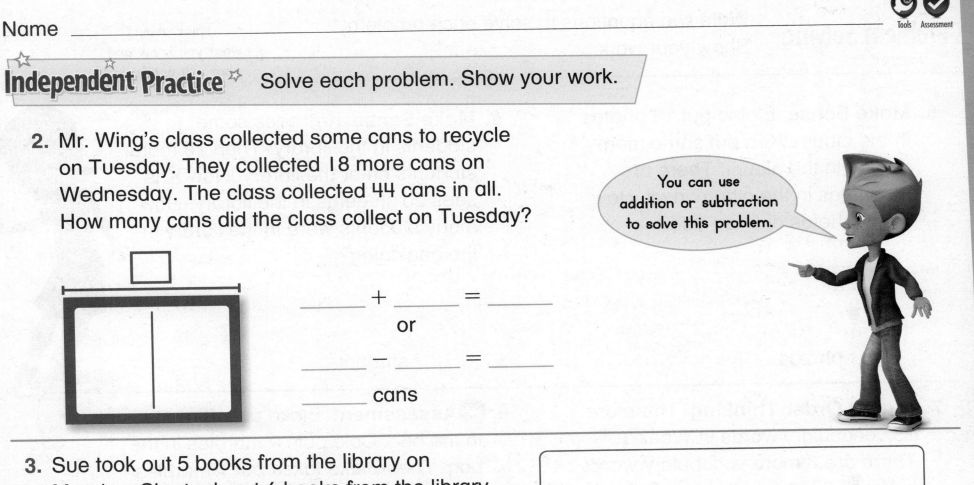

_____ + _____ = _____

or

_____ − _____ = _____

_____ cans

3. Sue took out 5 books from the library on Monday. She took out 6 books from the library on Tuesday. Then she returned 3 books on Wednesday. How many books does Sue have on Thursday?

_____ books

4. **Higher Order Thinking** There are 24 peas on Kim's plate. Kim eats 15 peas. Then Kim's mother puts 8 more peas on her plate. How many peas are on Kim's plate now?

Step 1

_____ − _____ = _____

Step 2

_____ + _____ = _____

_____ peas

Write two equations to solve each problem. Show your work.

Think about what you know and what you are trying to find.

5. **Make Sense** Elaine put 13 photos in the album. Ken put some more photos in the album. There are 32 photos in the album in all. How many photos did Ken add?

_____ photos

6. **Make Sense** Kris sees some students in the library. Then 10 more students enter the library. Now Kris sees 20 students in the library. How many students were in the library in the beginning?

_____ students

7. **Higher Order Thinking** There are 15 vocabulary words in Week 1. There are 8 more vocabulary words in Week 2 than in Week 1.

How many words are there in both weeks?

Step 1: _____ + _____ = _____

Step 2: _____ + _____ = _____

_____ words

8. ✅ **Assessment** Blake puts 8 marbles in the bag. Cole puts 9 marbles in the bag. Then Blake takes out 7 marbles from the bag. How many marbles are in the bag now?

Solve. Show your work in the table.

Step 1
Step 2
Answer: _____ marbles

© Pearson Education, Inc. 2

Name _____

Help   Tools   Games

Homework
& Practice 5-8

Solve One-Step and Two-Step Problems

Another Look! You can solve a two-step problem by writing two equations.

Rena counts 6 birds in the tree. 3 birds fly away. Then 8 more birds land in the tree. How many birds does Rena count in the tree now?

HOME ACTIVITY Make up a two-step story problem for your child to solve.

Step 1
Subtract to find how many birds are in the tree after 3 birds fly away.

$$\underline{6} - \underline{3} = \underline{3}$$

Step 2
Add the number of birds that landed in the tree.

$$\underline{3} + \underline{8} = \underline{11}$$

$$\underline{11} \text{ birds}$$

 Complete both equations to solve each problem.

1. Lucy collects 9 rocks. She gives 4 rocks to Sam. Then Lucy collects 7 more rocks. How many rocks does Lucy have now?

_____ rocks

Step 1:

_____ – _____ = _____

Step 2:

_____ + _____ = _____

2. 4 boys ride their bicycles to the park. 6 more boys ride their bicycles to the park. Then 2 boys go home. How many boys are at the park now?

_____ boys

Step 1:

_____ + _____ = _____

Step 2:

_____ – _____ = _____

Topic 5 | Lesson 8   Digital Resources at PearsonRealize.com   three hundred one **301**

Solve each problem. Show your work.

3. **Model** Michael put some of the dishes away. Scott put 17 dishes away. They put away 32 dishes in all. Use the bar diagram to model the story. Then write 2 equations the model shows. How many dishes did Michael put away?

_____ + _____ = _____

_____ − _____ = _____

_____ dishes

4. **Higher Order Thinking** Kina picked 14 green apples. Her dad picked 8 red apples. Then they each ate 2 apples. How many apples do they have now? Explain how you solved the problem.

_____
_____
_____
_____
_____
_____

_____ apples

5. ✅ **Assessment** 3 black cats were in the alley. 5 cats joined them. Then 6 cats walked away. How many cats are still in the alley?

Solve. Show your work in the table.

Step 1
Step 2
Answer: _____ cats

Name _____

Solve & Share

Bill collects and sells seashells. He has 45 shells, finds 29 shells, and sells 20 shells. How many seashells does Bill have now?

Tara says you have to subtract 45 − 29 and then add 20 to solve the problem. Do you agree with Tara's thinking? Circle your answer. Use pictures, words, or equations to explain.

I can ...
critique the thinking of others by using what I know about addition and subtraction.

I can also add and subtract two-digit numbers.

Agree   **Do Not Agree**

Thinking Habits

What questions can I ask to understand other people's thinking?

Are there mistakes in other people's thinking?

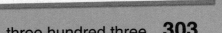

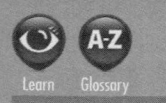
42 people are swimming. Some people leave. Now 15 people are swimming.

Kelly added up to subtract and she says 17 people left.

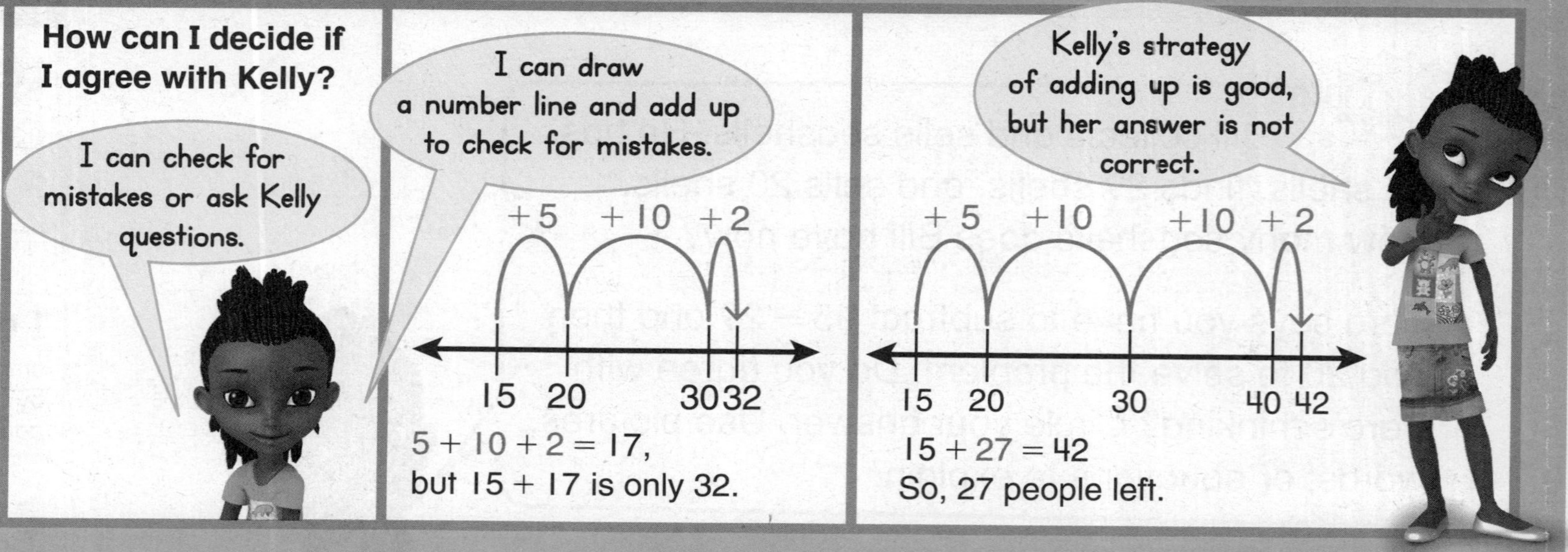

How can I decide if I agree with Kelly?

I can check for mistakes or ask Kelly questions.

I can draw a number line and add up to check for mistakes.

+5   +10   +2

15   20   30 32

$5 + 10 + 2 = 17$,
but $15 + 17$ is only 32.

Kelly's strategy of adding up is good, but her answer is not correct.

+5   +10   +10   +2

15   20   30   40 42

$15 + 27 = 42$
So, 27 people left.

Do You Understand?

Show Me! What question would you ask Kelly to help her check her reasoning?

☆ Guided Practice ☆

Circle the answer. Use pictures, words, or equations to explain your reasoning.

1. 51 people were on a train. 33 people left the train. How many people are on the train now?

   Ryan says 18 people. He broke apart 33 into 30 and 3. Then he subtracted each number. Does Ryan's reasoning make sense?

   Agree   **Do Not Agree**

Independent Practice Circle the answer. Use pictures, words, or equations to explain your reasoning.

2. Jill put 53 buttons in a box. Marci put 17 buttons in another box.

   Jarod says Marci has 33 fewer buttons than Jill. He thinks 53 − 20 is easier to subtract than 53 − 17. He subtracts 53 − 20 and gets 33.

   Do you agree or not agree with Jarod's thinking?

   Agree   **Do Not Agree**

3. Rob has 68 more puzzle pieces than Gina. Rob has 90 puzzle pieces.

   Carol says Gina has 22 puzzle pieces. Carol says she found 90 − 68 using an open number line. She added up 2 and 20 more from 68 and got 90.

   Does Carol's reasoning make sense?

   Agree   **Do Not Agree**

Reading Books

Ricky read the first 3 chapters of a book. Chapter 1 has 11 pages. Chapter 2 has 7 pages. Chapter 3 has 9 pages.

Sally read 46 pages of her book. How many more pages did Sally read than Ricky?

4. Make Sense What steps do you need to take to solve the problem?

_____

_____

_____

5. Look for a Pattern Is there a shortcut to find how many pages Ricky read? Explain.

_____

_____

_____

6. Explain Sally drew this open number line. Sally says she read 21 more pages than Ricky. Do you agree? Explain.

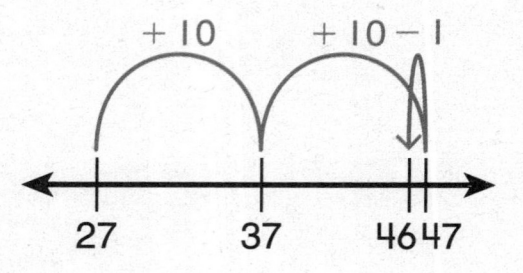

_____

_____

_____

_____

_____

© Pearson Education, Inc. 2

Help   Tools   Games

Another Look!

Shane has 62 stamps. Jake has 36 stamps.

Nita says Jake has 26 fewer stamps than Shane, because she can break apart 36 and subtract 62 − 30 = 32 and 32 − 6 = 26. Is Nita correct?

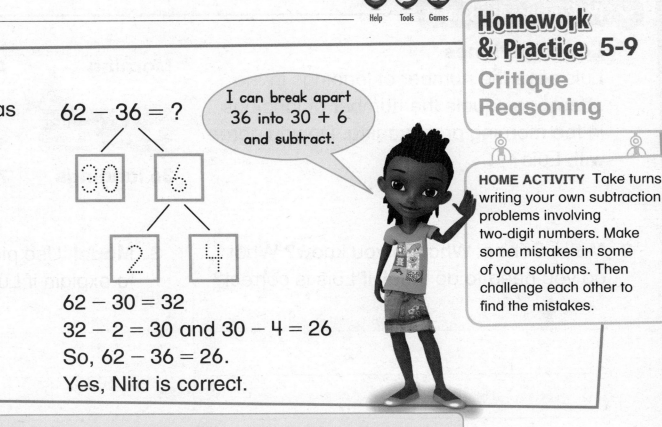

$62 - 36 = ?$

I can break apart 36 into 30 + 6 and subtract.

$62 - 30 = 32$
$32 - 2 = 30$ and $30 - 4 = 26$
So, $62 - 36 = 26$.
Yes, Nita is correct.

HOME ACTIVITY Take turns writing your own subtraction problems involving two-digit numbers. Make some mistakes in some of your solutions. Then challenge each other to find the mistakes.

Circle the answer. Use pictures, words, or equations to explain.

1. There were 64 runners in a race last year. This year there were 25 fewer runners.

   Latoya says 39 runners were in the race this year. She says 64 − 30 is easy to subtract. So she added 25 + 5 = 30. Then she found 64 − 30 = 34, and added 5 to 34 to get 39.

   Agree   **Do Not Agree**

Landing Planes

Luis says the number of landings in the afternoon equals the number of landings in the morning and evening. Do you agree with Luis?

Morning

36 landings

Afternoon

74 landings

Evening

38 landings

2. **Make Sense** What do you know? What do you need to do to tell if Luis is correct?

_____

_____

_____

3. **Model** Use pictures, words, or equations to explain if Luis's thinking is correct.

_____

_____

_____

4. **Explain** Luis got his answer by finding $74 - 38 = 36$.

Do you agree with Luis's thinking? Use pictures, words, or equations to explain.

© Pearson Education, Inc. 2

Find a Match

Find a partner. Point to a clue. Read the clue.

Look below the clues to find a match. Write the clue letter in the box next to the match.

Find a match for every clue.

Clues

A Every difference is 10.

B Every sum is 11.

C Every sum and difference is 6.

D Exactly three sums are the same.

E Exactly three differences are the same.

F Every sum is the same as 9 + 4.

G Every difference is odd.

H Exactly three sums are even.

☐	12 − 5 17 − 8 14 − 7 16 − 9	☐	10 − 0 20 − 10 14 − 4 19 − 9	☐	6 + 6 2 + 8 7 + 4 5 + 7	☐	14 − 8 3 + 3 15 − 9 0 + 6
☐	8 + 6 7 + 8 9 + 6 10 + 5	☐	15 − 8 18 − 9 12 − 7 13 − 6	☐	5 + 6 4 + 7 9 + 2 3 + 8	☐	7 + 6 3 + 10 8 + 5 4 + 9

A-Z
Glossary

Word List
- break apart
- compatible numbers
- compensation
- difference
- mental math
- ones
- open number line
- tens

Understand Vocabulary

Choose a term from the Word List to complete each sentence.

1. You can count back or add up to subtract on an

   _____.

2. To find $42 - 7$, you can _____ 7 into $2 + 5$.

3. The answer to a subtraction problem is called the _____.

4. There are 6 _____ in the number 36.

5. In 43, there are

   _____ tens.

6. In 76, there are

   _____ tens and

   _____ ones.

7. Break apart 8 to find $65 - 8$.

   _____

Use Vocabulary in Writing

8. Use words to tell how to find $54 - 19$. Use terms from the Word List.

   _____

   _____

   _____

   _____

   _____

Name _____

Set A

You can use a hundred chart to help you subtract. Find 65 − 31.

Start at 31. Move right 4 ones to 35.
Then move down 3 tens to 65.
3 tens and 4 ones is 34.

So, 65 − 31 = _34_ .

31	32	33	34	→35	36	37	38	39	40
41	42	43	44	45	46	47	48	49	50
51	52	53	54	55	56	57	58	59	60
61	62	63	64	65	66	67	68	69	70

Reteaching

Use a hundred chart to solve the problems.

1. 67 − 42 = _____

2. 70 − 33 = _____

3. 58 − 42 = _____

4. 63 − 38 = _____

Set B

You can use an open number line to find 85 − 30.

Place 85 on the number line.

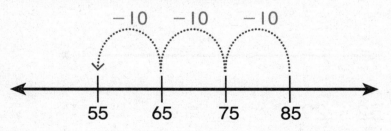

30 is 3 tens. Count back by 10 three times from 85.

So, 85 − 30 = _55_ .

Use an open number line to find each difference.

5. 60 − 20 = _____

6. 78 − 40 = _____

You can use an open number line to find 57 − 24.

Place 57 on the number line. There are 2 tens in 24. So, count back by 10 two times. There are 4 ones in 24. Then count back 4 from 37.

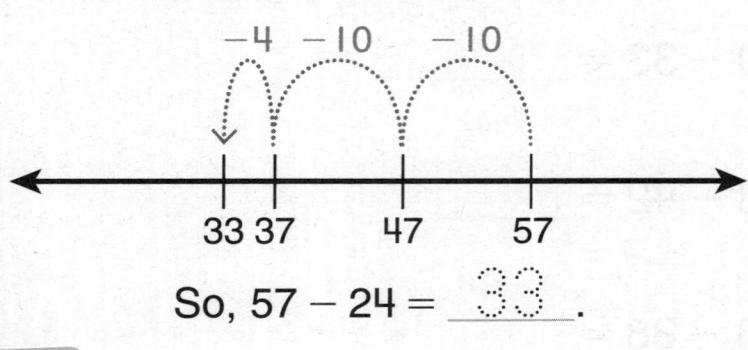

So, 57 − 24 = __33__ .

Find 62 − 37.

Place 37 on the line. Add 3 to get to 40. Then add two 10s to get to 60. Then add 2 to get to 62. Add the tens and ones: 3 + 10 + 10 + 2 = 25.

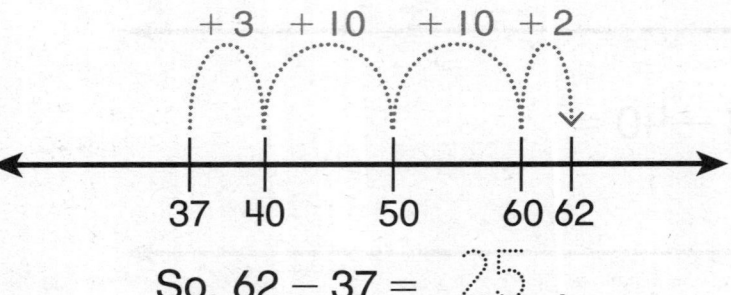

So, 62 − 37 = __25__ .

Use an open number line to find each difference.

7. 38 − 13 = _____

8. 93 − 36 = _____

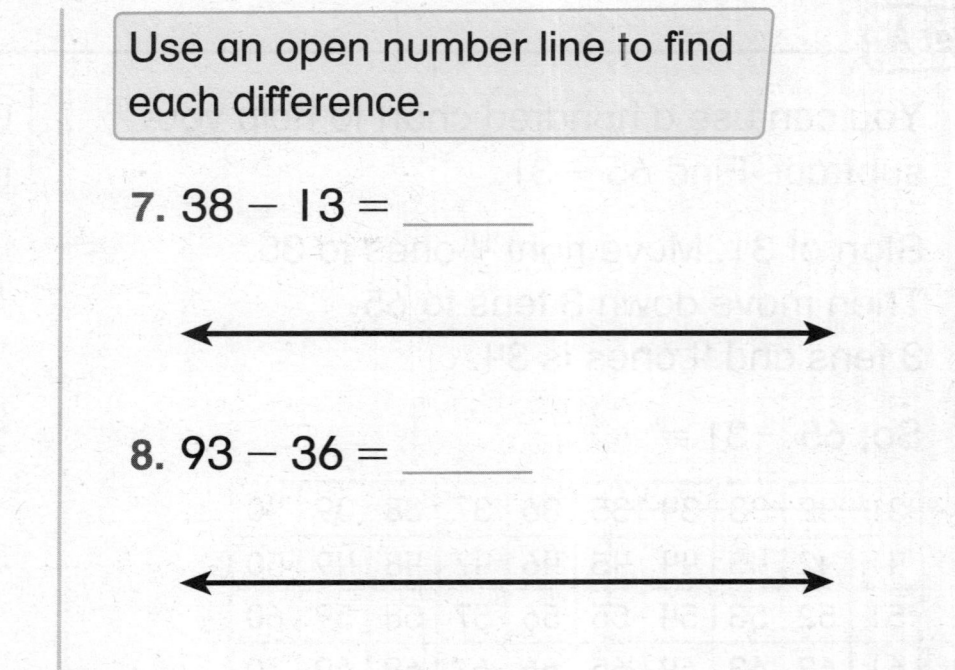

Add up on an open number line to find each difference.

9. 75 − 47 = _____

10. 52 − 29 = _____

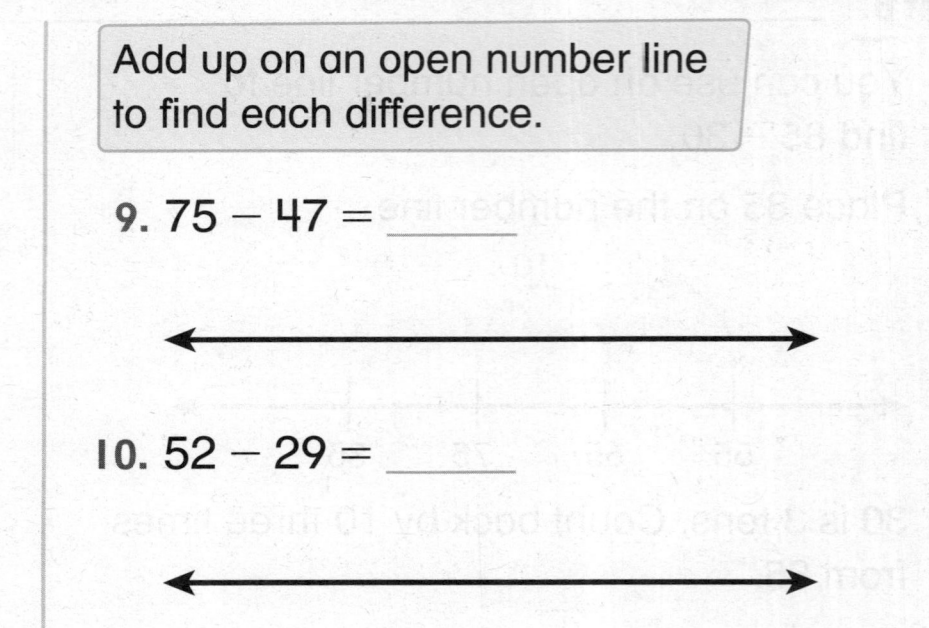

© Pearson Education, Inc. 2

Name _____

Set E

Break apart 17 to find 54 − 17.

21	22	23	24	25	26	27	28	29	30
31	32	33	34	35	36	37	38	39	40
41	42	43	44	45	46	47	48	49	50
51	52	53	54	55	56	57	58	59	60

Subtract. Break apart the number you are subtracting. Show your work.

54 − 17

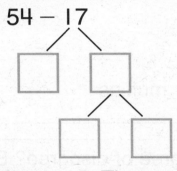

Start at 54. Subtract 10. Then subtract 4 to get to 40. Then subtract 3 more.

So, 54 − 17 = __37__.

11. 52 − 23 = _____

12. 45 − 19 = _____

Set F

74 − 27 = ?

Use compensation to solve.

74 − 27

↓ +3

74 − 30 = 44 ┈┈▶ 47

+3

So, 74 − 27 = __47__.

Use compensation to make numbers that are easier to subtract. Then solve.

13. 42 − 18 = _____

14. 84 − 37 = _____

Mason reads 34 pages in two days. He reads 8 of the pages on the second day. How many pages does Mason read the first day?

34

$26 + 8 = 34$ and
$34 - 8 = 26$

? | 8

_26_ pages

Thinking Habits

Critique Reasoning

What questions can I ask to understand other people's thinking?

Are there mistakes in other people's thinking?

Add or subtract to solve the problem. Show your work.

15. Gene bakes 60 muffins in one day. He bakes 24 of the muffins before lunch. How many muffins does he bake after lunch?

_____ ◯ _____ = _____

_____ muffins

Do you agree or disagree? Explain.

16. Ken has 29 more stamps than Jamie. Ken has 52 stamps. Lisa says Jamie has 23 stamps.

Lisa added up 1 from 29, then 20 more from 30, and 2 more to get to 52. Does Lisa's reasoning make sense?

Name _____

I. A store has 68 candles. Then they sell 29 of the candles.
How many candles are left?

Ⓐ 29   Ⓑ 38   Ⓒ 39   Ⓓ 97

---

2. Which does the number line show? Choose all that apply.

☐ Count back by 10 two times from 48.

☐ Count back by 10 three times from 48.

☐ 48 − 30 = 18

☐ 18 + 48 = 66

$$-10 \quad\quad -10 \quad\quad -10$$

18   28   38   48

---

3. Tony has 66 rocks.
He gives 23 rocks to Chris.

How many rocks does Tony have now?

_____ ◯ _____ = _____

_____ rocks

21	22	23	24	25	26	27	28	29	30
31	32	33	34	35	36	37	38	39	40
41	42	43	44	45	46	47	48	49	50
51	52	53	54	55	56	57	58	59	60
61	62	63	64	65	66	67	68	69	70

---

4. Raven solved a subtraction problem
using the number line. Write the equation
that the number line shows.

$$-2 \quad -10 \quad\quad -10 \quad\quad -10$$

50 52   62   72   82

_____ − _____ = _____

5. Ella has 7 carrots.
Ann has 34 carrots.
How many fewer carrots does
Ella have than Ann?

Ⓐ 7　　　　　　Ⓒ 34

Ⓑ 27　　　　　Ⓓ 41

6. Keena has 64 balloons.
28 of the balloons are red.
14 balloons are green.
The rest of the balloons are purple.
How many of the balloons are purple?

Ⓐ 22　　　　　Ⓒ 42

Ⓑ 36　　　　　Ⓓ 50

7. Break apart 48 to solve.
Show your work.

$$73 - 48 = ?$$

$73 - 48 = \underline{\hspace{2cm}}$

8. Joe has 43 stickers.
Then he gives away 9 stickers.
How many stickers does Joe have left?

Can you use the two equations to solve?
Choose Yes or No.

$43 + 7 = 50$　　　　○ Yes　○ No
$50 + 2 = 52$

$43 + 10 = 53$　　　○ Yes　○ No
$53 - 1 = 52$

$43 - 3 = 40$　　　　○ Yes　○ No
$40 - 6 = 34$

$43 - 10 = 33$　　　○ Yes　○ No
$33 + 1 = 34$

9. Which does the number line show?
Choose all that apply.

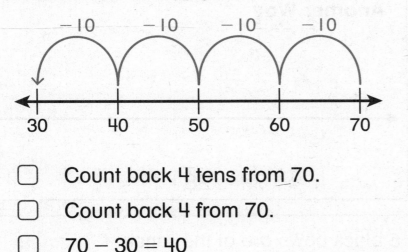

☐ Count back 4 tens from 70.

☐ Count back 4 from 70.

☐ $70 - 30 = 40$

☐ $70 - 40 = 30$

10. Use the open number line to find the difference.

$$80 - 42 = ?$$

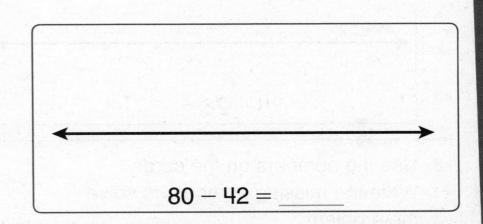

$80 - 42 = $ _____

11. Part A 33 ants are on a leaf. 15 ants leave. How many ants are left?
Jay adds 2 to 33 to make an easier problem, 35–15. He says 20 ants are left. Circle whether you agree or do not agree.

Agree   **Do Not Agree**

Part B Explain why you agree or do not agree with Jay's strategy.

12. Use the open number lines. Show two different ways to find 74 − 28.
Show your work.

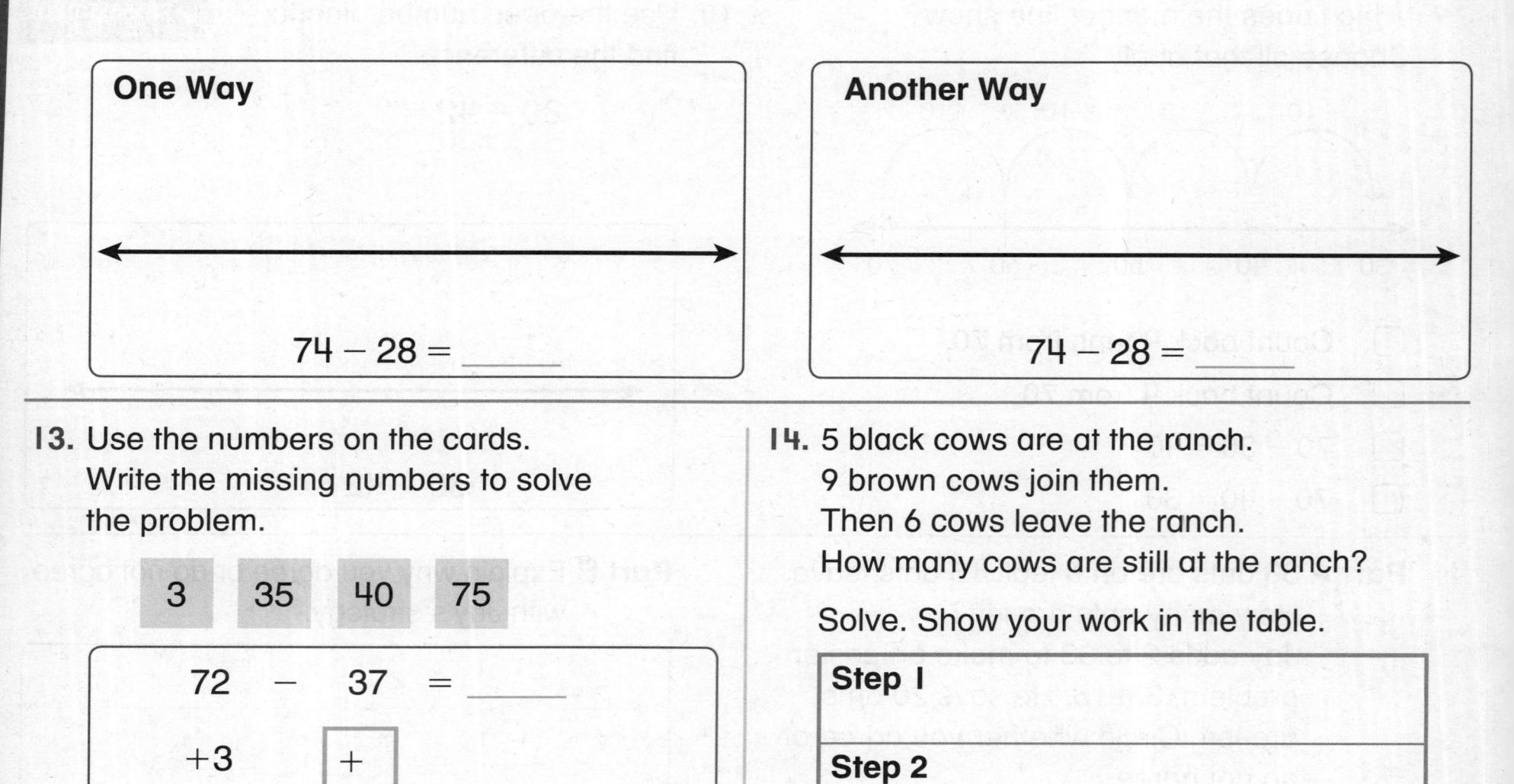

One Way

74 − 28 = _____

Another Way

74 − 28 = _____

13. Use the numbers on the cards.
Write the missing numbers to solve
the problem.

| 3 | 35 | 40 | 75 |

72 − 37 = _____

+3   + ☐

_____ − _____ = _____

14. 5 black cows are at the ranch.
9 brown cows join them.
Then 6 cows leave the ranch.
How many cows are still at the ranch?

Solve. Show your work in the table.

Step 1
Step 2
Answer
_____ cows

Name _____

Beautiful Boats

Chen's family goes to the lake for a vacation.
They count the boats that they see.

12 sailboats   28 rowboats   36 motorboats

1. How many more motorboats does
   Chen see than sailboats?

   Use the open number line to
   solve.

   <———————————————————————————>

   _____ more motorboats

2. Maria's family saw 57 rowboats
   on their vacation. How many
   more rowboats did they see
   than Chen's family?

   Use compensation to solve.
   Explain how you found your answer.

   _____ more rowboats

3. Chen's sisters play with toy boats at the lake. They have 21 yellow boats. They have 9 fewer red boats than yellow boats. How many boats do they have in all?

Write two equations to solve the problem.

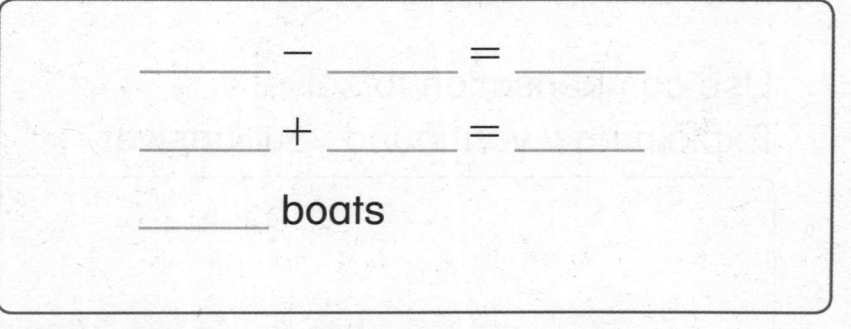

_____ − _____ = _____

_____ + _____ = _____

_____ boats

4. Julie's family saw 94 boats on their vacation. How many more boats did they see than Chen's family?

Part A What do you need to do to solve the problem?

Part B How many boats did Chen see? Show your work. Then explain how you found your answer.

_____ boats

Part C Julie said that her family saw 18 more boats than Chen's family. She broke apart 76 into 70 + 4 + 2. Then she subtracted each number from 94. Does Julie's reasoning make sense? Explain.

© Pearson Education, Inc. 2
Topic 5 | Performance Assessment

Fluently Subtract Within 100

Essential Question: What are strategies for subtracting numbers to 100?

Digital Resources

Solve   Learn   Glossary

Tools   Assessment   Help   Games

More of Earth is covered with water than with land!

And some of the land is covered with snow and ice!

Wow! Let's do this project and learn more.

Math and Science Project: Finding Water and Finding Differences

Find Out Use globes, maps, books, and other sources to find out where water, snow, and ice can be found on Earth. Make a list of different names of bodies of water and names of bodies of snow and ice.

Journal: Make a Book Show what you learn in a book. In your book, also:

• Tell about how globes are models that show where water is found on Earth.

• Tell about how to use a subtraction model to find differences.

Name _____

<table>
</table>

A-Z Vocabulary

1. **Break apart** 56 into tens and ones. Draw place value blocks to show the parts.

    56 = _____ + _____

2. Complete the drawing to show how to **regroup** 1 ten as ones.

    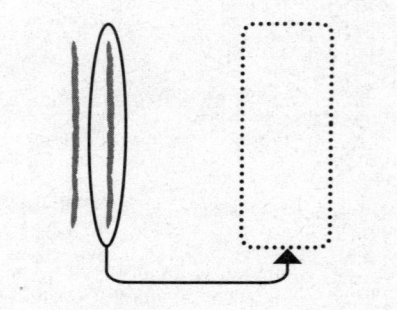

3. Complete the **bar diagram** to model 64 − 31 = ?

    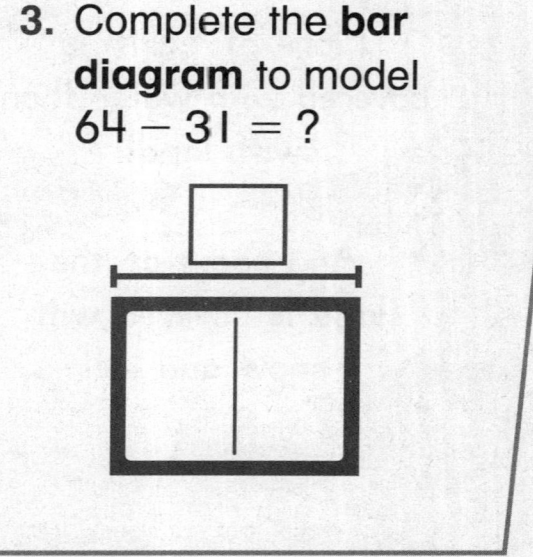

Open Number Lines

4. Find 40 − 25 by counting back on an open number line. Show your work.

    ⟷

    40 − 25 = _____

5. Find 45 − 22 by adding up on an open number line. Show your work.

    ⟷

    45 − 22 = _____

Math Story

6. Lea has 30 cookies. She gives 17 cookies to her friends. How many cookies does Lea have now?

    _____ cookies

Name _____

Solve & Share

How can you use tens and ones to find 23 − 6? Use place-value blocks to help you. Show your work.

I can ...
exchange 1 ten for 10 ones.

I can also use math tools correctly.

_____ − _____ = _____

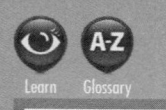

Find 34 − 6. Show 34. There are not enough ones to subtract 6.

You need to regroup.

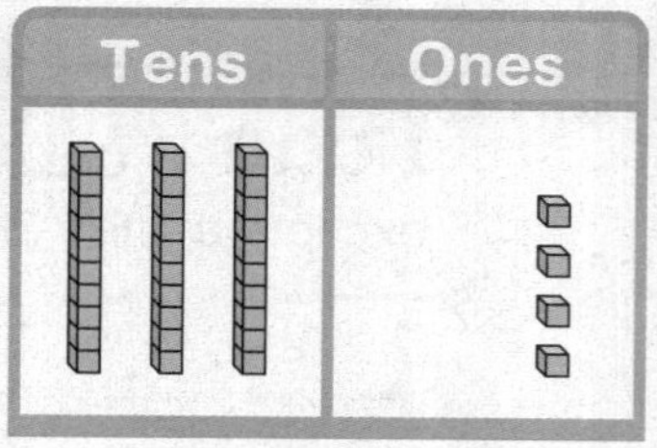

Tens	Ones

Regroup 1 ten as 10 ones.

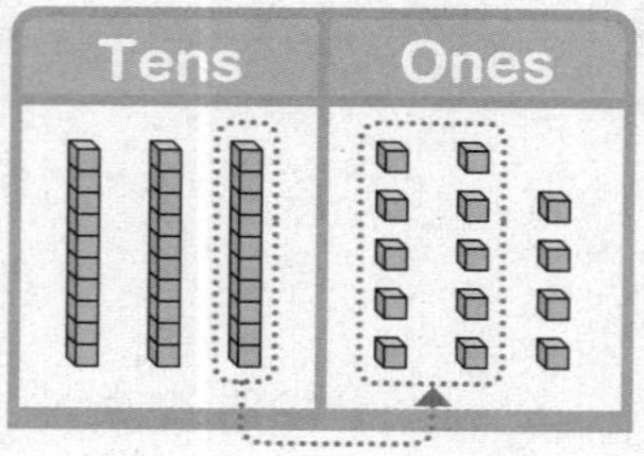

Tens	Ones

Subtract 6.

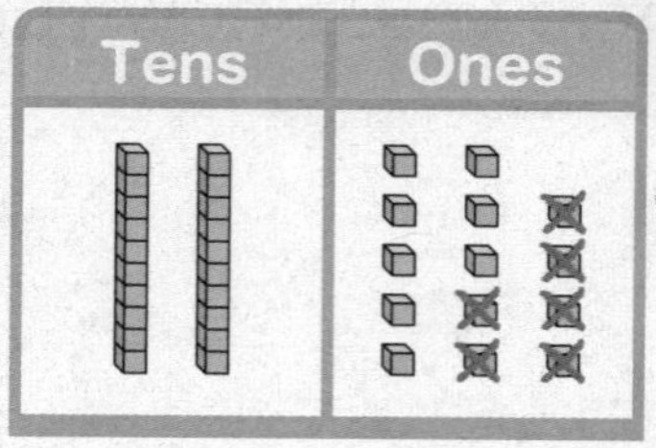

Tens	Ones

Cross out 6 ones to subtract. Now there are 2 tens and 8 ones left that show the difference.

$34 - 6 = \underline{28}$

Do You Understand?

Show Me! Do you need to regroup when you subtract 5 from 44? Explain why or why not.

★ **Guided Practice** ★ Subtract. Use your workmat and place-value blocks. Regroup if you need to.

	Show.	Subtract.	Do you need to regroup?	Find the difference.
1.	35	8	**Yes** No	$35 - 8 = \underline{27}$
2.	46	3	Yes No	$46 - 3 = \underline{}$
3.	62	4	Yes No	$62 - 4 = \underline{}$
4.	50	7	Yes No	$50 - 7 = \underline{}$

© Pearson Education, Inc. 2

Topic 6 | Lesson 1

Tools Assessment

Independent Practice

Subtract. Use your workmat and place-value blocks. Regroup if you need to.

Show.	Subtract.	Do you need to regroup?		Find the difference.
5. 81	2	Yes	No	$81 - 2 =$ _____
6. 29	1	Yes	No	$29 - 1 =$ _____
7. 60	4	Yes	No	$60 - 4 =$ _____
8. 24	9	Yes	No	$24 - 9 =$ _____
9. 75	3	Yes	No	$75 - 3 =$ _____
10. 43	5	Yes	No	$43 - 5 =$ _____

11. **Higher Order Thinking** Which one-digit numbers can you subtract from 74 without first regrouping? Explain how you know.

Think about what each digit stands for in 74.

_____

_____

12. **Make Sense** There are 21 snails in a garden. 6 snails leave. How many snails are still in the garden?

_____ snails

13. **Make Sense** Kate has 45 marbles. She gives 3 marbles to her brother. How many marbles does Kate have now?

_____ marbles

14. **Higher Order Thinking** Sammie has 9 fewer rings than Emilio.
Sammie has 7 more rings than Sara.
Emilio has 34 rings.
Complete the sentences below.
Draw a picture to explain your work.

Sammie has _____ rings.

Sara has _____ rings.

15. ✓ **Assessment** Malcolm has 38 seeds. Juan has 4 fewer seeds than Malcolm. Juan gives 8 seeds to his friend. How many seeds does Juan have now?

Ⓐ 22

Ⓑ 26

Ⓒ 36

Ⓓ 46

Think about what you know and what you are trying to find. Can drawing place-value blocks help?

© Pearson Education, Inc. 2

Name _____

Another Look! Use place-value blocks to find 42 − 7.

HOME ACTIVITY Ask your child to show you how to subtract 26 − 7 using small objects such as buttons, marbles, or paper clips. Have your child explain and show you how to regroup.

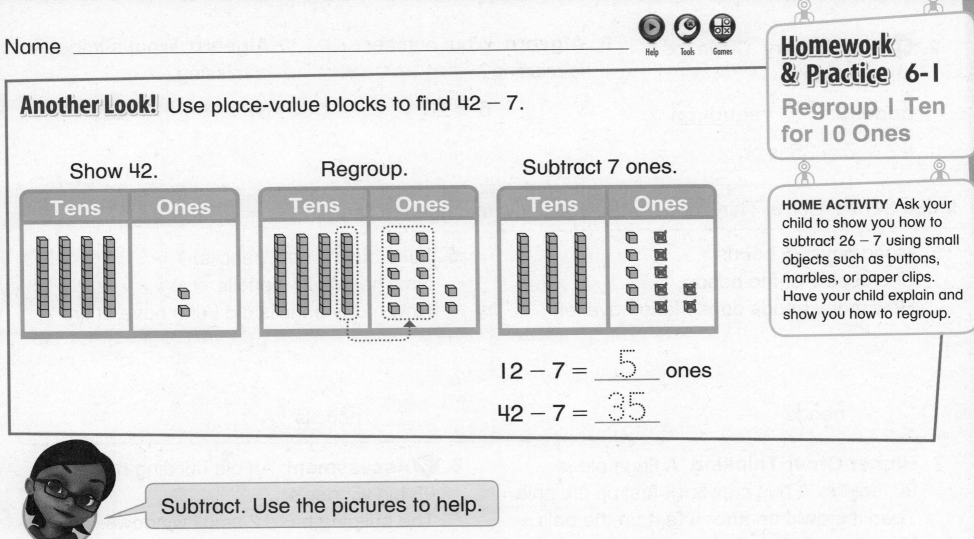

Show 42.

Regroup.

Subtract 7 ones.

Tens	Ones

$12 - 7 = \underline{5}$ ones

$42 - 7 = \underline{35}$

Subtract. Use the pictures to help.

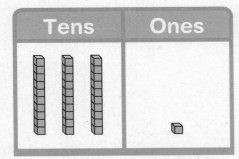

1. Subtract 5 from 31.

Show 31.

Regroup.

Subtract _____ ones.

Tens	Ones

$11 - 5 = \underline{}$ ones

$31 - 5 = \underline{}$

2. A-Z Vocabulary Circle the missing word.

addend   **equation**

$42 - 7 = 35$ is an _____.

3. Algebra What number is missing?

_____ $- 5 = 20$

4. Algebra What number is missing?

$37 -$ _____ $= 28$

Make Sense Solve. Think about what you know and need to find.

5. Maria buys 36 beads.
She uses 9 of the beads.
How many beads does Maria have left?

_____ beads

6. Luke buys 7 new pencils.
Now he has 21 pencils.
How many pencils did Luke have at first?

_____ pencils

---

7. Higher Order Thinking A flag pole is 30 feet tall. A bug crawls 14 feet up the pole. Then it crawls another 4 feet up the pole. How much farther must the bug crawl to get to the top?

_____ feet

8. ✓ Assessment An old building has 48 big windows.
The building has 12 small windows.
There are 9 broken windows.
How many windows are **NOT** broken?

Ⓐ 51

Ⓑ 48

Ⓒ 41

Ⓓ 37

© Pearson Education, Inc. 2

Name _____

Solve & Share

There are 22 students drawing pictures.
4 students finish drawing. How many students are still drawing?

Use place-value blocks to help you solve.
Show the tens and ones you have.

I can ...
use place value and models to subtract 2-digit and 1-digit numbers.

I can also use math tools correctly.

Tens	Ones

_____ tens   _____ ones

$$22 - 4 = \text{\_\_\_\_\_}$$

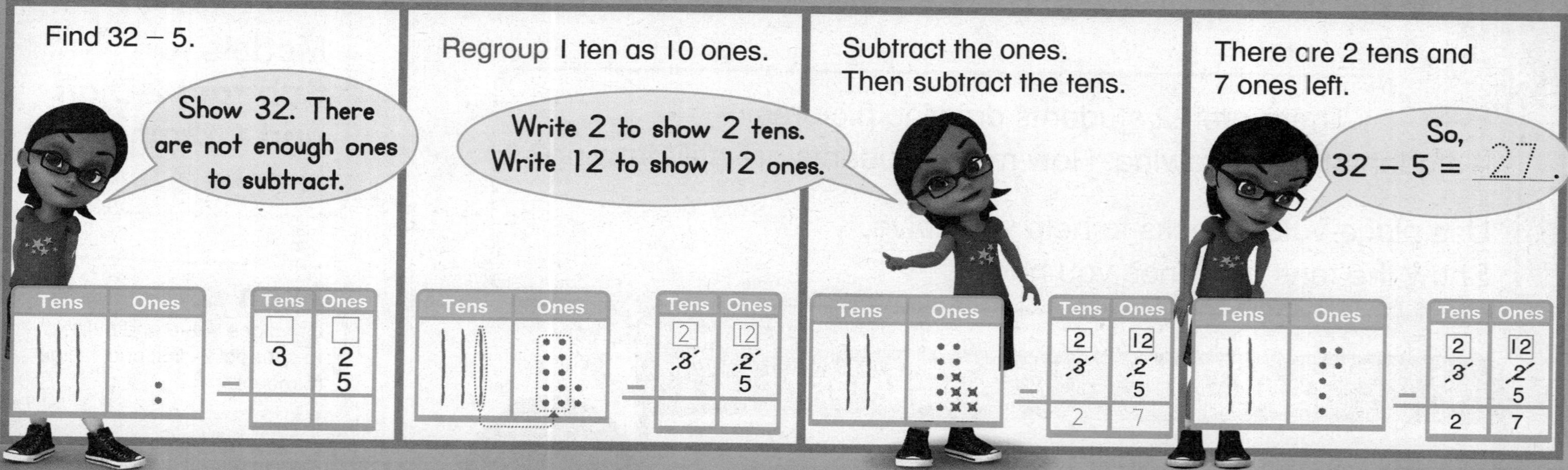

Find 32 − 5.

Show 32. There are not enough ones to subtract.

Tens	Ones
3	2
	5

Regroup 1 ten as 10 ones.

Write 2 to show 2 tens.
Write 12 to show 12 ones.

Tens	Ones
2	12
3	2
	5

Subtract the ones.
Then subtract the tens.

Tens	Ones
2	12
3	2
	5
2	7

There are 2 tens and 7 ones left.

So, 32 − 5 = 27 .

Tens	Ones
2	12
3	2
	5
2	7

Do You Understand?

Show Me! Why do you need to regroup when you subtract 32 − 5?

☆ **Guided Practice** ☆ Subtract. Draw place-value blocks to show your work. Regroup if needed.

1.

Tens	Ones
3	14
4	4
−	9
3	5

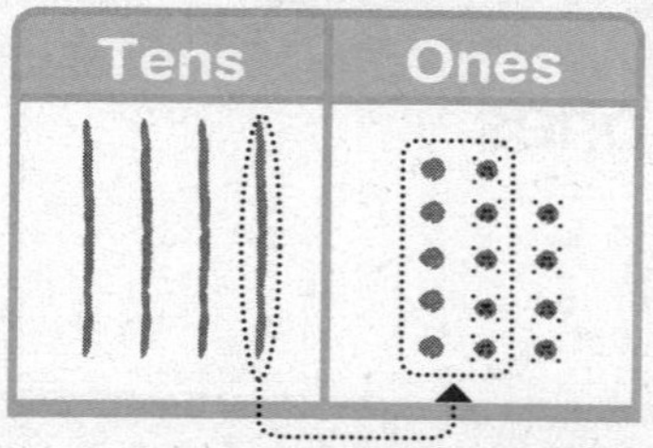

Tens	Ones

2.

Tens	Ones
2	3
−	5

Tens	Ones

3.

Tens	Ones
3	5
−	8

Tens	Ones

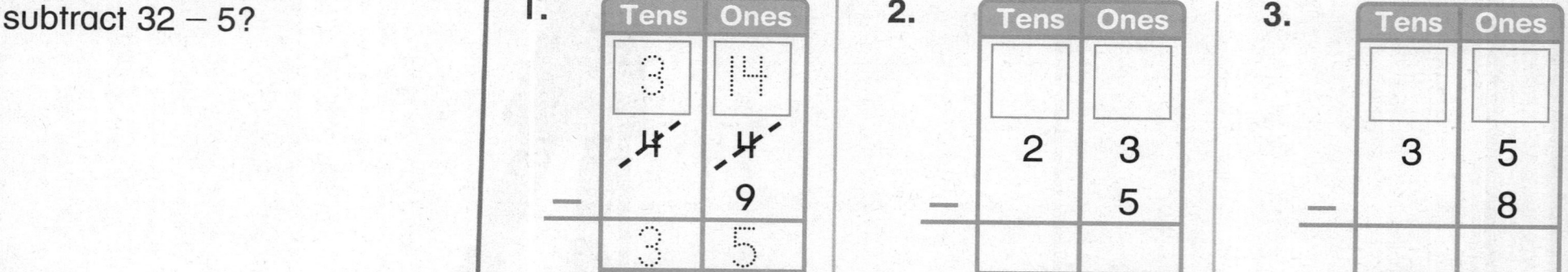

Topic 6 | Lesson 2

Independent Practice

Subtract. Draw place-value blocks to show your work. Regroup if needed.

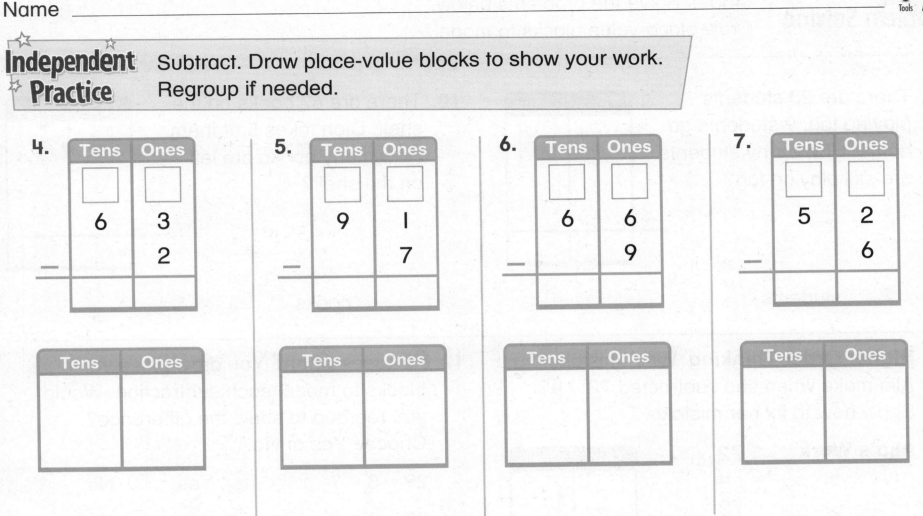

4.

Tens	Ones
6	3
−	2

Tens	Ones

5.

Tens	Ones
9	1
−	7

Tens	Ones

6.

Tens	Ones
6	6
−	9

Tens	Ones

7.

Tens	Ones
5	2
−	6

Tens	Ones

Write the missing numbers in the boxes. Draw a picture to show and explain your work.

8. Algebra What numbers will complete the subtraction equations?

$$\boxed{} - 8 = 17 \qquad 34 - \boxed{} = 29$$

Model Solve the problems below.
Draw place-value blocks to model.

9. There are 23 students playing tag. 9 students go home. How many students are still playing tag?

Tens	Ones

_____ students

10. There are 67 books on the shelf. Dion takes 5 of them. How many books are left on the shelf?

Tens	Ones

_____ books

11. **Higher Order Thinking** What mistake did Alia make when she subtracted 72 – 4? Show how to fix her mistake.

Alia's Work
$$72$$
$$-\ 4$$
$$\overline{72}$$

Tens	Ones

_____

_____

_____

_____

12. ✅**Assessment** You draw place value blocks to model each subtraction. Would you regroup to show the difference? Choose Yes or No.

29 – 3 = ?   ○ Yes   ○ No

30 – 0 = ?   ○ Yes   ○ No

77 – 8 = ?   ○ Yes   ○ No

55 – 5 = ?   ○ Yes   ○ No

© Pearson Education, Inc. 2

Topic 6 | Lesson 2

Name _____

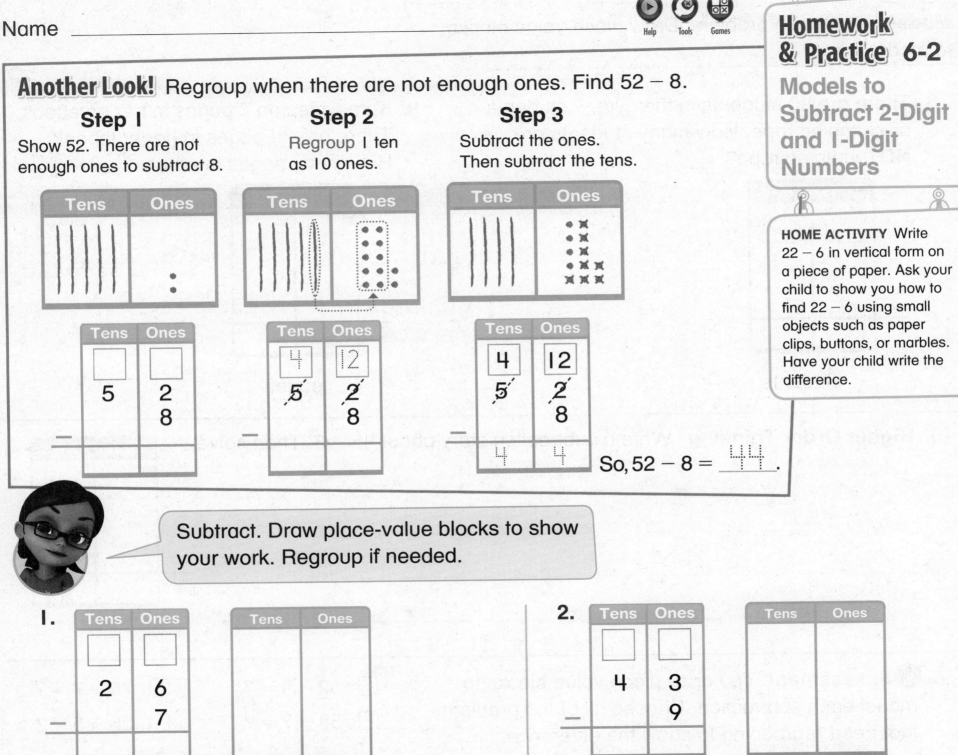

Another Look! Regroup when there are not enough ones. Find 52 − 8.

Step 1
Show 52. There are not enough ones to subtract 8.

Step 2
Regroup 1 ten as 10 ones.

Step 3
Subtract the ones. Then subtract the tens.

Tens	Ones

Tens	Ones
5	2
	8

Tens	Ones
4	12
5̷	2̷
	8

Tens	Ones
4	12
5̷	2̷
	8
4	4

So, 52 − 8 = __44__.

HOME ACTIVITY Write 22 − 6 in vertical form on a piece of paper. Ask your child to show you how to find 22 − 6 using small objects such as paper clips, buttons, or marbles. Have your child write the difference.

Subtract. Draw place-value blocks to show your work. Regroup if needed.

1.

Tens	Ones
2	6
	7

Tens	Ones

2.

Tens	Ones
4	3
	9

Tens	Ones

Model Solve each problem. Draw place-value blocks to model.

3. There are 40 students in the gym. 9 students are jumping rope. How many students are **NOT** jumping rope?

Tens	Ones

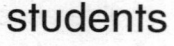

_____ students

4. Kate writes on 7 pages in her notebook. There are 34 pages in her notebook. How many pages are blank?

Tens	Ones

_____ pages

5. **Higher Order Thinking** Write a subtraction story about 45 − 8. Then solve.

_____

_____

_____

_____

Tens	Ones

6. ✓**Assessment** You draw place value blocks to model each subtraction. Choose all of the problems that need regrouping to show the difference.

☐ 62 − 4 = ?   ☐ 75 − 7 = ?

☐ 58 − 7 = ?   ☐ 35 − 5 = ?

© Pearson Education, Inc. 2

Solve & Share

Ari has 31 stickers.
He puts 8 of his stickers in a scrapbook.
How many stickers are left?

Solve. Explain why your strategy works.

I can ...
use place value and regrouping to subtract.

I can also look for things that repeat.

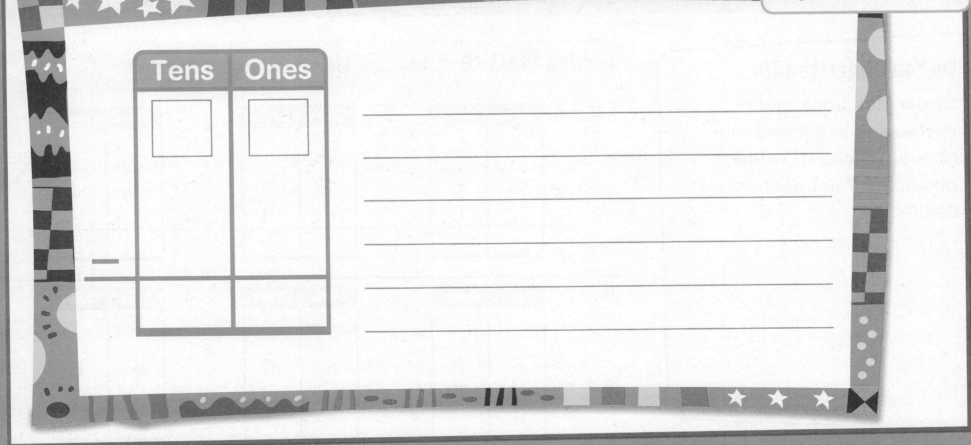

Tens	Ones
−	

Find 42 − 9.

Show 42.

Tens	Ones

Tens	Ones
4	2
	9

Look at the ones.
There are not enough
ones to subtract.

Regroup!

Tens	Ones

Tens	Ones
3	12
4	2
	9

Subtract the ones.
Then subtract the tens.

Tens	Ones

Tens	Ones
3	12
4	2
	9
3	3

There are 3 tens
and 3 ones left.

42 − 9 = 33

Tens	Ones
3	12
4	2
	9
3	3

Do You Understand?

Show Me! Look at the regrouping in the problem above. Why is 12 written above the 2 in the ones column?

☆ Guided Practice Subtract. Use drawings if needed.

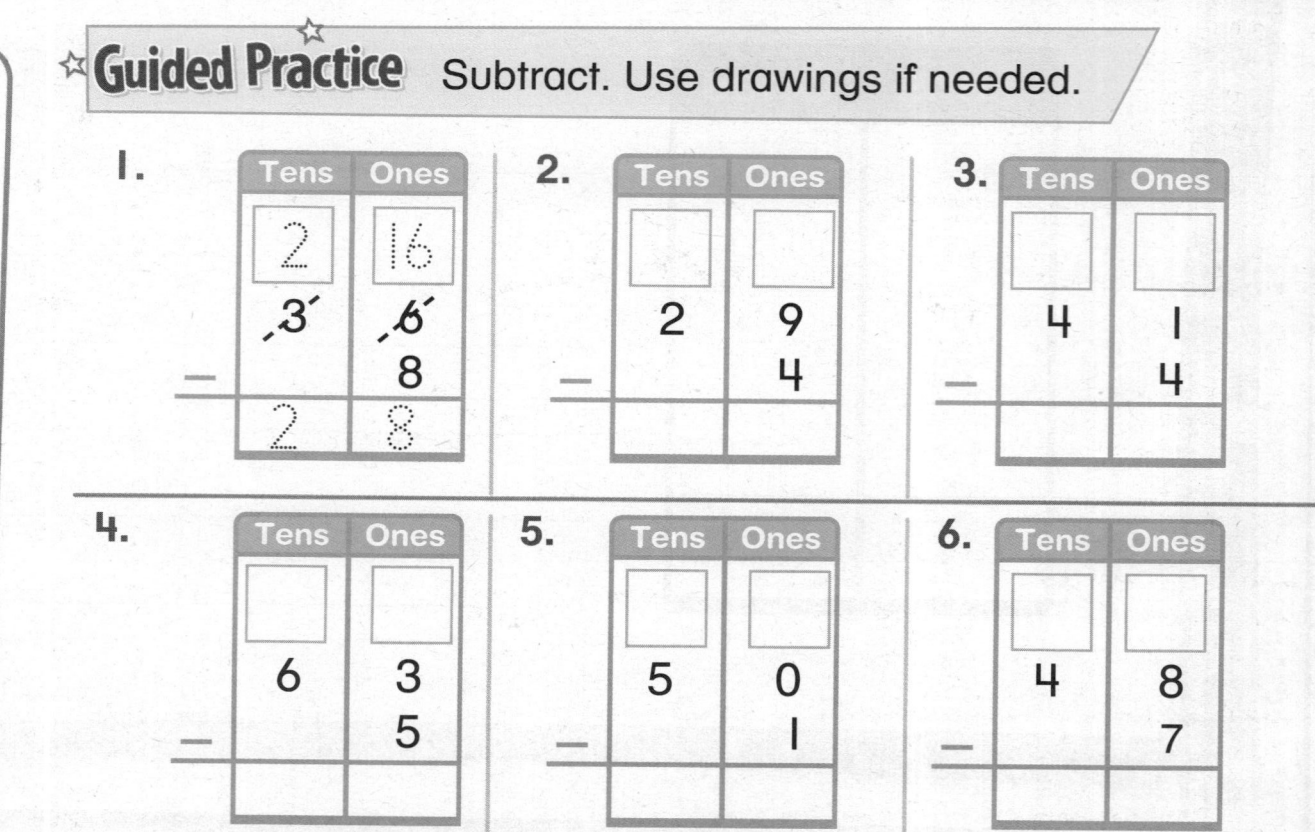

1.
Tens	Ones
2	16
3	6
	8
2	8

2.
Tens	Ones
2	9
	4

3.
Tens	Ones
4	1
	4

4.
Tens	Ones
6	3
	5

5.
Tens	Ones
5	0
	1

6.
Tens	Ones
4	8
	7

Independent Practice ⭐ Subtract. Use drawings if needed.

7.

Tens	Ones
□	□
3	2
	6

8.

Tens	Ones
□	□
2	0
	3

9.

Tens	Ones
□	□
6	7
	6

10.

Tens	Ones
□	□
5	2
	4

11.

Tens	Ones
□	□
3	5
	0

12.

Tens	Ones
□	□
7	5
	3

13.

Tens	Ones
□	□
5	6
	7

14.

Tens	Ones
□	□
8	5
	1

15.

Tens	Ones
□	□
9	8
	9

16.

Tens	Ones
□	□
7	7
	9

Use words or a picture to solve.

17. **Number Sense** What is the missing number? Explain how to solve.

$$45 - 9 = 46 - \boxed{}$$

18. **Generalize** There are 25 bikes at a bike store. The store owner sells 7 bikes. How many bikes are left?

Tens	Ones

–

_____ bikes

You can repeat steps to subtract. First subtract the ones. Regroup if needed. Then subtract the tens. 7 has zero tens.

19. **Higher Order Thinking** A bike store sold 10 fewer locks on Wednesday than on Tuesday. How many more locks did the store sell on Wednesday than on Monday?

Bike Locks Sold	
Monday	9
Tuesday	33
Wednesday	

Tens	Ones

–

_____ locks

20. ✅**Assessment** Use the numbers on the cards to find the missing numbers in the problem. Write the missing numbers.

| 15 | 9 | 3 |

Think: How will I regroup to subtract?

Tens	Ones
3	
4	5
–	6

© Pearson Education, Inc. 2

Topic 6 | Lesson 3

Name _____

Another Look! Find 42 − 6. You can subtract the ones first.

Think: Are there enough ones to subtract?

There are **NOT** enough ones to subtract.

Regroup if you need to. Then subtract the tens. Draw pictures if needed.

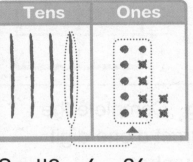

1-digit numbers have 0 tens.

Tens	Ones
3̶4̶	1̶2̶
−	6
3	6

Regroup? (Yes)   No

So, 42 − 6 = 36.

HOME ACTIVITY Write 34 − 9 in vertical form on a sheet of paper. Have your child use pencil and paper to solve.

Subtract. Use drawings if needed.

1.
Tens	Ones
□	□
2	5
−	4

2.
Tens	Ones
□	□
4	1
−	8

3.
Tens	Ones
□	□
6	5
−	7

4.
Tens	Ones
□	□
7	8
−	9

5.
Tens	Ones
□	□
8	3
−	6

Generalize Solve the problems. Show your work and regroup if needed.

6. 53 grapes are on a plate. Andrea eats 5 of them. How many grapes are on the plate now?

Tens	Ones
−	

_____ grapes

7. Chato reads 7 pages. His book has 67. How many pages does Chato have left to read?

Tens	Ones
−	

_____ pages

8. **Higher Order Thinking** Complete the subtraction frame. Subtract a one-digit number from a 2-digit number.

Tens	Ones
−	
7	6

You know the difference! Work backwards to check your work. There is more than one correct answer.

9. ✓**Assessment** Use the numbers on the cards to find the missing numbers in the problem. Write the missing numbers.

| I | 8 | II |

Tens	Ones
2	I
−	3
I	

© Pearson Education, Inc. 2

Name _____

Solve & Share

You have 42 pipe cleaners.
You use 19 of the pipe cleaners.
How many pipe cleaners do you have now?

Use place-value blocks to help you solve.
Draw your place-value blocks.
Tell if you need to regroup.

I can ...
use place value and models to subtract 2-digit numbers.

I can also use math tools correctly.

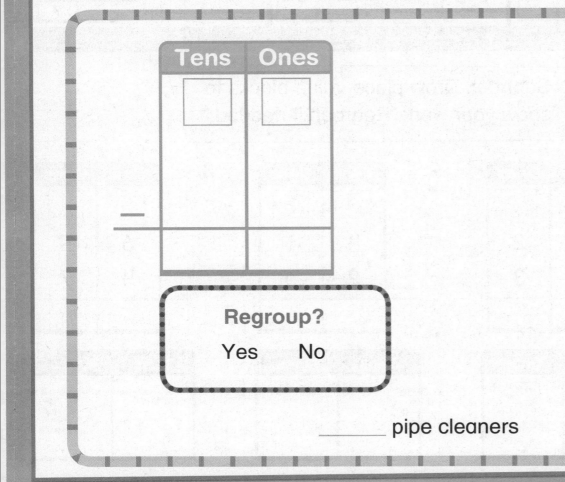

Tens	Ones
☐	☐
−	

Regroup?

Yes   No

_____ pipe cleaners

Topic 6 | Lesson 4
Digital Resources at PearsonRealize.com
three hundred forty-one **341**

Find 31 − 14.

Show 31. There are not enough ones to subtract.

Tens	Ones
|||	.

Tens	Ones
3	1
− | |

Regroup 1 ten as 10 ones.

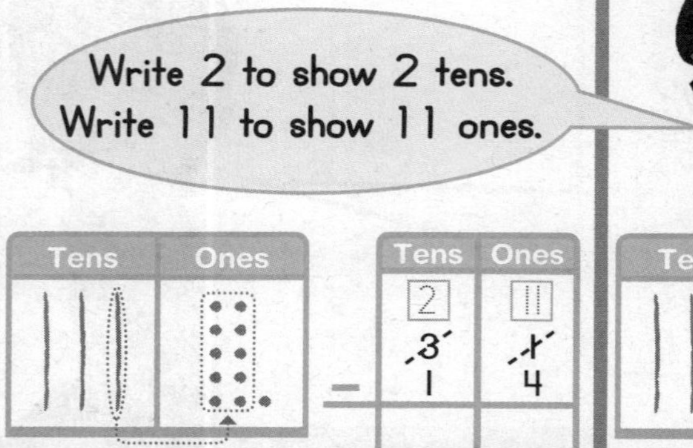

Write 2 to show 2 tens. Write 11 to show 11 ones.

Tens	Ones
|||	::::

Tens	Ones
2	11
3	1
− | 4 |

Subtract the ones.

 Tens	Ones
||	::::

Tens	Ones
2	11
3	1
−	4
	7

Subtract the tens.

So, 31 − 14 = ___17___ .

Tens	Ones
⋈	:::

Tens	Ones
2	11
3	1
−	4
1	7

Do You Understand?

Show Me! Explain why you need to regroup to find 65 − 17.

★ **Guided Practice** ★ Subtract. Draw place-value blocks to show your work. Regroup if needed.

1.

Tens	Ones
4	12
5	2
− 1	3
3	9

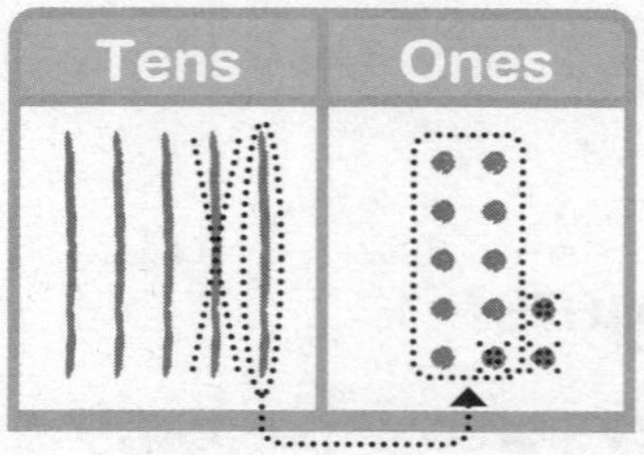

Tens	Ones
|||⋈	::::

2.

Tens	Ones
☐	☐
4	1
− 2 | 6 |

Tens	Ones

3.

Tens	Ones
☐	☐
6	4
− 4 | 7 |

Tens	Ones

Topic 6 | Lesson 4

Name _____

Independent Practice   Subtract. Draw place-value blocks to show your work. Regroup if needed.

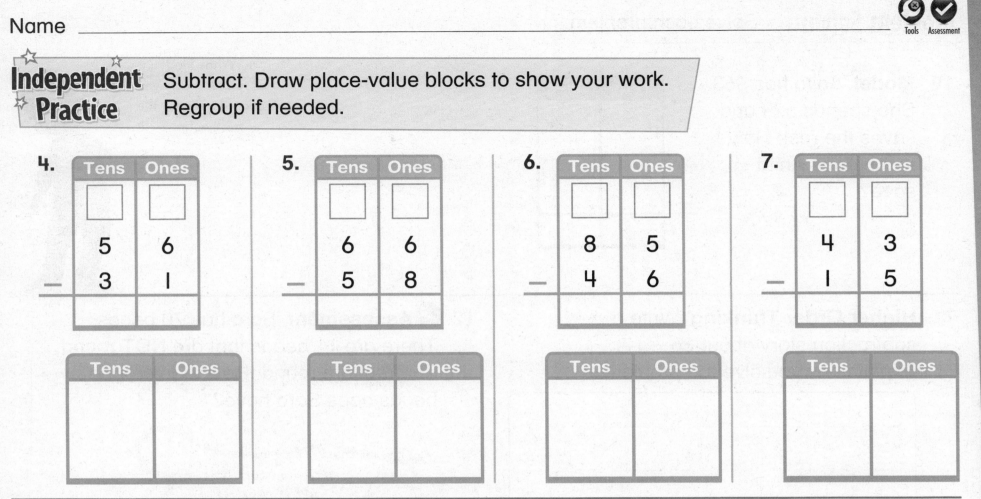

4.
Tens	Ones
☐	☐
5	6
− 3	1

Tens	Ones

5.
Tens	Ones
☐	☐
6	6
− 5	8

Tens	Ones

6.
Tens	Ones
☐	☐
8	5
− 4	6

Tens	Ones

7.
Tens	Ones
☐	☐
4	3
− 1	5

Tens	Ones

8. **Algebra** Write numbers to complete the equations. Draw pictures to help if needed.

$37 - 18 = \boxed{}$

$46 - \boxed{} = 18$

$\boxed{} - 17 = 16$

9. **Number Sense**
Do these models show the same value? Explain.

_____

_____

_____

_____

10. Model Anita has $63. She spends $24 and saves the rest. How much does Anita save?

$ _____

Tens	Ones

−

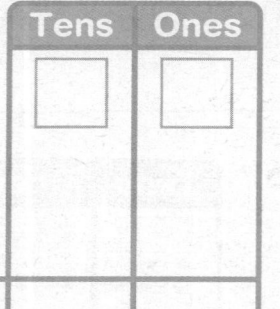

What kind of picture can you draw to model the subtraction?

11. Higher Order Thinking Write a subtraction story about $36 - 17$. Explain how to solve the problem.

_____

_____

_____

_____

_____

12. ✅ **Assessment** Sara has 70 beads. There are 11 beads that are **NOT** round. The rest are round. How many round beads does Sara have?

Ⓐ 59

Ⓑ 49

Ⓒ 47

Ⓓ 11

© Pearson Education, Inc. 2

Name _____

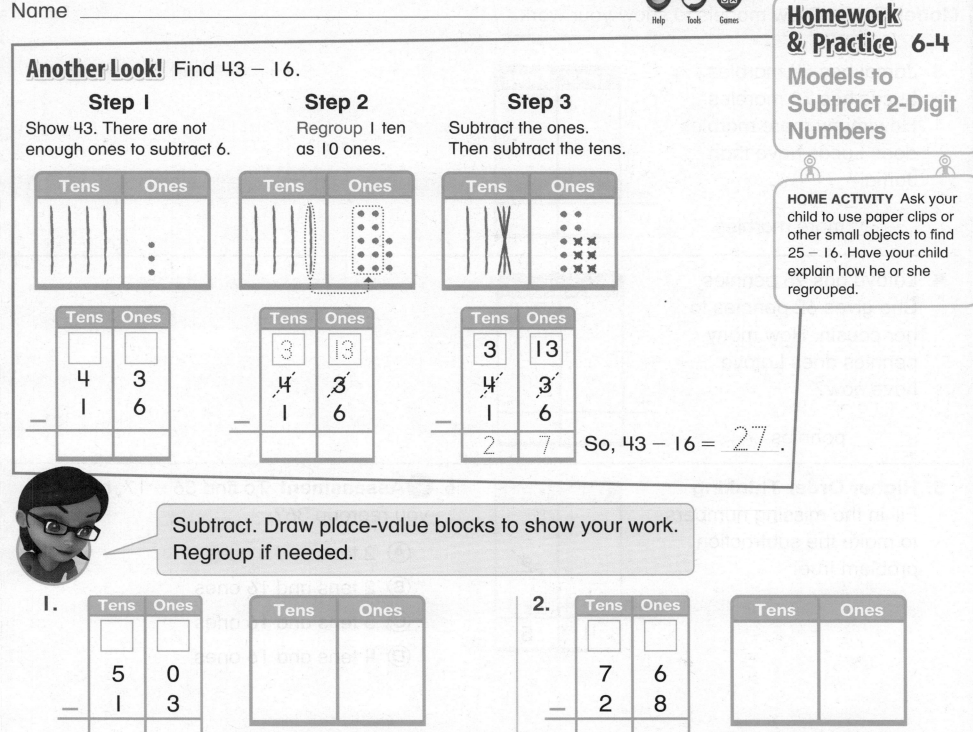

Another Look! Find 43 − 16.

Step I
Show 43. There are not enough ones to subtract 6.

Step 2
Regroup I ten as 10 ones.

Step 3
Subtract the ones. Then subtract the tens.

Tens	Ones
4	3
1	6

Tens	Ones
3̶ ₄̶	₁3 3̶
1	6

Tens	Ones
3 ₄̶	₁3 3̶
1	6
2	7

So, 43 − 16 = 27.

HOME ACTIVITY Ask your child to use paper clips or other small objects to find 25 − 16. Have your child explain how he or she regrouped.

Subtract. Draw place-value blocks to show your work. Regroup if needed.

I.
Tens	Ones
5	0
1	3

Tens	Ones

2.
Tens	Ones
7	6
2	8

Tens	Ones

3. Jamal has 54 marbles. Lucas has 70 marbles. How many more marbles does Lucas have than Jamal?

Tens	Ones

_____ more marbles

4. Latoya has 95 pennies. She gives 62 pennies to her cousin. How many pennies does Latoya have now?

Tens	Ones

_____ pennies

5. **Higher Order Thinking** Fill in the missing numbers to make the subtraction problem true.

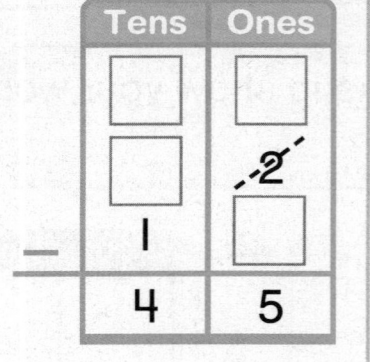

Tens	Ones
	~~2~~
1	
4	5

6. ✅**Assessment** To find $36 - 17$, how can you regroup 36?

Ⓐ 2 tens and 6 ones

Ⓑ 2 tens and 16 ones

Ⓒ 3 tens and 16 ones

Ⓓ 4 tens and 16 ones

Name _____

Solve & Share

How is subtracting 23 from 71 like subtracting 3 from 71? How is it different from subtracting 3 from 71? Explain. Find both differences. Use blocks if you need to.

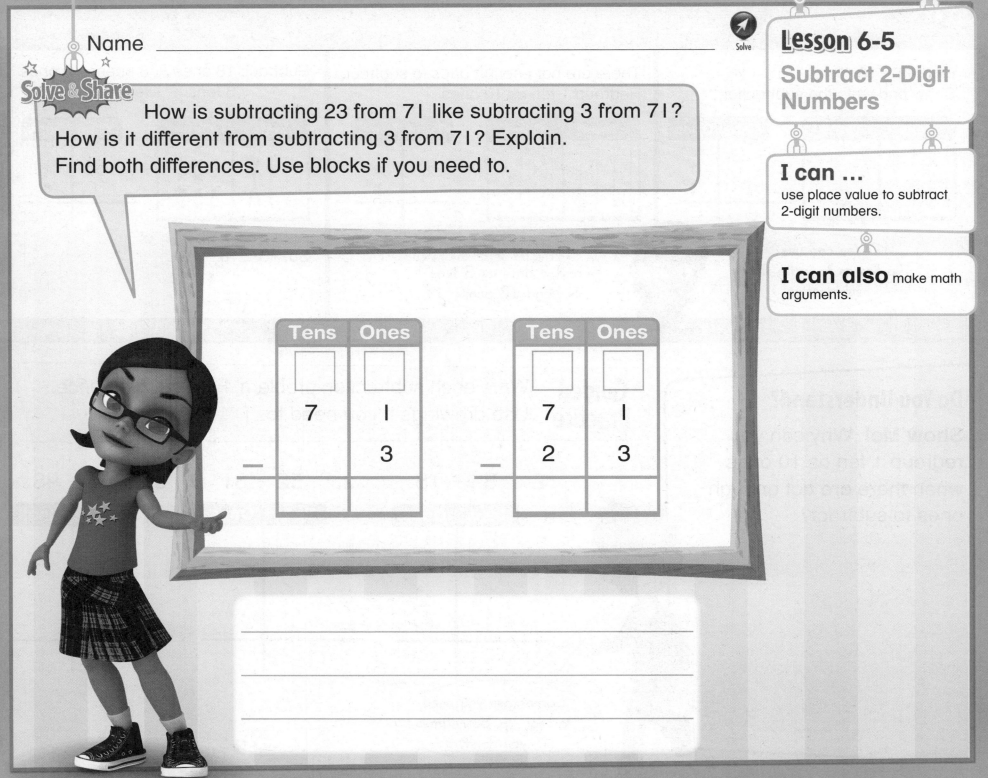

Tens	Ones
7	1
_	3

Tens	Ones
7	1
_ 2	3

Find 43 − 18.
Show and write the subtraction.

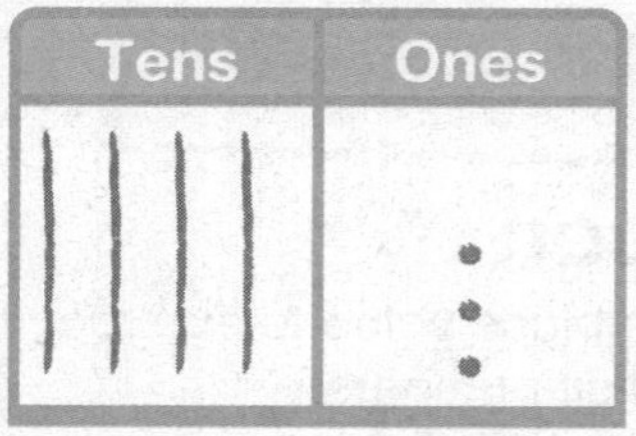

Tens	Ones
‖‖‖	⋮

	Tens	Ones
	□ 4	□ 3
−	1	8

You can use a frame to write the subtraction.

There are not enough ones to subtract.
Regroup 1 ten as 10 ones.

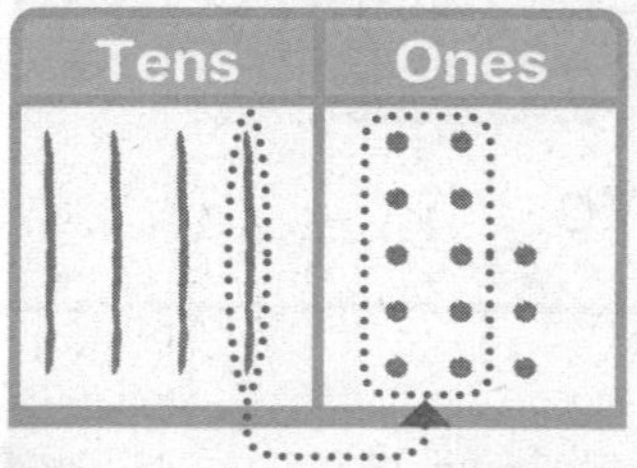

Tens	Ones
‖‖‖ ⦙	⦙ •••• ••••• •

	Tens	Ones
	3 4	13 3
−	1	8

Write 4 tens and 3 ones as 3 tens and 13 ones.

Subtract: 13 ones − 8 ones = 5 ones
3 tens − 1 ten = 2 tens

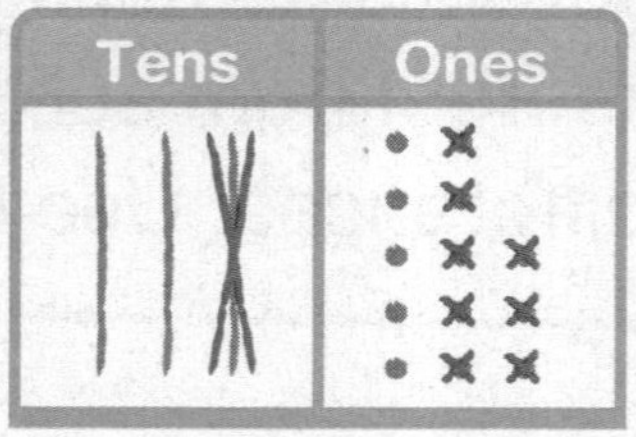

Tens	Ones
‖ ⨯	• ⨯ / • ⨯ / • ⨯ ⨯ / • ⨯ ⨯ / • ⨯ ⨯

	Tens	Ones
	3 4	13 3
−	1	8
	2	5

So, 43 − 18 = 25.

Do You Understand?

Show Me! Why can you regroup 1 ten as 10 ones when there are not enough ones to subtract?

☆ **Guided Practice** ☆
Write each subtraction problem. Find the difference. Use drawings if you need to.

1. 34 − 15

Tens	Ones
2 3	14 4
− 1	5
1	9

2. 52 − 31

Tens	Ones
□	□
−	

3. 67 − 48

Tens	Ones
□	□
−	

Sometimes you need to regroup. Sometimes you don't.

© Pearson Education, Inc. 2

Independent Practice

Write each subtraction problem. Find the difference.

4. 52 – 36

Tens	Ones
☐	☐

5. 94 – 54

Tens	Ones
☐	☐

6. 41 – 25

Tens	Ones
☐	☐

7. 33 – 28

Tens	Ones
☐	☐

8. 65 – 42

Tens	Ones
☐	☐

9. 70 – 48

Tens	Ones
☐	☐

10. 96 – 37

Tens	Ones
☐	☐

11. 87 – 45

Tens	Ones
☐	☐

Solve. Draw a model to help.

12. **Higher Order Thinking** Tia's basketball team scored 61 points. They won by 23 points. How many points did the other team score?

_____ points

13. **Model** Don has 72 marbles. Josie has 56 marbles. How many more marbles does Don have than Josie?

Tens	Ones

_____ more marbles

Can you use a drawing or objects to show the problem?

14. **Higher Order Thinking** Write a subtraction story using two two-digit numbers. Then solve the problem in your story.

_____

_____

_____

Tens	Ones

_____

_____

_____

15. ✓**Assessment** Eric can fit 90 cards in a scrapbook. He already has 46 cards in the scrapbook.

How many more cards will fit?

Ⓐ 44

Ⓑ 45

Ⓒ 46

Ⓓ 54

© Pearson Education, Inc. 2

Name _____

Another Look! Remember the steps for subtracting.

Step 1
Think: Are there enough ones to subtract?

Step 2
Regroup if you need to.

Step 3
Subtract the ones.
Subtract the tens.

HOME ACTIVITY Have your child use paper and pencil to solve 65 − 37. Have your child explain the steps he or she takes to subtract.

Write the problems in the frames. Find each difference.

38 − 13

Tens	Ones
3	8
− 1	3
2	5

54 − 17

Tens	Ones
4	14
5	4
− 1	7
3	7

Be sure to cross out if you regroup.

You can use drawings to help.

Write each problem in a frame. Find the difference.

1. 37 − 14

Tens	Ones

2. 64 − 18

Tens	Ones

3. 45 − 26

Tens	Ones

4. 73 − 25

Tens	Ones

Be Precise Decide which one item each child will buy. Subtract to find how much money is left.

Stickers 14¢

Craft sticks 36¢

Paint set 42¢

Crayons 58¢

---

5. Bonnie has 47¢. She buys the

Tens	Ones

_____.

Bonnie has _____ ¢ left.   −

---

6. Ricky has 59¢. He buys the

Tens	Ones

_____.

Ricky has _____ ¢ left.   −

---

7. Lani has 63 grapes. She gives 36 grapes to Carla. How many grapes does Lani have left?

_____ grapes

Tens	Ones

−

---

8. Write a number to make this a subtraction problem with regrouping. Then find the difference.

Tens	Ones

−   2   3

---

9. **Higher Order Thinking** Use each number below.

| 1 | 2 | 4 | 5 |

Write the subtraction problem that has the greatest difference. Then solve.

Tens	Ones

−

---

10. ✓**Assessment** Norma has 48 buttons. Grace has 14 buttons. Connie has 29 buttons. How many fewer buttons does Connie have than Norma?

34   29   19   15
Ⓐ   Ⓑ   Ⓒ   Ⓓ

© Pearson Education, Inc. 2

Lesson 6-6

Use Addition to Check Subtraction

I can ...
add to check my subtraction.

I can also reason about math.

Name _____

Solve & Share

Find 52 − 24.
Use the bar diagram and subtraction frame
to help you show and solve the problem.
How can you use addition to check your answer?

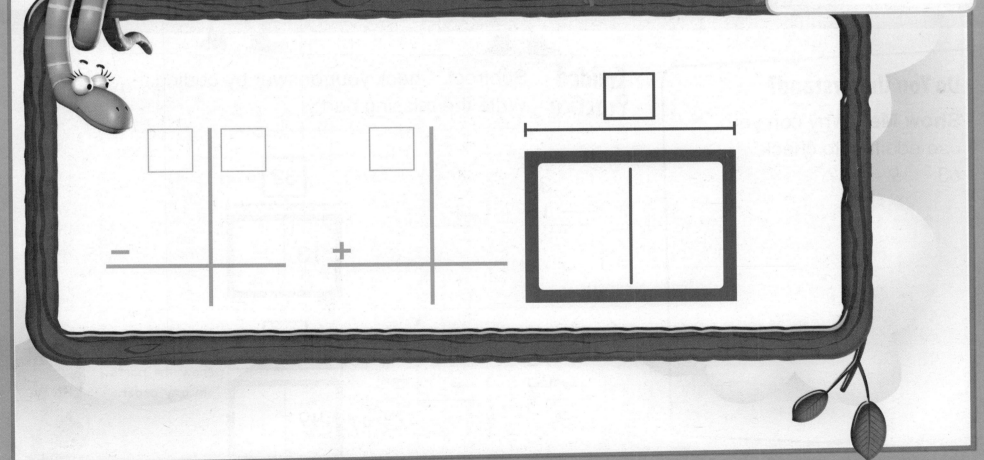

Topic 6 | Lesson 6
Digital Resources at PearsonRealize.com
three hundred fifty-three **353**

Remember that addition and subtraction are related. So, you can add to check subtraction.

Find 24 − 9.

The sum of the parts equals the whole.

$$\begin{array}{r} 1\;14 \\ 2\!\!\!/4 \\ -\;9 \\ \hline 15 \end{array} \qquad \begin{array}{r} 1 \\ 15 \\ +\;9 \\ \hline 24 \end{array}$$

24

9	15

Find 52 − 17.

Add to check your subtraction.

The two parts equal the whole!

$$\begin{array}{r} 4\;12 \\ 5\!\!\!/2 \\ -\;17 \\ \hline 35 \end{array} \qquad \begin{array}{r} 1 \\ 35 \\ +\;17 \\ \hline 52 \end{array}$$

52

17	35

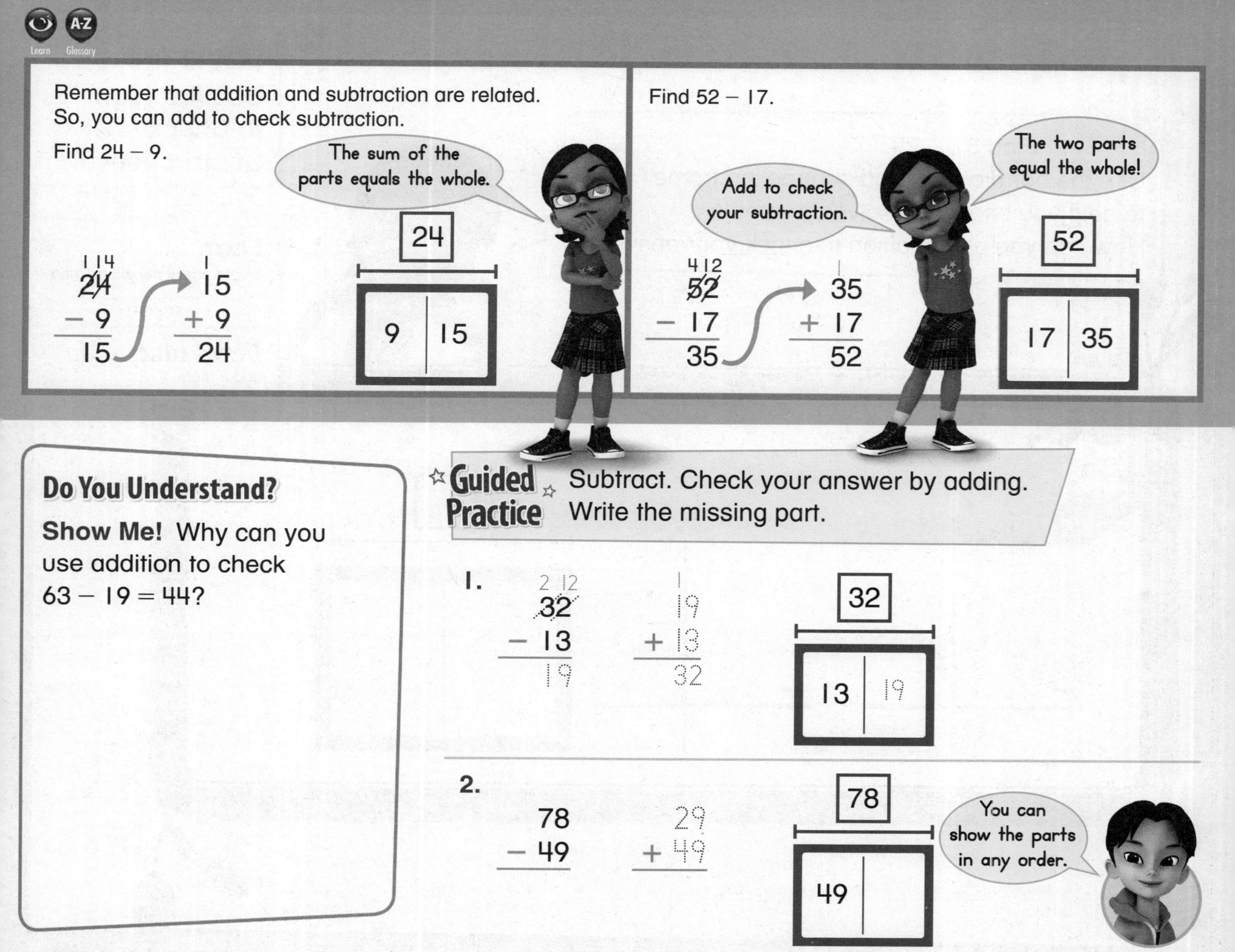

Do You Understand?

Show Me! Why can you use addition to check 63 − 19 = 44?

☆ Guided Practice ☆

Subtract. Check your answer by adding. Write the missing part.

1.

$$\begin{array}{r} 2\;12 \\ 3\!\!\!/2 \\ -\;13 \\ \hline 19 \end{array} \qquad \begin{array}{r} 1 \\ 19 \\ +\;13 \\ \hline 32 \end{array}$$

32

13	19

2.

$$\begin{array}{r} 78 \\ -\;49 \\ \hline \end{array} \qquad \begin{array}{r} 29 \\ +\;49 \\ \hline \end{array}$$

78

49	

You can show the parts in any order.

© Pearson Education, Inc. 2

Topic 6 | Lesson 6

Independent Practice Subtract. Check your answer by adding. Write the missing part.

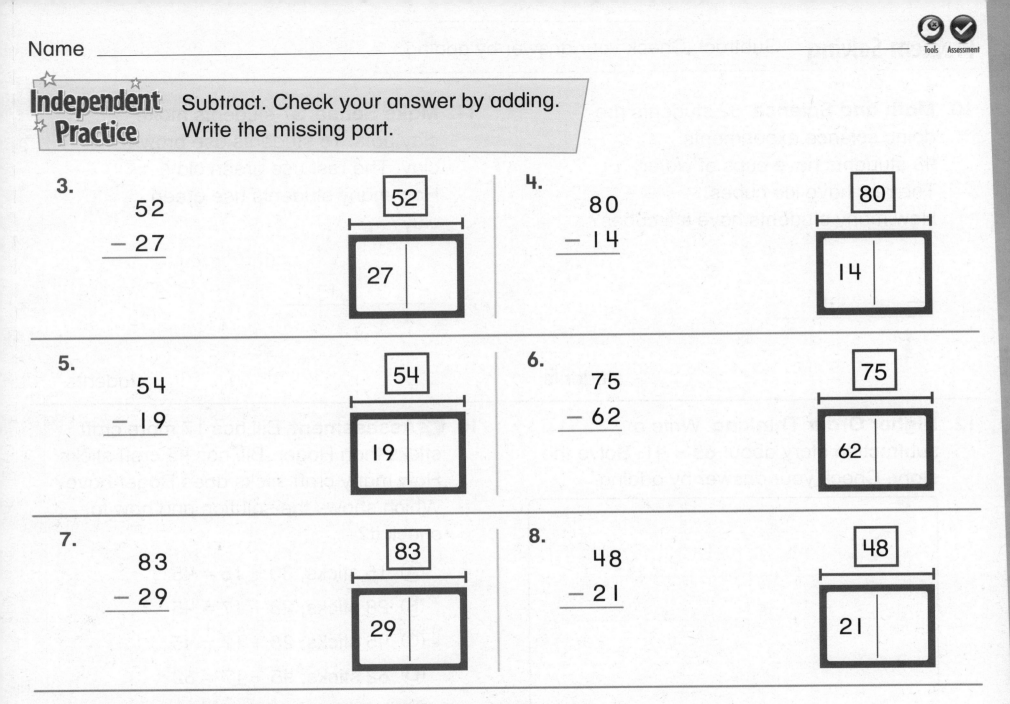

3.
　　52
　− 27

| 52 |
| 27 |

4.
　　80
　− 14

| 80 |
| 14 |

5.
　　54
　− 19

| 54 |
| 19 |

6.
　　75
　− 62

| 75 |
| 62 |

7.
　　83
　− 29

| 83 |
| 29 |

8.
　　48
　− 21

| 48 |
| 21 |

9. **Higher Order Thinking** Maria uses 35 + 24 to check her answer to a subtraction problem. Write two subtraction problems Maria could have solved.

10. Math and Science 62 students are
doing science experiments.
48 students have cups of water.
The rest have ice cubes.
How many students have ice cubes?

$-$ $+$

_____ students

11. Make Sense 37 students make
clay pots. 16 students use brown
clay. The rest use green clay.
How many students use green
clay?

$-$ $+$

_____ students

12. Higher Order Thinking Write a
subtraction story about $65 - 41$. Solve the
story. Check your answer by adding.

_____

_____

_____

13. ✓Assessment Bill has 17 more craft
sticks than Roger. Bill has 45 craft sticks.
How many craft sticks does Roger have?
Which shows the solution and how to
check it?

Ⓐ 15 sticks; $30 + 15 = 45$

Ⓑ 28 sticks; $28 + 17 = 45$

Ⓒ 45 sticks; $28 + 17 = 45$

Ⓓ 62 sticks; $45 + 17 = 62$

Another Look!

You can think of subtraction as starting with the whole. Then you take away one part. The other part is left.

```
  37    Whole
- 12    Part
  25    Part
```

```
  25    Part
+ 12    Part
  37    Whole
```

Tens	Ones

Tens	Ones
and	and

HOME ACTIVITY Ask your child to find 65 − 32. Then have him or her use addition to show you how to check the subtraction.

To check your work, add to put the parts back together. Your answer should be the whole.

If no regrouping is needed, then add or subtract the tens and the ones.

Subtract. Check your answer by adding.

1.
```
  86
-  9        +
```

2.
```
  54
- 19        +
```

3.
```
  63
- 37        +
```

4. Mei Ling has 71 marbles.
Then she loses 25 marbles.
How many marbles does Mei Ling have left?

Subtract   Check

_____ marbles

$-$ _____ $+$ _____

Think about how addition and subtraction are related.

5. Denise has 51 beads.
Then she uses 32 beads to make a bracelet.
How many of her beads does Denise have left to use?

Subtract   Check

_____ beads

$-$ _____ $+$ _____

6. Number Sense Write the number that makes each equation true.

$63 - 20 = 20 +$ _____

$58 - 40 = 18 +$ _____

$75 - 30 = 15 +$ _____

$89 - 46 = 30 +$ _____

In an equation, each side of the equals sign shows the same value.

7. ✔Assessment Lana subtracts to find $52 - 39$. Which addition equation could Lana use to check her answer?

Ⓐ $13 + 26 = 39$

Ⓑ $39 + 52 = 91$

Ⓒ $13 + 39 = 52$

Ⓓ $52 + 13 = 65$

Name _____

Solve & Share

Find 82 − 56. Use any strategy you have learned or your own strategy. Show your work. Explain why your strategy works.

I can ...
subtract 2-digit numbers and decide when to regroup and when not to regroup.

I can also reason about math.

Find 72 − 24.

One way is to break apart numbers.

72 − 24 = ?   72 − 20 = 52

20   4   52 − 2 = 50

2   2   50 − 2 = 48

So, 72 − 24 = 48.

Another way is to line up the numbers by place value.

$$\begin{array}{r} {}^{6\ 12} \\ \not7\,\not2 \\ -2\ 4 \\ \hline 4\ 8 \end{array}$$

I get the same difference either way!

So, 72 − 24 = 48.

You can check your subtraction with addition.

My work checks. My subtraction is correct.

$$\begin{array}{r} {}^{1} \\ 2\ 4 \\ +4\ 8 \\ \hline 7\ 2 \end{array}$$

Do You Understand?

Show Me! Could you solve 72 − 24 in another way? Explain.

Guided Practice   Use any strategy to subtract. Show your work. Check your work with addition.

1. 67 − 39 = _____

67 − 40 = 27

27 + 1 = 28

Check:

$$\begin{array}{r} {}^{1} \\ 2\ 8 \\ +3\ 9 \\ \hline 6\ 7 \end{array}$$

2. 78 − 42 = _____

© Pearson Education, Inc. 2

Tools Assessment

Independent Practice Use any strategy to subtract. Show your work. Check your work with addition.

3. 73 − 34 = _____

4. 78 − 25 = _____

5. 83 − 46 = _____

6. 36 − 27 = _____

7. 98 − 51 = _____

8. 45 − 34 = _____

9. 86 − 29 = _____

10. 71 − 38 = _____

11. 85 − 23 = _____

Algebra Find the missing number.

Look for a pattern. Use mental math.

12. 34 − 8 = 35 − ☐

13. 27 − 9 = 28 − ☐

Problem Solving

Make Sense Make a plan. Solve each problem. Show your work. Then check your work.

14. The hardware store has 32 hammers in stock. The store sells 16 hammers on Saturday. How many hammers are left?

_____ hammers

15. A barber does 15 haircuts on Monday. He does 28 haircuts on Friday. How many more haircuts does he do on Friday than on Monday?

_____ more haircuts

16. A-Z **Vocabulary** Complete each sentence. Use two of the words below.

addend   equation   difference   sum

$93 - 53 = 40$ is an _____.

40 is called the _____ of 93 and 53.

17. Higher Order Thinking
Fill in the missing digits.

$$\begin{array}{r} \square\ \square \\ -\ 2\quad 3 \\ \hline 2\quad 9 \end{array}$$

18. ✓**Assessment** Circle the problem that you will use regrouping to solve. Then find both differences. Show your work.

$56 - 38$ $74 - 52$

$$\begin{array}{r} 56 \\ -\ 38 \\ \hline \end{array} \qquad\qquad \begin{array}{r} 74 \\ -\ 52 \\ \hline \end{array}$$

© Pearson Education, Inc. 2

Another Look! Find 82 − 37.

$$\begin{array}{r} {\scriptstyle 7\,12} \\ \cancel{8}\cancel{2} \\ -\ 37 \\ \hline 45 \end{array}$$

Check

You can use addition to check your subtraction.

$$\begin{array}{r} 37 \\ +\ 45 \\ \hline 82 \end{array}$$

Or you can break apart the numbers to check your work.

82 − 37 = ?

30   7

2   5

82 − 30 = 52

52 − 2 = 50

50 − 5 = 45

So, 82 − 37 = 45.

I can subtract in different ways. I will line up the numbers by place value!

There is more than one way to check your subtraction.

HOME ACTIVITY Write 78 − 29 on a sheet of paper. Have your child use pencil and paper to solve the problem. Then ask your child to explain how he or she found the difference.

Use any strategy to subtract. Show your work. Check your work.

1. 56 − 37 = _____

2. 46 − 18 = _____

3. 75 − 22 = _____

Make Sense Make a plan. Solve each problem.
Show your work.
Then check your work.

4. 45 basketballs are in a closet.
38 basketballs are full of air.
The rest need air.
How many basketballs need air?

_____ basketballs

5. Sue buys a box of 60 craft sticks.
She uses 37 craft sticks for her project.
How many craft sticks are left?

_____ craft sticks

6. **Higher Order Thinking** 36 berries are in a
bowl. James eats 21 of the berries. Then he
puts 14 more berries in the bowl. How many
fewer berries are in the bowl now?

Is there a shortcut you can use?

_____ fewer berries

7. ✅**Assessment** Circle the problem that
you will use regrouping to solve. Then
find both differences. Show your work.

$83 - 45 =$ _____

$65 - 33 =$ _____

© Pearson Education, Inc. 2

Name _____

Solve & Share

Trevor made 20 apple muffins for the bake sale. Ryan made 15 banana muffins. They sold 23 muffins in all. How many muffins are left?

Solve any way you choose. Then write two equations to show your work.

Solve

Lesson 6-8
Solve One-Step and Two-Step Problems

I can ...
use models and equations to solve word problems.

I can also model with math.

_____ ◯ _____ = _____

_____ ◯ _____ = _____

 _____ muffins

Learn   Glossary

Some students are in the gym. 13 students leave. Now there are 15 students in the gym.

How many students were in the gym at the start?

What is happening in the story?

You can write an equation. First, think about what you need to find.

How many students were in the gym at the start?

You can use a ? for the unknown.

$? - 13 = 15$

You can also use a bar diagram to show the parts and the whole.

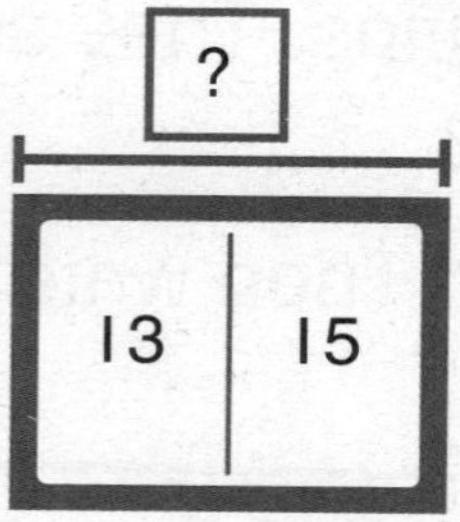

?

13	15

You can add to solve the problem.

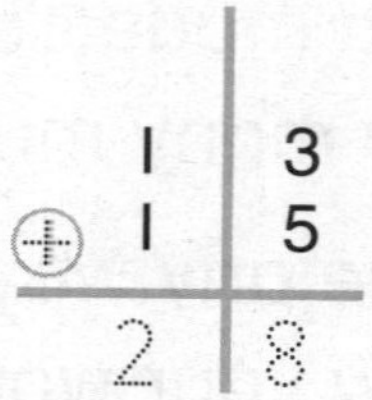

```
   1  3
 + 1  5
 ─────
   2  8
```

So, 28 students were in the gym at the start.

Do You Understand?

Show Me! How does the bar diagram show what happens in the story problem?

☆ Guided Practice   Solve each problem. Show your work.

1. Some key chains are in a bag. Aki takes out 17 key chains. 14 key chains are left in the bag. How many key chains were in the bag at the start?

?

17	14

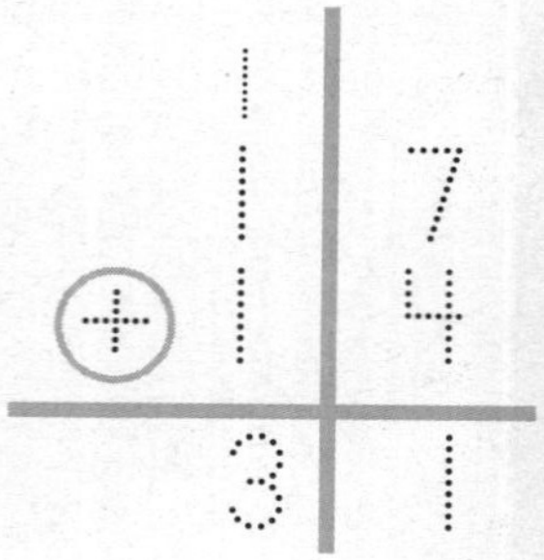

```
   1  7
 + 1  4
 ─────
   3  1
```

_____ key chains

2. Some leaves are in a pile. 26 leaves blow away. 22 leaves are left. How many leaves were in the pile at the start?

?

26	22

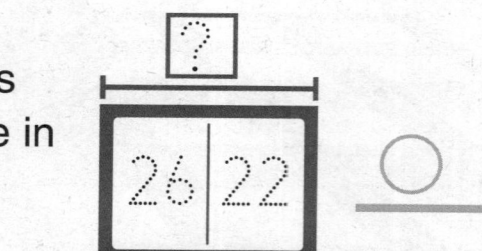

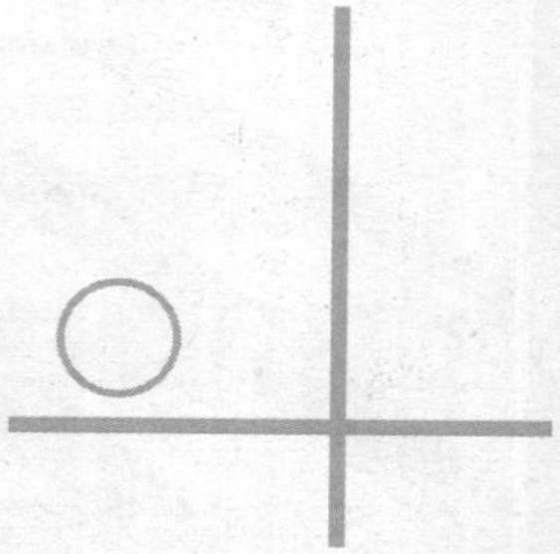

_____ leaves

© Pearson Education, Inc. 2

Independent Practice ⭐

Use a bar diagram to solve each problem. Show your work.

3. Some balls are in the closet. Mr. Thomas takes out 15 balls for class. Now there are 56 balls in the closet. How many balls were in the closet in the beginning?

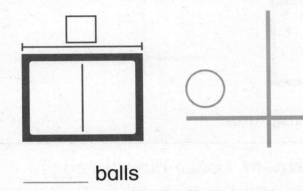

_____ balls

4. Corey buys a box of 96 paper clips from the store. He uses 34 paper clips. How many paper clips does Corey have left?

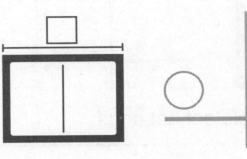

_____ paper clips

5. A.J. counts 44 acorns in his yard. He picks up 27 acorns. Then 16 more acorns fall from the tree. How many acorns are in the yard now? Show your work.

Think about what to find first. Then use that answer to solve the problem.

Step 1

_____ ◯ _____ = _____

Step 2

_____ ◯ _____ = _____

_____ acorns

Make Sense Make a plan. Solve each problem. Show your work. Then check your work.

6. 27 people are at a picnic. 14 people eat hamburgers. The rest eat hot dogs. How many people eat hot dogs?

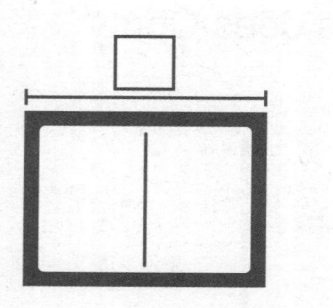

_____ people eat hot dogs

7. Some pumpkins are in a patch. 41 pumpkins are picked. Now there are 33 pumpkins in the patch. How many pumpkins were in the patch at the start?

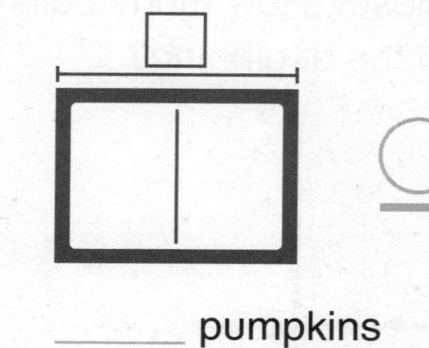

_____ pumpkins

8. **Higher Order Thinking** Lauren has a stamp collection. She gives Kristen 12 stamps and Ethan 15 stamps. Lauren has 22 stamps left. How many stamps did she have at the start?

Step 1

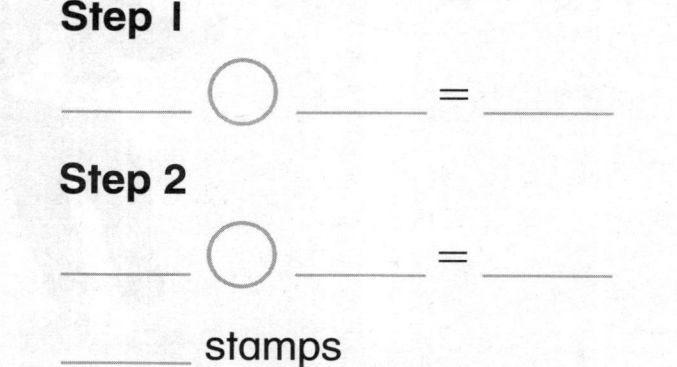

____ ◯ ____ = ____

Step 2

____ ◯ ____ = ____

_____ stamps

9. ✓**Assessment** Lance buys 48 eggs. He uses 24 of them for baking. Then he buys 12 more eggs. How many eggs does Lance have now?

Which set of equations can you use to solve this problem?

Ⓐ $48 + 24 = 72$
$72 - 12 = 60$

Ⓒ $48 + 24 = 72$
$72 + 12 = 84$

Ⓑ $48 - 24 = 24$
$24 + 12 = 36$

Ⓓ $48 - 24 = 24$
$24 - 12 = 12$

Help   Tools   Games

Another Look! 52 cars are parked in the lot. 18 cars leave. Then 10 more cars leave. How many cars are in the lot now?

Use the answer from Step 1 to solve Step 2.

Step 1: Subtract to find how many cars are still in the lot after 18 cars leave.

52

18 | ?

$$\begin{array}{cc} 4 & 12 \\ .5. & 2.. \\ -1 & 8 \\ \hline 3 & 4 \end{array}$$

Step 2: Then subtract to find how many cars are still in the lot after 10 more cars leave.

34

10 | ?

$$\begin{array}{cc} 3 & 4 \\ -1 & 0 \\ \hline 2 & 4 \end{array}$$

HOME ACTIVITY Have your child solve this problem: Some birds are sitting on the roof. Then thunder scares away 12 birds. Now there are 32 birds sitting on the roof. How many birds were sitting on the roof at the start?

Use the answer from Step 1 to solve Step 2.

1. 73 people are on the train. At a train stop 24 people get off and 19 people get on. How many people are on the train now?

Step 1

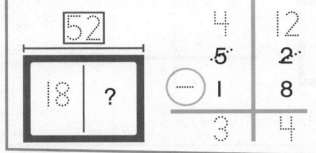

Step 2

_____ people

Make Sense Make a plan. Solve each problem. Show your work. Check your work.

2. Rosa's book has 88 pages in all. She reads some pages on Monday. She has 59 pages left to read. How many pages did she read on Monday?

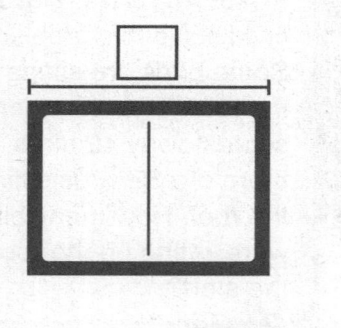

_____ pages

3. Jackie runs 19 laps on Monday. She runs 12 laps on Tuesday. How many laps did she run on both days?

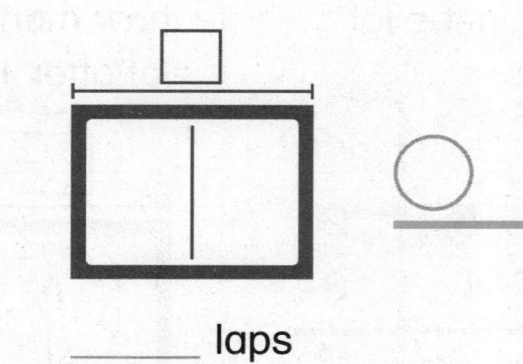

_____ laps

4. **Higher Order Thinking** Zak has a bag of cherries. He gives away 18 cherries to Tim and 18 cherries to Janet. Now he has 25 cherries. How many cherries did Zak have at the start?

Step 1

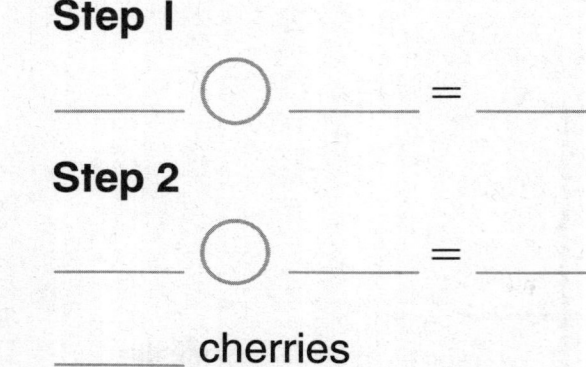

_____ ◯ _____ = _____

Step 2

_____ ◯ _____ = _____

_____ cherries

5. ✓**Assessment** There are 68 runners in a marathon. 28 runners finish the race. Then 22 more runners finish the race. How many runners have **NOT** finished the race?

Which pair of equations can you use to solve this problem?

Ⓐ $68 + 28 = 96$;
$96 - 22 = 74$

Ⓑ $68 + 28 = 96$;
$28 + 22 = 50$

Ⓒ $68 - 28 = 40$;
$40 - 22 = 18$

Ⓓ $68 - 28 = 40$;
$40 + 22 = 66$

© Pearson Education, Inc. 2

Topic 6 | Lesson 8

Name _____

Solve & Share

Farmer Davis has 52 chickens.
He sells 15 chickens at the market.
How many chickens does Farmer Davis have now?

Use the bar diagram and equation to help you solve.
Be ready to explain how the numbers in the problem are related.

I can ...
reason about word problems, and use bar diagrams and equations to solve them.

I can also add and subtract two-digit numbers.

Thinking Habits

How are the numbers in the problem related?

How can I show a word problem using pictures or numbers?

_____ ○ _____ ○ _____ chickens

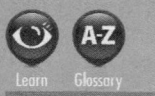

45 beads are in a jar. Jenny uses some beads to make a necklace.

Now 17 beads are in the jar.

How many beads does Jenny use to make the necklace?

How can I use reasoning to solve the problem?

45 beads − beads in = 17 beads
          necklace   left

I can think about how the numbers are related. 45 − ? = 17 A bar diagram can show this.

I know the whole. So, I can subtract the part I know to find the missing part.

45

? | 17

$$\overset{3\,15}{\cancel{4}\,5}$$
$$-\ 1\,7$$
$$\overline{2\,8}$$

$45 - 17 = 28$ beads

My bar diagram and equation show how the numbers relate.

Do You Understand?

Show Me! Why can you subtract 45 − 17 to solve 45 − ? = 17?

Reason about the numbers in each problem. Complete the bar diagram and write an equation to solve. Show your work.

1. Wendy has 38 cents to spend on a snack. She buys an apple that costs 22 cents. How many cents does Wendy have left?

   38 ⊖ 22 ⊜ _____ cents

   38

   22 | ?

2. Joe has 46 crayons. Tamila has 18 more crayons than Joe. How many crayons does Tamila have?

   _____ ◯ _____ ◯ _____ crayons

Topic 6 | Lesson 9